AFTER INJURY

AFTER INJURY

A Historical Anatomy of Forgiveness, Resentment, and Apology

Ashraf H. A. Rushdy

OXFORD
UNIVERSITY PRESS

OXFORD
UNIVERSITY PRESS

Oxford University Press is a department of the University of Oxford. It furthers
the University's objective of excellence in research, scholarship, and education
by publishing worldwide. Oxford is a registered trade mark of Oxford University
Press in the UK and certain other countries.

Published in the United States of America by Oxford University Press
198 Madison Avenue, New York, NY 10016, United States of America.

CIP data is on file at the Library of Congress
ISBN 978–0–19–085197–2

9 8 7 6 5 4 3 2 1

Printed by Sheridan Books, Inc., United States of America

For My Beloved Sons,
Zidane Amgad and Aziz Senai

CONTENTS

ACKNOWLEDGMENTS

It is a pleasure to thank all those who made this book possible, and those who made it and my life immeasurably better.

At Oxford University Press, Peter Ohlin has been a thoroughly thoughtful and supportive editor. I have read many, many books whose authors thank him for doing what the best editors do. I am truly happy to add mine to that list of books that have benefited—and been made possible—by his conscientious attention. It has indeed been as much a pleasure as it is an honor to work with him. Isla Ng has been enthusiastic and very helpful; I thank her, especially, for finding a way to get the permissions for the Ingres painting on the cover. I would like to thank Andrew Pachuta for his painstaking copy-editing work. Finally, I am grateful for the terrific work Rajesh Kathamuthu has done as the project manager who has expertly and generously overseen the process of producing this book.

I could not have been more fortunate in having the Press readers I have had. Stephen Darwall is a philosopher for whom I have tremendous respect. His work on the history of ethics and on the foundations of moral obligation has deeply informed and enlarged my thinking, as it has that of so many others. One of the things that most impresses me in reading his essays and books is both how brilliant and yet also how generous he consistently is in his assessment of the ideas of other philosophers. I am deeply thankful to him for his very helpful suggestions in improving my work, and for teaching me so effectively through his own.

This book would not exist without Jeffrie Murphy. His always profoundly illuminating and incisive essays first inspired me to think about the topics I take up in this book. That is not surprising, of course, since no contemporary philosopher has done more to inform the work of those who wrote after him on the subjects of forgiveness and resentment. What I find even more inspiring than his pioneering writing on those subjects, though, is the empathy, integrity, and considerable open-mindedness he exhibits in that remarkable body of work. He exemplifies for me what it means to be alive to moral ideas about retribution and forgiveness and the societies by which these ideas are created and the ones they help to create. The intellectual debts I owe him are great, as indeed are the ones that are more than intellectual.

It is indeed gratifying to discover that the philosophers I admire most are indeed most admirable—and not only for their ideas about the importance and place of ethics, but in their exemplary kindness and generosity of spirit.

I have been equally fortunate in having colleagues and friends at Wesleyan who have been unstintingly supportive in every possible way. I would like especially to thank Khachig Tölölyan, Nat and Erness Brody, Sean McCann, Joel Pfister, Stephanie Weiner, Lisa Cohen, Ellen Nerenberg, and Christina Crosby. Wesleyan's Provost, Joyce Jacobsen, has generously supported this work in every way any academic could possibly wish—materially and intellectually. I deeply thank her. I am also grateful for the support and expertise of Elizabeth Tinker, Amy Bello, Maureen Zimmer, Eloise Glick, Megan Flagg, and Joy Vodak.

I would like to thank the remarkably talented librarians at Wesleyan University's Olin Library, and at Yale's Sterling Library.

As always, I am profoundly grateful for my friends Ted Abel, Jeff Kerr-Ritchie, Shani Mott, Nathan Connolly, and Robert Greenhill. I owe a special debt to Rochelle Gurstein and Jack Barth, who found the Ingres painting which graces the cover of this book. It is but the latest act of kindness these dear friends have shown me in the decades I have known them.

Finally, I would like to thank my family, immediate and far-flung. The family into which I was born—my mother, father, and brother—created in me the desire for knowledge, the sense of hope, and the feeling of responsibility that have formed me into the person I am. The extended families I inherited and into which I married have made me want to be an even better person. I thank them all for sharing with me a love that has sustained me.

My beloved wife Kidan is a luminous presence in everything I do, and everything I do she makes better. I am grateful for her mind, her heart, her soul. Her conversation about everyday matters in the world we occupy and her particular insights about the life and intelligence of emotions have inspired and helped me in my thinking in ways that I cannot describe. Without Kidan, so many more and more important things than this book would not be possible. With her, and because of her, many things have become possible. I love and admire her courage, her nobility of spirit, and her compassion for others. You are the reason, my love.

I dedicate this book to our sons, Zidane and Aziz. I love and treasure every single thing about them—their good-humor, their endless creativity, their unstinting and unconditional love. They bless our life and expand our spirits. Their laughter and playfulness remind me daily of what is most valuable in life. The sight of them every morning gives me a joy that I cannot compare to anything else. At the time of this book, they have inhabited our world for ten and eight years, respectively, and I cannot imagine a world without them; they make me want to do whatever I can to make the world with them a fairer and more just one.

INTRODUCTION

On December 14, 1989, two South African security police-men, Mbambalala Glen Mgoduka and Amos Themba Faku, and one askari, Sheperd Shakati, were killed by a car bomb near Port Elizabeth, in what became known as the Motherwell bombing. Although at the time they blamed it on the African National Congress, the South African Police Security Branch had actually ordered the action because they suspected that the three might re-veal the Security Branch's involvement in the 1985 murder of the Cradock Four. In 1996, five members of the South African Police were indicted and found guilty of the Motherwell bombing mur-ders. On October 1, 1997, one of them, Eugene de Kock, the head of Vlakplaas, as the Security Branch was known, appeared before South Africa's Truth and Reconciliation Commission (TRC) to testify about the Motherwell bombing and appeal for amnesty. At the end of his testimony, he asked if he could express his deep con-trition to the widows of the two police officers whose murders he had planned. This was not the first, nor would it be the last time de Kock apologized to the survivors of his victims. The judge at his trial had noted that de Kock felt impelled to "reveal all the details which had been weighing heavily on his mind for many years." De Kock presented himself as a tormented soldier who sought expia-tion from his trauma through contrition. At later appearances be-fore the TRC and after, from his prison cell, de Kock continued to seek out and apologize to the South African families whose lives he had destroyed. Many of those families felt that his apologies were sincere—"His apology came from his soul," as one put it in 2014— and they supported his repeated appeals for parole. In early 2015, having served almost twenty years of his sentence of two terms of life imprisonment, and an additional 212 years, de Kock was released on parole.[1]

Unlike the TRC hearing, de Kock's apology to the widows was not broadcast on national television. It took place in a private room, arranged by the TRC, with the parties attended by their respective lawyers. After he had apologized for murdering their husbands, Doreen Mgoduka and Pearl Faku felt the relief of finally knowing the truth of what happened. Mgoduka said that she could now "mourn properly" for her husband, and Faku sobbed tears she had held in for years. Each also responded to de Kock's apology by forgiving him. "I was profoundly touched by him," Faku reported. "I couldn't control my tears. I could hear him, but I was overwhelmed by emotion, and I was just nodding, as a way of saying yes, I forgive you. I hope that when he sees our tears, he knows that they are not only tears for our husbands, but tears for him as well. . . . I would like to hold him by the hand, and show him that there is a future, and that he can still change." Even in the rarified climate of that moment in South African history awash with grace and emotion, this episode stood out as a particularly shining example. One of the TRC commissioners, Pumla Gobodo-Madikizela, said that "there was something divine about forgiveness expressed in the context of tragedy" and that what the widows did "had no equal" in her experience of the TRC hearings.[2]

It may have had no equal, but it was certainly not isolated. Many South Africans were eager to forgive those who had tortured, brutalized, and killed their loved ones. Nombuyiselo Mhlauli and her daughter Babalwa, for instance, ended their testimony to the TRC by stating: "We do want to forgive, but we don't know whom to forgive."[3] It is not surprising that the commission should have made forgiveness so essential to its work. The Xhosa term used to translate 'reconciliation' in the publicity for the commission was *uxolelwano*, which according to clinical psychologist Nomfundo Walaza "is much closer

---

1. For de Kock's testimony and Judge Van Rensburg's statement at his trial, see "Truth and Reconciliation Commission Amnesty Hearings" (October 1, 1997, Case No. 0066/96), http://www.justice.gov.za/trc/amntrans%5Cpe/mother3.htm. For the appeal to the Motherwell widows, see Pumla Gobodo-Madikizela, *A Human Being Died that Night: A South African Story of Forgiveness* (Boston: Houghton Mifflin, 2003), pp. 14–15; Sapa, "De Kock's Apology 'Came from His Soul," *IOL News* (October 7, 2014), http://www.iol.co.za/news/crime-courts/de-kock-s-apology-came-from-his-soul-1.1761026#.Verj77xVhBc; David Smith, "South African Death Squad Leader Eugene de Kock to Be Freed from Jail," *The Guardian* (January 30, 2015).

2. Doreen Mgoduka and Pearl Faku, quoted in Gobodo-Madikizela, *A Human Being Died that Night*, pp. 14–15, 97; also pp. 94–95.

3. Nombuyiselo Mhlauli and her daughter Babalwa are quoted in Desmond Tutu, *No Future Without Forgiveness* (New York: Doubleday, 1999), pp. 148–49.

in meaning to 'forgiveness.'" Reverend Bongani Finca inaugurated the first hearing of the commission with the Xhosa hymn "*Lizalise idinga lakho*" ('The Forgiveness of Sins Makes a Person Whole'). And those who led the commission strongly endorsed forgiveness as the only means of salvaging South Africa. The chairperson of the commission, Reverend Desmond Tutu, titled his book on the commission's work *No Future Without Forgiveness*. The vice-chairperson, Dr. Alex Boraine, noted at the end of his book that without "forgiveness as a means of assisting individuals and societies to overcome the evil of their past," there "can be very little hope in the world."[4] Here, then, was a commission that for many who told their stories to it had "forgiveness" in the title, that began with a hymn to forgiveness, and that was led by prominent advocates of political forgiveness as the only way to establish peace, the only path to the future.

The final report of the TRC even defined the explicit terms for forgiveness when it stated outright that forgiveness required "renouncing resentment, moving past old hurt."[5] While many South Africans did renounce resentment, as we see in those examples above, many also did not. Some felt coerced by the climate of the hearings and the unexpected apologies offered them. They, like Jubulisiwe Ngubane, for instance, whose mother and children were killed in the Trust Fields Massacre, felt they "have no choice" because the person who committed the crimes, Brian Mitchell in this case, "stepped forward and asked for forgiveness." They were surprised by the apology and felt constrained by the commission setting. Others felt coerced by the commissioners themselves. One woman named Kalu clearly resented what she described as the commission's effort "to dictate my forgiveness" when she was not ready to grant it. Kalu reported her frustration after her TRC hearing: "What really makes me angry about the TRC and Tutu is that they are putting pressure on me to forgive. . . . I don't know if I will ever be able to forgive. I carry this ball of anger within me and I don't know where to begin dealing with it. The oppression was bad, but what is much worse, what makes me even angrier, is that they are trying to dictate my forgiveness."[6] Kalu is a good representative

---

4. Antjie Krog, *Country of My Skull: Guilt, Sorrow, and the Limits of Forgiveness in the New South Africa* (1998; New York: Three Rivers Press, 2000), pp. 37, 212; Tutu, *No Future Without Forgiveness*; Alex Boraine, *A Country Unmasked: Inside South Africa's Truth and Reconciliation Commission* (Oxford: Oxford University Press, 2000), p. 439.

5. *Truth and Reconciliation Commission of South Africa Final Report* (Cape Town: Juta, 1998), Volume 1, p. 116 (Chapter 5, paragraph 50).

6. Jubulisiwe Ngubane and Kalu, quoted in Charles Villa-Vicencio, "Living in the Wake of the Truth and Reconciliation Commission: A Retroactive Reflection," *Law, Democracy, and*

of the secular witnesses who found themselves annoyed by the prayer-filled ethos of the TRC, since they were seeking more justice and less amnesty and forgiveness. And their resentment, lingering and justified, struck them as something they should *not* renounce since it was the sign of their injury and the motive for their seeking justice.

I

Here, then, are the three practices with which this study is concerned: *resentment* as a response to injury, *apology* as an expression of remorse and responsibility for the injury, and *forgiveness* as an act of rehabilitation and reconciliation in the wake of the injury. These are neither discrete events nor assured and final ones. We should consider, at first separately, each of these elements.

Kalu was doubly resentful for what she perceived as two separate insults. The first was the crime committed, and the second the insinuation that she was unreasonable in holding onto that resentment. The TRC was created by the Government of National Unity a year after the legal end of apartheid and held its hearings shortly thereafter. For some, it provided the mechanisms and impetus to save the nation—to produce reconciliation through truth. For others, it seemed an evasion in the way that all mechanisms of transitional justice could be—it risked producing injustice through amnesty. The critics' argument was effectively that amnesty produces amnesia—that forgiving would lead to forgetting (as the conventional wisdom counsels us). Was this feasible in a nation seeking "truth"? Would the truth, as the Biblical injunction puts it, set us free? Or would it only set *them* free, those who committed the crimes? What Kalu's response suggests is that she was not yet ready to forgive; her continuing resentment was what it was, that is, a sign of that festering wound of the oppression that had legally ended a year or two earlier. Giving it up prematurely struck her as a betrayal of her genuine emotions, not an opportunity to open herself up to new ones. She was not alone, nor was South Africa's an isolated case of coerced forgiveness. Some survivors of the Holocaust likewise expressed profound resentment that so hastily, so

---

Development: Journal of the Faculty of Law 3.2 (1999): 195–207, esp. pp. 203, 198 (ellipsis in text in Kalu quotation). Also see Charles Villa-Vicencio and Willhelm Verwoerd, Eds., *Looking Back, Reaching Forward: Reflections on the Truth and Reconciliation Commission of South Africa* (Cape Town: University of Cape Town Press, 2000), p. 201. Charles Villa-Vicencia was a theologian who served as National Research Director of the TRC.

precipitously, so shortly after the end of World War II, they were asked to participate and frequently did participate in collective rituals of forgiveness. Some refused because what they still felt, deeply felt, was what one survivor, Jean Améry, described as "resentment" as the "existential dominant" of their lives.[7] They felt they were justifiably resentful.

Resentment is often cast as a stalled state; one is stuck in resentment and expected ultimately to be free of it. Those who retain their resentment are seen as reveling in their negativity, wallowing in their pain, unwilling to release themselves from the past ("to let bygones be bygones"). Resentment is a moral sentiment that we accept in others only as temporary—as a sign of their having been injured and then, if it lingers, as a symptom of their having a spiteful character. We counsel those who hold on to their grudges that it is time to let them go and free themselves. Tutu's counsel to Kalu—or at least her perception of whatever it was he did say to her—probably amounted to the same thing. It is time to forgive, he urged; I am not ready, she maintained. To appreciate how resentment is widely understood as being connected to some abstract but intuited sense of time, let us turn to the second of the three practices—forgiveness—and consider two cases from the United States.

In the first, in October 2006, an armed gunman entered the West Nickel Mines School in Lancaster County, Pennsylvania, and killed five Amish girls in revenge on God for having taken his firstborn daughter nine years earlier. The Amish community expressed its forgiveness almost immediately. Within hours, several community representatives had sought out members of the gunman's family and comforted them by telling them that they held no grudges. A man whose two granddaughters were among the slain told media reporters that he had already forgiven the gunman. "I don't think there's anybody here that wants to do anything but forgive," one Lancaster County resident was quoted as saying. "We don't need to think about judgment; we need to think about forgiveness and going on." The media were mostly fascinated by this response and quickly made the Nickel Mines Amish community into "the world's most forgiving people." Others were skeptical because they felt that the forgiveness was given with what they deemed to be unseemly haste. How could one forgive a crime of this magnitude in a matter of hours or days? In the second case, in June 2015, a gunman entered a prayer service at Emanuel African Methodist Episcopal Church in Charleston, South Carolina, and

---

7. Jean Améry, "Resentments," in *At The Mind's Limits: Contemplations by a Survivor of Auschwitz and Its Realities*, translated by Sidney Rosenfeld and Stella P. Rosenfeld (Bloomington: Indiana University Press, 1980), pp. 62–81, esp. p. 65.

killed nine of the congregants. Two days after the tragedy, at the bond hearing of the killer, a self-described white supremacist who was hoping to incite a race war, the survivors of the slain expressed their forgiveness. Again, some felt that the forgiveness came too quickly.[8] If people forgive so hastily, are they really forgiving, asked the critics, or are they exhibiting stoic apathy or acting on some other philosophy in which they have insufficient respect for the victims and a too dulled resentment at the crime?

Here, then, we can see the conflicting claims on these practices—forgiving too quickly betrays one as unfeeling; too slowly, as spiteful. As we will see in the chapters that follow, this question of what we can call *measure* is an important one in the contemporary debates about what forgiveness entails and, for some, requires.

The Nickel Mines community and the Charleston congregation forgave the assaults on their institutions and lives quickly; had they not done so, had they continued in expressing resentment at these crimes, one wonders whether the media that applauded them might have instead criticized them. There is a widespread sensibility that people *should* forgive; that is not surprising since most of the world's people belong to one of the Abrahamic faiths, in each of which forgiveness is a stated principle, duty, and obligation. Indeed the sentiment that some express in the wake of tragedies like this one—"I, for one, am done forgiving," wrote Roxane Gay after the Charleston shooting—is in response to a perceived *expectation* that forgiveness is forthcoming. That expectation—sometimes coerced, as we saw in the Kalu case, but most often just understood—produces an additional resentment in the victims. Améry, for instance, had expressed resentment at this expectation that he and other Jews ought to forgive the perpetrators of the Holocaust. Whoever "lazily and cheaply forgives," he wrote, is denying something in himself, and the act of denial involved in such forgiveness, he suggested, is "*anti*moral in character."

---

8. The Lancaster County resident is quoted in Jeff Jacoby, "Undeserved Forgiveness," *Boston Globe* (October 8, 2006). My account of the Nickel Mines story is taken from Donald B. Kraybill, Steven M. Nolt, and David L. Weaver-Zercher's *Amish Grace: How Forgiveness Transcended Tragedy* (San Francisco: Jossey-Bass, 2007). Also see "Lost Angels: The Untold Stories of the Amish School Shootings," a three-part series that appeared in the *Lancaster New Era* (December 13, 14, 15, 2006), and then was issued as a pamphlet; Cindy Stauffer, "Widow of Amish Schoolhouse Shooter Charlie Roberts Tells Story of Her Life and That Day in New Book," *Lancaster New Era* (October 1, 2013); and Marie Monville with Cindy Lambert, *One Light Still Shines: My Life Beyond the Shadow of the Amish Schoolhouse Shooting* (Grand Rapids, MI: Zondervan Publishers, 2013). My account of the Charleston story is taken from "White Man Arrested in Slaying of Nine Blacks at South Carolina Church," *New York Times* (June 18, 2015); "Families of South Carolina Church Massacre Victims Offer Forgiveness," *New York Times* (June 19, 2015).

He condemned those who were "trembling with the pathos of forgiveness and reconciliation" at the end of the war, as he seethed with resentment twenty years after it. Forgiveness in our culture is an assumed norm, what we feel to be the proper and fitting conclusion to an episode. Another Holocaust survivor, Simon Wiesenthal, was so haunted by his refusal to forgive a dying SS Nazi who asked him for forgiveness while Wiesenthal was still in a concentration camp that he talked incessantly about it to his campmates and then sought out the responses of dozens of spiritual leaders and intellectuals about what he *should* have done.[9] Forgiveness, in other words, is an expectation, and it is one that determines how we can think about the dynamic of events that produce resentment and sometimes elicit apologies.

What many of these examples share is that the crimes for which the victims are resentful and expected to forgive are crimes that are historic—in two senses. They are historic in their magnitude; these are atrocities, some of them mass atrocities that redefined the world. They are also historic in that they are expressions of enduring forms of targeted hatred and oppression: notably anti-Semitism and anti-black racism. The shootings and mass killings are events that occur against the backdrop of, and emphatically as a result of, long-standing philosophies and political practices that sometimes take legal form (ghettoization, segregation, or apartheid) and sometimes murderous (police terrorism, white supremacist lynching, or pogroms). And when apologies are offered for those events, there is a question of what specifically these apologies are addressing—the events only, or also the intellectual foundations that made them possible? Consider *Dabru Emet*, for example, a millennial statement signed by a group of 170 interdenominational Jewish scholars that addressed the apologies that Christian churches were making for their inaction during the Holocaust. While seeking reconciliation with these remorseful churches and acknowledging their apology for a specific event, the group also insisted on addressing the long and desolate history of what it called "Christian anti-Judaism."[10] An apology, they hinted, was meaningful when it provided a full accounting of motivations for, as well as talking about the effects of, the wrong, sin, or mass atrocity.

---

9. Roxane Gay, "Why I Can't Forgive the Killer in Charleston," *New York Times* (June 24, 2015); Améry, "Resentment," pp. 72, 65; Simon Wiesenthal, *The Sunflower: On the Possibilities and Limits of Forgiveness* (revised and expanded ed.; New York: Schocken Books, 1998).

10. Tivka Frymer-Kensky, David Novak, Peter W. Ochs, and Michael A. Signer, "Dabru Emet," *New York Times* (September 10, 2000). Also see Victoria Barnett, "Provocative Reconciliation: A Jewish Statement on Christianity," *The Christian Century* (September 27–October 4, 2000). *Dabru Emet* ("Speak the truth," Zechariah 8:16).

That kind of apology is rare, of course. In the numerous apologies made to people of African descent in what Wole Soyinka called the "*fin de millénaire* fever of atonement," such acknowledgment was simply absent. Pope John Paul II, President Bill Clinton, and President George W. Bush all apologized or expressed remorse and regret for the slave trade; but they were focused on the trade rather than the white supremacy that made it possible and supported it for centuries.[11] These were apologies for what these church and national leaders considered a historic event that was in the past, while the people to whom they addressed these apologies, the descendants of the victims, many of them at least, were focused less on the event and more on the backdrop that made it possible, and continues to make possible an entire repertoire of ongoing oppressions. Why apologize for a historic event, they ask, when the effects of that history and the underlying cause of that event are still with us? An apology is seen as sincere and meaningful when it addresses something that has ended, since it is an expression of remorse for behavior that is now acknowledged to be wrong. Someone apologizing for an activity that he continues to exhibit can hardly be said to be apologizing, or at least sincerely. Likewise, a politician apologizing for an event in her nation's past that has discernible ongoing effects and was itself an expression of an enduring intellectual legacy of hatred is going to meet with skepticism from those who feel those effects and are victims of that legacy. An apology that "comes from the soul" is going to express something deeper and reflect a more probing analysis of the past of the person, church, or nation making it.

What these accounts reveal about each of these separate practices is that resentment has layers, apologies can occlude as much as they express, and forgiveness can in some ways be a coercive and illusive ideal. This might be surprising, since we often think of resentment as a shallow emotion, apologies as straightforward, and forgiveness as more of an opportunity than an enforced practice. It is likely that we expect forgiveness to happen because we are sociable creatures who desire a moral and social equilibrium that forgiveness seems to bespeak. We are often uncomfortable in a state of social irresolution, and, sometimes, whole households or communities are rendered anxious while awaiting the comforting reassurance of resolution to conflicts in which we do not necessarily have a part other than witnesses. It is possible that we are trained to expect and seek forgiveness because it represents the

---

11. Wole Soyinka, *The Burden of Memory, the Muse of Forgiveness* (New York: Oxford University Press, 1999), p. 90. I have written about these apologies in Ashraf H. A. Rushdy, *A Guilted Age: Apologies for the Past* (Philadelphia: Temple University Press, 2015).

kind of denouement that centuries of exposure to a particular narrative form have educated us to desire (although it is equally possible that we have created that narrative form because of our desire for tidy resolution in our lives). In any case, seen separately, then, there is a great deal of profound meaning in each of these practices of resenting, apologizing, and forgiving.

There is a large and robust body of writing on these practices. Philosophers, psychologists, sociologists, linguists, and historians have written about each of them; and in recent years, that body of writing has grown considerably, especially in the study of apology and forgiveness as concepts and practices.

The least studied of the three practices is resentment, primarily, one suspects, because of the bad reputation it has in general and because of the particular nastiness it has assumed in the Western philosophical tradition since Nietzsche. Philosophers who have focused on emotions and passions have briefly studied resentment, sometimes to support and sometimes to contest Nietzsche's representation of it. Some social historians have recently turned their attention to it to see how we can understand particular historical phenomena (revolutions and other forms of social transformation) as manifestations of class resentments of all sorts. Some intellectuals have affirmed the value of resentment in general. One sort, like Améry, who write about historical atrocities from a personal or interested position, have maintained that the resentment they feel is justified both because of the magnitude of the atrocity and because a lingering resentment is one of the few ways for a person or group to keep alive the memory of the past in an amnesiac age. A second group, philosophers who are either committed or reluctant retributivists, has asserted that it is the emotion that is at the core of our sense of justice.

Forgiveness—usually defined, since Bishop Butler in the early eighteenth century, as the forswearing of resentment—is the most studied topic of the triad. And both the intellectuals who celebrate and the philosophers who affirm the value of resentment tend to do so while writing about forgiveness. This is the case in both French and American philosophy—notably, Vladimir Jankélévitch and Jeffrie Murphy—where resentment assumes a distinctly minor role in the discussion of the more significant practice of forgiveness. These philosophers—some retributivists or recovering retributivists—write about what forgiveness means when it is performed in a way congruent with the values of justice and condemn what they feel are the travesties of forgiveness when it is done for reasons they deem immoral. They tend to focus on the conditions in which forgiving is moral and the conditions when it is not forgiving at all. Others, often writing from a religious perspective, challenge this representation and argue for a less restrictive set of conditions for when forgiveness can be forgiveness and not something else like condonation, acceptance, or otherwise a manifestation of weakness or failure of self-esteem. They value forgiveness for what it accomplishes, what reconciliation and hope it inspires, and what it represents for the forgiver and the forgiven.

Apology, like forgiveness, is receiving renewed interest from philosophers and sociologists. It is worth noting the difference between an earlier moment when these intellectuals attended to the subject of apology and our current moment. When philosophers and sociologists wrote about apology in the 1950s, they wrote about what kind of speech act or what sort of interactive communication it was; they focused on what apologies did, what work they performed, what communicative norms served as a backdrop, and what these ritual practices meant in a secular setting. And their focus was exclusively on apologies that individuals made to each other, most often privately. Sometime in the postwar period, there emerged the new social practice of the public apology. Politicians—Nixon in his famous "Checkers" speech in 1952, for instance—began to make apologies, or statements that appeared somewhat apologetic, for actions related to their roles as public figures. Representatives of states, congregations, and other social groups began to make apologies for how their nations, churches, or corporate bodies had mistreated others in the near and then the distant past. Public apologies—for political malfeasance, for tragic historical episodes, and, by celebrities, for being caught in rude or unruly behavior or being overheard uttering racist or homophobic slurs—are now a routine feature of our culture. And so, when philosophers and sociologists write about apology now, they tend to focus on these *public* apologies in order to see whether they meet some strict set of criteria for authenticity, sincerity, and plausibility. There is certainly good reason for us to be suspicious of the numerous public apologies that celebrities and politicians routinely offer; they are often shoddy, ill-conceived, and practiced theatrical events. If being in love means never having to say you're sorry, as *Love Story* affirmed, being famous means having to say it regularly but not really caring. It's not clear yet which is better—the foolishness of that sentiment in *Love Story* or the folly of our apologetic culture. The problem, though, is that these public apologies are only one kind of apology, and there are, conceivably, more promising ways of approaching the topic of apology as a practice than by focusing on whether public acts of penance resemble, or should resemble, private acts.

II

Two things stand out in these studies of the practices of apology and forgiveness. First, they are studied separately. Those who write about each practice tend to imply that there is something important about the relationship of the given practice to the ones to which it is related. Those who write about forgiveness mention resentment as the emotion that forgiveness forgoes or apology as the necessary or unnecessary precursor to the granting of forgiveness, but neither resentment nor apology constitutes a significant part of their studies. Likewise, those who write about apology sometimes make passing reference to what apology is intended to alleviate and what it is meant to elicit—respectively, the resentment and the forgiveness of the offended party—but their focus is less on the context of apologizing and more on the constituent features that an apology must have in order to be defined as a successful and not a faux one.

That is the second thing that stands out in these studies. To use two metaphors, they tend to dissect and police the practices they study. They identify just what makes an apology or an act of forgiveness that, and not something else, by designating what are its necessary parts. Usually, and understandably, they focus on the parts that are apparent (what is said and how it is said) rather than the parts that are impossible to verify (the emotional backdrop). This dissection, however, sometimes misses the point because it assumes that there is only one form the practice may take, and likewise that that form of communication follows only one set of rules and norms. Or, in the terms of the other metaphor, they police the definition of the practice in ways that are understandable—in the age of rampant public apologies—in order to protect its integrity from what they (most often correctly) see as illegitimate use. But, again, the policing of the terrain suggests that we are thinking of the practice in a particular way—in need of protection or possessing an inviolate integrity, for instance. The policing of these practices means we don't appreciate the ways they operate in the communities, where they often don and doff different roles, just as dissecting them as species of things means we can't understand them as part of a larger, more vibrant ecosystem in which they are at play with others.

Let me be clear: there is value in identifying what constitutes an apology or an act of forgiveness and in showing in what ways particular deviances from the accepted norms reveal something that cannot meaningfully be called an apology or an act of forgiveness but must be designated either as something else or, more often, as a failed or infelicitous or faux apology or forgiveness.

And I am deeply indebted to those studies that have performed that important work. Yet, there is also something quite promising and potentially illuminating in opening up the terrain and approaching these practices with a different sensibility—of an anthropologist, say—in order to see what possible work they do in the situations in which they operate.

This study makes such an attempt, first by looking at these three practices *together*. It takes seriously what connects them. They are, after all, serial responses to what precedes them—resentment to injury, apology to resentment, and forgiveness to apology. There is a logic in their connection that I hope to tease out by devoting equal space to each of them in order to draw out what is implied in the practice in its relationship to the others it either precedes, produces, or both. I should note, though, that I am not studying them as an *ensemble*, that is, looking at particular moments in which all three are involved. I have two reasons for avoiding that strategy. First, I think such case studies limit what can be said about the practices, separately or together. Rather, I limn out each practice in its own section in order to reveal what is particularly important about it and then address in the conclusion what we can make of the dynamic interactions among the three practices. Second, the only evidence one readily has for producing such case studies is of *public* acts—public apologies and publicly given or publicly withheld forgiveness—and the distinction between private and public apologies, as I discuss in the second and third sections, is profound. Such case studies necessarily limit the study. One could, I suppose, draw on acts of resentment, apology, and forgiveness from one's private life with those one loves; but I suspect that one would then truly test the fortune cookie wisdom of *Love Story*.

Second, this study recognizes that these practices are evolving and polysemantic. There is no one single way to feel resentment, express apology, or forgive; and there is no single set of meanings for those practices. Consider the case of forgiveness, for instance. There is a healthy debate about whether it is an emotion (a change of heart), a speech-act (saying, "I forgive you"), a gesture of another sort (a waving of the hand, say), a process (with stages toward fulfillment), or a disposition (to be a forgiving person). Each of these determinations of what forgiveness is (or should be) as an *entity* provides one way of defining when forgiveness happens or doesn't as an *event*.

Moreover, these practices are intrinsically more complicated and more polysemantic (if such an idea is possible) because they involve us in the insoluble problem of "other minds" (I discuss this point more fully in later chapters). We might begin by stating the obvious, first about resentment and then about apology and forgiveness. First: resentment is an *emotion*, and therefore requires us to approach it in a way respectful of that determination. All emotions, including resentment, have their own logic; what they know cannot be known in the way our "reason" knows "facts." Indeed, their status is something that challenges and perhaps makes possible the practice of knowing itself. As both neuroscientists and philosophers have shown us in the last few decades, emotions are in themselves cognitive, not failures of cognition. Neuroscientists have recently attended to the ways that "emotions and feelings may not be intruders in the bastion of reason at all" but rather "enmeshed in its networks," as Antonio Damasio puts it. Damasio studied the relation of emotion to cognition by focusing on patients with injuries to their orbital cortex who have diminished capacity for processing emotional information. Joseph LeDoux studies different parts of the brain (the lateral, anterior cingulate, and orbital prefrontal regions) that make up the integrated working memory system, and his findings too are that our conscious emotional feelings and our conscious thoughts are not that different, can be studied through the same mechanisms, and all take place in what he calls "the emotional brain."[12]

Philosophers, too, have rejected the long tradition of seeing emotions as the enemies of reason. Jean-Paul Sartre argues that an emotion is, in fact, another form of reason, "a certain way of apprehending the world," as he puts it. "Emotion is not an accident," he concludes, not an aberration to rational thinking and understanding but rather "a mode of existence of consciousness," one of the ways consciousness "*understands* (in the Heideggerian sense of *Verstehen*) its 'being-in-the-world.'" *Reason* itself, as Robert Solomon wisely puts it, "is nothing other than perspicacious passion." Emotions do not distract us from rational thinking; they enable it and are it. Our passions, he concludes, are "judgments, *constitutive* judgments according to which our reality is given its shape and structure."[13] So, when we say that resentment is

---

12. Antonio R. Damasio, *Descartes' Error: Emotion, Reason, and the Human Brain* (New York: G. P. Putnam's Sons, 1994), p. xii; Joseph LeDoux, *Synaptic Self: How Our Brains Become Who We Are* (New York: Viking Penguin, 2002); and LeDoux, *The Emotional Brain: The Mysterious Underpinnings of Emotional Life* (New York: Simon & Schuster, 1996). Cf. Damasio, *The Feeling of What Happens: Body and Emotion in the Making of Consciousness* (New York: Harcourt, Brace & Co., 1999); and Damasio, *Self Comes to Mind: Constructing the Conscious Brain* (New York: Pantheon, 2010).

13. Jean-Paul Sartre, *The Emotions: Outline of a Theory*, translated by Bernard Frechtman (New York: Philosophical Library, 1948), pp. 52, 91; Robert C. Solomon, *The Passions: Emotions and the Meaning of Life* (1976; Indianapolis: Hackett Publishing, 1993), pp. 58, xvii. Cf. Martha Nussbaum, *Political Emotions: Why Love Matters for Justice* (Cambridge, MA: Belknap Press of Harvard University Press, 2103). Also see the cautionary essay by Cheshire Calhoun, "Cognitive Emotions?" in *What Is an Emotion: Classic Readings in Philosophical Psychology*, edited by Solomon and Calhoun (New York: Oxford University Press, 1984), pp. 327–42.

an emotion, we do not render it beyond the pale of cognition. We instead recognize the need to approach it with an appreciation for what it is, how it is constituted, and what might prove more fruitful for us to ask of it in order to understand better what it is, does, and reveals.

Or, to state the obvious about the other two practices: forgiveness and apology are matters of *belief*, not knowledge. There is simply no way for us to "know" that the person forgiving us has indeed had a change of heart toward our offense, nor is there any way for us to "know" that the remorse we hear in the voice and gestures of the person apologizing to us is indeed sincere and means the same thing that we mean by remorse. Most people, I think, would grant this and then dismiss it as either obvious or unimportant in, and to, our philosophical discussions of apology and forgiveness. But this point should not be dismissed, I think, since it reveals something about these practices that seems to go unnoticed, or is actively disregarded, in those discussions. In a word, many studies treat these matters as if they were indeed practices that involve knowing and not believing. The most obvious way this sensibility is manifest is that scholars of apologizing and forgiving forge definitions that clearly do treat the concepts as being matters of knowledge, and not belief.

Let me use as an example two recent books, both very fine and intelligent studies from which I have learned a great deal but that also demonstrate this tendency. Charles Griswold's *Forgiveness* (2007) and Nick Smith's *I Was Wrong* (2008) both offer what are accurately called "categorical definitions" of forgiveness and apology, respectively. Smith deserves the credit for this term, since he offers the neologism "categorical apology" to describe what he calls "a kind of *prescriptive stipulation*," or "regulative ideal." Smith is quite open in acknowledging the terms of his project. His interest, as he says at the outset, is not in "asking what an apology *is*" but rather in arguing "what an apology *should be* in various contexts." Given this premise, it is not surprising that he defines apology by designating what twelve elements it possesses (thirteen in his later book). And while he is open to accepting that certain practices might be apologies in an unusual sense, his "categorical apology" remains just that— *categorical*—not only unambiguous but, as I argue later, somewhat Kantian. Griswold uses more tempered terms but abides by the same principles. He sometimes refers to "forgiveness at its best" and "imperfect forgiveness," which suggests that he sees forgiveness as a practice that falls into a spectrum, which I think is a promising model, but that spectrum quickly becomes something much less open. His more common usage is to refer to "paradigmatic forgiveness" and "non-paradigmatic forgiveness," and his own practice is to establish what he calls "threshold conditions."[14]

These are the strategies I referred to above as *policing* the terms and meanings of the practice. If, as they believe, *apology* or *forgiveness* means a particular thing (that is, one is sorry or forgiving) and expresses and requires a relatively stable set of sentiments (one repents the wrongdoing or forgoes resentment over it), then these terms are meaningful only when these sentiments are present. When they are not evident, the terms *apology* and *forgiveness* are used promiscuously, improperly, or meaninglessly. I have some sympathy with the policing sensibility (what teacher doesn't?), and I am troubled, as they are, when it is clear that someone is using either term to describe an activity that is not recognizably either apologizing or forgiving. Yet, I am also aware of the very narrow limitations (and effectiveness) of that policing strategy when it comes to terms that describe emotions or beliefs. And it is not because people will simply abuse those terms, calling things what they are not. It is because there is no way to *prove* the absence of the emotion or belief that the sentiment is supposed to express. We are inevitably confronted, as I will discuss later, with the problem of "other minds."

Given that these practices are interrelated and that we can tease out their potentially deeper meaning by attending to them as vibrant practices rather than static ones, we might approach them by focusing on them *together* and by focusing on them as *evolving*. In this study, then, I will attempt that. Rather than striving to define the borders and boundaries beyond which an act cannot be described as resentment, apology, or forgiveness, I instead explore the premises, assumptions, and traditions of these practices.

III

This is, admittedly, a hybrid study (in a presustainable economy, it would have less generously been called an unorthodox study). It is unorthodox in a general way, as I have said, because it is organized around all three practices and implicitly argues that they can be understood in a more meaningful

---

14. Nick Smith, *I Was Wrong: The Meanings of Apologies* (New York: Cambridge University Press, 2008), pp. 17, 25; see Smith, *Justice Through Apologies: Remorse, Reform, and Punishment* (New York: Cambridge University Press, 2014); Charles L. Griswold, *Forgiveness: A Philosophical Exploration* (New York: Cambridge University Press, 2007), pp. 38, 113, 114–15.

way when they are studied together than when they are studied separately. In addition, though, I should note three particular unorthodoxies in the structure of the book.

First, I do not study three practices in what is their serial relationship to each other—that is, resentment, first, and then the apology in response, and the forgiveness as the finale. I begin with forgiveness, then turn to resentment, and finally to apology. I do so because I think it is important for us to see first what possible meanings there are in the *culmination* of the dynamic interaction and because we can better understand that dynamic interaction by seeing what is its *expected* culmination. I then turn to resentment in order to show how there are two discernible traditions in the philosophical thinking about this subject that help us see what happens when we turn from thinking of resentment as an individual sentiment and think of it as a social condition. Finally, I examine the practice of apology by again employing that distinction—between private, individual apologies and collective, public apologies—to show what a range of apologies can mean in different sites and situations.

Second, I situate the study of each practice in a different way. I introduce each of the three sections with an opening chapter (Chapters 1, 4, and 7) by looking at a set of texts from different traditions and media. In Chapter 1, I examine two moments in the New Testament—Jesus' ministry and Paul's and deutero-Paul's epistles—to tease out what are two distinct models of forgiveness that have very different implications. In Chapter 4, I draw on two literary works, a nineteenth-century Russian story and an ancient Greek tragedy, to reveal the continuities and discontinuities in our understanding of resentment and to discern the primary divisions in how resentment has been rendered as either a form of spiteful envy or hopeful striving for justice. In Chapter 7, I examine two contemporary films in order to explore two different renderings of what social conditions permit and enable, or prohibit and disable, the act of repentance.

Finally, and most significantly, I do not approach each of these practices in the same way, with the same questions or methodology. My study of forgiveness is more philosophical and polemical, my study of resentment more obviously historical, and my study of apology more typological. I wish to reveal the premises in arguments concerning what forgiveness may be said to be, to discern the trajectory in thinking about what resentment may be said to represent morally, and to explore the variety of different forms apology may be said to assume.

In the first section, on forgiveness, I am involved in a set of debates with philosophers about the nature of secular forgiveness. Some affirm that forgiveness is *impossible*, while others argue that it is possible but that it cannot be described as forgiveness when the act is premised on or motivated by some set of desires that fall outside the narrow range they designate. I wish to suggest that these arguments are premised on a particular understanding of what forgiveness is that we can trace to a very particular origin. In this section, then, I am mostly limning out the debates, revealing the premises supporting them, and showing how these premises are traceable to an earlier moment that is perhaps the origin of our modern understanding of forgiveness in a secular sense. In the first chapter, then, I discern and tease out the implications of what I believe to be two distinct models of thinking about forgiveness—one that we can find in Jesus' statements and the other in Paul's epistles. After showing what is implied in these two models, I then turn, in Chapter 2, to the first question of whether forgiveness is indeed impossible, as several philosophers argue, and then, in Chapter 3, to the question of what conditions, if any, make forgiveness possible.

In the second section, I pursue a more historical approach to the ways we can understand the evolution of resentment as a moral concept. My primary concern here is to reveal two things—first, that resentment is a deeply complicated emotion that has the potential to stifle and stall us in a self-involved anguish or to liberate and open us to seek greater justice and, second, that there is an important and revelatory trajectory in the evolution of the concept of resentment. In the opening chapter of the section, I look at some literary works that help us appreciate the complexity of the emotion, drawing on two very different worlds. Once we have a sense of the major issues involved in resentment's complexity, I offer a historical survey of the evolution of the moral concept. In Chapter 5, I trace the writings of a set of eighteenth-century British moralists who represent resentment as primarily the condition of an individual conscience. In Chapter 6, I examine the writings of nineteenth-century Continental existentialists who argue that resentment is best conceived as the condition of a collective society. I should also be clear that this evolution, like ours, is not one that is directed toward a particular end, nor one in which one species inevitably gives way to another that replaces it. The resentment described by the British moralists who wished to see it as a source of our search for justice continues to exist in robust ways at the same time as, and after, the appearance of a Nietzschean species of resentment as a debilitating cultural condition and source of weakness.

In the third section, I offer a taxonomy of apologies in their two forms, private and public. My interest in this section is to make what I think are necessary distinctions that will assist us in appreciating better what to make of practices of apologizing. We tend to expect certain properties in particular events that permit us to judge whether that event is successful or not. In the case of apologies, though, we have largely—and, I think, mistakenly—applied our norms for private apologies to our expectations of public ones. Many of us are dissatisfied with most public apologies, I believe, because we have thought that they should resemble in form and sincerity and meaning the ones we make and receive in private life. I offer, instead, this taxonomy in order to reveal in what different spheres we can find different norms for and meanings of apologies. In the opening chapter, I look at two films in order to discuss how certain social conditions produce an ethos that makes apologizing more or less possible. In Chapter 8, I focus on private apologies, and my discussion is largely theoretical as I examine the conceptions of what work an apology can do in an interpersonal relationship. In Chapter 9, my theorizing is buttressed by a series of case studies as I attempt to identify the variety of different types and sites of public apologies.

IV

While the term *historical anatomy* in the subtitle of this book reflects an obvious desire on my part to echo Nietzsche's "genealogy" of morals, I am also making an important distinction between what we can say about the historical evolution of the formation of these three practices and what we wish to understand about the relationship of the parts to each other within our present formation. I am interested in, and dwell at length on, critical moments in the historical development of these ideas (the genealogy of them), but my primary intent is to reveal what properties each practice contains so that we can better understand the interactive dynamic in the interplay of the three of them. In one central aspect of our moral life—that concerning how we respond to injuries we caused or suffered—we face a series of choices. Injured, we can respond with resentment or stoic apathy. Recognizing that we have injured another, we can feel remorse and offer an apology or feel indifferent and offer nothing. Faced with an apology, we can forgive or continue to resent what the original injury signified about our place in the world. These are by no means the only choices or the only possibilities for organizing these choices. But they are the ones most of us face, and the terms most of us use in the aftermath of injury. My interest, after giving some genealogy of these terms, is to see what kind of moral body they together assemble. Like Dr. Frankenstein, but, one hopes, with better results, the best way to approach that work is through anatomy.

FORGIVENESS

1 FORGIVENESS

JESUS AND PAUL

The search for origins sometimes, as in mythic and religious texts, explains what a phenomenon is and sometimes, as in Darwin, helps explain a process that makes defining a phenomenon difficult. I am here involved in that second task, and I begin with three accounts of the origins of forgiveness.

In his most recent book, Robert Enright, who arguably pioneered the psychological study of forgiveness with the creation of the Human Development Study Group at the University of Wisconsin-Madison in 1985 and the International Forgiveness Institute in 1994, argued that forgiveness as a human, secular practice emerged "over 3,000 years ago." He seems to put that date on its origin only because we have no textual evidence from "written history" to place it even earlier. It is likely that most people, were they to consider the question, would express agreement with Enright—they would hold that forgiveness originated either with Judaism or human nature, either with the religious textual records that establish it as a religious principle in the first Abrahamic faith tradition or as a documentation of what had already been a social practice in the earliest prehistoric human moral orders.[1]

Enright made this statement four years after David Konstan had challenged that conventional wisdom. To understand what forgiveness means now, that is, broadly, since the Enlightenment, Konstan argues, we have to understand what it meant to classical

---

1. Robert D. Enright, *The Forgiving Life: A Pathway to Overcoming Resentment and Creating a Legacy of Love* (Washington, DC: American Psychological Association, 2014), p. 307. For the creation of the Human Study Group and the International Forgiveness Institute, see Enright, *Forgiveness Is a Choice: A Step-by-Step Process for Resolving Anger and Restoring Hope* (Washington, DC: American Psychological Association, 2001).

antiquity, to ancient Judaism and Christianity, and to medieval rabbinic and patristic writers. His argument is that the "modern concept of forgiveness" (that is, specifically, "interpersonal forgiveness") did not exist for any of these schools of thinking and emerged, as so much of modern thinking did, only as a post-Kantian phenomenon. Konstan defines *interpersonal forgiveness* as follows: whoever beseeches forgiveness "must repudiate the act of wrongdoing together with the values that permitted it," and whoever grants forgiveness "must come round" to "seeing the offender and oneself in a new light."[2] That kind of interpersonal forgiveness, he argues, simply did not exist in classical antiquity and had only a rudimentary existence in the sacred texts of and commentators on Judaism and Christianity, rarely articulated and always in the context of some other practice, until the nineteenth century. What came before then was either not interpersonal (it was divine forgiveness of human sinfulness) or not forgiveness (it was some other form of appeasement or ritual of reconciliation used to shed or mark the shedding of enmities).

Konstan made that statement fifty years after Hannah Arendt had begun this particular debate about origins. What Arendt did that was remarkably original is define forgiveness in terms of its function in relationship to the evolution of the human condition, namely, to provide a means of redress that allowed humans to escape a temporality based on cycles. Arendt claimed, in a famous passage, that the "discoverer of the role of forgiveness in the realm of human affairs was Jesus of Nazareth." The fact that Jesus "made this discovery in a religious context and articulated it in religious language," she contends, "is no reason to take it any less seriously in a strictly secular sense." We should be clear in understanding just what Arendt is saying that is strikingly original. She is not saying what theologians had been saying for centuries, that Christianity brought cosmic mercy to answer the strictures of cosmic justice or that forgiveness, as so many theologians also claim, is central to Christianity as the historical response to original sin. Drawing strictly from the philosophical practices of Jesus, she is arguing that Jesus gave the secular world its first model of interpersonal forgiveness.[3]

---

2. David Konstan, *Before Forgiveness: The Origins of a Moral Idea* (Cambridge: Cambridge University Press, 2010), pp. ix, xi, 99. In the last passage in the definition of forgiveness, Konstan is quoting Charles L. Griswold, *Forgiveness: A Philosophical Exploration* (Cambridge: Cambridge University Press, 2007), p. 53.

3. Hannah Arendt, *The Human Condition* (Chicago: University of Chicago Press, 1958), p. 238.

We have, then, at least three different origins for forgiveness as a human practice, and each of them posits a distinctive development to which it can be traced. Either it emerged with human nature itself and was formalized in religious scriptures some three thousand years ago, or it was inaugurated with Jesus' ministry and meant to create a model of political behavior for a "small and closely knit community of his followers" two thousand years ago, or it began less than two hundred years ago as an Enlightenment phenomenon in a post-Kantian world that valued "moral autonomy."[4]

We should be clear that Konstan, Arendt, and Enright are not talking about different *forms* of forgiveness (secular or not) or different *effects* of forgiveness (permitting or not the reevaluation of the offender and the offended self). They are not. All of them conceive of forgiveness as a secular, social practice in which the action or process of forgiveness between humans involves a change in the person who forgives (most commonly defined, since the eighteenth century, as the repudiation of resentment or, before that, as a *metanoia*, or 'change of heart'). If they do not differ on what they mean by forgiveness, we cannot resolve this debate by suggesting that they are describing different points on an evolutionary continuum. They simply disagree in their assessments of when that one kind of forgiveness was inaugurated. So, who is right? I believe, in the end, that Arendt is right, for reasons that will be made clear below. But it is less my intention to prove Arendt correct than to return to that key moment she identified as the origin of interpersonal forgiveness and see in what ways Jesus provided a model for it and in what ways that model of forgiveness was challenged, and in many ways superseded, by another, that of the Apostle Paul. That moment in the early Christian era defined what I will argue are two discrepant ideas about forgiveness, two distinct models of the practice.

Most theologians who write about forgiveness in the New Testament do not see, or at least do not acknowledge, a discrepancy between what Jesus says and what Paul says. My argument is not only that there is a discrepancy, and a meaningful one, but that what I will characterize as Paul's interpretation of Jesus' most consistent and resonant statements on forgiveness does nothing less than undermine the meaning of those statements and alter the key terms that Jesus had articulated about the nature and meaning of forgiveness. There is today a healthy debate over whether Paul can be considered the "founder of

4. Arendt, *The Human Condition*, p. 239; Konstan, *Before Forgiveness*, pp. 152, xi.

Christianity" or to what degree he "transformed" it.[5] This is not a debate I will enter directly. My interest, rather, is to see first the terms that Jesus and Paul employ, to develop two models from those terms, and to see the implications that each model makes about the nature of forgiveness. In this chapter, then, we can see briefly the ways that the Pauline model has largely replaced the model Jesus provides in modern theological conceptions of forgiveness, and in the following chapter we can see just how much that Pauline model is the one implicitly assumed in the modern, secular study of forgiveness.

I

In order to understand the crucial difference between Paul and Jesus on the topic of forgiveness, we need first to appreciate two puzzling things and one historical development. The first puzzling thing is the infrequency of references to "forgiveness" in the New Testament, which is surprising, of course, given how theologians insist that forgiveness is central to Christianity. The "essence of Christianity," writes H. R. Mackintosh in a representative statement, "might fairly be summed up" in the following credo: "I believe in God who forgives sins through Jesus Christ." Such a statement should surprise no one possessing a passing familiarity with Christianity. These are the terms, after all, that have defined the early Christian church, the terms, indeed, that come down from the Apostle's Creed: "I believe in God the Father Almighty . . . And in Jesus Christ his only Son our Lord . . . I believe in . . . The Forgiveness of Sins." They are the terms found in the Nicene Creed as amended at the First Council of Constantinople in 381: 'forgiveness of sins' (*aphesin hamartiōn*). And, of course, they are the terms we find in the New Testament itself, and indeed the words Jesus uses in the Lord's Supper: "For this is my blood of the new testament, which is shed for many for the remission of sins" (Matthew 26:28).[6] What the King James Version translates

---

5. See, for instance, Joel Carmichael, *The Birth of Christianity: Reality and Myth* (Dorchester, UK: Dorset Press, 1989); David Wenham, *Paul: Follower of Jesus or Founder of Christianity?* (Grand Rapids, MI: Wm. B. Eerdmans, 1995); N. T. Wright, *What Saint Paul Really Said: Was Paul of Tarsus the Real Founder of Christianity?* (Grand Rapids, MI: Wm. B. Eerdmans, 1997); and Gerd Lüdemann, *Paul: The Founder of Christianity* (Amherst, NY: Prometheus Books, 2002). Also see James D. Tabor, *Paul and Jesus: How the Apostle Transformed Christianity* (New York: Simon & Schuster, 2012).

6. All quotations from the New Testament will be taken from the King James Version, except where I draw on the Greek terms to make the point clearer (which I do in the discussion of Ephesians 5:1 and 1 Corinthians 11:1 and 4:16 below).

as 'remission' is that same word, *aphesin*, which in other translations of the New Testament is more accurately rendered 'forgiveness' (the Latin translation of the Niceno–Constantinopolitan Creed has it *remissionem peccatorum*). Given its focal point in Christianity, then, we might be disconcerted to discover that the terms denoting "forgiveness" occur only forty-five times in the Gospels (including Acts) and fourteen times in the rest of the New Testament.[7]

The root word used by Matthew in the scene of the Lord's Supper and the other Gospel writers in other statements of Jesus (*aphesis*) is one of the four Greek words used in the New Testament to denote forgiveness: *charizomai, aphiemi, aphesis,* and *apoluo,* the last of which, with one notable exception, usually means 'dismiss' or 'put away.' The first, *charizomai,* as Anthony Bash notes, is rare. In cases where the context makes it clear that it means 'forgive'— and not 'bestow' or 'give'—it occurs twelve times in the New Testament.[8] Of these twelve usages, two are to be found in Luke 7:42–43 and the remaining ten in the Pauline and the deutero-Pauline epistles: 2 Corinthians 2:7 and 2:10 (thrice), 12:13, Ephesians 4:32 (twice), Colossians 2:13 and 3:13 (twice).[9] Paul does not use the other terms found in the Gospels. Commentators have marveled at the fact that the Gospel terms for 'forgiveness' (*aphesis* and *aphiemi*) are, as Krister Stendahl phrases it, "spectacularly absent" in the undisputed Pauline epistles. Some have found this absence "inexplicable," while

---

7. H. R. Mackintosh, *The Christian Experience of Forgiveness* (London: Nisbet & Co., 1927), pp. 1–2. The translation of the Apostle's Creed is taken from the 1662 edition of *The Book of Common Prayer* (New York: Church Publishing Incorporated, 2007), p. 96. On the infrequency of *forgiveness* in the New Testament, see Anthony Bash, *Just Forgiveness: Exploring the Bible, Weighing the Issues* (London: SPCK, 2011), pp. 59, 70–71, 85, 13. Cf. Harvey Cox, "Repentance and Forgiveness: A Christian Perspective," in *Repentance: A Comparative Perspective,* edited by Amitai Etzioni and David E. Carney (Lanham, MD: Rowman & Littlefield, 2000), pp. 21–30, esp. p. 23.

8. Bash, *Just Forgiveness,* pp. 41, 43–49; V. Norskov Olsen, "Forgiveness in the New Testament," *Ministry Magazine* (July, 1963). The word *apoluo* is also translated as 'forgive' (it is usually rendered as 'let go,' or 'put away,' or 'dismiss'), but it is used only twice in the New Testament. As well, *aspondia* is used twice as 'unforgiving' (Bash, *Just Forgiveness,* p. 53).

9. I will be using *Paul* and *Pauline* to refer to all the epistles ascribed to Paul in the New Testament. I will not take up the debate about what are and are not Paul's epistles; the orthodoxy seems to be that there are seven undisputed epistles, and the rest are debatable. Both of the epistles I will be focusing on here fall into the debatable category: Ephesians and Colossians. The point of authenticity of authorship is unimportant for my purposes since the deutero-Pauline epistles have been ascribed to Paul, and therefore had the influence they had as Pauline writings, and it is this influence that is important for the argument I am making here. For the debates on the letters, see Günther Bornkamm, *Paul Paulus,* translated by D. M. G. Stalker (New York: Harper & Row Publishers, 1971), pp. 241–47.

others have explained it away by arguing that Paul means "forgiveness" when he uses the term *justification*.[10] We will return to this point presently.

The second puzzling thing is the New Testament representation of the idea of the *unforgivable*, which Jesus introduces in curious circumstances. In the Gospel of Mark, when the scribes try to dismiss Jesus' miraculous work by claiming that it is the work of Satan, Jesus first demonstrates the illogic of their claim—"How can Satan cast out Satan?"—and then makes the following contradictory statement: "All sins shall be forgiven unto the sons of men, and blasphemies wherewith soever they shall blaspheme: But he that shall blaspheme against the Holy Ghost hath never forgiveness, but is in danger of eternal damnation" (Mark 3:28–29).[11] In context, it is clear that the sin against the Holy Ghost is for someone to deny the work of the Spirit (and, as the scribes do, to insist that it comes from other, evil sources). After that, things become a little less clear. In context, it might be that Jesus is emphasizing the depth of depravity in that particular sin by noting that all *other* sins are forgivable. But he does not say "other"; he says "all" (*panta*). Here, then, we find ourselves confronted with either a paradox (all sins shall be forgiven, but not all) or a mystery (all sins shall be forgiven, even the unforgivable). One reading sees the second verse qualifying the first; the paradox is that "all" is contradicted by the exception. The second reading sees the first verse qualifying the second; the mystery is that forgiveness is possible for even that which is unforgivable. Bash, for example, supports the latter reading, which effectively renders the category of the "unforgivable" empty of significance.[12] The "unforgivable" is forgivable, under the right circumstances. What Jesus' statement

---

10. Krister Stendahl, "Paul Among Jews and Gentiles," in *Paul Among Jews and Gentiles and Other Essays* (Minneapolis: Fortress Press, 1976), pp. 1–77, esp. p. 23; George Foot Moore, *Judaism in the First Centuries of the Christian Era* (Cambridge, MA: Harvard University Press, 1954), III, p. 151; William Sanday and Arthur C. Headlam, *A Critical and Exegetical Commentary on the Epistle to the Romans* (Edinburgh: T&T Clark, 1958), p. 36.

11. The other Gospels do not much help clarify the issue of the unforgivable sin against the Holy Spirit. In Matthew, the context is the same as in Mark. Jesus addresses the scribes who suggest the power to heal is satanic, and he responds the same way. The contradiction is even more apparent in Matthew, since Jesus says that "All manner of sin and blasphemy shall be forgiven unto men," before he says: "whosoever speaketh against the Holy Ghost, it shall not be forgiven him, neither in this world, neither in the *world* to come" (Matthew 12:32). In Luke, the context is different; the scribes are not addressed at that moment in that Gospel, and there is no contradiction. Jesus does not say that "all sins" will be forgiven when he states that the sin against the Holy Ghost "shall not be forgiven" (Luke 12:8–10). The Greek phrase in the Gospel of Mark is *ouk echei aphesin* (literally, 'not have forgiveness'); in Matthew and Luke, *ouk aphethēsetai* ('will not be forgiven').

12. Bash, *Just Forgiveness*, pp. 61–62.

on the sin against the Holy Ghost indisputably does, however we choose to read those differing and either paradoxical or mystical accounts, is complicate the vision we have of forgiveness in the New Testament. Forgiveness is not unconditional; there are conditions in which it is not granted and conditions in which it might never be granted.

The historical development that is important for us here to note is that the terms used in the Pauline epistles and the Gospels denote *both* divine and interpersonal forgiveness. When Paul uses the term *charizomai*, he uses the same term to talk about the divine act of remission of sins, justification, and salvation that he argues Christ brought into the world and to talk about the kinds of social acts of reconciliation that are necessary in the young Christian communities to which he addresses his epistles. As an example of the first usage, he notes that Christ has "forgiven you all trespasses" (Colossians 2:13); of the second, he urges the community in Colossians to be "forbearing" and "forgiving [to] one another" (Colossians 3:13). He also uses the same word when he talks about his own acts of forgiveness. He does this when he self-mockingly apologizes to the Corinthians—"forgive me this wrong"—for being insufficiently "burdensome" to them (2 Corinthians 12:13). And, finally, he uses it when he describes an intricate relationship among the community, the pastor (himself), and Christ: "To whom ye forgive any thing, I *forgive* also: for if I forgave any thing, to whom I forgave *it*, for your sakes *forgave I it*" in the person of Christ" (2 Corinthians 2:10).[13] The same term, *charizomai*, describes two distinct kinds of forgiveness. So, too, when Jesus uses the terms *aphesis* in the Lord's Prayer or *apoluo* in the Sermon on the Plain, he uses it to describe the forgiveness that one may expect from God and the forgiveness that one must extend to one's brother.[14]

We can see the importance of this point by returning to the Hebrew Bible, which employs two distinct terms to denote the two kinds of forgiveness. The Hebrew word for forgiveness used in the instances of divine forgiveness either is or has the root *salakh* (or *salach*) and it is a verb that, as Konstan and David Montgomery note, "always has God as the subject." The Hebrew word used in the cases of interpersonal forgiveness, in the story of Joseph and his

---

13. Cf. Colossians 3:13: "Forbearing [*anechomenoi*] one another, and forgiving [*charizomenoi*] one another, if any man have a quarrel against any: even as Christ forgave [*echarisato*] you, so also *do* ye."

14. The one usage in John 20:22–23 is as follows: "he breathed on them, and saith unto them, Receive ye the Holy Ghost: Whose soever sins ye remit [*aphēte*], they are remitted [*apheōntai*] unto them; and whose soever sins ye retain, they are retained."

brothers, for instance, is *nasa*, a word that usually has God as the subject but sometimes other humans, like Joseph.[15] Likewise, in the rabbinical tradition, distinct terms denote distinct kinds and degrees of forgiveness. Maimonides, for instance, uses *mechilá* for interpersonal forgiveness and *kappará* for divine atonement. As David Blumenthal points out, these are two of the three kinds of forgiveness in the Jewish tradition. *Mechilá*, like other terms for "forgiving" in other languages, implies a "forgoing the other's indebtedness," and it is the most basic kind of forgiveness that one human extends to another. *Kappará*, on the other hand, like *tahorá* (purification), is "a total wiping away of all sinfulness" and can be given only by God. The middle form of forgiveness (*selichá*) is more profound than *mechilá* in that it implies a greater degree of empathy for the sinner, but it is still "closer to an act of mercy than to an act of grace."[16] We will note shortly in what ways the difference between divine and human acts of forgiveness is marked in the New Testament, but it is important to see that both Paul and Jesus use the same term to describe the two kinds of forgiveness that the Hebrew Bible had denoted with distinct terms.

II

We can now turn to where Paul and Jesus differ in their models of forgiveness, which is precisely on that idea of the relationship of interpersonal to divine forgiveness. The focal text on which each model seems to be based is precisely that statement in the Lord's Prayer that defines the relationship. In Matthew, the Lord's Prayer reads: "forgive us our debts, as we forgive our debtors" (Matthew 6:12).[17]

15. David Montgomery, *Forgiveness in the Old Testament* (Belfast: Center for Contemporary Christianity in Ireland, nd), pp. 3, 7–11; Konstan, *Before Forgiveness*, pp. 105–11. Cf. Michael L. Morgan, "Mercy, Repentance, and Forgiveness in Ancient Judaism," in *Ancient Forgiveness: Classical, Judaic, and Christian*, edited by Charles L. Griswold and David Konstan (Cambridge: Cambridge University Press, 2012), pp. 137–57, esp. p. 138. Montgomery's tract is one of a series of papers published as the *Forgiveness Papers* under the *Embodying Forgiveness* project run by the Centre for Contemporary Christianity in Ireland.

16. David R. Blumenthal, "Repentance and Forgiveness," *Cross Currents* 48.1 (Spring, 1998): 75–82, esp. pp. 79–80. Cf. Solomon Schimmel, "Interpersonal Forgiveness and Repentance in Judaism," in *Forgiveness in Context: Theology and Psychology in Creative Dialogue*, edited by Fraser Watts and Liz Guildford (London: Bloomsbury, 2004), p. 20.

17. In Luke it reads: "forgive us our sins; for we also forgive every one that is indebted to us" (Luke 11:4). There seems to be a potentially meaningful difference in the two Gospels ("as" or "for") that requires some explanation here. In Matthew, the Greek word *hōs* is translated as 'as,' while in Luke the word *gar* is translated as 'for.' *Hōs* is an adverb, while *gar* is a conjunction, and, according to *Strong's Concordance hōs* is an adverb meaning "as, like as, even as, since, as

Paul implicitly interprets this statement with two subtle modifications. In his letter to the community in Ephesians, he states: "be ye kind one to another, tenderhearted, forgiving one another, even as God for Christ's sake hath forgiven you" (Ephesians 4:32). And in the epistle to Colossians 3:13, he writes: "even as Christ forgave you, so also *do* ye" (Colossians 3:13). What Paul does is emphasize Christ's role in divine forgiveness: "as God for Christ's sake" in Ephesians, "as Christ" in Colossians. As he does throughout this corpus, Paul uses this verse to elaborate his Christ-based soteriology, his focus on Christ as the sole source of salvation. The second thing that Paul does is emphasize the relationship in a particular direction, making it even more into an exhortation for us to forgive our fellow humans as an *effect* of our having received divine forgiveness. We should forgive *because* we have been forgiven.

Jesus explicitly interprets the statement in the Lord's Prayer with one emphatic modification. The text that says "forgive us our debts, as we forgive our debtors," Jesus explains immediately after reciting the prayer, means that "if ye forgive men their trespasses, your heavenly Father will also forgive you: But if ye forgive not men their trespasses, neither will your Father forgive your trespasses" (Matthew 6:14–15). Only in Matthew does this account of forgiveness follow directly after the Lord's Prayer. In Luke, the Lord's Prayer appears in one place (11:2–4), and the statement about forgiveness is stated in the Sermon on the Plain, when Jesus describes the beatitudes of responding to wrongdoing with love: "Judge not, and ye shall not be judged: condemn not, and ye shall not be condemned: forgive [*apoyete*], and ye shall be forgiven [*apolythēsesthe*]" (Luke 6:37). (This is the only use of *apoluo* to denote forgiveness.) In Mark, where the Lord's Prayer does not appear, the statement is made during Jesus' entry into Jerusalem for Passover: "when you stand praying, forgive, if ye have ought against any: that your Father also which is in heaven may forgive you your trespasses. But if you do not forgive, neither will your Father, which is in heaven forgive your trespasses" (Mark 11:25–26).

That statement, then, constitutes Jesus' model of forgiveness, just as the sentiment in Ephesians and Colossians constitutes Paul's. It is the same sentiment Jesus expresses after the parable in which the servant was forgiven his debt of ten thousand talents by the king, but then that servant in turn refused

---

along as," while *gar* is used to express "cause, explanation, inference or continuation." Some translators see no difference; Wycliffe, for instance, translates *gar* as 'as.' As we will see, Paul uses a different word (*kathōs*) to replace either *gar* or *hōs*. Matthew: *kai aphes hēmin ta opheilēmata hēmōn hōs kai hēmeis aphēkamen tois opheiletais hēmōn.* Luke: *kai aphes hēmin tas hamartias hēmōn kai gar autoi aphiomen panti opheilonti hēmin.*

to forgive his fellow servant a debt of one hundred pence. When the king is told of this ungrateful behavior, that is, this servant's failure to forgive debts as he was forgiven, the king reinstated the debt and delivered the servant to the tormentors until he paid what he owed. Jesus draws the lesson for Peter: "So likewise shall my heavenly Father do also unto you, if ye from your hearts forgive not every one his brother their trespasses" (Matthew 18:35). This parable is told immediately after Jesus answers Peter's question about the duty to forgive. "Then came Peter to him, and said, Lord, how oft shall my brother sin against me, and I forgive him? till seven times? Jesus saith unto him, I say not unto thee, Until seven times: but, Until seventy times seven" (Matthew 18:21–22).

While both statements insist that the human imperative to forgive those who commit wrongs against them has a direct relationship with divine forgiveness, the two statements offer drastically different dynamics of that relationship. Paul had urged the congregations to forgive because God had forgiven them, while Jesus implies that God might forgive us if we had forgiven others. In Paul, divine forgiveness *stimulates* interpersonal forgiveness, while in Jesus divine forgiveness *presupposes* and *requires* it.

In Jesus' description, as opposed to Paul's, the relationship between divine and interpersonal forgiveness is considerably more fraught. Divine forgiveness is conditional on our own acts of forgiving, and those acts are not measured or limited by the actions of others; repeated wrongs must receive repeated forgiveness. (Jeffrie Murphy does wittily note that Jesus does not say "always forgive" but *only* four hundred and ninety times.)[18] Jesus' point, then, is that interpersonal forgiveness must be unconditional, recurrent, and pervasive, while divine forgiveness is conditional—precisely, on the exhibition of interpersonal forgiveness. Such a reading, I think, does not deny that salvation (forgiveness of sins) is a gift, as theologians like to say, but that it is a particular kind of gift that is premised on its recipients' giving something in anticipation of it.[19]

---

18. Jeffrie G. Murphy, "Forgiveness and Resentment," *Midwest Studies in Philosophy* 7 (1982): 503–16, esp. p. 513.

19. There is one place in the New Testament where Jesus stipulates a condition. It is the passage in Luke where he answers a disciple's question about how frequently one must forgive (the same as Matthew 18:21–22). In Luke, Jesus states: "if thy brother trespass against thee, rebuke him; and if he repent [*metanoēsē*], forgive him. And if he trespass against thee seven times in a day, and seven times in a day turn again to thee, saying, I repent [*metanoō*]; thou shalt forgive him" (Luke 17:3–4). The word *repent* (*metanoia*) suggests something like a change of heart, an acknowledgment that what one did was morally wrong; and it is the same term Jesus

What is it, then, that we can make of this difference between Jesus' and Paul's exhortations? Jesus' model of forgiving places more emphasis on interpersonal forgiving, by making it the condition for receiving divine forgiveness, while Paul's model places more emphasis on divine forgiveness since it implicitly becomes the precondition. Paul's version is clearly less demanding of what it is people are expected to do. Forgiving *because* we have been forgiven implies that the original forgiveness (divine) is a gift that makes it possible for us to forgive and that we are commanded to respect that original gift by emulating it. It is a gift in the conventional sense of something we receive. Jesus' version is more demanding in making our forgiving others the precondition for our receiving divine forgiveness. Forgiving "so that" we may be forgiven implies that the divine forgiveness is conditional (the sentence of course is conditional in mood: 'if' [*Ean*]) and that the condition is what is required for us to receive the gift. In other words, it is a gift in an unconventional sense.

Paul's version, to use other terms than *conditional* or not, is based on faith, while Jesus' is based on works. And that might of course be part of the reason that Protestant theologians have overwhelmingly favored Paul's version. The focus here is not on what import to place on our work of forgiving others but rather on how we should do so as a sign of our already having been the recipients of God's forgiveness.

We need to explore more deeply and systematically this dynamic exchange in which we are urged to give the gift of forgiveness to others because we have received it from God. First, what precisely is forgiveness in this model? We can think of interpersonal forgiveness as a genuine gift; that is, we are truly giving something away for a disinterested reason because we have been inspired to do so by the example of having received a divine gift. In the conditional reading, the gift of interpersonal forgiveness does not feel like a genuine gift since the presupposition is that we are doing it in order to receive a greater gift from God. The difference is that in the conditional reading we give a gift in the expectation of receiving one, while in the unconditional reading we give a gift in appreciation of already having received one. So, the gift is a gift, not an act of aspiration.

---

uses when he urges people to repent because the kingdom of heaven is near (cf. Matthew 4:17, *Metanoeite* [imperative mood] and Luke 24:47, *metanoian* [noun] among other places). But Luke 17:3–4 is the solitary instance in which Jesus speaks of the conditions of interpersonal forgiveness. It is a passage many philosophers use to buttress their accounts of why forgiveness requires the wrongdoer's penitence in order to avoid being condonation. I write about this debate elsewhere.

III

There is, then, a significant difference between what Paul and Jesus say about forgiveness. How has that difference been explained? It has largely *not* been explained, or indeed much recognized. The most common response of theologians who write on forgiveness has been to ignore the difference and implicitly to accept Paul's model over that of Jesus (we will turn to that response in a moment). The difference is so little noticed that sometimes writers cite Paul's words as if they express Jesus' sentiments. As astute a Biblical scholar as David Augsburger, for instance, notes that the statement "Forgive us our debts as we forgive our debtors" is "the only condition in the Lord's Prayer," the only item in the prayer on which Jesus offers a commentary, and the only "condition which is repeatedly underscored in Jesus' teaching." All of these teachings, he writes, "limit God's forgiveness to those who forgive their brothers and sisters," and this point, he continues, is found "repeated in all of the crucial passages on forgiving (see Mark 11:25, Ephesians 4:32, Colossians 3:13)."[20] But, as we have seen, what Paul says in the verses in Ephesians and Colossians that Augsburger cites is precisely *not* that.

What many modern writers on forgiveness find objectionable in Jesus' model is that it seems too crassly economic—we will receive forgiveness because we forgive others. It is likewise the objection they make to the language of "debt" in the Lord's Prayer ("forgive us our debts") since it makes forgiveness into an exchange and transaction that is based on economics rather than a gift based on generosity and grace. We have to earn our forgiveness rather than graciously be given it. It seems to make salvation less an act of grace, less a gift, and more a reward, more a repayment. If God may or may not grant forgiveness—and it depends on our actions—then God's actions are bound to human ones. In this extreme version, human free will undermines God's power. The Pauline model, on the other hand, puts the power solely and firmly in God, who forgives us and thereby gives us the power and ability and model for forgiving others.

If we accept what Jesus says, then forgiveness becomes for many commentators, as John Patton puts it, "a manipulative ploy for influencing God." Jesus is appealing to our reason and effectively offering us a deal in which a lesser

---

20. David Augsburger, *Caring Enough to Not Forgive: False Forgiveness/Caring Enough to Forgive: True Forgiveness* (Ventura, CA: Regal Books, 1981), p. 34. This volume has separate pagination for each of the sections; the passage is taken from the *Caring Enough to Not Forgive* section. Cf. Augsburger, *The New Freedom of Forgiveness* (3rd. ed.; Chicago: Moody Press, 2000), p. 29.

investment, forgiving others, produces a more advantageous return, eternal salvation. In other words, the offer is based on an exchange and premised on rational calculation.[21] It is, in a word, *conditional*. Jesus makes divine forgiveness *conditional* on interpersonal forgiveness.

Patton, for instance, finds "highly questionable" what he calls "the conditional nature of forgiveness" that the Lord's Prayer appears to express, which he argues is a misinterpretation of the prayer. According to many Christian theologians, we have to understand that the Lord's Prayer is expressing not only an ethics (forgive others) but also an eschatology (you will be forgiven in the kingdom of the end times), and we can understand the ethics (what should you do now) only in light of the temporal framework provided by the *eschaton* (what will happen at the end times). So, they argue, what appears to provide one temporal framework (forgive others *first*, so that you will *then* be forgiven) is actually providing a different one that assumes the future in the present, that is, in the "kingdom come." For Norman Perrin, that dissolves what appears to be a condition (if you do this, then you will get this) into something else that is wrought out of the "eschatological tension between present and future." Likewise, Raymond Brown focuses on the *eschaton* to understand the impetus for interpersonal forgiveness: "In the last days the followers of Christ will receive the fullness of divine sonship. Their forgiveness of one another as brothers and their forgiveness by their Father are both parts of this great gift." Both Perrin and Brown thereby avoid what Brown calls the "*quid pro quo*" that Jesus seems to describe in insisting on the "priority of human forgiveness." In this reading of the Lord's Prayer through the temporal lens of the *eschaton*, what had appeared to be an order based on a prior and later action (forgive others now, you will then be forgiven) becomes instead, as Patton puts it, an atemporal situation in which "God's forgiveness and ours may be simultaneous."[22]

Even the idea of "simultaneous" forgiving seems too much of a compromise, however, as theologians go on to argue the priority of God's forgiveness. What had appeared to be commanded as prior (interpersonal forgiveness), writes David Norris, is in fact evidence that we are already the recipients of

21. John Patton, *Is Human Forgiveness Possible? A Pastoral Care Perspective* (Nashville: Abingdon Press, 1985), p. 122.

22. Patton, *Is Human Forgiveness Possible?*, p. 153; Norman Perrin, *The Kingdom of God in the Teaching of Jesus* (Philadelphia: Westminster Press, 1963), pp. 196, 201–202; Raymond Brown, *New Testament Essays* (Milwaukee: Bruce Publishing Company, 1965), p. 248; Patton, *Is Human Forgiveness Possible?*, p. 157. I am indebted to Patton's book for this discussion of the *eschaton* in the Lord's Prayer.

God's forgiveness: "forgiving one another is made possible by the deep reception of God's forgiveness, and is therefore ultimately the work of God in us." And Patton, who had earlier in his book suggested simultaneity as a possibility, eventually concludes in favor of the priority of God's actions: "we are forgiven and can *thereby* be forgiving" (emphasis added).[23]

What this theological argument does is curious not so much because it pursues a strategy that makes the words on the page appear to say something entirely opposite—we all do that as interpreters of texts sacred and secular—but rather because it is precisely based on what Paul had argued. They take what Jesus expressed as a rigorous imperative condition of what one needs to do to attain salvation (*do this if*) and render it into a benign exhortation of what one should do as a result of salvation (*do this because*). What Jesus had represented as a *cause* was now cast as an *effect*. What each of these writers falls into is emphatically a Pauline interpretation of Jesus' words.

That dynamic, in which Paul's commentary trumps Jesus' words has a fairly long history in theological writing, of course, and it is especially pronounced on the topic of forgiveness. Paul, after all, had formulated the idea that became the basis of Protestant theology—the idea of justification by faith, not works. That idea, writes Günther Bornkamm, what he calls the "gospel of justification by faith alone," is not a product of the early primitive church but rather "a specifically Pauline creation." And it is a Pauline creation that has exerted enormous influence and largely displaced Jesus' texts on which it was offered as an interpretive commentary. It is noteworthy that even those who criticize that tendency in theologians to value Paul's interpretations over Jesus' statements frequently fall into it. In his massive *fin de siècle* tome of systematic theology, for instance, Albrecht Ritschl commented that "the authority of Jesus . . . deserves to be set above that of Paul." He is here talking about the idea of the Kingdom of God. But when it comes to talking about forgiveness, Ritschl distinctly sets the authority of Paul over that of Jesus. Jesus spoke of "forgiveness of sins," writes Ritschl, while Paul speaks of "justification." While he considers these terms synonymous, Ritschl nonetheless says that the Pauline term is the "positive" formulation, while Jesus' is the "negative" one. Jesus, "like the men of the Old Testament," might "rest satisfied with the negative term," but those interested in the New Testament, and invested in distinguishing Christianity from Judaism, must turn to Paul

---

23. David Amherst Norris, "Forgiving from the Heart: A Biblical and Psychotherapeutic Exploration" (Ph.D. dissertation, Union Theological Seminary, 1983), pp. 184–85; Patton, *Is Human Forgiveness Possible?*, p. 169.

instead. Indeed, Ritschl concludes, "it would be a mistaken purism were anyone, in this respect, to prefer the less developed statements of Jesus" to what
he calls the "most developed forms of the Pauline system." So much, then, for
the "authority of Jesus."[24]

IV

Rather than following that example of preferring Paul's sentiments over Jesus',
or the example of mistaking Paul's sentiments for Jesus', we are better advised
to return to that moment when Paul interpreted Jesus on what forgiveness
means and discern just what is expressed in these two distinct models of forgiveness. Once we understand just where they differ, we can see what precisely
is implied in these different models.

We can begin with Jesus' parable of the unforgiving servant. As he does
in other parables, Jesus begins and ends that parable by noting that it is
meant to represent heaven: he starts the story by noting that "the kingdom
of heaven likened unto a certain king, which would take account of his ser-
vants" (Matthew 18:23); and he concludes the account of the unforgiving
servant's being cast into jail with an object lesson: "So likewise shall my heavenly Father do also unto you, if ye from your hearts forgive not every one his
brother their trespasses" (18:35). The parable expresses two points in particular that Paul's model will alter. One has to do with *priority* and the other
with *power*.

The question of priority, of course, had been at the crux of the question of
the conditional reading. While I have been stressing that Jesus makes divine
forgiveness conditional on interpersonal forgiveness (and therefore suggests
that interpersonal forgiveness is prior to divine forgiveness), it is important
to clarify that Jesus does not deny the prevenient grace of God for those who
are told to forgive their brothers and sisters as a condition for their salvation.
In the parable of the unforgiving servant, most emphatically, he shows us a
servant who has been forgiven by the king and, presumably, is *therefore* morally bound to forgive his own debtor. In the parable, the priority of the king's
forgiveness is meant to indicate the priority of God's forgiveness. The parable
continues, though, and shows us what happens when the gift of forgiveness is

---

24. Bornkamm, *Paul Paulus*, p. 115; Albrecht Ritschl, *The Christian Doctrine of Justification and Reconciliation: The Positive Development of the Doctrine*, edited by H. R. Mackintosh and A. B. Macauley (Edinburgh: T. & T. Clark, 1900), pp. 313, 38, 3–4. The Ritschl volume does not note the name of the translator.

not appreciated, when we do not forgive our fellow-servants. In other words, Jesus returns to the *conditional*. That we have been the recipients of God's forgiveness does not mean we are eternally assured of it; if we do not forgive others, we will lose it. And presumably if we do forgive others, we will continue to be worthy of it. Jesus states forgiveness, then, as an *ethical* imperative; we must do something for the end we seek.

Paul's model, on the other hand, and the theologians who draw on it, contests that very point. Justification is not by deeds (or by actions that follow ethical or legal dictates) but by faith alone. Priority, in this model, assures salvation eternally. It is for this reason that the theologians focus on eschatology rather than ethics, on the eternal and endless Kingdom of God rather on the present moral activity in these earthly kingdoms we occupy. What in Jesus was conditional and ethical, in Paul becomes an effect and a sign of grace. We don't forgive so that we can be forgiven; we forgive *because* we have been forgiven.

If the question of priority focuses on the temporal relationship between divine and interpersonal forgiveness, the second question, concerning power, focuses on the possible equivalence between them. We should remember that both Jesus and Paul had departed from the Hebrew Bible's and Jewish tradition of using distinct terms for divine and secular forgiveness. Paul and Jesus employ the same terms (*aphesis, apoluo,* or *charizomai*) to describe both. The question is: is it implied that these two forms of forgiveness are somehow the same? To appreciate better what is implied, we might note the dynamics of the *Imitatio Dei* tradition, that is, the religious principle that we ought to imitate God as a way of achieving our own holiness. As Jesus phrases it in the Sermon on the Mount, "Be ye therefore perfect, even as your Father which is in heaven is perfect" (Matthew 5:48), or, in the Sermon on the Plain, "Be ye therefore merciful, as your Father also is merciful" (Luke 6:36). There are two possible ways of reading these exhortations to imitate God—the worshipful and the blasphemous. In the worshipful sense, God provides an exalted example to which we aspire. God is the exemplar for perfection and mercy, and we are to follow that model in our own way and at our own level. In the blasphemous sense, though, this might be an instance of our being told to act *like* God, to perform our duties *as if* they expressed the same power as God's. This sense of imitation, we recall, is the basis of human sinfulness in the Biblical account. When the serpent in Genesis seduces Eve, he tells her that eating of the forbidden fruit will give her precisely this power: "ye shall be as gods" (Genesis 3:5). In other words, there is a dangerously thin line between the two understandings of *imitation*—one of falling humanity's desire to have a power like God's, and the other of rising humanity's desire to behave morally in a way God models and sanctions.

In Jesus' model of forgiveness, this ambiguity is largely absent. Since he provides his followers with a conditional imperative, he alerts them to what they must do, not to how their activity is akin to God's. Again, if we look at the parable of the unforgiving servant, we see precisely how Jesus focuses on *differences*. Yes, the relationship between interpersonal and divine forgiveness is conditional, but it is not imitative. Jesus emphasizes the distinctions between those who represent divine and secular forgiveness by noting their difference in class (one is a king, the other a servant), in depth (one forgives an enormous amount, the other a pittance), and in power (one judges and can condemn the other to prison, the other cannot). So, Jesus makes clear that we should understand how different these two kinds of forgiveness are.

In the Pauline model, though, it is not so clear. The word *as* in Paul's epistle is *kathōs*, and *Thayer's Greek Lexicon* defines it as "according as, just as, even as," in cases where it is followed by *kai* (as it is in Paul's usage in Ephesians 4:32). *Strong's Dictionary* defines it as "precisely as, in proportion as" and "just or inasmuch as" when it is followed by *kai*.[25] There is some ambiguity here, which neither Thayer nor Strong dissipate, since *as* in this case can mean "inasmuch as" (that is, *given that* God has forgiven us), or it can mean "like" (that is, *in the same way as* God has forgiven us). Put more strongly, Paul might be asking us to forgive *because* God has forgiven us, or he might be urging us to forgive *like* God. That second reading, of course, would constitute the blasphemous sense of the *Imitatio Dei* tradition.

It is worth noting that Paul articulated the *Imitatio Dei* principle in the very next verse after telling the congregation to forgive "even as God": "Be ye therefore *imitators* of God, as dear children" (Ephesians 5:1, KJV, emphasized word altered). The word used is *mimētai*, which the King James Version translates as 'followers' but is more accurately rendered as 'imitators.' It is, moreover, a word that occurs only six times in the New Testament, and all six are from the Pauline writings. The most notable instance of his using it is in 1 Corinthians where he first exhorts the community, "be ye *imitators* of me" (4:16, KJV altered), and then, "Be ye *imitators* of me, even as I am also of

---

25. *A Greek–English Lexicon of the New Testament Being Grimm's Wilke's Clavis Novi Testamenti, Translated Revised and Enlarged by John Henry Thayer* (New York: Harper & Brothers, 1887), pp. 314–15; *The New Strong's Complete Dictionary of Bible Words* (Nashville: Thomas Nelson Publishers, 1996), pp. 134, 89.

Christ" (11:1, KJV altered). Paul, in other words, seems to offer himself as a mediator to the mediator to God.

Even Paul's most fervent admirers see in these statements and others like them something quite troubling, something that reveals aspects of him as a thinker that are deeply disturbing. What Bornkamm calls "the very embarrassing traits of his personality" tend to come out in what Stendahl refers to on one occasion as Paul's "ego trip" and on another as his "arrogant exuberance." This arrogance is to be found throughout the Pauline writings, and it seems to go in one direction, namely, comparing himself to either Christ or God. When Paul says in Colossians that "in my flesh I complete what is lacking in Christ's afflictions" (Colossians 1:24), Stendahl correctly notes that to "any proper theologian this must be strange language," employing terms that are frankly "shocking." Does Paul think himself *like* Christ? Stendahl thinks not, but he implies that there is in Paul certainly a capacity for that thought, especially when he contemplates his weakness and sickness. "Paul's sickness," writes Stendahl, "is a little—and perhaps not so little—Golgotha, a Calvary of his own." In other words, when it comes to comparing himself to God, Paul might sometimes mistake a simile for reality, misconstrue "as" into "is."[26]

Now, let's return to the question of forgiveness and see in what way this Pauline tendency inflects his conception of forgiveness. As Stendahl notes, *forgiveness* is the "term for salvation used least in all of the Pauline writings," and yet one that is "frequent in the Jesus tradition." Stendahl reads this fact through what he argues is Paul's psychological condition, that is, someone who possessed a "robust conscience" but was "not plagued by much introspection."[27] Forgiveness as a human practice is simply less resonant for Paul, and thus presumably becomes an *effect* of salvation rather than its premise. That, alone, I suppose, might make us wonder why the Pauline model of forgiveness should have assumed the place it has in theological writing. Here was someone who used the term infrequently, and lacked the introspection to appreciate what it meant most profoundly. But, even more, I think, is the fact that the Pauline model seems, like his other expressions, to imply that we

26. Bornkamm, *Paul Paulus*, p. 239; Stendahl, "Paul Among Jews and Gentiles," p. 62; Stendahl, "Glossolalia—The New Testament Evidence," in *Paul Among Jews and Gentiles and Other Essays*, pp. 109–24, esp. p. 110; Stendahl, "Paul Among Jews and Gentiles," p. 44. I am taking the quotation of Colossians 1:24 from the Revised Standard Version, which is the one Stendahl quotes.

27. Stendahl, "Paul and the Introspective Conscience of the West," in *Paul Among Jews and Gentiles and Other Essays*, pp. 78–96, esp. p. 82; Stendahl, "Paul Among Jews and Gentiles," pp. 25, 40.

can "imitate" God, not in the worshipful sense of acknowledging our distance from the ideal, but in the less worshipful sense of sometimes becoming confused about precisely what our status is.

When Paul counsels the community to forgive "as" God has done, is he implying that God provides a model for our blasphemous imitation? Should we think of our acts of forgiveness as modeled on and equivalent to God's? In this reading, Paul's exhortation for us to forgive *as* God forgives us comes to mean we will exhibit the same power in forgiving *as* God has done. In other words, what becomes attractive in Paul's version is that human forgiveness assumes divine power. Jesus' model, on the other hand, implies a very different dynamic. Our acts of forgiveness may have the power to inspire divine forgiveness, but it is not implied that they resemble divine forgiveness; and indeed, the parable of the unforgiving servant demonstrates just how unequal the two forms of forgiveness are.[28] Perhaps, that is what makes the Pauline model so insidiously seductive. An essential element of mysticism, Bornkamm notes, "is the blurring of the boundary between God and man." Bornkamm argues that Paul was not a mystic in this sense, since he insisted on the distinction: "Christ remains Lord; the believer is his property."[29] But, as we have seen, Paul blurs the boundaries in other ways and sometimes seems to imply that the "property" possesses the power of the Lord.

In the end, it is actually not that important to my argument whether or not Paul meant to suggest, inadvertently imply, or blasphemously assume that we *emulate* God in our acts of interpersonal forgiving. It is also relatively unimportant whether it is Paul himself, or deutero-Paul, who makes the suggestion and whether or not it is an expression of arrogance or mysticism. What is important is that we distinguish the Pauline model from the one provided by Jesus and that we appreciate the implications in each model. The reason this is important for those of us interested in forgiveness as a philosophical problem is that it is not only theologians but also modern scholars of forgiveness who have been seduced by the Pauline model and implicitly incorporated it into the modern secular discourse on forgiveness.

---

28. It is possible, I suppose, to argue that human forgiveness in Jesus' model would appear to be *stronger* than divine forgiveness, since it can *cause* it, but that reading seems to require a certain model of causality that is nowhere apparent in Jesus' description.

29. Bornkamm, *Paul Paulus*, p. 155.

V

To sum up, then, we can distinguish two major differences between Jesus' and Paul's models of forgiveness.

First, Jesus had clearly distinguished the difference in *power* of the two kinds of forgiveness by showing us, in the homely terms of the parable, that divine forgiveness is worth considerably more than our acts of forgiving our fellow-servants. Paul, on the other hand, had implicitly conflated the value and power of the kinds by invoking the *Imitatio Dei* tradition immediately after exhorting the congregation to forgive "as God" has. In both cases, Jesus emphasizes the necessity and defines the specific scope of interpersonal forgiveness, while Paul reduces the pressing imperative of interpersonal forgiveness at the same time as he exalts it beyond its boundaries by suggesting its shared attributes with divine forgiveness.

Second, Jesus makes the work of forgiveness *purposeful*. It is meant to do something both for the human beings who receive it and for those who offer it; in the first case, it creates reconciliation amidst community, and in the second, it produces a receptive soul for divine forgiveness. Paul, on the other hand, does not make the forgiveness purposeful in nearly the same way, and it is telling that the exhortation to forgive is based on what *has* happened rather than what *will* happen (it is an imitation and not a condition). Jesus had likewise noted that we are already the recipients of divine forgiveness in his model, but the difference is that he insists on the *ongoing work* that forgiveness performs. Because of that emphasis, Jesus' model is emphatically *conditional*, while Paul's is not. Whereas Jesus had glossed the statement in the Lord's Prayer to suggest that our offering to others interpersonal forgiveness was a precondition of our receiving divine forgiveness, Paul implicitly makes interpersonal forgiveness an effect of our receiving Christ's forgiveness.

These two points of contention, I will argue in the chapters that follow, are at the heart of, and largely define, the modern, secular debates over the possibility and meaning of forgiveness.

The question of *power* is implicitly at the core of the debate over whether forgiveness is possible or not. If we understand forgiveness to contain a particular dynamic and power—either to efface or to undo a wrong—can we say that this exercise is possible, given the characteristics of temporality that define human existence? We can't (yet) go back in time to change what we have done, and so forgiveness that presumes to do that is a futile gesture. Moreover, because we do exist in a time that flows forward, it is possible to say that we are not the same person we were when we committed the wrong, and so, in some sense the person forgiven is not the same person as the wrongdoer. For some philosophers, that makes forgiveness futile, for others impossible. The key question in this debate is *whether* forgiveness can ever be. In the next chapter, we will take up this debate and examine what is implied in the arguments of those philosophers who argue that forgiveness is *impossible*.

The question of *conditional* is at the heart of the debate over whether forgiveness is desirable or whether retribution based on a justified resentment is preferable. This debate focuses on the question of whether forgiveness can or should or must be conditional—in somewhat different but related senses of what conditions obtain. Those debates contest whether some act that does not abide by a stipulated set of conditions can be considered forgiveness or whether it is more accurately described as a different form of tolerance or acceptance or submissiveness. The key question in those debates is *what* forgiveness is and its relationship to other moral and ethical practices. In the third chapter, we will look at what is implied when we think of forgiveness in terms of the conditions and practices with which it has consistently been aligned, especially repentance and retribution.

2 THE BANALITY OF FORGIVENESS

In the 1980s, two strikingly different theologians published books on forgiveness. The two authors differed in substantial ways. One was Protestant (a Methodist pastor), the other Catholic (a nun in the order of the Franciscan Sisters of Joy); one taught and wrote books on pastoral theology, the other on systematic theology. Yet divided as they were by sectarian affiliation and intellectual affinities, they shared a belief in what we in the previous chapter characterized as the Pauline model of forgiveness. The key question between what Jesus said and what Paul said, as we saw, was whether human forgiveness is a condition of God's forgiveness (Jesus' model) or whether human forgiveness imitates God's forgiveness (Pauline model). The first theologian, John Patton, challenged what he called the "misinterpretation of the Lord's Prayer" based on the "conditional" reading of Jesus' words. The way he explains what he calls "the close connection of human and divine forgiveness in the Christian tradition" is by seeing human forgiveness as something "discovered rather than done." The second theologian, Joan Mueller, likewise implicitly dismisses the "conditional" model when she writes that Christians "are called to forgive as unconditionally as God does." The only verse she cites in support of her reading is Paul's epistle to the Colossians (3:13). And, even more than Patton, Mueller affirms the Pauline model of forgiveness as an act of *Imitatio Dei*. "The model of human forgiveness," writes Mueller, "is the forgiveness of God." Divine forgiveness is the "model" and the way ("as"). Both, then, propose a Pauline model of forgiveness in books that share an almost identical title: *Is Human Forgiveness Possible?*[1]

---

1. John Patton, *Is Human Forgiveness Possible?* (Nashville: Abingdon Press, 1985), pp. 157, 132, 12, 173–76; Joan Mueller, *Is Forgiveness Possible?* (Collegeville, MN: Liturgical Press, 1989), p. 6.

The answer they give to that question is complicated: it depends, largely, on what we mean by "human." If we mean simply "by the power of being human," then the answer both give is "no, it is not possible." Humans cannot forgive without the power of God acting through them and the model of God's forgiveness guiding them. Forgiveness, in other words, is only one kind of thing, one practice, and one model. As another advocate of the Pauline model, David Augsburger, puts it: "All forgiveness, human or divine, operates from the same model." In other words, we can forgive *only* as God does. And if we understand "human" in those terms—as reflecting the glory of God in our acts of forgiveness (as discovering rather than performing it)—then human forgiveness is possible. The danger, as I suggested in the previous chapter, is that the Pauline model and its *Imitatio Dei* exhortation seem to invite us to think that we can forgive like God. And, like Paul, theologians are frequently untroubled by the implications of this idea. Consider, for instance, how Paul Jensen describes divine forgiveness: "when God forgives, God determines to absorb into his own being the consequences of human sin and thus exhaust its virulence." And so, Jensen concludes, humans must do much the same: "to forgive means to exhaust in one's own being the consequences one has suffered so that those consequences will not cause further damage . . . to the victimizer."[2] There is a troubling implication in this model, as I suggested in the previous chapter—troubling both for our practices of forgiving and for what we may presume about our sense of ourselves when we do forgive.

One possible way of escaping the troubling implications in this idea is for us to make a distinction between two kinds of forgiveness. F. LeRon Shults, for instance, takes issue with Jensen's idea because, as he puts it, "humans do not have enough *being* for this kind of forgiveness." To try and forgive by ourselves is doomed to fail, because, as Shults phrases it, we have insufficient "ontic weight." The danger, he recognizes, is precisely that the *Imitatio Dei* tradition can lead to the "apotheosizing of humanity," to believe ourselves capable of acting "as God." In order to avoid that danger, one might imagine that Shults would here apply a distinction that he had made earlier between two kinds of forgiveness—forensic and redemptive. Lacking the ontic weight of God, we could see our acts of forgiveness as forensic and God's as redemptive. But Shults denies that possibility, emphatically. He understands cosmic history as showing us that forensic forgiveness is "subsumed" into redemptive.

---

2. David Augsburger, *Helping People Forgive* (Louisville, KY: Westminster John Knox Press, 1996), p. 117; Paul Jensen, "Forgiveness and Atonement," *Scottish Journal of Theology* 46 (1993): 141–59, esp. p. 154.

The "whole of Scripture," he writes, "leads us toward an understanding of divine forgiveness as manifesting grace and of human forgiveness as sharing in that grace." And so what had seemed a promising way of avoiding "apotheosizing" human forgiveness is dismissed, as Shults then resorts to a Pauline formulation that we forgive as God: "Sharing in the divine glory with Christ radically frees the one who hopes, empowering her to face the other with promising grace—to forgive."[3]

It is perhaps unsurprising to find theologians of various denominations adhering to a Pauline model of forgiveness—sometimes, like Paul, blithely asserting the human capacity for imitating God and sometimes, more temperately, seeing the pitfalls of presuming to imitate God while nonetheless urging us to do just that in our conceptions of what it is we do when we forgive. It is simply a sign of how hegemonic Paul has become in theology—he was, after all, the first theologian of Christianity—and, for the more critical, a troubling sign of how Pauline theology has altered rather than deepened the message of Christ. What I would like to do here is show how this Pauline conception has indeed spread beyond theology and seeped into the more secular philosophy that takes up the topic of forgiveness as a concept and practice. I will turn to three philosophers here, who share virtually nothing in common and who disagree publicly with each other on almost everything they say about forgiveness. Even as they make wildly different presuppositions about what forgiveness is and contest each other about what it means, they all, it turns out, share in common an unspoken but fundamental allegiance to the Pauline model of forgiveness. And for each of them, in different but related ways, the result of their commitment to the Pauline model is that forgiveness, in the end, turns out to be *impossible*.

I

We can start with John Milbank, who is both a theologian and a philosopher and the founder of "Radical Orthodoxy," a movement, according to one commentator, that responds to the "impersonal chaos" of postmodernity by affirming the value of "credal Christianity and the exemplarity of its patristic

---

3. F. LeRon Shults and Steven J. Sandage, *The Faces of Forgiveness: Searching for Wholeness and Salvation* (Grand Rapids, MI: Baker Academic, 2003), pp. 211 (emphasis added), 221, 213, 139, 221. Shults also denies the conditional reading of the Lord's Prayer, arguing that it must be read "within the semantic field of redemptive forgiveness." If it is read in "the forensic domain," the text that we "will be forgiven as we forgive others" becomes "a tool for manipulating victims through fear" (235).

matrix." At the moment when he was most engaged on the topic of forgiveness, for our purposes at the dawn of the twenty-first century, Milbank asked a set of questions concerning the possibility of a certain kind of reconciliation in the age of postmodernity. "How can we bring about peaceful reconciliation in the contemporary world?" he asks, and if "we are to perform peace, then how are we to be forgiven and how are we to mediate forgiveness?" Postmodernity, not as a philosophy or an index of intellectuals but as a "set of cultural circumstances," seems to militate against the possibility of reconciliation because of its "obliteration of boundaries" and "confusion of categories." Milbank's argument is that reconciliation and forgiveness are to be found in the Incarnation, and the way for us to understand the mystical meaning of that event requires us to accept what postmodernity proscribes, what he calls "super-hierarchical transcendence." And for us to understand that kind of transcendence, we need a premodern set of guides that includes, for him, the patristic, doctrinal writings of Aquinas, Anselm, and Maximus the Confessor (but not Duns Scotus).[4]

That argument of his 2003 book *Being Reconciled* had been limned out in his talk in October 1999 at Villanova University at the conference on "Religion and Postmodernism." In that talk, entitled "Forgiveness and Incarnation," Milbanks begins by foregrounding Kierkegaard's idea that forgiveness is miraculous like the Creation because it brings "being out of nothing." Forgiveness, he writes, "with equal miraculousness decreates, and causes what is not merely to be as if it were not, but literally not to be." I have written elsewhere just what to make of this idea, commonly and persistently found in forgiveness studies, of the work of forgiveness to "undo," its capacity for countering what Hannah Arendt called the "predicament of irreversibility," the human condition of living in ceaselessly flowing time. It is enough to recognize that Milbank begins as he will end by insisting on the mystical quality of forgiveness, which is for him not a human performance but essentially a divine one manifest only in the Incarnation. He describes what he calls the "five major aporias" of forgiveness—involving who can forgive, when forgiveness can happen, the relationship of forgiving to forgetting, the "trade" of forgiveness in what he calls "the aneconomic economy of pardon," and the illusory idea of human forgiveness having any finality. After demonstrating the illogic,

---

4. Mark Dooley, "The Catastrophe of Memory: Derrida, Milbank, and the (Im)possibility of Forgiveness," in *Questioning God*, edited by John D. Caputo, Mark Dooley, and Michael J. Scanlon (Bloomington: Indiana University Press, 2001), pp. 129–49, esp. pp. 129–31; John Milbank, *Being Reconciled: Ontology and Pardon* (London: Routledge, 2003), pp. 187, 211.

the "futility," of human forgiveness, Milbank concludes that a "purely inter-human forgiveness" appears to be "impossible." His answer to the question posed in the titles of Patton's and Mueller's books is, no, "there is no human forgiveness."[5]

Milbank's arguments about the paradoxes of forgiveness were not original, and many earlier philosophers had dealt with the paradoxes he describes, most notably Aurel Kolnai who was the first to define several of them and identify in what ways they rendered forgiveness impossible.[6] Of course, Milbank, as we might expect of someone whose movement is called "Radical Orthodoxy" and whose primary theorists are patristic writers, is not striving for originality. And the answer he offers—what he calls the "prime paradigm for positive forgiveness"—is also not original. It is the "the Incarnation and atonement." He is insistent that he is not talking about *divine* forgiveness (that he argues is likewise impossible), but only that very specific forgiveness found in the Christ: "for us in the West, forgiveness began as the work of, and was made possible by, precisely a God-Man." Only with Christ, only in the form of the Incarnation, do we finally find manifest in the world "pure forgiveness" which also "really *surpasses* forgiveness." Milbank's argument is that the Incarnation represents forgiveness precisely because "in Christ it is *not* God forgiving us" but rather "humanity forgiving humanity." Milbank's Christology is not my concern here, and others have written about it; but it is worthwhile pointing out that the animosity he shows toward Duns Scotus is based on the differences between their Christologies and what each of their conceptions of the relationship of the human and the divine in Christ means for the possibility of forgiveness.[7]

In the end, forgiveness *seems* possible in Milbank, but in a way that appears deceptive. As for the kinds of practices that we assume constitute forgiveness in our daily lives and interactions, Milbank's answer is that they are always illusory, not really forgiveness in any meaningful sense. The reason that "there is no human forgiveness," as he phrases it, is that *forgiveness* can mean only

---

5. Milbank, "Forgiveness and Incarnation," in *Questioning God*, pp. 92–128, esp. pp. 93, 98–107, 98, 99; Hannah Arendt, *The Human Condition* (Chicago: University of Chicago Press, 1958), p. 237; see Ashraf H. A. Rushdy, *A Guilted Age: Apologies for the Past* (Philadelphia: Temple University Press, 2015), Chapter 6.

6. Aurel Kolnai, "Forgiveness," *Proceedings of the Aristotelean Society*, New Series, 74 (1973): 91–106.

7. Milbank, "Forgiveness and Incarnation," pp. 108, 109, 121–25. For a critique, see N. Vorster, "A Critical Assessment of John Milbank's Christology," *Acta Theologica* 32.2 (2012): 277–98.

one kind of act, a historically singular act. Other acts that we perform that we think of as forgiving are delusive, false, or "nominal," as he puts it in *Being Reconciled*, but not forgiveness in the sense he means it.[8] I would suggest that the sense in which he means it is strictly Pauline. It is the cosmic forgiveness that Paul used as the basis of his theology of justification, and that clearly tempered his statements about what forgiveness means in human interactions. It is the forgiveness of Christ that permits—and is not conditional on—our forgiveness of our fellow beings. It is the kind of forgiveness that Milbank sees as either a unique instance (the Incarnation) or deferred (to the *eschaton*). It is hard not to see his argument as positing that secular, human, interpersonal forgiveness as impossible—and impossible precisely because he can imagine only a Pauline version of what forgiveness is and does.

II

Shortly after the end of World War II, Vladimir Jankélévitch started to explore the topic of forgiveness, starting with a brief discussion in his 1947 book *Le Mal* and then with a full explication in his 1967 study *Le Pardon*.[9] In between these two philosophical studies, Jankélévitch participated in an important public, political debate in 1965 over the statute of limitations on World War II crimes. When France was considering whether to extend the statute of limitations beyond twenty years or whether to render these crimes eternally *imprescriptible*, Jankélévitch took a strong stance to argue that these crimes must remain *imprescriptible* and used the occasion to make some important comments about forgiveness or, more accurately, about what is unforgivable. He first published a letter in the "*Opinion libre*" section of *Le Monde* on January 3, 1965, which he then augmented and published as an essay entitled "L'imprescriptible" in *La revue administrative* in the February 1965 issue of that journal. He then revised this essay and published it as a chapter in his 1971 book *Pardonner?*, and then again in his 1986 book *L'imprescriptible*.[10] There is strong disagreement among scholars who write on Jankélévitch

8. Milbank, *Being Reconciled*, p. 60.

9. Andrew Kelley, "Translator's Introduction," to Vladimir Jankélévitch, *Forgiveness*, translated by Kelley (Chicago: University of Chicago Press, 2005), pp. vii-xxvii, esp. p. xix.

10. Vladimir Jankélévitch, "Opinion libre," *Le Monde* (January 3, 1965); Jankélévitch, "L'imprescriptible," *La revue administrative* 103 (January–February, 1965): 37–42; Jankélévitch, *Pardonner?* (Paris: Éditions Le Pavillion, 1971); Jankélévitch, *L'Imprescriptible* (Paris: Éditions du Seuil, 1986).

whether it is possible to reconcile his political commentary and his philosophical meditations on forgiveness. Some see a strong contradiction, and others see a seamless continuity in which any discrepancy can be explained by the fact that he is talking about political, juridical concerns in one case and ethical, philosophical ones in the other.[11]

The main point of contention has to do with what Jankélévitch says about the concept of the "unforgivable." For Jankélévitch, the Holocaust is simply that; it is unforgivable because of its depth, its magnitude, the sheer moral horror that led to its conception and execution. His most famous comment is not only that what happened in Auschwitz is unforgivable, but that in fact "forgiveness died in the death camps" ("*Le pardon est mort dans les camps de la mort*").[12] That was what he wrote in his polemical commentary. In his philosophical book, he seemed to ring a very different note, as he there celebrates forgiveness with fulsome lyricism. Forgiveness, he writes, is "initial, sudden, and spontaneous." Like love, it is either absolute or it is nothing at all. He insists that it must be instantaneous and freely given (its grace comes from its "gratuitousness and suddenness"). If one waits for an apology, or waits for some explanation of the wrong committed before forgiving—in other words, if one has *reason* to forgive—then forgiveness is compromised. As he wittily puts it, "Reasons for forgiveness abolish the raison d'être of forgiveness."[13] It is hard to reconcile these two postures toward forgiveness—in one case, dead, and in the other, exceptionally vibrant and encompassing.

It is also excessive. Jankélévitch insists that forgiveness is more, much more than what others have thought. He says that forgiveness is not an act or practice that can be replicated. Those who believe that each wrong must be separately forgiven are wrong. He argues that forgiveness is more global: "Forgiveness forgives one time, and this time is literally *one time for all*!" Forgiveness, in other words, is preemptive, and this conception of forgiveness goes against the grain of most models of forgiving. If we forgive ahead of time the wrong

---

11. In an interview, Jankélévitch suggests that there "seems" be a contradiction. The interview occurs in Renée de Tryon-Montalembert, "Entretien avec le Professeur Jankélévitch," *La vie spirituelle* 619 (March–April, 1977): 194–95; quoted and translated in Joëlle Hansel, "Forgiveness and 'Should We Pardon Them?': The Pardon and the Imprescriptible," in *Vladimir Jankélévitch and the Question of Forgiveness*, edited by Alan Udoff (Lanham, MD: Lexington Books, 2013), pp. 111–25, esp. p. 111. For two contrasting opinions, see Jacques Derrida, "To Forgive: The Unforgivable and the Imprescriptible," translated by Elizabeth Rottenberg, in *Questioning God*, pp. 21–51; and Kelley, "Translator's Introduction."

12. Jankélévitch, *L'Imprescriptible*, p. 50. Cf. *Pardonner?*, p. 47.

13. Jankélévitch, *Forgiveness*, pp. 3, 100, 10, 96, 107.

that is to come, have we *forgiven* or have we *licensed* that act? For Jankélévitch, that question is moot because forgiveness operates in such a way that it "forgives all of the misdeeds that this guilty person would be able to commit or still will commit." There are two other philosophical schools that might be comparable. The Stoics believe that one must be durable in the expectation of future pain and this apathy is akin to a preemptive forgiving. And, likewise, Hegel argues that it is possible for a subject to do something similar: "A heart thus lifted above the ties of rights, disentangled from everything objective, has nothing to forgive the offender, for it sacrificed its right as soon as the object over which it had a right was assailed, and thus the offender has done no injury to any right at all." There is a difference, of course, since the Stoics and Hegel are working from a position in which forgiveness does not need to be extended since rights are renounced prior to the offense, while Jankélévitch sees the act of forgiveness as hereafter renouncing the rights.[14]

In this case, the issue is time, but it is also something more. Hegel and the Stoics first renounce rights and make the later forgiveness unnecessary, while Jankélévitch offers the forgiveness first, and that forgiveness, as he puts it, "cuts the temporal continuation." The something more is that the act of forgiveness, in his terms, *erases* the later wrongs. What happens when we forgive, he writes, is that the "*misdeed* vanishes as if by magic!" Forgiveness not only erases the past, but it also "converts the sinners whom it pardons to innocence." What was done is undone; what was wrong is transformed into innocence. Both time and state are transformed by the power of forgiveness. Such a power, as we might now suspect, is otherworldly: it is beyond human reason, total, redemptive, and eternal. What Jankélévitch is describing, of course, is divine forgiveness; and his model for forgiveness is distinctly Pauline. Forgiveness, he writes, "initiates a change *of all into all*." In "one fell swoop and in a single, indivisible *élan*," it "pardons undividedly; in a single, radical, and incomprehensible movement, forgiveness effaces all, sweeps away all, and forgets all."[15] These, obviously, are the rhythms of Paul's most famous paean to charity: "Beareth all things, believeth all things, hopeth all things, endureth all things" (1 Corinthians 13:7).[16] It is more than the rhythms of the

---

14. Jankélévitch, *Forgiveness*, pp. 153–54, 153; Georg Wilhelm Friedrich Hegel, "The Spirit of Christianity," in *Early Theological Writings*, translated by T. M. Knox (Chicago: University of Chicago Press, 1948), p. 236.

15. Jankélévitch, *Forgiveness*, pp. 153, 154, 145.

16. The French text reads: "le pardon efface tout, balaye tout, oublie tout." And the French translation of 1 Corinthians 13:7 is: "elle excuse tout, elle croit tout, elle espère tout, elle

prose that are Pauline in Jankélévitch, however; it is the very mysticism of the sentiments about a power to forgive "as God."

Given these premises and descriptions of what it is forgiveness can do, it is not surprising that Jankélévitch opens his book with a statement that forgiveness is indeed impossible. He begins by stating that "forgiveness is an event that has never come to pass in history, an act for which there is no place in space, a gesture of the soul that does not exist in our contemporary psychology." As he puts it later, what he calls "pure forgiveness is an event that has perhaps never occurred in the history of man; pure forgiveness is a limit that is barely psychological, a peak state that is hardly lived."[17] Here, perhaps, we can see the continuity between the polemical and philosophical Jankélévitch: the one argues that forgiveness died, while the other argues that it never existed. That may be a kind of existential paradox of the sort some French philosophers enjoy, but it is a statement of another kind of impossibility—the impossibility of forgiveness. Killed amidst the horrors or too exalted to be found in the terrestrial world, forgiveness is rendered absent, missing, and therefore nonexistent. It is impossible in the first case because the atrocity is too great, and in the second because forgiveness is too pure.

III

The one moment when John Milbank seemed most affirmative about the possibility of forgiveness was when he challenged Jankélévitch's claim that the Holocaust was unforgivable, that forgiveness, as he puts it, "died in the concentration camps." Milbank strongly disagrees with Jankélévitch, and he invokes the "Christian ontology of forgiveness" as his reason for disagreeing. Not to forgive the Holocaust, or the purveyors of it, would render the event and the people beyond "all comprehension whatsoever" and perpetuate the event's "terror, since what is unredeemed remains in force." To insist that the Holocaust is unforgivable both "falsely glamorizes" and "absolutizes it," he writes. What all these denials of any event's being unforgivable amount to, in the end, for Milbank, is a denial of the unique status of Christ. Seeing an event as unforgivable grants "it a demonic state *equivalent to divinity*" (emphasis added). Although using quite different terms, a different logical

---

supporte tout" (this is the Louis Segond, 1910, translation; the Martin Bible of 1707 differs only in employing "endure" instead of "excuse" in the first clause). See Jankélévitch, *Le Pardon* (Paris: Aubier-Montaigne, 1967), p. 199.

17. Jankélévitch, *Forgiveness*, pp. 1, 114.

strategy, and for a very different end, Jacques Derrida agrees with Milbank about Jankélévitch. He offers a critical, disruptive, and somewhat ad hominem reading of Jankélévitch that took him to task for "hypostasizing" the terms he uses, including the terms *Jew*, *German*, and *inexpiable*. Derrida goes even further, though, and affirms what many have seen to be an ingenious argument about what it means to forgive.[18]

Toward the end of his life, about forty years after he first introduced the concepts of deconstruction, Derrida undertook a series of lectures, essays, and seminars that took up the question of forgiveness. In the late 1990s, he taught a seminar in Paris entitled "Forgiveness and Perjury" ("Pardon et Parjure") and co-taught a seminar at New York University with Avital Ronell entitled "Forgiveness and Violence." (He apparently wanted to call it "Forgiveness," and Ronell added the second term, and then they quarreled and reconciled, appropriately enough, I guess.) He had also published about forgiveness, including, especially, the keynote talk he delivered at the Villanova conference, the roundtable discussion in which he participated the next day, and an essay that took the form of a response to five queries put to him by Michel Wieviorka and published as "Le siècle et le pardon" in the December 1999 issue of *Le Monde des débats*, a leading French intellectual journal (that was translated as "On Forgiveness" in Derrida's 2001 collection, *On Cosmopolitanism and Forgiveness*).[19]

What moves Derrida to examine forgiveness is the postwar rise of a wave of ritualistic collective apologies that governments and churches were offering for past atrocities. Like other commentators around the millennium, which was a jubilee year and therefore gave rise to even more concerted church apologies, Derrida was bemused by what struck him and many others as an insincere moment in the development of globalization. These rituals of apology

---

18. Milbank, "Forgiveness and Incarnation," p. 102. Derrida, "To Forgive," pp. 34–44.

19. On the Paris seminar, see *Questioning God*, pp. 3, 67. On the NYU seminar, and the amusing exchanges between Derrida and Ronell, see Benoît Peeters, *Derrida: A Biography* (Cambridge: Polity Press, 2012), p. 487; also see Mary-Jane Rubenstein, "Of Ghosts and Angels: Derrida, Kushner, and the Impossibility of Forgiveness," *Journal for Cultural and Religious Theory* 9.1 (Winter, 2008): 79–95; Derrida, "To Forgive"; also "On Forgiveness: A Roundtable Discussion with Jacques Derrida," moderated by Richard Kearney, in *Questioning God*, pp. 52–71; Derrida, "Le siècle et le pardon," *Le Monde des debats* (December 1999); Derrida, "On Forgiveness," translated by Michael Hughes, in *On Cosmopolitanism and Forgiveness* (London and New York: Routledge, 2001), pp. 27–60. He also touched on forgiveness in Derrida, *Given Time: I. Counterfeit Money*, translated by Peggy Kamuf (Chicago: University of Chicago Press, 1992), but only tangentially in his reading of a couple of phrases on forgiveness in the Baudelaire story that he discusses in that text.

were staged events, and in their "very theatricality" Derrida found "the traits of a grand convulsion," a "frenetic compulsion." Moreover, he found in them a profoundly troubling "process of Christianisation." The "'globalization' of forgiveness," he writes, resembles an immense scene of confession in progress, thus a virtually Christian convulsion–conversion–confession." His critique, then, is motivated by what he sees as an unseemly incursion of Christianity, and other Abrahamic faiths, into global politics, into what he now fears is a diminished secular civil society.[20]

He then applies to the concept of forgiveness what have been recognized as the hallmark strategies of deconstruction, discerning and then teasing out the deeper meanings of etymological puns, affirming and deepening particularly telling aporias, and then reveling in irresolvable paradoxes. The etymological pun that starts his essay concerns the "gift." In both French and English, the words for forgiving contain in their etymologies the idea of the gift (*don* in *le pardon*, *giving* in *forgiving*). This is likewise true of German and classical New Testament Greek (*geben* in *vergeben, charis* in *Charizomai*). With Jankélévitch, this idea that true forgiveness is what he calls "a *gracious gift* from the offended to the offender" provides sanction for considering what to make of a mystical relation that is beyond conventional economic exchanges. For Jankélévitch, forgiveness is a gift of grace; it is not simply a human relation. For Derrida, though, the forgiveness that contains a gift in it (etymologically) makes it "undecidedly equivocal," not just "ambiguous, shady, or twilit," he insists, but rather "heterogeneous to any determination in the order of knowledge." Both the gift and forgiveness, he concludes, contain what he calls "an aporetic logic."[21]

That "aporetic logic" of forgiveness seems to consist of three elements, three states, let's say, in which forgiveness is compromised: the states of exchange, finality, sovereignty.

First, Derrida offers a variation of the paradox that Kolnai had identified some thirty years earlier. For Kolnai, forgiveness given to someone penitent is unnecessary, and given to someone impenitent unconscionable; in one case redundant, in the other condoning. Derrida agrees with the distinction, calling one a "conditional forgiveness" (*un pardon conditionnel*) and the other

---

20. Derrida, "On Forgiveness," pp. 29, 31: "la 'mondialisation' du pardon ressemble à une immense scène de confession en cours, donc à une convulsion–conversion–confession virtuellement chrétienne."

21. Derrida "To Forgive," pp. 21–22; Jankélévitch, *Forgiveness*, pp. 5, 9. Derrida "To Forgive," p. 36.

"unconditional" (*du pardon inconditionnel*). He then extends the argument and notes that any forgiveness that is conditional is to that extent invidiously caught in the meshes of an "economy," what he calls the "*conditional* logic of the *exchange*" (*cette logique conditionnelle de l'echange*) where forgiveness becomes a traded commodity, losing its efficacy and betraying, to some extent, its heritage. Only unconditional forgiveness, forgiveness offered for no reason, "gracious, infinite, aneconomic forgiveness granted *to the guilty as guilty*, without counterpart, even to those who do not repent or ask forgiveness" is a forgiveness worthy the name and heritage. (The Abrahamic heritage, he notes, contains both kinds of forgiveness.)[22]

Second, Derrida likewise sees an aporia in a particular kind of work that forgiveness purports to do in contemporary politics, that is, provide an opportunity for nations and churches to address and *resolve* crimes of the past. Such opportune uses of forgiveness likewise betray the practice. At first critical of these contemporary political moments of apology and forgiveness in the political sphere, Derrida then extends his commentary to any use of the "language of forgiveness" in the "service of determined finalities" (*au service de finalités déterminés*). Every occasion at which "forgiveness is at a service of a finality, be it noble and spiritual (atonement or redemption, reconciliation, salvation), each time that it aims to re-establish a normality (social, national, political, psychological) . . . then the 'forgiveness' is not pure." As he had concluded about conditional forgiveness, such forgiveness seeking "finality" is likewise a betrayal that evinces a human desire that is not for forgiveness, but for resolution. And his response to both conditional and resolving forgiveness is to take up a mystical notion of forgiveness. "Forgiveness," he concludes, "is not, it *should not be*, normal, normative, normalising. It *should* remain exceptional and extraordinary."[23]

Third, Derrida takes up the question, as he puts it, of "whether forgiveness should or should not be 'sovereign.'" Beginning with the historical practice in which actual sovereigns wielded the power of pardon in a legal sense, Derrida then shifts to the ways sovereignty as a particular form of subjectivity is to be found in interpersonal forgiveness. The granting of forgiveness can feel like it is replicating that original sense of sovereignty, in which the penitent is absolved by a superior power. What "makes the 'I forgive you' sometimes unbearable or

---

22. Derrida, "On Forgiveness," p. 34: "du pardon, gracieux, infini, anéconomique, accordé au coupable en tant que coupable, sans contrepartie, même à qui ne se repent pas ou ne demande pas pardon."

23. Derrida, "On Forgiveness," pp. 31–32.

odious, even obscene," Derrida insists in his concluding remarks to the questions put to him by *Le monde des débats*, "is the affirmation of sovereignty" (*l'affirmation de souveraineté*). As with the earlier cases of conditional forgiveness, and forgiveness that seeks a finality, sovereign forgiveness strikes Derrida as impure, a violation of the concept. "What I dream of, what I try to think as the 'purity' of a forgiveness worthy of its name," he states, "would be a forgiveness without power: *unconditional but without sovereignty*."[24]

Having identified three moments in which we can discover the "aporetic logic" of forgiveness, Derrida then makes his paradoxical claim that the only place we can find genuine and pure forgiveness, forgiveness beyond the states of exchange, finality, and sovereignty, would be in the category of the *unforgivable*. Taking up Jankélévitch's contention that forgiveness "died in the death camps," that the Holocaust constitutes what is beyond human remorse and human expiation as well as human comprehension, Derrida counters that "forgiveness, if there is such a thing, must and can forgive only the unforgivable, the inexpiable." To "forgive the forgivable," he insists, "is not to forgive," since those acts are premised on the condition of a penitent wrongdoer, a desire for resolution, or a granting that betrays a will to power; in other words, each such instance would fall into the states of exchange, finality, or sovereignty. He presents his case in language that dispenses with sovereignty at every level (syntactic, semantic, moral): "forgiveness forgives only the unforgivable. One cannot, or should not, forgive; there is only forgiveness, if there is any, where there is the unforgivable."[25] The subject of forgiving, like other subjects in deconstruction, has disappeared: one does not forgive; forgiveness forgives. And the only thing it can forgive is that which renders it impossible.

Derrida seems to take flight into the aery realms of the mystic when he insists, in his commentary on the aporias, that forgiveness must be unconditional, exceptional, extraordinary, and without sovereignty, and then to ascend even higher into the mystical when he says that forgiveness can forgive only the unforgivable. In his discourse, it is hard to distinguish his commentary from that of Jankélévitch or that of Milbank, even as he profoundly disagrees with each of them. So, is Derrida a mystic, then? I would argue that he is not. He adopts the mystic discourse, but his strategy in the end is that of

24. Derrida, "To Forgive," p. 33; "On Forgiveness," pp. 58, 59.

25. Derrida, "To Forgive," p. 30; "On Forgiveness," pp. 32–33: "le pardon pardonne seulement l'impardonnable. On ne peut ou ne devrait pardonner, il n'y a de pardon, s'il y en a, que là où il y a de l'impardonnable."

the skeptic. Milbank is a mystic because he wants to identify a key moment (the Incarnation) in cosmic history, before which forgiveness was not possible and after which forgiveness was conditioned exclusively by that moment and deferred until the *eschaton*. Jankélévitch is a mystic because he wants to exalt forgiveness as a practice that is likewise too exquisite for a material world, its properties too fine for this space; it is literally utopic. Derrida, while echoing the discourse of the mystic, comes to a quite different conclusion. He uses the mystical language of forgiveness in order to affirm that, in the end, it does not exist. The point of claiming that there "is only forgiveness, if there is such a thing, of the unforgivable" is not to celebrate or exalt the extent to which forgiveness can overcome all, or to make a claim for its fulfillment in the *eschaton*. It is rather to affirm that "forgiveness, if it is possible, if there is such a thing, is not possible, it does not exist as possible, it only exists by exempting itself from the law of the possible, by impossibilizing itself, so to speak."[26]

Forgiveness for Derrida is a delusion, like other affirmative acts, strategies, aspirations—like the moment of presence itself as such. In this case, he is intent on showing it as a delusion because of the specific and noxious and theatrical uses to which it was being put in the modern world, and the instances in which less grandiose humans likewise thought of it as a particular kind of humble, gracious practice when it in fact betrayed the economies and powers that governed other aspects of our lives. He noted that he likes to use the qualifying phrase "if there is such a thing" (*s'il y en a*) to describe those moments "when an impossible something happens or becomes possible *as* impossible."[27] It is not entirely clear, at least to this reader, whether a happening assumes the status of possible because it has happened or remains impossible because it is misunderstood as being something other than what people think happened. That, in any case, is someone else's problem, if it is a problem, if there is such a thing, one might say.

The point that is important for us here is to notice that what looked like Derrida's challenge to Jankélévitch turns out, then, to be largely an agreement on a basic philosophical principle—namely, forgiveness is impossible.

---

26. Derrida, "To Forgive," p. 48. There is a wonderful photograph of Derrida sitting next to Jankélévitch at a June 1979 panel in the extended obituary of Derrida that *Le Monde* published as a supplement three days after his death (Octobre 12, 2004, p. IV). It is only the seriousness of the fact of an obituary that keeps me from reflecting on the propriety of his having his obituary as a *supplement* to *Le Monde*; only a Derrida, I think, would have fully appreciated the humor in that.

27. "On Forgiveness: A Roundtable Discussion with Jacques Derrida," pp. 52–53.

The reason it is impossible is that Derrida has, like Jankélévitch, described a strictly Pauline sense of divine forgiveness and eschewed any secular, humane forgiveness as impure and false. The curious thing is why Derrida, of all people, should do that. He insists on using the term *pure forgiveness* (as do both Jankélévitch and Milbank). It is only because he cannot find any instances or possibility for pure forgiveness that he concludes that forgiveness is impossible. What is "pure" in the forgiveness Derrida imagines, of course, is precisely what we have come to see marks the Pauline model. A forgiveness that is "pure" is a forgiveness in which one forgives "as God." The Pauline model, as we recall, is based on the assumption that what humans do when they forgive is imitate God, and it carries with it the dangers we see regularly manifest here, that they believe that their acts of forgiveness are somehow similar to divine acts.

Like Jankélévitch, Derrida too implicitly adopts a model in which "pure forgiveness" possesses divine attributes, and it is precisely the confusion between what are sacred and secular practices of forgiveness that makes forgiveness impossible for him. Derrida may not draw on Paul's rhythms, as Jankélévitch does, or Paul's Christology, as Milbank does, but he is as committed to the Pauline model of forgiveness as they are. All three use the same very curious term—*pure forgiveness*—that reveals just what is at stake in their understanding of it. Derrida is critical of those who believe, as he puts it, "that forgiveness is a human thing."[28] He claims that this is the belief shared by Jankélévitch and Arendt; we have seen how Jankélévitch does not, in the end, have that belief. What we can tease out of Derrida's insights is revealing: it is that we misunderstand what secular forgiveness means when we expect it to replicate or have the same properties and powers as sacred forgiveness. It is no wonder that Derrida claims forgiveness is impossible, in the same way that omniscience or omnipotence or any other divine attribute is impossible. Our expectations of forgiveness are what make it impossible. What is curious is that we should have those expectations.

IV

I have suggested that those expectations are part of our Pauline inheritance and that the Pauline model is implicitly based on a misinterpretation of Jesus'

---

28. Derrida, "To Forgive," p. 30.

model of forgiveness. Forgiveness is indeed "impossible" if we think of it as "pure," as a divine rather than a human expression; when Jankélévitch claims that "pure forgiveness is an event that has perhaps never occurred in the history of man," he is right because the forgiveness he is describing is beyond human capacity, and we are assured of disappointment if we imagine ourselves capable of forgiving "as God."

The philosopher who seems most aware of that distinction between the Pauline and Jesus' models, Hannah Arendt, is also the one who most clearly articulated in just what way Jesus can rightly be identified as the "discoverer of the role of forgiveness in the realm of human affairs." What Jesus argued, Arendt notes, are two important points: "first that it is not true that only God has the power to forgive, and second that this power does not derive from God . . . but on the contrary must be mobilized by men toward each other before they can hope to be forgiven by God also."[29] That is what Jesus says: if you forgive others, God will forgive you; if you don't, He won't. This implies that we possess the power to forgive (not only God), and it states indisputably that it is a condition for our receiving divine forgiveness. Those operating under the Pauline inheritance have trouble seeing that, however. The theologian John Patton argues that "Arendt's theological judgments" are at odds with "Christian theological understanding."[30]

What they are odds with, more accurately, is the Pauline misinterpretation that has exerted an undue and deleterious influence over both "Christian theological understanding" and the modern, secular philosophers who seek purity where it is not be found. Arendt gets Jesus right. That is indeed what Jesus said and what is implied in what he said. His warning is not to imagine ourselves forgiving "as God," but to imagine ourselves forgiving repeatedly as humans for whom forgiveness is both possible and essential in order to create the conditions for creative and productive activity. Jesus' point is that the

---

29. Arendt, *The Human Condition*, pp. 238–39. There are two ways to understand what we have been calling the "conditional" relationship between human and divine forgiveness. In one, humans have the capacity to forgive without any divine assistance or prevenient grace; and once they do forgive their fellow humans, they can receive divine forgiveness. In the other, humans have the capacity to forgive because they have been forgiven; and if they do forgive their fellow human beings, they continue to receive divine forgiveness. In the first way, divine forgiveness is newly granted, in the second it is renewed. Forgiveness remains conditional in both cases, and in both cases is wholly at odds with the Pauline model. Arendt supports the first case. I think Jesus is expressing the second case, especially in his parable on the unforgiving servant.

30. Patton, *Is Human Forgiveness Possible?*, p. 122.

forgiveness to which we aspire is not the same thing as that which we express. Arendt's point is that it is not the purity of forgiveness on which we should focus and celebrate and use to deny its existence but the banality of it to understand the limits and necessity of it for what Arendt appropriately called "the *human* condition."

3 FORGIVING RETRIBUTION

Immanuel Kant took the occasion of the preface to his 1798 tract *The Conflict of the Faculties* to offer a final statement in his late-life battle over censorship with the Prussian state. The state's Commission of Faith tested potential candidates for ecclesiastical offices by grilling them with a strict catechism to ensure doctrinal orthodoxy. The example Kant gives is as follows: a person who has sinned must repent in order to be forgiven. The repentance involves what Kant calls 'grief of soul' (*maeror animi*) and "an overwhelming remorse." The question the Commission of Faith asks the candidates is: can the person attain "this grief by himself"? The answer the board expected of successful candidates is: never. In the scholastic Latin of the commission's text, the *Schema Examinationis*, this suggestion of autonomy on the part of the sinner 'should be denied and denied altogether' (*negandum ac pernegandum*). The proper way to find remorse, the commission concludes, is by petitioning heaven for it. Kant mordantly observes that the commission does not seem to realize that "anyone who still has to beg for this *repentance* (for his transgressions) does not really *repent* of his deeds." Repentance, for Kant, is something the transgressor has, and therefore need not beg to receive, or does not have, and would not get by begging for it (nor logically would she or he be capable of begging for it without possessing it). Examinations like this, Kant concludes, are precisely what "drove conscientious candidates in theology away from ecclesiastical offices in flocks" and led, instead, to the overpopulation of "the faculty of law"—a "kind of migration," Kant noted with amusement, that "may have had its advantages."[1]

---

1. Immanuel Kant, *The Conflict of the Faculties*, translated by Mary J. Gregor and Robert Anchor, in *Religion and Rational Theology*, edited by Alan W. Wood and George Di Giovanni (Cambridge: Cambridge University Press, 1996), p. 243.

One of the key presuppositions in the commission examination still continues to haunt the contemporary debate over repentance and forgiveness. When Kant took up the commission's logic, he focused on the question of who is best able to determine one's psychic state: if one felt remorseful, then one could be said to be remorseful. If one did not and had to beg heaven for the feeling of remorse, then one could not be said to possess that feeling. For Kant, *where* the feeling resides is what matters, what gives it its potency in the exchange. A genuinely remorseful person knows by his or her own reason what remorse is felt, and expresses that feeling. For the commission, on the other hand, remorse is an emotion we can easily delude ourselves into thinking we can generate, but we can only be certain of its sincerity when it is the product not of our treacherous reason but only of our full submission to a higher, divine power. In the contemporary debate, we continue to be baffled by that question: who can determine sincerity? For Kant, reason, the guide for all morals, is able to determine how it feels; and sincerity is not that important a question. For the commission, humanity's bottomless capacity for self-delusion can be circumvented only when the entire exchange takes place outside of our all too fallible reason. For the contemporary debate, whose contours we will trace below, the question is slightly different and the proposed answers are less certain than either Kant's or the commission's.

The question we take up in this chapter is not where repentance is to be found, but what relation it has to the forgiveness it is meant to elicit. In other words, in the formulation posed by contemporary scholars who take up this question: does forgiveness require or not require repentance? In the formulation of those who can be called *retributivists*, whatever is expressed without a sign and expression of sincere repentance is *not* forgiveness but something else; in the most common expressions of that belief, without repentance, we condone or accept or excuse rather than forgive a transgression. In the formulation of those who challenge the retributivists on this ground, whom we will hereafter call the *unconditionalists*, forgiveness must be unconditional and therefore cannot *require* an expression of repentance. If it is conditional on repentance, then what would have been an act of gracious forgiveness becomes something else, the somewhat grudging fulfilling of a social contract. It would be a wonderful coincidence if those who held the retributivist position came from law schools and those who held to the unconditionalist position came from theological seminaries, but, alas, that is not the case. Many of the retributivists do indeed work in law faculties, and some in theology departments do indeed hold that forgiveness must be unconditional; but the majority of the participants in this debate either are housed in philosophy departments or have joint appointments in philosophy departments as well as law schools. That fact is enough to suggest that the academic migration within the faculties that Kant identified two centuries ago might still be exerting its influence.

I

We can begin by noting that there is a way of thinking—a wrong one, I argue—that sees the tension between retribution and forgiveness as a tension between reason and passion. For some retributivists, the reasonable response to injustice is punishment and the desire to forgive is simply an intrusive merciful emotion. Seen from the other perspective, the reasonable response to injustice is forgiveness and the desire to punish is simply an uncontrollable vindictive emotion. That dichotomy between reason and passion is a false one. Neither mercy nor vengeance is a passionate response that reason can properly resist and cast into more appropriate channels. And reason itself is not a cool incapacity to feel what should anger us and drive us to vengeful sentiments, or melt us and deliver us to forgiving ones. Robert Solomon has written an invigorating series of insightful books that demonstrated that passions are not uncontrolled, unreasonable features of our being but rather, as he put it, "ways of coping, products of assessment and evaluation, modes of rational action." Emotions *are* reasonable; they are not what reason has to quell. As Michael Moore put it, there is a "rationality of the emotions that can make them trustworthy guides to moral insight." And that goes, as both of them insist, for justice. As Solomon argued, "Justice is not, first of all, a set of principles or policies; it is, first of all, a set of personal feelings, a way of participating in the world." We have, as he put it in the title of one of his books, *A Passion for Justice*, because that is what moves us.[2] That "passion" is at the root of how we interact with the world.

2. Robert C. Solomon, *In Defense of Sentimentality* (New York: Oxford University Press, 2004), p. 23; Michael S. Moore, "The Moral Worth of Retribution," in *Responsibility, Character, and the Emotions: New Essays in Moral Psychology*, edited by Ferdinand Schoeman (New York: Cambridge University Press, 1987), pp. 179–219, esp. p. 190; Solomon, *In Defense of Sentimentality*, p. 22; Solomon, *A Passion for Justice: Emotions and the Origins of the Social Contract* (Reading, MA: Addison-Wesley, 1990). Cf. Robert C. Roberts, "Justice as an Emotion Disposition," in *On Emotions: Philosophical Essays*, edited by John Deigh (New York: Oxford University Press, 2013), pp. 14–28. Also see Martha C. Nussbaum, *Upheavals of Thought: The Intelligence of Emotions* (Cambridge: Cambridge University Press, 2001) and *Political Emotions: Why Love Matters for Justice* (Cambridge, MA: Belknap Press of Harvard University Press, 2013). Solomon exposes the same false tension between justice and vengeance (the former motivated by reason, the latter by passion) in his "Justice vs. Vengeance: On Law and

Once we better understand what emotions are, we can, I think, be better equipped to appreciate to what we can trace the profound interaction and interdependence of these two emotions: the passion to punish and the passion to forgive. I will give a very brief survey here of four important moments—one evolutionary, one scriptural, one early modern, and a final modern one—that will help us orient our thinking about that relationship.

Solomon did not, but later writers have turned to evolutionary psychology to attempt to explain the source of the passion for justice; and their argument is that it constitutes part of our species' genetic inheritance. Morris Hoffman, in his recent book *The Punisher's Brain*, writes that "natural selection has bequeathed us" what he calls a "three-pronged punishment strategy": we punish ourselves with guilt, we punish our tormenters with retaliation, and as a group we punish wrongdoers with retribution. It is instinctual for us to be retributivists, and, as Judge Hoffman argues in concluding his book, "our evolved retributive feelings will continue to be the best proxies we have" for establishing what is, and for meting out, justice. A passion for retribution might be part of our evolutionary heritage but so too, it turns out, is a passion for forgiving. What Michael McCullough calls the "evolution of the forgiveness instinct" is an important part of the growing sociability of the human species. Drawing on the recent discoveries of animal researchers who have found that conflicts in other "group-living animals" often end with reconciliation and peacemaking and on theoretical biological models that involve computer simulations of game theories, McCullough finds that humans too possess what he calls "something that looks an awful lot like a 'forgiveness instinct.'" Helping "individuals preserve their valuable relationships" and therefore preserve the communal order necessary for survival, he writes, seems to be the "main adaptive function of forgiveness." We might be instinctually retributive, but we are also instinctually forgiving. And indeed, as Hoffman concludes, "forgiveness and punishment are really just two sides of the same evolutionary coin."[3]

When we turn to scripture, we find something similar. As retributivists are fond of pointing out, what looks like forgiveness in the traditions that most

the Satisfaction of Emotion," in *The Passions of Law*, edited by Susan A. Bandes (New York and London: New York University Press, 1999), pp. 123–48, esp. p. 130.

3. Morris B. Hoffman, *The Punisher's Brain: The Evolution of Judge and Jury* (Cambridge: Cambridge University Press, 2014), pp. 8, 345; Michael E. McCullough, *Beyond Revenge: The Evolution of the Forgiveness Instinct* (San Francisco: Jossey-Bass, 2008), pp. 114–16; Hoffman, *The Punisher's Brain*, p. 188.

validate it, especially Christianity, sometimes reveals more than its share of vindictiveness in it. In his epistle to the Romans, for example, Paul urges his congregation in the following terms: "Dearly beloved, avenge not yourselves, but rather give place unto wrath: for it is written, Vengeance is mine; I will repay, saith the Lord. Therefore if thine enemy hunger, feed him; if he thirst, give him drink." What the Roman congregation should do, turn the other cheek, "overcome good with evil," as Paul states it, would seem to constitute forgiveness, that is, forgoing resentment for those who harm us. And yet, when Paul adds that "in so doing thou shalt heap coals of fire on his head"— that is, the head of the person who wronged us—what had seemed selflessly forgiving suddenly acquired an edge that we cannot call anything but vengeful (Romans 12:19–21). The idea of killing with kindness is premised on the belief that behind the merciful emotions we can often find the retributive ones.[4] That, argue the retributivists, shows how the desire for retribution is a valid one; and the lesson that critics of retribution might draw from this moment of slippage in Paul's discourse is that the desire to forgive requires vengefulness to give it measure and meaning.[5]

---

4. Susan Jacoby, *Wild Justice: The Evolution of Revenge* (New York: Harper & Row, 1984), pp. 331–62; William Ian Miller, *Eye for an Eye* (Cambridge: Cambridge University Press, 2006), pp. 152–53; Peter A. French, *The Virtues of Vengeance* (Lawrence: University Press of Kansas, 2001), pp. 18–20.

One way that retributivists reveal the connection of vengeance to justice is by showing us how we sometimes misunderstand one for the other. A notable instance of this is when they remind us that the Mosaic law of "an eye for an eye" is not only about the search for the proportionate in justice but also about *limiting* the extent of vengeance. One who has lost his eye takes a wrongdoer's eye, not his life or those of his family or tribe. A phrase that has come to represent vengeance ("an eye for an eye") is more accurately understood as directing vengeance into a system of justice.

Theologians have alternative readings of the passage from Paul about heaping coals of fire on the heads of the forgiven: some see it as an expression for how the forgiving might shame the enemies into repentance, and others see it as rendering the enemies even more culpable for the *eschaton*, the Day of Judgment. See Gordon Zerbe, "Paul's Ethic of Retaliation and Peace," in *The Love of Enemy and Nonretaliation in the New Testament*, edited by Willard Swartley (Louisville, KY: Westminster/John Knox, 1992), pp. 177–222, esp. p. 183; and L. Gregory Jones, *Embodying Forgiveness: A Theological Analysis* (Grand Rapids, MI: William B. Eerdmans, 1995), pp. 255–57.

5. Martha C. Nussbaum, *Anger and Forgiveness: Resentment, Generosity, Justice* (New York: Oxford University Press, 2016), has argued that what she calls the "transactional model" of forgiveness—that is, the kind of forgiveness that requires the wrongdoer's repentance—is premised on particular kinds of traumatic emotional violence (pp. 72–73). In its classic form, she writes, "forgiveness exhibits a mentality that is all too inquisitorial and disciplinary" (p. 10).

We can represent the third moment, the early modern, by looking at an underappreciated scene in *Macbeth* that addresses this question of retribution and forgiveness. When Macduff first learns that Macbeth has murdered his wife and all his children, he invokes heaven three times. In the first instance, he pursues a question about theodicy, asking effectively what kind of divinity can permit such crimes against the innocent: "Did heaven look on / And would not take their part?" (IV.3.223–24).[6] Immediately thereafter, he accepts responsibility and acknowledges that they were killed because of who he was (a rebel to Macbeth) and what he did (flee Scotland). Having come to terms with the divinity he had just invoked plaintively, he then invokes heaven a second time and bids "Heaven rest them now" (IV.3.228). Having first questioned and then accepted divine justice, Macduff sets himself to avenge the loss of his family, and he expresses that final thought, and makes his final invocation to heaven, by stating the terms to which he accedes. Put him and Macbeth together in single, mortal combat and see who wins. "If he scape," says Macduff, "Heaven forgive him too" (IV.3.234–35). It is a profoundly curious moment in the play, since it seems to be setting up a contradiction between retribution and forgiveness but simultaneously placing the whole affair in divine hands. If Macduff kills Macbeth, justice will be served because the murderer of innocents will have been killed; there is no forgiveness. If he fails to kill him, then by asking heaven to forgive Macbeth, Macduff is effectively saying that Macbeth will deserve the same forgiveness he has just requested for his own slaughtered wife and children.[7]

It is notable that *Macbeth* is Shakespeare's most concentrated meditation on the meaning and nature of *destiny* and of *consequences*, that is, questions of whether we are predetermined in our actions and whether our actions determine further ones. Once Macbeth has information from the witches about his future fate, his thoughts immediately turn to what would happen if he did anything, and what might or might not happen if he didn't. He would perform the act of killing the king, he thinks, but only if that act did not necessarily lead to something else, in Macbeth's words, if the act itself "Could trammel up the consequence." Macbeth drily notes this point in a

---

6. William Shakespeare, *Macbeth*, edited by Stephen Orgel (New York: Penguin, 2000). All further references will be taken from this edition and noted parenthetically.

7. I am reading the key word "too" to refer to Macduff's family, but it might also be read as saying that if Macbeth escapes Macduff's sword, he (Macbeth) will be forgiven by both Macduff and heaven. This second reading seems less plausible to me.

pun explaining his dilatoriness in acting: "If it were done [finished] when 'tis done [performed]," then he would do it gladly, but he recognizes that as a fond and false hope (I.7.1–6). And Lady Macbeth's final words in the play—"What's done cannot be undone" (V.1.67)—reinforce the point that consequences matter (they cannot be trammeled up) and that what is done (performed) is never done (finished) because those consequences continue to produce further consequences. In this play about the meaning and nature of consequences, then, Macduff establishes two options—earthly retribution or divine forgiveness—that serve to show us that what are presented as polarities of possible consequences are, in this case, determined in the same act.

The final moment comes to us from Kant, appropriately, since Kant provides the inspiration for much modern retributivism. Kantian justice— premised on perfect duties, categorical imperatives, and undeviating commitment to right—often seems like a wholly unforgiving concept. That, though, is not wholly accurate, as we can see in examining three instances of what Kant says about justice.

The first, in the passage that is most frequently cited in the literature, is that in which Kant describes a counterfactual to give substance to his insistence that "the law of punishment is a categorical imperative":

> Even if a civil society were to be dissolved by the consent of all its members (e.g. if a people inhabiting an island decided to separate and disperse throughout the world), the last murderer remaining in prison would first have to be executed, so that each has done to him what his deeds deserve and blood guilt does not cling to the people for not having insisted upon this punishment; for otherwise the people can be regarded as collaborators in this public violation of justice.

Justice is based on desert (the murderer deserves to be executed), and there are virtually no conditions in which it should be tempered (literally, even if the state disbands). It is worth emphasizing precisely what Kant sees as the ultimate result of deviating from strict justice—that the burden of responsibility is placed on the whole (everyone is *complicit* if the deserved punishment is not inflicted). If all the murderers are not executed, those who failed to do it are "collaborators." We might be reminded of the other famous counterfactual Kant proposed, which follows the same logic: the categorical imperative never to lie, even if your friend's life depends on it. The person who lies to save another's life becomes "responsible" and "legally accountable for all the consequences that might arise" from the lie.[8] We are all potentially complicit in the kingdom of ends.

Of course, this is not Kant's only word on retribution. He offers examples of when murder can be justified and of when extenuating circumstances permit a lesser judgment than capital punishment. And he also, tellingly, offers an example of a situation in which executive clemency of a sort may be allowable. This constitutes the second instance we can consider. Kant imagines a scenario in which the act of murder is accomplished by a great number of people who are 'accomplices' (*correi*) to the deed. In fact, there are so many accomplices that sentencing them all to death would literally depopulate the state. In this 'case of necessity' (*casus necessitatis*), Kant says, the sovereign must possess the power to commute the sentence of capital punishment and decree a sentence that "still preserves the population." Kant's reasoning is that if the civil society were depopulated, it would "pass over into the state of nature, which is far worse because there is not external justice at all in it."[9]

This is a curious moment in Kant, since it was the very concept of *complicity* that he had earlier wielded as a weapon against such commutation of death penalty sentences. Why should it be that those who fail to execute the last murderer in the island civil society be considered collaborators, while the actual collaborators in this sovereign-led civil society can have their sentences commuted in order to preserve the civil society? Is it that one civil society would be dissolved by consent, while the other would be involuntarily depopulated? Or is it that one is a kingdom with a sovereign, while the other might not be? Whatever might be the case, it is worthwhile noting that Kant emphasizes the fact about the *number* of people who are accomplices. Perhaps complicity becomes less complicitous when enough people are guilty of it.

In the final instance, Kant meditates specifically on the interrelationship of retribution and forgiveness. He begins by spelling out the general theory of retribution: "Every deed that violates a human being's right deserves punishment, the function of which is to *avenge* a crime on the one who committed it." In then thinking about the application of this general principle, Kant considers an expanding set of authorities who can perform that vengeance. He dismisses the idea that the injured party might pursue vengeance alone;

---

8. Kant, *The Metaphysics of Morals*, in *Practical Philosophy*, translated and edited by Mary J. Gregor (Cambridge: Cambridge University Press, 1996), pp. 473, 474. For the counterfactual on lying, see Kant, "On a Supposed Right to Lie from Philanthropy," in *Practical Philosophy*, pp. 611–15, esp. pp. 612–13.

9. Kant, *Metaphysics of Morals*, p. 475.

that would simply repeat the wrong (of someone's using another as a means rather than an end). Instead, the vengeance must be pursued by a court of civil society, which "gives effect to the law of a *supreme authority* over all those subject to it." Kant then extrapolates from this situation, in which a society may and an individual may not inflict punishment, to consider the question from the purview of the "*laws of reason* (not civil laws)." From that perspective, he concludes, "no one is authorized to inflict punishment and to avenge the wrongs sustained by them except him who is also the supreme moral lawgiver." Only God, then, can punish. The conclusion Kant draws from this logical exercise is that it is the "duty of human beings to be *forgiving* (*placabilitis*)," precisely because every human being "has enough guilt of his own to be greatly in need of pardon."[10] In other words, none of us can punish because each of us is guilty; that is the human condition.

A shared, universal guilt is not the same thing as complicity, but Kant makes a suggestive point in this series of arguments about retribution. Kant has rendered three different models of justice, based to some extent on the concept of complicity: (1) we are complicit if we do not perform strict and implacable justice; (2) if enough people are complicit, there is a necessity for justice to be tempered by commutation of too strict a sentence; and (3) finally, if we are all complicit—that is, all guilty by dint of the human condition— there is a necessity for us all to be forgiving. Kant, in the end, seems to suggest that forgiveness is equally a duty as retribution and that it is so for the same reason—our complicity.

We see, then, a complicated interdependence between retribution and forgiveness in a range of thinkers—from the apostolic moralist Paul to the enlightenment arch-retributivist Kant—in which merciful forgiveness sometimes hides a vengeful desire and sometimes subverts it. Moreover, it becomes clear that the intricate dance between these two options for putting to rights or rest past crimes is emblematic of how they are deeply interconnected at a profound level in our psyches and, arguably, in our genetic heritage. It is telling that when Macduff prays to heaven for retribution or forgiveness for Macbeth, he does so in the immediate aftermath of the decimation of his family and genetic posterity ("all my pretty chickens and their dam / At one fell swoop?"). When he is urged to seek "great revenge" for this crime, his remarkable response—"He has no children" (IV.3.216)—suggests that his retribution would have been frighteningly full, as he would have murdered

---

10. Kant, *Metaphysics of Morals*, p. 578.

not only Macbeth and his lady but all their children too. The retribution he sought would have destroyed the Macbeth lineage as surely and completely as Macbeth destroyed Macduff's. An eye for an eye, a tooth for a tooth, a gene for a gene—that is one side of the evolutionary coin, whose other side also gave us the capacity not to avenge and instead to seek reconciliation with those who injure our eyes, our teeth, and those things more precious than ourselves.

II

When a philosophical justification for retribution returned as a respectable intellectual position in the late 1960s, it returned with this same dialectic with forgiveness. It is worth briefly returning to that moment. Herbert Morris' influential 1968 article, "Persons and Punishment," according to someone who first agreed and then contested its premises, "almost single-handedly rescued robust retributivism from obscurity and rendered it philosophically respectable again." Morris presented a theory of retribution that attempted to justify desert on the principle of *fairness*. As Morris put it: a "person who violates the rules has something others have—the benefits of the system—but by renouncing what others have assumed, the burdens of self-restraint, he has acquired an unfair advantage." The point of punishment, then, is to restore "the equilibrium of benefits and burdens by taking from that individual what he owes, that is, exacting the debt." Morris built his case for a robust retributivism on four bold propositions: we have a right to punishment; this right derives from a fundamental human right to be treated as a person; this fundamental right is a natural, inalienable, and absolute right; and the denial of this right implies a denial of all moral rights and duties. The major intellectual trend against which Morris leveled his retributivism was one that presumed that criminals should be rehabilitated and drew on the discourse of therapy to explain the sources and treatment of crime. Therapy, for Morris, simply failed to respect rights and choices and personhood; and it is the therapeutic model that he spends most of his article dismantling.

Morris begins his article by spelling out his premises, offering his model, and then recognizing one other model that also works to restore equilibrium to a social order disrupted by unfair actions. "Forgiveness," he writes, "while not the righting of an unfair distribution by making one pay his debt is, nevertheless, a restoring of the equilibrium by forgiving the debt." In his model, forgiveness is not simply present-oriented, which is part of his critique of therapy, namely, being insufficiently attentive to the past. Rather, in an ingenious and felicitous turn, Morris argues that forgiveness can be seen "as a gift after the fact, erasing a debt, which had the gift been given before the fact, would not have created a debt."[11] Therapy ignores the debt; forgiveness erases it through a gift, just as punishment erases it through demanding payment. In its most recent resurrection, retributivism was again in an inevitable *pas de deux* with its evolutionary twin or nemesis.[12]

Here, then, is where things stood when the contemporary retributivists appeared on the scene a generation ago. So, who are these retributivists, and how can we recognize them? We can recognize them, first, by their tastes in entertainment. By their own admissions, they tend to favor the more bloodthirsty genres—"revenge drama" from ancient Greece to early modern England, Icelandic sagas, and American films that celebrate vengeful violence in the form of westerns or movies about organized crime (*The Godfather*) or contemporary vigilantism (*Death Wish*). In classical and popular forms, these are texts that value revenge and justice and *lex talionis* ('law of retaliation'), where bad guys always get theirs in the end at the hands of a lonely and justified avenger. A partial list of some influential retributivists includes Susan Jacoby (*Wild Justice*), Peter French (*The Virtues of Vengeance*), William Ian Miller (*Eye for an Eye*), and Jeffrie Murphy (*Getting Even*).[13] Unlike French (westerns), Miller (Icelandic sagas), and Jacoby (all the rest), Murphy does not draw on classical literature or popular culture as his inspiration for holding to retribution. He claims, instead, that he was subjected to "a classic Protestant upbringing," read Kant early in life, and was "born a natural hater," which, he

11. Jeffrie G. Murphy, "Legal Moralism and Retribution Revisited," in *Punishment and the Moral Emotions: Essays in Law, Morality, and Religion* (New York: Oxford University Press, 2014), pp. 66–93, esp. p. 78 (this essay originally appeared in 2007); Herbert Morris, "Persons and Punishment," *The Monist* 52.4 (October, 1968): 475–501, esp. pp. 478, 476, 478; Michael Davis, "Punishment Theory's Golden Half Century: A Survey of Developments from (About) 1957 to 2007," *Journal of Ethics* 13.1 (2009): 73–100, esp. p. 93 and 93 (note 47), questions whether Morris' article was indeed the first to state the "fairness theory."

12. Consider the dialectic Cesare Beccaria, the founder of modern penology, established between retribution (punishment had to be "proportioned to the crime, and determined by the laws") and forgiveness (a small crime "is sometimes pardoned, if the person offended chuses to forgive the offender" [*sic*]). Beccaria believed that these private acts of forgiveness were "contrary to the good of the public." See Cesare Beccaria, *An Essay on Crimes and Punishments: by the Marquis Beccaria of Milan. With a Commentary by M. de Voltaire* (Philadelphia: William Young, 1793), pp. 160, 159.

13. Jacoby, *Wild Justice: The Evolution of Revenge*; French, *Virtues of Vengeance*; Miller, *Eye for an Eye*; Murphy, *Getting Even: Forgiveness and Its Limits* (New York: Oxford University Press, 2003).

hints, might be "genetic with the Irish."[14] I am sure this is just not true; people of many nations read Kant.

We can also recognize retributivists by how they identify their antagonists. Retributivists tend to be critical of certain professions—especially the professions of theology and psychotherapy—because they feel that what is professed in those fields about the role of forgiveness in what the first call "restorative justice" and the second "healing" is dismissive of and dangerous to a sense of justice. It is noteworthy that theologians (Anthony Bash) and psychologists (Everett Worthington) have recently responded to this charge in books that claim, in their almost identical titles, the possibility of *A Just Forgiveness*. They want to affirm the place forgiveness should occupy in the administration of justice, as a tempering mechanism to soften the harshness of sentencing for criminals, as a therapeutic strategy to establish the humane involvement in the judicial process by victims. The retributivists, however, are troubled by this migration of ideas about mercy and forgiveness from what they consider their proper realms (the relation of soul to creator, say, or domestic relations between individuals). In the most emphatic statement, French argues that a lone vigilante out for justified vengeance for harms personally suffered is less dangerous to justice than "good people, anesthetized by moral insensitivity" or "moral cowardice" and "brimming over with Christian forgiveness," accepting and bearing the harms they suffer instead of affirming their right to retribution.[15]

Although without French's relish, retributivists also uniformly salvage the reputation of revenge and the value of resentment from the long history of denigration they have suffered at the hands of moralist writers. Most of these writers return us to formative scenes in the literature of the Western heritage (Homer, Euripides, Icelandic sagas) in order to reveal the equally long history of celebrating vengeance *as* a form of justice. They also draw our attention to the meanings of "satisfaction" in all senses in retribution and demonstrate how our sense of justice is premised on ideas that are dissociable from vengeance.

When they do, inevitably, turn to the question of the relationship between retribution and forgiveness, retributivists offer different answers. French, as we saw, dismissed forgiveness as contrary to justice. Others, like Kathleen

---

14. Murphy and Jean Hampton, *Forgiveness and Mercy* (New York: Oxford University Press, 1988), pp. 184–85.

15. Everett L. Worthington, Jr., *A Just Forgiveness: Responsible Healing Without Excusing Injustice* (Downers Grove, IL: InterVarsity Press, 2009); Anthony Bash, *Just Forgiveness: Exploring the Bible, Weighing the Issues* (London: SPCK, 2011); French, *Virtues of Vengeance*, p. 111.

Dean Moore, place them in different realms. Criminal justice is for apportioning punishment based on fitness, whereas forgiveness is an act of mercy based precisely on *disproportion* (a gift of grace for an injury). "Retributivism does not forbid forgiveness," Moore concludes, simply because they differ in what they are and in where they appear. Retributive justice is about acts that constitute proportionality; in other words, it is about the requirement of "punishment under specified circumstances." Forgiveness, on the other hand, is an emotion (how people "feel toward someone who wrongs them"), and retributivists, like everyone else, can maintain "an attitude of goodwill toward a transgressor."[16]

Forgiveness, then, is a virtue that has no place in the courtroom. And yet it has certainly been present. In 1972, for instance, Hermine Braunsteiner was on trial for having lied about her past (before she married an American serviceman and emigrated from Germany, she had been an officer at the Maidanek death camp during the war). In order to have her deportation case dismissed, her lawyer wanted to suggest that those testifying against her were motivated by vengeance. In one exchange with a witness, after the witness denied that she "hated" or was motivated by "vengeance," the lawyer asked: "Can you sit here now and forgive the person who hit you?" When he eventually got the undesired answer of "Yes," he wanted to make sure that it was with "all your heart." When the witness said "That's right, forgiveness is my religion," the lawyer had no further questions. Such attention to the categories of "forgiveness" and "love," as Jacoby noted, held these witnesses to a standard that had little to do with justice, which is what the court trial was putatively trying to establish. Forty years after the Braunsteiner case, the *New York Times Magazine* ran an article on restorative justice with the suggestive title "Can Forgiveness Play a Role in Criminal Justice?"[17]

---

16. Kathleen Dean Moore, *Pardons: Justice, Mercy, and the Public Interest* (New York: Oxford University Press, 1989), p. 196.

17. Jacoby, *Wild Justice*, pp. 346–47; Paul Tullis, "Can Forgiveness Play a Role in Criminal Justice?" *New York Times Magazine* (January 4, 2013). For more on restorative justice, see Christopher Bennett, "Taking the Sincerity Out of Saying Sorry: Restorative Justice as Ritual," *Journal of Applied Philosophy* 23.2 (2006): 127–43; Bennett, *The Apology Ritual: A Philosophical Theory of Punishment* (Cambridge: Cambridge University Press, 2008); Barbara Hudson, "Restorative Justice: The Challenge of Sexual and Racial Violence," *Journal of Law and Society* 25.2 (June, 1998): 237–56; and the essays in the collection *Forgiveness, Mercy, and Clemency*, edited by Austin Sarat and Nasser Hussain (Stanford, CA: Stanford University Press, 2007).

III

The retributivists who seem to me best to appreciate just how long and enduring, and ingrained, is the relationship between forgiveness and retribution have been those who, like Jacoby, see forgiveness and revenge not in a false opposition but rather in a delicate balance or dialectic, but not one in which justice is sacrificed. On the issue of forgiveness specifically, then, when the retributivists accept it as congruent with vengeance, they insist that it is a practice that makes sense only when it is a response to some act of appeasement like repentance and apology. In other words, the retributivist position is: forgiveness *requires* repentance. And they hold that position because they argue that it is both logical (without repentance, forgiveness has to be something else) and fair (if forgiveness is the payment of the debt, repentance is a promissory note that the wrong will not be repeated).

The question of the logic of forgiveness, as we saw in the previous chapter, focused on the conditions in which forgiveness could be said to be forgiveness and the absence of conditions in which it devolved into something else that resembled forgiveness. Aurel Kolnai had articulated this logic when he defined what he called the "paradox of forgiveness." And, as we saw, those who approached the topic of forgiveness from a mystical or skeptical bent centered their analyses of forgiveness on this paradox, and concluded ultimately that forgiveness was impossible. The retributivists approach the question of the logic of forgiveness with considerably less mysticism and somewhat less skepticism. Part of the reason, one suspects, is that because they are retributivists, and therefore by definition concerned with the justification for punishing wrongdoers, they do not easily accept the kind of metaphysical arguments that Kolnai presupposed.

Consider, for instance, Morris' series of propositions for defining the concept of "culpable responsibility for wrongdoing": "There must be a *doing*; it must be a *conscious* doing; it must be a *free* doing; there must be *wrong*doing; there must be a *moral* wrongdoing; it must be by a *person*; it must be by a *moral person*; this person must be *responsible* for the wrongdoing; the guilty person must be the *self-same* person as the one responsible for the wrongdoing; the person must be *at fault* with respect to wrongdoing." It is the penultimate proposition that is at issue here. For the mystics and skeptics, the idea of a "*self-same* person" was a troubling one. For Kolnai, if someone repented of the wrong, then the person who had been the wrongdoer was now someone else, not the "self-same" person. The act of penitence was transformative, and therefore the forgiving of a penitent soul could not make sense. Retributivists do not accept this logic, understandably, since it would mean that whoever is being punished would always be the wrong person. The less dogmatic retributivists accept the complexity in the metaphysical problem of identity—as Morris puts it, it may be difficult to provide "a philosophically satisfying account of personal identity"—but they nonetheless see it as a "principal assumption" necessary to criminal justice. "We assume such identity," writes Morris; "we take responsibility for what we have done and view ourselves, the guilty person, as the self-same person responsible for wrongdoing."[18]

Forgiveness, then, for retributivists is less transformative, at least less metaphysically transformative, than it is for skeptics and mystics. When they take up Kolnai's second proposition, though, they are fully in agreement with him that forgiveness requires repentance in order to be forgiveness. In the absence of repentance, we do not forgive but rather condone, excuse, or justify a wrongdoing. That, of course, is the logic that the unconditionalists contest, and it is also a logic that is widely held by those who cannot accurately be described as retributivists. Kolnai, who seems first to have articulated the paradox, certainly was not; nor have been the most recent commentators on forgiveness who insist that forgiveness without apology is not forgiveness. Joram Haber, Charles Griswold, David Konstan, and a series of other writers have made repentance (or apology, as an expression of repentance or remorse or both) a precondition for forgiveness. Griswold, for instance, argues that one of the key "threshold conditions required of any forgiveness whatever" is precisely the offender's repentance, or at least "the offender's taking minimal steps" toward that repentance. He outlines six such steps: acknowledging responsibility, repudiating the wrongdoing, expressing regret, committing to future amendment of behavior, showing empathy with the victim, and offering a narrative encompassing the wrong and explaining why that action does not define the wrongdoer.[19] Without such repentance, we witness someone condoning rather than forgiving a wrong. Retributivists agree with this logic

---

18. Morris, "Nonmoral Guilt," in *Responsibility, Character, and the Emotions: New Essays in Moral Psychology*, pp. 220–40, esp. pp. 225, 240.

19. Charles L. Griswold, *Forgiveness: A Philosophical Exploration* (Cambridge: Cambridge University Press, 2007), pp. 115, 149–50. Cf. Joram Graf Haber, *Forgiveness: A Philosophical Study* (Lanham, MD: Rowman & Littlefield Publishers, 1991); David Konstan, *Before Forgiveness: The Origins of a Moral Idea* (Cambridge: Cambridge University Press, 2010). For an elegant critique of the arguments that insist on the necessity of penitence and apology for an act of forgiveness to have significance, see Glen Pettigrove, *Forgiveness and Love* (New York: Oxford University Press, 2012), pp. 108–24.

of forgiveness (even as they disagree with the metaphysics that might be said to subtend it).

What, then, about the *fairness* involved in making forgiveness conditional on repentance? Probably no writer on forgiveness has given more attention, and made more elegant and insightful arguments, for the question of fairness as a feature of the forgiveness dynamic than has Jeffrie Murphy. We need to note at the outset that Murphy has been a far from dogmatic writer, showing a remarkable readiness to amend or dismiss a position he had earlier presented and defended. And since he began his career as a robust Kantian retributivist, went through a middle Humean skeptical phase, and seems to be concluding it with an increased interest in Christianity and the moral emotions, and because he is acutely and generously open to critics of his arguments, he has made some *significant* modifications to his commentary on forgiveness. He has throughout remained committed to retribution, albeit having moved from a more robust to a more diffident kind of retribution. Some have called him an "erstwhile retributivist," and he calls himself, in his most recent essays, a "reluctant retributivist," that is, someone who holds the positions he had held more cautiously and with greater moral humility.[20]

Murphy makes two key arguments in defense of requiring repentance as a condition for forgiveness. The first is that without remorse and repentance and apology, the wrongdoing stands as an uncontested kind of communication. Murphy's point is that wrongdoing is not just an abstract *doing* with no implications or presuppositions; each wrongdoing is rather what he calls "a *communicative* act." What it communicates to the victim is the message: "I matter more than you and can use you, like a mere object or thing, for my

---

20. Anthony Ellis, "Recent Work on Punishment," *Philosophical Quarterly* 45 (April 1995): 225–33, esp. p. 227; Murphy, "Legal Moralism and Retribution Revisited," p. 86. Also see Murphy, "Moral Epistemology, the Retributive Emotions, and the 'Clumsy Moral Philosophy' of Jesus Christ," in *Punishment and the Moral Emotions*, pp. 21–42; and Murphy, "Christian Love and Criminal Punishment," in *Punishment and the Moral Emotions*, pp. 43–65. Cf. Murphy, "Cognitive and Moral Obstacles to Imputation," in *Character, Liberty, and Law: Kantian Essays in Theory and Practice* (Dordrecht, the Netherlands: Kluwer Academic Publishers, 1998), pp. 43–57, esp. p. 55: "The effect of such humility should rather be the introduction of greater care and uncertainty in our retributive practices—making us tentative retributivists rather than supremely confident retributivists—and should prompt empathetic inquiry into the actual characters and life circumstances faced by criminal defendants before we pronounce on what they deserve." For Murphy's earlier views, see especially his "Kant's Theory of Criminal Punishment," in *Retribution, Justice, and Therapy: Essays in the Philosophy of Law* (Dordrecht, the Netherlands: D. Reidel Publishing Company, 1979), pp. 82–92; Murphy, "Marxism and Retribution," in *Retribution, Justice, and Therapy: Essays in the Philosophy of Law*, pp. 93–115; and Murphy, *Kant: The Philosophy of Right* (London: Macmillan, 1970).

own purposes." A remorseful wrongdoer who offers repentance "repudiates this message, stands with his victim in its repudiation, and acknowledges moral equality with the victim."[21] In other words, the repentance stands as a self-admitted indictment of the wrongdoing, and a clear rejection of what the wrongdoing had implied. In Kantian terms, repentance acknowledges the failure to respect the dignity of the victim as an end since the wrongdoing had made her a means. Repentance, we might say, acknowledges her as a subject in the kingdom of ends.

The second argument takes the same position from the perspective of the victim, and Murphy's contribution here is to see the value of the vindictive attitudes that injury inspires (and forgiveness dissipates). He argues that to forego resentment without having some evidence of the change of heart of the wrongdoer, without a reflective act of repentance that indicates that the wrongdoer precisely shares the victim's understanding and condemnation of the injury, and an apology that acknowledges that fact, is to manifest a failure of self-esteem. He, more than anybody else, reminds us that Joseph Butler had noted in the eighteenth century that resentment is an appropriate response to the extent that it expresses righteousness in the face of immorality. Murphy adds that it should also be seen as a proper and healthy response that demonstrates the integrity of the harmed subject. The reactive or vindictive passions, in other words, are healthy expressions of what we take seriously, or, as Murphy elegantly puts it, they are "instruments of our self-defense, our self-respect, and our respect for the demands of morality."[22] Too hasty an act of forgiveness indicates that someone has not sufficiently appreciated the meaning of the injury, the presuppositions it bespeaks, and the importance of having valid evidence that the presupposition has been revoked.

Murphy has offered three important modifications to his ideas about forgiveness that affect both these arguments. First, he now feels that forgiveness is not, as Butler and others have maintained, simply the overcoming of only "resentment." He sees that wrongdoing inspires a range of emotions including "sadness, disappointment, insecurity, anger, and even hatred or loathing." What this change has done is forced Murphy to admit that forgiveness is no longer the sole right of the victim. When resentment was the only emotion that forgiveness overcame, it made no sense to speak of "third-party

---

21. Murphy, "Remorse, Apology, and Mercy," in *Punishment and the Moral Emotions*, pp. 129–80, esp. pp. 153–54. This essay was originally published in the 2007 issue of the *Ohio State Journal of Criminal Law*.

22. Murphy, *Getting Even*, p. 115.

forgiveness," that is, forgiveness by people who were not directly injured by the wrongdoing (and therefore could not *resent* the wrongdoing, although they could feel *indignation* at it).[23] This change, then, opens up the field for who can forgive, but it does not change significantly his argument that feeling resentment (and the other reactive attitudes) is an expression of self-respect.

Second, Murphy has now "come to have doubts" about the argument that the injury represents a "symbolic message" to the victim—"you do not matter"—that the act of sincere repentance withdraws. He believes that this model does not "seem to work at all for some crimes" and that he "may have overestimated the importance of symbolic messaging even in the crimes for which it does seem to work." His argument, at this point, is primarily about sentence reduction—that is, that repentance might be a determining factor in what sentence a judge will mete out—and less about the act of forgiveness in interpersonal relations outside the court system.[24]

Finally, and more significantly, Murphy now claims that he no longer holds so tenaciously to the basic retributive idea that forgiveness requires repentance. Although he still believes that "repentance by the wrongdoer is the best way to open a door to forgiveness by the wronged," he writes, he now sees that he had tended "to overestimate its role and gave rather short shrift to other possible doors." He now considers "with sympathy" the possibility that there are acts of forgiveness—"in at least some meaningful senses of the concept of forgiveness—that do not demand repentance as a precondition." This strikes me as a more significant change than his openness to third-party forgiveness, precisely because it now alters the very dynamic of forgiveness that Murphy had earlier presented. We will return to this point presently.[25]

What, then, can we make of these revisions in Murphy's considered judgment about forgiveness? First of all, we must note that he remains a retributivist, even if a cautious and morally humble one. He remains committed to the self-esteem of the victim and does believe that the best way to affirm that self-esteem is through an act of repentance by the wrongdoer. He sees that there is often a malignant message that wrongdoing can send and that repentance can help send a different message. And while he does consider the

---

23. Murphy, "The Case of Dostoevsky's General: Some Ruminations on Forgiving the Unforgivable," in *Punishment and the Moral Emotions*, pp. 181–214, esp. pp. 185–86.

24. Murphy, "Legal Moralism and Retribution Revisited," p. 76.

25. Murphy, "Introduction," in *Punishment and the Moral Emotions*, pp. x–xvii, esp. p. xi; Murphy, "Response to Neu, Zipursky, and Steiker," in *Punishment and the Moral Emotions*, pp. 215–33, esp. p. 217.

possibility of forgiveness without repentance, it does not seem that he accepts that this model would be the norm, or even the preferred one. It is something that he sees as feasible in situations in which it is better for the victim to forgive in order to move on with her life. In other words, it is better to be freed of the vindictive passions than to be bound to them by the reluctance of an unrepentant wrongdoer. I think these revisions all attest to an openness to consider alternate models of forgiving rather than a dismissal of the model he had earlier presented. As he puts it in his most recent work, he is now no longer interested in presenting a "general theory of forgiveness" since that would produce what he, using H. L. A. Hart's phrase, calls "uniformity at the price of distortion."[26] That is why he is open to considering new ways of imagining forgiveness that are not bound to repentance.

Finally, it is also indicates, I think, a recognition that there are irreconcilable tensions within the retributive and forgiveness models to which Murphy had been drawn—and repentance, I suspect, was the crux in both. Uneasy with the kind of character retributivism that declared some people to be depraved or tainted, and always generously liberal in his assessment of the social conditions that produced certain kinds of criminality, Murphy could not remain comfortable with legal or social practices that were fundamentally based on examining and judging the *inner* state of wrongdoers. He took issue, for example, with Michael Moore's contention that unrepentant criminals deserved a harsher sentence because they lacked the "virtue of feeling guilty," as Moore puts it, because Murphy believed it a violation of a "right of moral independence." In other words, he asked, what kind of liberal state would punish rather than permit "a right to be morally shallow, hard of heart, or unrepentant?"[27] It was not the kind of liberal state he imagined, or desired. And, in interpersonal relations, he also began to question what kind of practice forgiveness would have to be if it too was premised on only one sort of interaction, and one that presumed a capacity to determine the depth of sincerity of repentance when it was offered and the meaning of its absence when it was not. What we see in Murphy's later work, then, is a consistent effort to expand the parameters of what forgiveness is, to broaden the range of vindictive emotions it overcomes, and to be more open to the variety of factors that invite it.

---

26. Murphy, "Introduction," p. xi.

27. Murphy, "Legal Moralism and Liberalism," in *Character, Liberty, and Law: Kantian Essays in Theory and Practice*, pp. 90–117, esp. p. 103.

IV

Retributivists, then, value resentment for the values it declares and indicates about the self-esteem of the victim, the seriousness of the wrongdoing, and the larger question of justice itself. What the reactive emotion of resentment often seeks—*vengeance*—is something retributivists see as also possessing a particular value. In their thinking, vengeance is not an irrational, out of control vindictiveness, but rather, as R. S. Gerstein puts it, a passion that contains a "kernel of rationality" that should be included in "any just system of laws." Vengeance, in other words, is not a vice but rather a potential virtue. What Thomas Brudholm, in a book of that title, calls *Resentment's Virtue* is resentment's capacity for expressing our sense that violations are not to be tolerated. What Peter French, in an even more vigorous defense, calls *The Virtues of Vengeance* are likewise that vengeance, and vindictive passions more generally, are indications of our respect for our selves and our sense of justice. Retributivists see vengeance as reasonable and temperate; vengeance is not just "the desire to harm," notes Solomon, but rather "the desire to punish for good reason and to the right measure."[28]

The critics of retributivism find fault precisely with this idea that resentment can indeed become vengeful. What both Martha Minow and Trudy Govier imply in the titles of their books taking issue with this idea is that there is a tension *Between Vengeance and Forgiveness* or between *Forgiveness and Revenge* that, if resolved in favor of vengefulness, leads to a vicious cycle of reactive hatred and violence. Unconditionalists see vengeance as unreasonable, socially disruptive, and carrying the potential for being endlessly cyclical since it produces conditions in which it reproduces and reinforces itself. While acknowledging that vengeance is the "wellspring of a notion of equivalence that animates justice," Minow, for instance, nonetheless emphasizes the dangers that it "leads people to exact more than is necessary, to be maliciously spiteful or dangerously aggressive, or to become hateful themselves by committing reciprocal acts of violence." Vengeance, in other words, "carries with it potential insatiability."[29]

---

28. R. S. Gerstein, "Capital Punishment: A Retributivist Response," *Ethics* 85 (1985): 75–79; Thomas Brudholm, *Resentment's Virtue: Jean Améry and the Refusal to Forgive* (Philadelphia: Temple University Press, 2008); Solomon, "Justice vs. Vengeance," p. 142.

29. Martha Minow, *Between Vengeance and Forgiveness: Facing History After Genocide and Mass Violence* (Boston: Beacon Press, 1998); Trudy Govier, *Forgiveness and Revenge* (London and New York: Routledge, 2002); Minow, *Between Vengeance and Forgiveness*, p. 10.

Because they see the virtue or vice of vengeance in such starkly opposed terms, retributivists and unconditionalists set quite different terms for what threshold conditions are necessary for forgiveness. Retributivists, as we saw, value repentance as an indication of remorse for the wrong done, revocation of what that act implied about the victim, and a promise for future right conduct. In the face of an unrepentant wrongdoer, they see revenge as a better way to gain the goals of assuring respect for victim and justice. Unconditionalists, on the other hand, believe that revenge cannot gain those goals and can only produce conditions for the next inevitable act of revenge. In the face of an unrepentant wrongdoer, unconditionalists see forgiveness as a means of gaining those goals and preventing the spiral of descent into endless feuding; given the dangers of vengeance, and the need for stability, they argue that forgiveness should therefore be extended even without repentance.[30]

It is not only the fear of the cyclical violence that vengeance can promote that motivates unconditionalists, of course; it is not even the prime motivation for most of them. Rather, most believe that unconditional forgiveness is required by either the religious or philosophical principles they hold dear. The terms were set early in the contemporary study of forgiveness, in a debate between Anne Minas and Meirlys Lewis. Minas argued that forgiveness had to occur *between* people. "Repentance as an overt sign of remorse makes such a difference in forgiveness," she concludes, that "it is sometimes difficult to see how forgiveness can take place without it." Lewis disagreed and argued that forgiveness emphatically did not have to be between two people. A defining feature of what she called "the uniqueness of Christian forgiveness" was that it was "unconditional," including the condition of communication with the wrongdoer. "Christian forgiveness," she concludes, "does not require the repentance of the one who is to be forgiven."[31] It could be performed in

---

30. Nussbaum, *Anger and Forgiveness*, offers a different take on this question, since she is critical of both the kind of forgiveness that requires penitence and the kind of forgiveness that does not. She argues that "unconditional forgiveness has some advantages over transactional forgiveness, but it is not free of moral danger" (77). At least part of the reason is that unconditional forgiveness for Nussbaum requires that "the wronged party have angry feelings first, and then choose to waive them" (86). Her view is that those initial angry feelings are problematic enough and can potentially stall the process of re-establishing the relationship, and that they also exhibit at least some of the "moral dangers" of the transactional model of forgiveness. The proper response to injury, she writes, should be "forward-looking and welfarist" (176). Therefore, she argues for what she calls "an ethic of unconditional love" in which the wronged party exhibits (and feels) "a kind of generous letting-go" (78, 110).

31. Anne C. Minas, "God and Forgiveness," *Philosophical Quarterly* 25 (April 1975): 138–50, esp. pp. 147, 150, 147; Meirlys Lewis, "On Forgiveness," *Philosophical Quarterly* (July 1980): 236–45, esp. p. 243. An earlier writer, Joseph Beatty, had proposed a rather ingenious,

isolation and without the apology or repentance of the wrongdoer. One side maintains that forgiveness is inherently interpersonal since it requires repentance or apology or acknowledgment of some sort from the wrongdoer, while the other insists that forgiveness is unilateral since it must be unconditional and requires nothing more than the genuine change of heart of the injured party. Those terms governed the debates that took place through the 1980s and 1990s, between Joanna North and John Wilson in the journal *Philosophy*, for instance, and then later in the three convened discussions that followed the publication of Charles Griswold's 2007 *Forgiveness: A Philosophical Exploration*.[32]

Margaret Holmgren has most recently made the fullest case for what she calls "unconditional genuine forgiveness." The term *genuine* is crucial to Holmgren, since she wishes to address directly the main ideas put forth by the retributivists that support their claim that forgiveness without repentance

---

but not altogether clear, model of interpersonal forgiveness that paradoxically threatened to collapse into something unilateral (although it is difficult to say just what). He maintained that what one sought in seeking forgiveness was for the injured party to "see me as I see myself, or as she herself once saw me, or as others who like me see me." This involves two people, but only to an extent since what the wrongdoer seeks is actually *one* perspective (his). Moreover, Beatty continued, what we really ask for when we ask for forgiveness is to make the injured party feel guilty (and therefore have to seek our forgiveness). Here, then, what seemed like a regular exchange between two clearly defined positions (injured, wrongdoer) becomes a convoluted network that seems premised on only one viewpoint. It is easy to see how such an idea could lead to a sense of unilateral forgiveness. See Joseph Beatty, "Forgiveness," *American Philosophical Quarterly* 7.3 (July, 1970): 246–52, esp. p. 251.

32. Joanna North, "Wrongdoing and Forgiveness," *Philosophy* 62 (October, 1987): 499–508; John Wilson, "Why Forgiveness Requires Repentance," *Philosophy* 63 (October 1988): 534–35; William Meninger, "Why Unconditional Forgiveness IS Needed," *Tikkun* (March/April 2008): 26, 62–63, esp. p. 63; Griswold, "Unconditional Forgiveness?: Reply to Father Meninger," *Tikkun* (March/April 2008): 63–64; Griswold, "Forgiveness, Secular and Religious: A Reply to My Critics," *Proceedings of the ACPA* 82 (2009): 303–13; Michele Moody-Adams, "Reply to Griswold, Forgiveness: A Philosophical Exploration," *Philosophia* 38 (2010): 429–37, esp. p. 434; Griswold, "Debating Forgiveness: A Reply to My Critics," *Philosophia* 38 (2010): 457–73.

In the first *Tikkun* exchange, Meninger argued that forgiveness is "essentially something we do for ourselves," not primarily "for the sake of the perpetrator." Griswold maintained that forgiveness without repentance fell into the category of condonation. The same issues arose in the roundtable panel organized by the American Catholic Philosophical Association, where Griswold and his critics addressed the question of "unconditional" and "unilateral" forgiveness. In the last roundtable discussion, published in *Philosophia* in 2010, Michele Moody-Adams maintained that while forgiveness recognized "the humanity of the wrongdoer," it did not require any evidence of that humanity through acts like repentance. She too, perhaps more cautiously, saw the value of "an unconditional *willingness* to forgive." In each case, Griswold affirmed his skepticism about any form of forgiveness that was not premised on an expression of repentance, and thereby not bilateral.

is not genuine forgiveness but something else. Holmgren defines forgiveness as genuine only if the victim "regards herself with sufficient self-respect, and if she does not condone the wrong, engage in self-deception, or evade any of the issues she needs to address with the offender as a result of his offense." With this rigorous definition in place, then, Holmgren takes up the two major points raised by the retributivists. Resentment (again, shorthand for all the reactive attitudes) is *not* a virtue in representing the victim's self-respect, she writes. Indeed, repeating a point Nietzsche made about *ressentiment*, a victim's resentment might well grant too much power to the wrongdoer and fail to "assign sufficient importance to *her own* assessment of her worth."[33] Resentment here is itself a sign of the victim's ceding to the wrongdoer the power to define what she is worth; it is not a response to the wrong that demands justice, but one that empowers the wrongdoer's will and evaluation over her own.

When Holmgren takes up the retributivists' second argument—that without repentance, victims condone rather than forgive—she does so with the same focus on the interior process that she believes to be at the heart of forgiving. Genuine unconditional forgiveness, she writes, does not "condone" the wrong because the victim "recognizes the wrongness of *the offense* at the same time that she extends an attitude of respect, compassion, and real goodwill toward *the offender*."[34] For the retributivists, one condones an act if one attempts to appease the wrongdoer before any expression of repentance, which, for Holmgren, means that the retributivists have granted a particular power to the wrongdoer to define the act. Only if the wrongdoer defines the act as evil does there develop a shared definition of it as evil. Holmgren argues that the one whose definition is more important in this process is the victim; if the victim defines the act as evil, she does not require the supporting or shared belief of the wrongdoer. To condone in this case means not so much to permit to continue (that is the retributivists' implicit point) but rather who gets to define an act as beyond the moral pale (that is Holmgren's point).

For Holmgren, then, forgiveness is "unconditional and unilateral." The victim "*unilaterally* cultivates *her own* attitude of genuine forgiveness *independent* of the offender's actions and attitudes." There are two points worth making about Holmgren's model of forgiveness. First, it is focused almost

---

33. Margaret R. Holmgren, *Forgiveness and Retribution: Responding to Wrongdoing* (Cambridge: Cambridge University Press, 2012), pp. 74, 63, 67.

34. Holmgren, *Forgiveness and Retribution*, p. 76.

exclusively on the interior processes of the victim. The "moral appropriate-
ness of forgiveness," she insists, "turns only on the internal preparation of
the person who forgives." Second, it seems to be based on a Kantian imperative, not only in its discourse but also in its primary motivation. From what
Holmgren calls "the moral point of view," it is always appropriate and desirable" for someone to forgive precisely because not forgiving—holding onto
resentment and thereby fixing the wrongdoer in his act—fails to respect the
wrongdoer as a "sentient being and moral agent."[35] In other words, resentment
treats others as means and not ends, while forgiveness does not. Forgiveness is
a duty, then, something "always appropriate," because in any kind of reflective
equilibrium, Kantian to Rawlsian, it is what each of us would want to exist in
the world since it is premised on the idea that each of us is an end in ourselves,
and thereby facilitates the kingdom of ends.

V

The fact that both the retributivists and the unconditionalists can draw on
Kant suggests that these two positions are not entirely incommensurable
in terms of what they believe necessary for forgiveness. Let me clarify: the
two positions would be incommensurable if the unconditionalists held that
forgiveness is forgiveness if and only if it is given in the absence of repentance. But that is not what the unconditionalists hold; nor could they logically hold that, since such a condition would render their position not one
of unconditional forgiveness. In that way, then, both the retributivists and
the unconditionalists believe that if the wrongdoer repents, the victim's forgiveness is still precisely the same thing—a gracious act of forgiveness. They
do not agree on the opposite point: if the wrongdoer does not repent, the
victim's forgiveness for the unconditionalists is still a gracious act of forgiveness, while for the retributivists it would be an act of excusing, justifying, or
condoning the wrong that the victim wrongly believes herself to be forgiving.
There are, then, situations in which the unconditionalist and the retributivist
agree on forgiveness. And it is unsurprising that they do both draw on Kant to
provide the grounding for their cases since Kant fully endorsed each of these
imperatives—the duty to punish and the duty to forgive.

There are two points on which I would like to conclude this discussion
of these two positions: first, what *is* the forgiveness that each of these models

---

35. Holmgren, *Forgiveness and Retribution*, pp. 65, 66, 65, 95, 65, 98–99.

holds and, second, in what ways do they frame the question of *sincerity* that we saw Kant raised in his debate with the commission and that in many ways is at the heart of the contemporary debate over forgiveness.

To appreciate the first point—that each model differs in what it holds forgiveness *to be*—we can return to Murphy and see how he articulates the different stances he has taken in his turn away from being a strict to becoming a more reluctant retributivist. When it required repentance, forgiveness for Murphy had been an *act*. It was something one did. Now, he sees it as something more than, or perhaps something behind, the act. He argues that forgiveness is better thought of as a "disposition of *character*—a *virtue* in something like the Aristotelian sense." We work to habituate ourselves to particular views, and we can and ought to work at developing "a *forgiving character*—a character that is disposed to constrain resentment within reasonable and moral bounds."[36] These two conceptions of forgiveness, I think, adequately describe the two models. Retributivists see it as an act, while unconditionalists see it as a disposition.

At a deeper level, we can say that retributivists see it emerging in a social process while unconditionalists see it evolving within an interior drama. The retributivist believes that forgiveness becomes what it is within a particular social context, in which repentance is expressed and accepted and forgiveness is granted. Forgiveness may be, or may be based on, a change of heart—retributivists differ on the point—but the change of heart can be characterized as forgiveness only when it is a result of the wrongdoer's sincere repentance. The retributivist answer, then, is: forgiveness *becomes* forgiveness when it responds to repentance.

The unconditionalist, on the other hand, believes that forgiveness is what it is within a particular emotional or cognitive framework, in which the forgiver feels what he or she feels. For many unconditionalists, forgiveness is not an expressed emotion in an interaction but a continuous conviction about the basis of what it means to live as a flawed being. Unconditionalists implicitly believe that forgiveness that is withheld until the wrongdoer offers repentance is not forgiveness but also something else. If the victim feels forgiving but waits for the repentance, then the victim has transformed the feeling of forgiveness into an agency of empowerment. The withholding is an act of failed mercy and affirmed

---

36. Murphy, "Introduction," pp. x-xvii, esp. p. xi; Murphy, "Response to Neu, Zipursky, and Steiker," p. 217.

power.[37] If the victim does not feel forgiving and waits for an expression of repentance to inspire that feeling, then the victim cannot be said to have forgiven when that expression comes; rather, the victim is fulfilling a contract instead of revealing her sincere change of heart. The unconditionalist answer, then, is: forgiveness is forgiveness when it is felt and not when it responds to anything else.[38]

The second issue is sincerity. If we make sincere repentance the precondition for forgiveness, as the retributivists do, who gets to say that it is sincere? And, from the other side, who can likewise say that an act of forgiveness in the absence of repentance is full and sincere, and not a delusive attempt to curtail or end an uncomfortable failure of communication? The question about who can judge sincerity is necessarily different in these two scenarios. The question for retributivists is: who can judge the sincerity of the repentance, and the answer they give is: the one who forgives. Since the retributivist model is based on an open exchange, the one who is positioned to forgive weighs the wrongdoer's expression of repentance to see if it sufficiently contains sincere remorse for the wrong. The question for the unconditionalists is different because the question is not about the sincerity of someone else's emotion but the sincerity of one's own. The question for the victim is whether the forgiveness—the change of heart—is full and sincere, that is, not a preemptive attempt to forestall the gnawing resentment but instead a feeling of genuine absence of resentment (or any of the vindictive emotions).

It is clear that each of these models is focused in a particular way: the retributivist is focused outwardly and socially, while the unconditionalist is focused inwardly and emotionally. Each of these models, then, implies a particular order—both a sequence of events and a model of the world—and each of these orders has, I think, a particular set of problems and, likewise, a particular appeal.

---

37. Nussbaum, *Anger and Forgiveness*, makes this point elegantly in her critique of the "transactional model" of forgiveness.

38. Jeffrey M. Blustein, *Forgiveness and Remembrance: Remembering Wrongdoing in Personal and Public Life* (New York: Oxford University Press, 2014), offers an insightful intervention in this debate between those I have been calling retributivists and unconditionalists. He defines what he calls an "expanded sentiment-based account of forgiveness," in which he sees the possibility of a forgiveness that does not wholly eradicate a lingering sense of "non-retributive negative feelings," and in which it is possible to feel forgiving and yet feel also a sense of the propriety of finding "blame" in the wrongdoer (88, 47). He argues, as well, that the "most plausible account of interpersonal forgiveness" is "partly sentiment-based but partly relational" (155).

For retributivists, because of the intense focus on social exchange, forgiveness becomes less about the process of evaluating the reactive attitudes to which the wrong gave rise, and then ridding ourselves of them, and more about the demands and conditions that must be met for the process to work. The problem in the retributivist model is that forgiveness becomes a contractual process that in meaningful ways is determined by the wrongdoer.

For unconditionalists, because the process is focused on interior processes, forgiveness becomes less about the relationships that are damaged by the wrong that forgiveness is meant to repair. Since it is "unilateral," unconditionalist forgiveness is something that can sometimes be unknown to its recipient and is, in some extreme cases, expressly something that is simply not communicated to its recipient. In some models of forgiveness therapy, for instance, clients are advised to forgive an empty chair that represents the wrongdoer and write a letter of forgiveness that they are not to send to the wrongdoer.[39] Here are cases, then, of extreme interiority, in which the drama takes place with stand-ins rather than with actual people. If forgiveness is something only felt and not communicated, can it be said to be *given* (and recall that in all European languages the root of forgiveness is "gift")? Can it be a gift if it remains sealed within the soul of the forgiver? Those, then, are some of the problems in each model.

The appeal of each model is also based on the focus that gives rise to its problems. The retributivist model is appealing because it addresses the question of sincerity as a question about retrospection. When the victim evaluates whether the wrongdoer is sincere, the victim is ascertaining whether they have a shared understanding of the past, of the event for which remorse is expressed. They are together looking at that event—one using repentance as a way of expressing his sense of the wrongness of the act, and the other using forgiveness as a way of expressing her merciful agreement with that sense. They are both looking backward, and both agree. Again, this is possible only because it is a shared process, not an interior one only. The person who forgives makes the forgiveness conditional because she values the relationship with the other enough to wish the other to repent and for the reconciliation to be fully interpersonal, that is, shared between the repentant wrongdoer and the now reconciled and forgiving victim. The retributivist might respond to Holmgren's challenge by arguing that the demand for repentance is not

---

39. See Worthington, *A Just Forgiveness*, pp. 103–104; and Robert D. Enright, *Forgiveness Is a Choice: A Step-by-Step Process for Resolving Anger and Restoring Hope* (Washington, DC: American Psychological Association, 2001), pp. 87, 104.

an example of the victim's thinking of someone as a means, or a failure to see her as an autonomous moral agent. It is rather precisely because the victim respects the wrongdoer as a moral agent that she expects repentance; repentance opens the path to the wrongdoer's achieving an end.

The unconditionalist model is appealing because it treats the question as one of introspection. The person forgiving must delve deep into herself in order to ascertain that the change of heart is genuine, and not an expression of a different desire. Those who criticize the idea of unconditional forgiveness as too easy because it is done in isolation miss this crucial point that the person who forgives presumably undertakes a searching analysis of precisely what she feels about the wrongdoing, the wrongdoer, and herself, the victim. She has to probe deeply into her precise feelings: does she really forgive, and is she genuinely forgiving a wrong whose seriousness she has correctly evaluated, and does she forgive the wrongdoer for reasons she deems legitimate? What removing the question of repentance does, I suggest, is focus more on the question of what the forgiver *feels*. Of course, we feel something when we hear someone apologizing to us, and that feeling assuages our previous feeling (resentment, say) and conditions our future feeling (forgiveness); and it would be a curious model that made feeling possible outside of a social condition. But solitude, as several literary and meditative traditions have taught us, is particularly efficacious for acts of assessing and achieving particular interior states; and that, for the unconditionalists, gives the victim room and space and time to perform the reflective act that we call forgiveness.

VI

While the retributivist and the unconditionalist models are not entirely incommensurable, there are deep conflicts between them, and, at points, they simply disagree on what forgiveness is and when it can be said to become. My interest here is certainly not to attempt to erase those conflicts, nor is to suggest that there is some possible ground for reconciling them, nor, finally, is it to suggest that one model is preferable or the only acceptable one. Since forgiveness is not one thing, we can expect, and should welcome, a diverse set of models that define what, in their model, forgiveness is, what requisites it has, and what work it performs. Both the retributivist and the unconditionalist models do that. My interest here has been to reveal the inner workings of both models, and then to examine what those premises imply about the vision of the world each model embodies—its focus on mercy or justice, obviously, but also its ideals about what set of behaviors, focused patiently inwardly or expectantly outwardly, it upholds as the more desirable in that world.

We can return one last time to Kant, on whom both retributivists and unconditionalists base their models, and consider three late comments he offered about repentance. The first is a theory. In the final section of *The Metaphysics of Morals*, Kant made a distinction between repentance and penitence. These two things, "morally speaking," he notes, are very different. "To repent of a past transgression," he writes, is a "duty" and it helps keep in our recollection our past misdeeds; "doing penance," on the other hand, "makes virtue itself hated and drives adherents away from it" since it is "cheerless, gloomy, and sullen." Repentance, Kant's theory holds, should neither be depressing nor follow a set, orthodox pattern (as the commission had demanded); that, for Kant, would be either irrational, because it removes the incentive to be virtuous, or not virtuous, because it was not rational so much as formulaic.

The second comment was about doctrinal practice. In *The Conflict of the Faculties*, Kant criticized both the Moravians and the Pietists for what he held to be "mystical theories of feeling." The Pietists believe that supernatural grace is required for conversion, and Kant notes that their model of penance "therefore, begins with a *miracle*." The Moravians believe that one can turn away from sin through reason but that it takes supernatural grace to persevere in this course, and Kant notes that in their model this resolution to persevere is likewise based on "a *miracle*." Here, he concludes, "we have two mystical theories of feeling offered as keys to the problem of becoming a new man." In his critique of models of repentance, then, Kant found fault with those who largely agreed with the commission's idea of where repentance was to be sought. He believed that repentance was not something mystical in its origin or its resolution; it was not something institutionalized or orthodox, as penitence was, nor something mystical as the Pietists and Moravians had it. He sought something else, something not crushed "between *orthodoxy* which has no soul and *mysticism* which kills reason."[40]

Kant had considered the problem of conversion on his own terms in *Religion Within the Boundaries of Mere Reason*—the very book whose publication led to his conflicts with the Prussian censors. In that volume, he took up the same question raised by those sects whose mysticism he decried and considered the question of repentance, and, as we might expect from Kant,

40. Kant, *Metaphysics of Morals*, p. 598; Kant, *Conflict of the Faculties*, pp. 277–278, 280.

he took it up in light of the question of retribution. Since all humans begin in "*radical* evil"—that is, at the root each one "started from evil"—the "*infinity* of guilt*," Kant calculates, must deserve "*infinite* punishment." But if one is penitent, and therefore converted, what happens? For Kant, one becomes a different person. Here is the problem facing a retributivist: *who* deserves punishment? An impenitent sinner deserves the punishment meted out to him, but once that sinner undergoes repentance and has become a "new man" then "the punishment cannot be considered appropriate." The problem, then, is how "satisfaction" has been "rendered to Supreme Justice, in whose sight no one deserving of punishment can go unpunished." If Supreme Justice requires punishment, and the penitent is no longer the right person to be punished since he is no longer the same person, what can be done? Kant resolves the dilemma by suggesting that the "punishment" is "adequately executed" in the process of repentance itself (the "conversion"). In the act of penitence, the "old man" is put to death and the "new man" emerges.[41] The penitent is no longer deserving of punishment because the process of change itself has punished the older version of him.

Unlike the Prussian Commission of Faith, the Moravians, and the Pietists, whose questions were focused on the source of penance, Kant asks a different question about the *work* that repentance does. What it does is transformative; it changes "the old human being" into someone with a different "disposition" and therefore a "new human being." Physically, one remains the "same human being," but the conversion and the new *disposition* make him or her "*morally* another being." Kant's resolution to the problem might convince some, and probably does not convince others, who might see in its processes of transformative conversion just as much mysticism as in the orthodox accounts he had criticized. What is important for the analysis we have been pursuing here, though, is that Kant manages to resolve not only the problem of what repentance can do but also the metaphysical problems involved in the dynamic between retribution and forgiveness. We saw earlier that Kant argued that we have a duty to punish and a duty to forgive; he had attempted no resolution to the problems that arise in having what might appear to be conflicting duties. He merely suggested that the notion of a shared complicity made forgiveness a duty, just as the fear of complicity made punishment one. What remained

---

41. Kant, *Religion Within the Boundaries of Mere Reason*, translated by George di Giovanni, in *Religion and Rational Theology*, pp. 55–215, esp. pp. 113, 112, 113–14. Cf. David Sussman, "Kantian Forgiveness," *Kant-Studien* 96 (2005): 85–107, esp. p. 106.

residually problematic in that formulation is now ingeniously solved *by making punishment itself the process of forgiving.*[42]

Forgiveness—the acceptance of repentance as sincere, by an omniscient being who knows it is sincere—effectively becomes part of a protocol that can be described only as a capital punishment. The "old human being" is executed, and the new one born. The terms that Christian theologians have used to describe conversion have likewise emphasized death (mortification) and rebirth (regeneration), and so Kant is not breaking any new ground here. What is striking, though, is that he has used this discourse to reconcile retribution with forgiveness, by making forgiveness itself a death sentence.

There are two final observations I would like to make about Kant's model of retributive forgiveness. First, Kant makes it clear that he is talking about two different spheres. The process of repentance does produce two distinct beings—the "physical" and the "moral"—but that does not mean that the reborn soul can now escape earthly justice. The *physical* person "still is the same human being liable to punishment" at the hands of any "moral tribunal of justice," and by her own conscience also. The *moral* being, on the other hand, who is "another being," will be weighed "in the sight of a divine judge." What is most significant about that divine judge, for Kant, is that He prevails over a tribunal in which "the disposition takes the place of the deed." The retributivists might read this as suggesting that in our earthly moral tribunals—our human exchanges with each other—we should not permit the disposition to take the place of the deed; we should punish the deed. And they are likely right. The unconditionalists might respond that Kant is suggesting that we should indeed model our earthly moral tribunals on the divine one, and demonstrate in our forgiveness our own disposition rather than focus on deeds (the wrongdoing as one deed, the act of forgiveness as another). And they are likely right too. What is significant, though, for my purposes here, is that Kant, unlike the mystics and skeptics whose thinking we explored in the previous chapter, did not mistake a Pauline model of forgiving for a Christian one. Forgiveness is not impossible—for Kant, or for the retributivists and the unconditionalists who follow him—precisely because they all appreciate that

---

42. Kant, *Religion Within the Boundaries of Mere Reason*, p. 114; Kant, *Metaphysics of Morals*, of course, was published after *Religion*. My argument is not that Kant developed the solution later; he explained later the deeper problem that his earlier formulation had resolved.

our human forgiveness is limited to being human, and that what we do when we forgive here is not what a divine judge does elsewhere.[43]

Finally, what Kant provides us with in this model of the work of repentance is what we can call a *myth*, that is, an account or story or usable fiction that a state or group or community tells itself about either its formation or its most distinguished accomplishments to fortify its members and provide them with exemplars. For his larger project about the rationality of morality, Kant had of course offered his take on the social contract, namely, the imagined story of a judge who can formulate a universal law. For this specific moment of morality—the relationship of forgiveness and retribution—Kant offers a story of transformation in which retribution becomes forgiveness, and forgiveness retribution, in the process by which we are changed from physical to moral beings. Some of the most insightful commentators on forgiveness have emphasized that the process of forgiveness requires us to give an account of what the wrong was and an account that implicitly endorses the moral order that it violated. The retributivists insist that the repentance is required precisely because it is an account that endorses our forgiving account—yes, what I did was wrong and, yes, it was wrong because it did not fulfill these expected duties that our morality holds dear.

VII

A crucially important reason that the *account* is so important in the dynamic of forgiveness is that the whole exchange between forgiver and forgiven is fraught with the possibility of misunderstanding. When someone forgives another, it is quite possible that the forgiver assumes that what has been forgiven is a narrowly conceived misdeed, while the forgiven assumes that it is an entire personality and way of being. This is likely the case in acts of private and interpersonal forgiveness, and almost assuredly the case of public and collective ones. Let us return to the cases with which we opened our study. When South African widows forgave the man who widowed them, what precisely were they forgiving? The words they use strongly suggest that they were forgiving *him* and the individual evil act he performed. But lurking in the background, and not subtly lurking but anxiously, was a widely held social belief

---

43. Kant, *Religion Within the Boundaries of Mere Reason*, p. 114. See Kant, *Lectures on the Philosophical Doctrine of Religion*, translated by Wood, in *Religion and Rational Theology*, pp. 341–451, for the discussion of how God's holiness, benevolence, and justice differ from humans'.

that these individual acts of forgiveness embodied and represented the whole process of social reconciliation for a nation. Forgiveness, as both the chair and vice-chair of the Truth and Reconciliation Commission insisted, made possible the future. And so it is particularly important to know just what was being forgiven and what different weights these individual acts of forgiveness were being given by differently situated groups in the nation.

What the widows forgave, it seems to me, is the act of pulling a trigger or setting a bomb, or whatever other nefarious means these state-sanctioned terrorists devised for what they termed their "security." What assuredly they were not forgiving was the state-sanctioned policy of apartheid or the white supremacy on which it was based. It was not always clear that this was a shared understanding in a nation that was indeed divided in its excitement and worry, divided in its anticipation and fear, and divided in its racial makeup. Likewise, when the congregants of Charleston's Emanuel African Methodist Episcopal Church forgave Dylann Roof, they forgave him the evil he did, but not the evil he represented. They forgave him his slaughtering of the worshipful innocents, not the white supremacy to which he had erected his altar. But, as was the case in South Africa, there was a nagging feeling that these moments of forgiveness were being uttered in one way and perhaps understood in another. As Roxane Gay insightfully put it in an editorial in the wake of Charleston, "What white people are really asking for when they demand forgiveness from a traumatized community is absolution. . . . They want to believe it is possible to heal from such profound and malingering trauma because to face the openness of the wounds racism has created in our society is too much." Forgiveness, as Gay put it, is easier than the widespread recognition of widespread complicity.[44] I would add that it is a complicity that is not just individual or even collective in any simple sense, but instead institutional and foundational. It is the complicity that created race itself on which the white supremacy that manifest itself in different forms in South Africa and the United States was based—the belief that certain peoples distinguished in certain ways possess certain cultural traits.

Has forgiveness become one of those traits? "Black people forgive because we need to survive," writes Gay. For her it is a mechanism of socially negotiating dangerous terrain, and one she says has failed to end or erode the source of the crimes for which forgiveness is given. For others, though, it has become

---

44. Roxane Gay, "Why I Can't Forgive the Killer in Charleston," *New York Times* (June 23, 2015).

more than a mechanism, but a trait that certain people exemplify. Let me offer an example. In response to Lord Gifford's motion for reparations in the British House of Lords, the Viscount of Falklands stated: "I have worked for a long time in central and eastern Africa. . . . In my experience, the African people are immensely forgiving. They have forgiven the indignities that they suffered in recent times. To encourage the kind of attitude of fervent desire for reparation suggested here would go against the grain, certainly among Africans, *because it is not in their nature*" (my emphasis). What Gay sees as a means the viscount understands as an inherent property; what for her was a historical strategy for him was a natural condition. What for her was social for him was something close to racial. In a very different way, some people of African descent have contributed to this belief. Archbishop Desmond Tutu's comment that forgiveness was in fact "a central feature of the African *Weltsanschauung*"—what was called *Ubuntu* in the Nguni group of languages and *Botho* in the Sotho ones—differed significantly from the viscount's, but it possibly also provided cover and support for beliefs like his.[45]

Wole Soyinka has noted the dangers of such beliefs in his mordant summary of them: "To err is human, to forgive, African." He hews to the position that Africa's nations need more than reconciliation through forgiveness and more than amnesty in exchange for truth. They need what the viscount saw as unnatural. Reparation, Soyinka writes, is "a structure of memory and critique"—a means, a strategy, a social position that might and should replace forgiveness for confronting historical crimes. He is profoundly troubled by what he calls the "culture of impunity in race relations," in which reconciliation is valued more than retribution, and wonders whether the African continent's "humanity [is] of such bottomless reserves that it can truly accommodate" such forgiveness. Instead of a "charter of forgiveness," he writes, perhaps we should instead demand "a bill of indictment."[46] Soyinka's point is to challenge the idea that forgiveness is "natural" to African peoples, but it is

---

45. "The Official Record from Hansard of the Debate Initiated by Lord Gifford, QC in the House of Lords of the British Parliament on 14th March 1996 Concerning the African Reparations," In *Reparations for Slavery: A Reader*, edited by Ronald P. Salzberger and Mary C. Turck (Lanham, MD: Rowman and Littlefield Publishers, 2004), pp. 96–115, esp. p. 106; Desmond Tutu, *No Future Without Forgiveness* (New York: Random House, 1999), p. 31. For Lord Gifford's statements on reparations, see Anthony Gifford, *The Passionate Advocate* (Kingston, Jamaica: Arawak, 2007), pp. 243–68; and Hilary McD. Beckles, *Britain's Black Debt: Reparations for Caribbean Slavery and Native Genocide* (Kingston, Jamaica: University of the West Indies Press, 2013), pp. 177–82.

46. Wole Soyinka, *The Burden of Memory, The Muse of Forgiveness* (New York: Oxford University Press, 1999), pp. 21, 39, 37, 22, 109.

also to urge a harmony and equilibrium in what we have seen to be an intricate dance between forgiveness and retribution. By returning the question of restitution and justice to the debate, Soyinka seeks a balance. So, too, does the Black Lives Matter movement. In the cases we have been discussing here, such equilibrium would help ensure greater clarity between the forgiver and forgiven in identifying just precisely what crime the forgiveness addressed: an act—not a disposition, not a structure of thinking, not an institutional or political force. It would also help us understand that there is no absolution of the sort Gay rightly notes that many people in the world seek. The absolution from history and its effects is impossible—an impossibility, we might say, based on a confusion similar to the one that holds that human forgiveness can resemble divine. What we are then left with—a forgiveness that neither absolves history nor effaces the events of our own pasts—is, in the end, a forgiveness that is only human. That is all—and that is much.

II RESENTMENT

4

RESENTMENT

THE WOUND OF PHILOCTETES

At an early point in Dostoevsky's *Notes from Underground*, the narrator considers the difference between "*l'homme de la nature et de la vérité*" (a Rousseau-like "man of nature and truth") and a timid, resourceless mouse. When injured by someone, *l'homme de la nature et de la vérité* exacts revenge and calls it *justice*. The mouse, on the other hand, "as a result of its heightened consciousness, denies it any justice" and responds only with bitter "spite." The narrator sees himself as that mouse. "There, in its loathsome, stinking underground," he writes, "our offended, beaten-down, and derided mouse at once immerses itself in cold, venomous, and, above all, everlasting spite." The Russian word for 'spiteful' is "*zloi*," and it is a crucial term in the Underground Man's self-representation. It is how he begins his story: "I am a sick man. . . . I am a spiteful man." And it is how he explicitly defines each of his relationships—with nameless strangers and estranged friends, with men and women, with those higher and those lower than him in class. Spite is his response to the world that he inhabits and creates; it is his underground. "For forty years on end," the Underground Man writes, the mouse "will recall its offense to the last, most shameful details of its own, spitefully taunting and chafing itself with its fantasies. It will be ashamed of its fantasies, but all the same it will recall everything, go over everything, heap all sorts of figments on itself, under the pretext that they, too, could have happened, and forgive nothing."[1]

---

1. Fyodor Dostoevsky, *Notes from Underground*, translated by Richard Pevear and Larissa Volokhonsky (New York: Everyman, 2004), p. 12. The first sentence of the story in the Pevear and Volokhonsky translation is: "I am a sick man. . . . I am a wicked man." I have drawn on the translation by David Magarshack for the more famous rendition of that line. Dostoevsky, *The Best Short Stories of Dostoevsky*, translated by David Magarshack (New York: Modern Library, 1992), p. 115.

Dostoevsky published *Notes from Underground* in 1864, and it was translated into French the same year. The translators, Ely Halpérine-Kaminsky
and Charles Morice, usually rendered the term *zloi* (and its cognate forms)
with the French word *méchanceté* (and its cognate forms) (as they do in the
opening line: "*Je suis malade. . . . Je suis méchant, très-désagréable*"). They also
used the term *ressentiment*, which some, including Richard Weisberg, believe
more closely approximates what *zloi* connotes. That, in fact, is the term they
did use when they translated the passage comparing the mouse to the man of
nature and truth; and it is the first of the two times the term appears in their
translation. In 1887, Nietzsche read Dostoevsky's novella in French translation
and adopted the term the translators less frequently used—*ressentiment*—for
a project on which he was then working. That book was published the following summer as *The Genealogy of Morals*. In the first essay of that book,
Nietzsche argued that the "slave revolt in morals began when *ressentiment*
itself becomes creative and ordains values: the *ressentiment* of creatures to
whom the real reaction, that of the deed, is denied and who find compensation in an imaginary revenge." Both Dostoevsky and Nietzsche focused
on resentment as a malady, an illness; and in these two short late-nineteenth
century books, *Notes From Underground* and *The Genealogy of Morals*, the
first what someone has called the "most paradigmatic novelistic expression"
of *ressentiment*, and the second its most influential philosophical explication,
we find fully rendered the idea of resentment as a sickness and a product of a
brooding, febrile imagination as incapable of comprehending the reality outside its fevered brain as it is "*capable de ressentiment*" for the insults and hurts
that brain imagines.[2]

2. Fedor Mikhaïlovitch Dostoïevski, *L'Esprit Souterrain*, traduction et adaptation Ely
Halpérine-Kaminsky and Charles Morice (1864; Libraire Plon, 1886), pp. 117, 109: "*Voyons
maintenant le rat aux prises avec l'action. Supposons par exemple qu'il soit offensé (il l'est presque
toujours): il veut se venger. Il est peut-être plus capable de ressentiment que l'homme de la nature
et de la vérité*" (117). Richard H. Weisberg, *The Failure of the Word: The Protagonist as Lawyer
in Modern Fiction* (New Haven: Yale University Press, 1984), pp. 29–30; Friedrich Nietzsche,
On the Genealogy of Morals, translated by Douglas Smith (New York: Oxford University Press,
1996), p. 22. See Robert C. Solomon and Kathleen M. Higgins, *What Nietzsche Really Said*
(New York: Schocken Books, 2000), pp. 141–42; and Yamina Oudai Celso, "Nietzsche: The
'First Psychologist' and the Genealogist of Resentment," in *On Resentment: Past and Present*,
edited by Bernardino Fantini, Dolores Martín Moruno, and Javier Moscoso (Newcastle upon
Tyne, UK: Cambridge Scholars Publishing, 2013), pp. 37–54, esp. p. 37. Nietzsche wrote in
a letter to Overbeck (dated February 21, 1887) that he had read *Notes from Underground*.
Weisberg, *The Failure of the Word*, p. 28, calls *Notes from Underground* the paradigmatic novelistic expression of *ressentiment*.

That is one model of resentment—as an illness, as a neurosis that is based on a collection of imagined harms by an uncaring world. Largely because of Nietzsche's influence, that has become perhaps the primary meaning of the term.[3] So, it is unsurprising that it is a term that is regularly used in medical parlance. In a survey of twenty years of articles in the journal *Psychosomatic Medicine*, Pilar León-Sanz discovered over 270 articles on resentment. It is a term that physicians employ when they diagnose patients on their couches and in their offices, but also one they employ when they diagnose history. The Spanish physician Gregorio Marañón y Posadillo published his book *Tiberius: The Resentful Caesar* in 1939, an auspicious time for a Spanish doctor to look around him at the rise of a particular kind of sick leadership in Rome, Berlin, and his own Madrid. He diagnosed Tiberius as perhaps syphilitic, certainly "schizoid," but "*not* mad" (emphasis added). What he was instead, argued Marañón, was *resentful*, and resentment, the good doctor wrote, is "incurable."[4]

There is, though, another model of resentment. In that model, resentment is what one feels in response to injury, not imagined or enlarged by imagination but actual and purposeful injury. That is the idea implicit in Bishop Joseph Butler's description of it in 1729: "it is not suffering, but injury, which raises that anger or resentment, which is of any continuance." Butler at first suggests that we are resentful of anyone "who has been in a moral sense injurious either to ourselves or others." He will later suggest that we are *resentful* of injuries to ourselves and *indignant* at injuries to others (but the distinction is not hard and fast). A century later, George Combe follows suit and identifies resentment as "the result of wounded Self-esteem." Combe would add a cautionary note and say that the emotion is "aided by destructiveness," but that is a cautionary note that had also been made a century earlier. Butler too had seen the danger of resentment when it becomes vengeful, but he insisted that it could with proper tempering also be "a weapon, put into our hands by nature, against injury, injustice, and cruelty." A little later in the nineteenth century, John Stuart Mill saw the same possibilities and dangers in resentment. On the one hand, there is the resentment "common to all animal

---

3. I discuss below what distinction is worth making about any difference between *ressentiment* and resentment.

4. Pilar León-Sanz, "Resentment in Psychosomatic Pathology (1939–1960)," in *On Resentment: Past and Present*, pp. 135–67, esp. p. 137; Gregorio Marañon, *Tiberius: The Resentful Caesar*, translated by Warre Bradley Wells (1939; New York: Duell, Sloan and Pearce, 1956), pp. 212, 18.

nature," which seeks to retaliate against injury to self or kin; and, on the other, the resentment that "is *made* moral by the social feeling," that is, the recognition that justice demands that one "resents a hurt to society even if it isn't directly a hurt to him." A little less than a century after Mill, the Oxford philosopher Peter Frederick Strawson gave modern impetus to this model when he argued that resentment, as one of a repertoire of what he calls "reactive attitudes," is "a reaction to injury or indifference." It is, in other words, itself a moral attitude, and one not to be dismissed as an aberration of one, but rather to be appreciated as a source of our considered conceptions of how we respect ourselves and others—ourselves for what we deserve, and others for their moral accountability.[5]

Philosophers after, and influenced by, Strawson have given us robust models of morality that take seriously the idea of resentment as a guide to our sense of justice. Jeffrie Murphy has been the most consistent and elegant defender of resentment as a supremely beneficial emotion that is part of a suite of retributive emotions that serve to affirm and defend our sense of moral justice and buttress our self-esteem and self-respect. Stephen Darwall has likewise generated his deeply important model of "second-person standpoint" by drawing out how resentment, and other reactive attitudes, "presuppose the authority to demand and hold one another responsible for compliance with moral obligations." It is, then, a response that helps constitute our sense of ourselves as having certain rights, our sense of others as possessing particular responsibilities, and our sense of a moral community that is premised on a recognition of equality.[6] In this model, then, resentment is not an illness but rather an affirmative and righteous response to injustice. Indeed, as later commentators insist, anyone who does not feel resentful at injury might be considered ill in another sense—that is, notably lacking the moral self-esteem to know that she deserves better treatment.

---

5. Joseph Butler, *Fifteen Sermons*, in *The Works of Joseph Butler, D.C.L. Sometime Lord Bishop of Durham*, edited by W. E. Gladstone (Oxford: Clarendon Press, 1896), II, 142–43; George Combe, *Essays on Phrenology* (Edinburgh: J. Anderson, 1830), p. 170. John Stuart Mill, *Utilitarianism*, edited by George Sher (2nd ed.; Indianapolis: Hackett Publishing Company, 2001), pp. 51–52; P. F. Strawson, "Freedom and Resentment," in *Freedom and Resentment and Other Essays* (London: Methuen, 1974), pp. 14, 6, 10. The paper was delivered as a talk in 1960 to the British Academy and originally published in 1962 in *Proceedings of the British Academy*.

6. Jeffrie G. Murphy, *Getting Even: Forgiveness and Its Limits* (New York: Oxford University Press, 2003), p. 115; Stephen Darwall, *The Second-Person Standpoint: Morality, Respect and Accountability* (Cambridge, MA: Harvard University Press, 2006), p. 17; and Darwall, "Bipolar Obligations," in *Morality, Authority, & Law: Essays in Second-Personal Ethics I* (New York: Oxford University Press, 2013), pp. 20–39, esp. pp. 22, 27.

These, then, we can identify as arguably the two most resonant models of resentment—as an unforgiving and incurable spiteful illness reacting to imagined evils, and as a righteous and justified response to actual injury. Both nineteenth- and twentieth-century philosophers sometimes call the first *envy* and the second *resentment*, but they often felt they needed to justify their usage by noting that it is not that *kind* of resentment, by which they mean its Nietzschean form. As we will see presently, it is not always easy to make that distinction, and it is sometimes very easy to discern how the two forms share a great deal in common, depending largely on what perspective one assumes.

I

Resentment, then, has assumed an important place in twentieth-century philosophy and politics, particularly the philosophy that deals with forgiveness and the politics that deals with reconciliation and transitional or restorative justice. It is difficult to say precisely why this is so, although it is likely deeply connected to the fact that we are living in what I have elsewhere called a "guilted age"—an age that not only has produced its own awful atrocities, as has every previous age, but one that feels a peculiar accountability for them and, indeed, for those of the previous ages. In this guilted age, which we can date from the end of World War II to the present, we regularly witness innumerable acts in scores of societies that attempt to produce some kind of reconciliation with past atrocities, past regimes, past epochs. Populations across the globe have experimented with and adopted a variety of strategies ranging from collective apologies to truth and reconciliation commissions to ritual pilgrimages of penitence to address local horrors, national shames, and crimes against humanity (a legal concept that arose at the outset of the guilted age and helped promote the sentiments that define that age).[7]

Resentment is a concept that has long assumed a place in that complex of ideas around apology, forgiveness, guilt, shame, and related states and emotions that are very much in play in this guilted age. It is not surprising, then, that it should re-emerge as what Martha Nussbaum calls a "political emotion" in current debates about the ways to address past crimes. As we saw in the Introduction, South Africa stated outright in its Truth and Reconciliation Commission Final Report that it was important for the nation to pursue

---

7. Ashraf H. A. Rushdy, *A Guilted Age: Apologies for the Past* (Philadelphia: Temple University Press, 2015).

a path of "renouncing resentment, moving past old hurt."[8] And those who proved unwilling to renounce resentment, and were urged by those in power to do so, found themselves resentful again at the applied pressure. Resentful of the harm done by the original injury, they became doubly resentful at the disrespect of being expected not to be resentful. The forgiveness that is sought feels rushed or coerced, and insufficient attention is paid to the injury that produced the resentment in the first place. That is a point that contemporary philosophers, especially Murphy, Peter French, and Thomas Brudholm, have emphasized as they develop a point that was, for our age, first and most influentially expressed by Strawson.[9]

In a much reprinted and much cited paper, "Freedom and Resentment," Strawson draws clearly the connection between injury and resentment. He notes that "resentment, or what I have called resentment, is a reaction to injury or indifference." And to forgive for the injured and resentful party is precisely "to forswear the resentment." It is interesting that Strawson's comments on resentment and the reactive attitudes should have played and continue to play so prominent a role in moral philosophy, particularly since he was not all that concerned with moral philosophy in general, and given that his primary subject in this essay was the debate over the freedom of the will. The question that most engages Strawson is, ultimately, in what ways the recognition of determinism (the absence of the *freedom* that is the second term in his title) affects *resentment* (the first term in his title), whether resentment can be dissipated by the recognition of the limited volition of those who hurt us. The answer, it turns out, is no.[10]

Resentment, for Strawson, like other reactive attitudes, reveals an "involvement or participation in a human relationship," and can thus be distinguished

---

8. Martha Nussbaum, *Political Emotions: Why Love Matters for Justice* (Cambridge, MA: Belknap Press, 2013); *Truth and Reconciliation Commission of South Africa Final Report* (Cape Town, South Africa: Juta, 1998), Volume 1, p. 116 (Chapter 5, paragraph 50).

9. Jeffrie G. Murphy and Jean Hampton, *Forgiveness and Mercy* (New York: Cambridge University Press, 1988); Murphy, *Getting Even*; Peter A. French, *The Virtues of Vengeance* (Lawrence: University Press of Kansas, 2001); Thomas Brudholm, *Resentment's Virtue: Jean Améry and the Refusal to Forgive* (Philadelphia: Temple University Press, 2008); Joram Graf Haber, *Forgiveness: A Philosophical Study* (Lanham, MD: Rowman & Littlefield, 1991), pp. 69–88, also offers a defense of the "ethics of resentment."

10. Strawson, "Freedom and Resentment," pp. 14, 6, 10; Strawson, "Intellectual Autobiography," in *Freedom and Resentment and Other Essays*, pp. xvi–xxxix, esp. pp. xxvi–xxvii, calls the 1962 paper "one of my very few ventures into moral philosophy," a field he recognizes as "important" but one that he "never found as intellectually gripping" as the ones to which he devoted more of his attention.

from what he terms an "objective attitude." We adopt the "objective attitude" toward those we cannot hold responsible for their actions—the delusional, say—and therefore do not think of them as individuals on whom we place moral demands and expectations. At its most extreme, the "purely objective view" sees such individuals as needing "intellectual understanding, management, treatment, and control." They are not seen as morally responsible agents, nor considered as members of the moral community. With those we do consider as rational beings, though, we have different responses. We do not excuse the injuries they cause; instead we resent them. That reactive attitude is also part of what constitutes the moral community. We resent the person who injures us, precisely because we continue to view that person "as a member of the moral community; only as one who has offended against its demands." For Strawson, then, resentment comes to play a crucial role in our sense of justice because it expresses "a certain sort of demand for inter-personal regard."[11]

Resentment, then, has assumed a prominent place in contemporary philosophy and politics, and it has been largely treated in those discourses as the effect of an injury and the necessary condition to forgiveness. The argument goes along the following lines: we can say that where we have not felt resentment we cannot forgive, and where we remain resentful we have not forgiven. First, we cannot forgive what we have not resented, since forgiveness requires an injury to be forgiven (and the injury does not become forgivable until it is felt, and the proper feeling is resentment). There are other responses to things we do not resent, but they cannot rightly be called forgiveness unless they begin in resentment. We may excuse or exempt or pardon or forget, but we do not forgive unless we have resented. Likewise, we cannot be said to have forgiven if we remain resentful since we retain the very emotion whose forswearing constitutes forgiveness. The contemporary philosophers of forgiveness from Vladimir Jankélévitch to Charles Griswold have shown us the complexity in our practices of forgiving and the relationship of forgiving to resentment.[12] And yet, I would argue, there are still missing complexities in this contemporary discourse on forgiveness, some of which, I believe, can be returned to the debates by tracing the evolution of philosophical thinking about resentment. In the next two chapters, I will trace first what can be designated as the eighteenth-century British moral tradition of resentment and

---

11. Strawson, "Freedom and Resentment," pp. 9, 18, 23, 17.

12. Vladimir Jankélévitch, *Forgiveness*, translated by Andrew Kelley (Chicago: University of Chicago Press, 2005); Charles L. Griswold, *Forgiveness: A Philosophical Exploration* (Cambridge: Cambridge University Press, 2007).

then the nineteenth-century Continental cultural tradition of *ressentiment*. That genealogy will, I hope, provide us with a greater appreciation of the conflicting meanings of resentment as an individual sentiment or a cultural habitus, and the dialectic within those conflicting meanings as it unfolds. In this chapter, then, we can begin by examining some of those conflicting meanings, and seeing what to make of those two models we have for thinking about resentment as a practice.

II

What I am designating as two distinct traditions of thinking about resentment—British and Continental—present us with two starkly opposed models of resentment. Although the following chapters will explore the connections more fully, it is worthwhile briefly noting here the remarkable differences between the two models with which we began this chapter—as neurotic illness and as justified indignation.

Robert Solomon—one of the foremost philosophers of emotions—begins his catalogue of resentment by calling it "the villain of the passions." He notes that it is "obsessive and enduring," that it poisons "the whole of subjectivity with its venom." What is "most vile about this all-pervasive emotion," he continues, is "its deviousness." It "rarely allows itself to be recognized as resentment," but instead puffs itself up "with moral armament" as it pretends to be "indignation, jealousy, and anger." He argues that the true polarity of our emotional lives is not "love and hate," but rather "love and resentment"— the "first an open and trusting acceptance of intersubjectivity and intimacy, the second a defensive and closed fortress of schemes and maliciousness." Resentment, he continues, "builds all of its strategies on a single principle—*to drag others down.*" For the resentful, whatever self-esteem she or he may have is a product largely of that negative view of others. The one thing resentment seems incapable of doing, he concludes, is considering its "starting point, the self-imposed judgment of oppression and inferiority upon which all these malevolent desires and strategies are built."[13]

---

13. Robert C. Solomon, *The Passions* (New York: Doubleday, 1976), pp. 350–55. Cf. Solomon, *The Passions: Emotions and the Meaning of Life* (Indianapolis: Hackett, 1993), pp. 290–95. Also see Solomon, *True to Our Feelings: What Our Emotions Are Really Telling Us* (New York: Oxford University Press, 2007), pp. 101–13, 208–12. I will be citing hereafter from the abridged second edition of *The Passions*, except where necessary to make a point about Solomon's revisions.

To get a sense of how to understand the particular dynamics of resent-ment, and the kind of self that feels such a brooding emotion, Solomon compares resentment to other possible responses to injury—hatred and con-tempt. Contempt involves a feeling of superiority, hatred a feeling of equality, and resentment one of inferiority. While contempt "frees itself altogether by constituting the other as utterly insignificant," and hatred "involves a mu-tual binding with the other" based on a sense of equality, resentment im-plicitly accepts its inferiority and "attaches itself to the other like a leech." Resentment, in other words, is parasitic on the other, weak, and fearful of confrontation. Resentment is most like a tarantula in its modality: "Its vicious appearance and poisonous bite, its constant stance of defensiveness and back-ward and sideward retreating movements, its ultimate cowardice and fear of actually attacking, all exemplify the impotent fury of resentment." This model of resentment and the metaphor of the tarantula are drawn from the philos-opher Solomon had studied prior to his work on emotions, Nietzsche, who most fully articulated what we will call the Continental tradition.[14] (We will discuss that model in Chapter 6.)

The second model, based on the British tradition, presents a vastly different idea of what resentment is and does. Later in his career, Solomon would come to appreciate that model of resentment in which the emotion was seen as not only and irredeemably parasitical and negative. Freed of what Solomon calls its "Neitzschean context," resentment can be interpreted to be "an extremely philosophical emotion" that is "quite conscious not only of how things are but of how they might be" and how "they ought to be." Its perspicacity leads it to desire fairness and a sense of giving each her due (what "ought" to hap-pen). What we can find in this "most philosophical of emotions," in other words, is "one key ingredient of our sense of justice."[15] This model of resent-ment comes to us from the eighteenth-century British moralist Joseph Butler, whom we will discuss in the next chapter. His work has informed much of the discussion of resentment and forgiveness in contemporary philosophy, and

---

14. Solomon, *The Passions: Emotions and the Meaning of Life*, pp. 207–208.

15. Solomon, *A Passion for Justice: Emotions and the Origins of the Social Contract* (Reading, MA: Addison-Wesley Publishing, 1990), pp. 269, 261. Also see Solomon, "One Hundred Years of *Ressentiment*: Nietzsche's *Genealogy of Morals*," in *Nietzsche, Genealogy, Morality: Essays on Nietzsche's Genealogy of Morals*, edited by Richard Schacht (Berkeley: University of California Press, 1994), pp. 95–126.

especially the work of Murphy, who has played an important part in making Butler's work familiar to contemporary readers.[16]

In that model, resentment is seen as an appropriate response to wrong-doing and mistreatment. We are resentful at being harmed not because we feel ourselves inferior, but because we value ourselves sufficiently to feel affronted at being treated in a disrespectful way that is meant to make us feel inferior. As Murphy elegantly puts it, "resentment and other vindictive passions" can ideally be "instruments of our self-defense, our self-respect, and our respect for the demands of morality."[17] Resentment, then, and the closely related passion of *indignation*, are affirmative emotions, spurring us on to seek correction and justice. It is precisely for this reason that this form of resentment demands an apology for a wrong and is open to forgiveness for that wrong. In the Nietzschean model, forgiveness is not an option because there is no direct wrong for the resentful to forgive—or, better, the perceived wrong is more correctly described as an existential one for which there is no one to forgive. But in the Butler model of resentment as an appropriate response based on a sense of justice, there is the possibility (and expectation) of forgiveness. Indeed, we tend to think of someone who refuses to forgive a wrong for which atonement has been made as a person prone to falling into the negative kind of resentment that broods on ills precisely because of the pleasure he or she gets from it. In other words, forgiveness becomes something like a fulcrum for determining what sort of resentment is in play—positive or negative, righteous indignation at or morose delectation in acts of injustice.

When Murphy first set out to define forgiveness, he established it as precisely the act of "overcoming resentment." Following Butler, he argues that "forgiveness is the forswearing of *resentment*." As we saw in the previous chapter, Murphy was to evolve his views on forgiveness. In regards to its relationship to resentment, he would modify his definition of forgiveness twice. First, in dialogue with Jean Hampton, he came to see that the forswearing of resentment by itself is not forgiveness, since one can cease to resent by forgetting the injury, for instance. "Forgiveness," he now wrote, "is not the

---

16. Also see Hastings Rashdall, "The Ethics of Forgiveness," *International Journal of Ethics* 10.2 (January, 1900): 193–206, esp. pp. 199–200.

17. Murphy, *Getting Even*, p. 115; Darwall, "Justice and Retaliation," in *Honor, History, & Relationship: Essays in Second-Personal Ethics II* (New York: Oxford University Press, 2013), pp. 50–71, esp. p. 52, makes the point that resentment need not imply vindictiveness, but presupposes accountability. Resentment's "object is not to retaliate against someone who has injured one, but to hold him responsible in a way that expresses respect for him as a member of a mutually accountable moral community."

overcoming of resentment *simpliciter*; it is rather this: forswearing resentment on moral grounds." Second, in a dialogue with Norvin Richards, Murphy altered his definition one more way by expanding the range of emotions that forgiveness forswears. "It is more illuminating—more loyal to the actual texture of our moral lives—to think of forgiveness as overcoming a variety of negative feelings that one might have towards a wrong-doer—resentment, yes, but also such feelings as anger, hatred, loathing, contempt, indifference, disappointment or even sadness." In his most recent work, he has defined forgiveness with those qualifications as "the overcoming, on moral grounds, of what I will call the *vindictive passions*—the passions of anger, resentment, and even hatred that are often occasioned when one has been deeply wronged by another."[18] *Resentment*, then, in Murphy, has come to represent an entire suite of retributive or vindictive emotions; and I will follow his example by using the term as connoting those other emotions.

In sum, then, the two models of resentment offer us two distinct ideas of just what that emotion entails and what it means about the things that inspire it and the person who feels it. It is either a morose sensibility brooding on imaginary ills and producing feelings of jealousy or rancor for not having access to what others have (that is, a violation of some cosmic sense of fairness that exists in our minds); or it is a righteous expression of self-esteem and the proper aggrieved response to injury brought on by a sense of having been misserved (that is, a violation of justice or fairness). These two primary meanings of resentment, then, can be designated as *resentment for perceived denial*, which is usually represented as the kind of cancerous, poisonous obsession that leads to *envy*, which is, for most, a narrower selfish sense of grief, and *resentment for injury*, which many argue leads to *indignation*, and therefore to a larger social sense of justice.

---

18. Murphy, "Forgiveness and Resentment," *Midwest Studies in Philosophy* 7 (1982): 503–16, esp. p. 504; Murphy and Hampton, *Forgiveness and Mercy*, pp. 23–24; Murphy, "Jean Hampton on Immorality, Self-Hatred, and Self-Forgiveness," *Philosophical Studies: An International Journal for Philosophy in the Analytic Tradition* 89.2/3 (March 1998): 215–36, esp. p. 217; Murphy, *Getting Even*, p. 16; see Norvin Richards, "Forgiveness," *Ethics* 99.1 (October, 1988): 77–97, esp. pp. 77–79. Even in his 1982 essay, Murphy had included "anger and hatred" as cognate emotions to resentment (204).

Murphy continued to explore this definition in debates with Herbert Morris as well. See Murphy, "Forgiveness, Mercy, and the Retributive Emotions," *Criminal Justice Ethics* 7.2 (Summer, 1988): 3–15; Herbert Morris, "Murphy on Forgiveness," *Criminal Justice Ethics* 7.2 (Summer, 1988): 15–19; Murphy, "A Rejoinder to Morris," *Criminal Justice Ethics* 7.2 (Summer, 1988): 20–22; Jeffrey M. Blustein, *Forgiveness and Remembrance: Remembering Wrongdoing in Personal and Public Life* (New York: Oxford University Press, 2014), develops the point of what forgiveness means once we expand the range of emotions it attempts to overcome.

While we make that distinction for the sake of clarity here, it is also important for us to insist that these two models are profoundly connected. Some philosophers wish to make clear distinctions between what we can call the injured resentful and the envious resentful. John Rawls, for example, notes that envy is "not a moral feeling," whereas "resentment is a moral feeling," and, he warns us to be "careful not to conflate envy and resentment." The difference Rawls spells out is noteworthy, but in the end not entirely persuasive. One can be either resentful at or envious of not having a fair share, and the difference can depend largely on "the sort of perspective from which the situation is viewed," as Rawls himself recognizes. The resentful person feels resentful because she or he feels that the unfairness is a result of others' misconduct or of unjust institutions. The envious person feels envious in the same circumstance without expressing a sense of where blame should be attached (others' crimes or structural injustices). These do not seem particularly strong grounds for making that distinction. After all, both resentment and envy are expressions of self-esteem: resentment as a violation of the self in being affronted, envy as a violation of the self in being denied. We tend to make the distinction or, more accurately, judge those who hold one or the other based on whether we agree or disagree that the self-esteem has merit.[19] We should keep this in mind, especially when we find some historians who seem to posit that all revolutions are products of envious resentment, while others of us might see many such attempts to reorder a society as an expression of an injured resentment in which revolutionaries see the structural injustices that had ordered the *ancien régime* or serfdom they are overthrowing.[20]

What also makes it difficult to hold that distinction too sharply is that the enviously resentful and the injured resentful frequently conflate the

---

19. John Rawls, *A Theory of Justice* (Cambridge, MA: Belknap Press, 1971), p. 533. Cf. Nussbaum, *Political Emotions,* pp. 341–42. Also see Gabrielle Taylor, *Deadly Vices* (Oxford: Clarendon Press, 2006), pp. 42, 88, 92, for the distinction between envy and resentment; Alice MacLachlan, "Unreasonable Resentments," *Journal of Social Philosophy* 41.4 (Winter, 2010): 422–41, makes a fine case that Rawls and others who make the distinction—between "reasonable" and "unreasonable" resentment, as she calls them—risk "overmoralizing and undermoralizing the work that resentment does" (437); Amélie Oksenberg Rorty, "The Dramas of Resentment," *Yale Review* 88.3 (July, 2000): 89–100, offers a lyrical and insightful description of the two models of resentment. What I am designating the British and Continental traditions, Didier Fassin calls *"ressentiment* in the Nietzschean lineage" and "resentment in the Smithian tradition." See Fassin, "On Resentment and *Ressentiment*: The Politics and Ethics of Moral Emotions," *Current Anthropology* 54.3 (June, 2013): 249–67 (including responses by five readers and an authorial rejoinder).

20. Marc Ferro, *Resentment in History*, translated by Steven Rendell (Cambridge: Polity Press, 2010).

two sources of resentment. Consider, for instance, Iago who is clearly envious of Othello for all the excellent qualities he detects in him. But he also feels the need to fabricate a background story of injury to give substance and heft to his envy. What feeds his desire for revenge, as he notes, is his suspicion that "the lusty Moor / Hath leap'd into my seat." This suspicion of having been cuckolded—which no one else in the play can give the least support—leads him to the kind of brooding that we identify particularly with envy: the suspicion "like a poisonous mineral," he says, does "gnaw my inwards." In other words, what he identifies as resentment due to injury (being cuckolded) he responds to with the conventional sensibility of envy. And his plan, as he says, is to produce exactly the same kind of envious jealousy in Othello. There are plenty of moments in the play where it is shown that Iago does not seriously believe himself to have been injured. He knows that he is working what he calls "double knavery," and one half of that knavery, it seems, is on himself. When he tells Cassio, for instance, that "oft my jealousy / Shapes faults that are not," we are meant to understand the statement as both a lure for Cassio as well as an unintentional self-revelation. Iago recognizes that he shapes injuries where there are none, that he, in other words, fabricates an account that permits him to think himself a resentfully injured person while he is a resentfully envious one.[21]

Finally, we should also note that the distinction is not simply from the English to the French term, from resentment to *ressentiment*. R. Jay Wallace, for example, maintains that "*ressentiment* is essentially *about* one's lack of some value or good, whereas resentment is *about* the breach of demands." In this usage, *ressentiment* becomes the equivalent of envy (as Rawls uses it), and resentment umbrage; and therefore one is and the other is not a moral emotion. As we saw, Rawls was not able to provide a compelling distinction for that difference, other than the subjective perspective of the injured party. The point, however, is that the French term somehow means something the English does not, which I think mistaken. Likewise, Charles Griswold writes that "*ressentiment*" has "connotations that are broader than 'resentment,'" including "malice, desire for revenge, envy," as well as "anxiety, suspicion, the holding of a grudge, a hatred of whatever one feels has called one's standing into question, a feeling of powerlessness, a loss of self-respect," and "a

---

21. William Shakespeare, *Othello*, edited by Ross McDonald (New York: Pelican), 2.1.280–85.

generalized sense that the world is unfair."[22] I think "resentment" does indeed connote many of these things as much as does *"ressentiment,"* and the rest are not connoted by the word *"ressentiment"* itself but rather by Nietzsche's particular use of the term. Nietzsche, who first used *"ressentiment"* in a philosophical sense, felt that he could find no German equivalent, and he also had personal reasons, having to do with his growing animosity for Wagner and his growing fondness for Dostoevsky, from whom he may have borrowed it, for preferring the French word. Philosophers since have borrowed either his term or his license. They have either used the French term because Nietzsche used it or offered suspect reasons for finding a deeper and more brooding meaning in it than the English word permits because they are thinking of Nietzsche's use of it rather than the French use of it.

I can fully understand the temptation for anyone—say, someone who has had to spend hours futilely arguing with a bureaucrat in a prefecture—to think that the French feel things differently. But the French term *"ressentiment,"* in the end, is not qualitatively different from the English "resentment." The entry for *ressentiment* in *Le Robert Illustré* (2012) is as follows: *"Fait de se souvenir avec animosité des torts qu'on a subis,"* and refers the reader to the synonymous words *rancœur* and *rancune.* And French–English *Le Grande Dictionnaire Hachette-Oxford* defines each term (*"ressentiment,"* "resentment") by the other. It is better, I think, to follow the examples of Robert Solomon and Jeffrie Murphy and Stephen Darwall, who are clear that they are drawing on "Nietzsche's use of the French" when they argue that there is something more in *"ressentiment"* than in "resentment."[23]

What resentment is, what range of emotions it expresses, will become clear as we see each of the philosophical traditions develop a case for it in the two chapters that follow. We have seen that the two primary senses include umbrage and envy and that in both cases the resentment expresses a response

---

22. R. Jay Wallace, *Responsibility and the Moral Sentiments* (Cambridge, MA: Harvard University Press, 1994), p. 247; Griswold, *Forgiveness,* pp. xix–xx; Solomon, *A Passion for Justice,* p. 265.

23. Murphy, "Moral Epistemology, the Retributive Emotions, and the 'Clumsy Moral Philosophy' of Jesus Christ," in *Punishment and the Moral Emotions: Essays in Law, Morality, and Religion* (New York: Oxford University Press, 2012), pp. 21–42, esp. p. 26, makes a distinction between *ressentiment* and resentment, but also makes it clear that he is talking about Nietzschean *ressentiment*; Darwall, "*Ressentiment* and Second-Personal Resentment," in *Honor, History, & Relationship,* pp. 72–88. Also see Bernard N. Meltzer and Gil Richard Musolf, "Resentment and *Ressentiment,*" *Sociological Inquiry* 72.2 (Spring, 2002): 240–55, esp. p. 242, who see no distinction in the French and English usage, but who employ "resentment" to describe a fleeting emotion and *"ressentiment"* for an enduring one.

to an injury, whether it is direct or indirect, felt or imagined, whether one can or cannot identify the maleficence that produced it. To be clear, this is not to deny the difference between a justified response to a genuine injury and a pervasive sense of being ill-served by the universe. We will see in what ways those two primary meanings emerge, merge, and produce a different set of connotations over the course of two centuries. We will also see how resentment is manifest as an individual and a collective sentiment, at times the emotion of an injured person, at others a society in malaise, and in others something in between. To appreciate better what it is to feel resentful in that complicated sense of somewhere between umbrage and envy, and to understand more about where resentment dwells and how it spreads, we can turn from the Underground Man to a predecessor twenty-four centuries earlier.

III

Sophocles' late play *Philoctetes* is one of the earliest and most poignant representations of resentment. The story centers on the attempt by Odysseus and Neoptolemus to get Philoctetes' famed bow (willed to him by Heracles), in order to fulfill the prophecy that this bow will give the Greeks victory in the Trojan War. Philoctetes has been exiled to the island of Lemnos for the past ten years, sent there against his will by the leaders of the Greek military, including Odysseus, whom he despises and wishes to kill. The background story—not told in Sophocles' play, but understood as its context—is that Philoctetes is exiled because of his wound. On the way to Troy at the outset of the war, Philoctetes had been bitten by a snake as he approached the shrine of a local deity on the island of Chrysè to make a sacrifice. The infected wound became so malodorous, and Philoctetes' groans of pain so jarring, that Agamemnon and Menelaus abandoned him on the island of Lemnos and went off to Troy without him. For ten years, then, he has nursed his chronically suppurating and odious-smelling wound, isolated from everyone.

The editors of the play rightly note that while Philoctetes is bitten while approaching a shrine, and the snake is a Greek symbol of godly power, we must also understand that Greek shrines were unmarked terrain and that what happened to Philoctetes was largely an accident. He was not punished for treading willfully on holy ground, nor marked by this wound—as Cain was, for instance—because of some evil act he performed. There is something irreducibly mysterious about Philoctetes' fate. As the editors note, he "becomes burdened with the mark of God's resentment without any explanation for it humanly cogent either for himself or for others." And, likewise, the end of the play reinforces this point that what happens cannot be explained as a result of human agency. After Philoctetes vows not to go to Troy, Heracles, in the form of a *deus ex machina*, descends and states his fate: Philoctetes will go to Troy, where "you shall find there the cure of your cruel sickness, / and then be adjudged the best warrior among the Greeks."[24] His cure, like his wound, is inexplicable.

Even so, it is hard not to see the physical wound as a metaphor for the sense of grievance, the resentment that Philoctetes carries with him. He refers to it as "my insatiable disease" (ll. 313–14), and the disease, we are meant to infer, is far more than physical. Indeed, in the warning he gives Neoptolemus as he lapses into one of his periodic bouts of anguished and tormented pain, he uses language that indicates a gnawing spite:

> I am lost, boy.
> I will not be able to hide it from you longer.
> Oh! Oh!
> It goes through me, right through me!
> Miserable, miserable!
> I am lost, boy. I am being eaten up. Oh! (ll. 742–47)

Sophocles also makes it clear that Philoctetes is nursing a resentment against the world. While he is consistent in expressing his hatred for Agamemnon, Menelaus, and Odysseus, the play suggests that these figures have become tokens of his resentment because the cause of his injury remains inexplicable. When he lashes out at the Chorus, they remind him of this point:

> It was the will of the Gods
> that has subdued you, no craft
> to which my hand was lent.
> Turn your hate, your ill-omened curses, elsewhere. (ll. 1118–21)

And likewise, the Chorus claims that Philoctetes' rancor against Odysseus is equally misplaced:

---

24. David Grene, "Introduction to *Philoctetes*," in *The Complete Greek Tragedies*, Vol. IV, edited by David Grene and Richmond Lattimore (New York: Modern Library, 1957), pp. 208–11, esp. p. 209; Sophocles, *Philoctetes*, in *The Complete Greek Tragedies*, Vol. IV, p. 277 (ll. 1425–26). Hereafter all quotations will be taken from this edition and the line numbers noted parenthetically in the body of the text.

A man should give careful heed to say what is just;
and when he has said it, restrain his tongue from rancor and taunt.
Odysseus was one man, appointed by many,
by their command he has done this, a service to his friends. (ll. 1140–43)

Even the most sympathetic of the characters in the play, Neoptolemus, chastises Philoctetes for holding a grudge that has literally unmanned him: "But men that cling wilfully to their sufferings / as you do, no one may forgive nor pity. / Your anger has made a savage of you" (ll. 1319–21).

Philoctetes may feel justifiable anger at having been subjected to his humiliating condition—inhumanly malodorous, isolated, abandoned, and in deep and abiding pain. But the play suggests that in holding his grudge so relentlessly he has become unbearable for reasons having nothing to do with his smell or his groans. He has become unbearable because he is unreasonably resentful, and frequently at the wrong people for the wrong things. In an engaging and spirited reading of the play, Edmund Wilson argues that the story offers us an account of two things—the bow and the wound. Philoctetes represents "a superhuman art which everybody has to respect" (the bow) and yet he is victim of an illness that renders him "abhorrent to society" (the wound). The play resolves this by making his cure depend on his ability "to forget his grievance and to devote his divine gifts to the service of his own people." What the *deus ex machina* represents, Wilson argues, is the "change of heart which has taken place in Philoctetes as a result of his having found a man who recognizes the wrong that has been done him and who is willing to champion his cause in defiance of all the Greek forces." The key figure in Wilson's reading is Neoptolemus, who recognizes the wrong, and "dissolves Philoctetes' stubbornness, and thus cures him and sets him free."[25]

Neoptolemus is one of the two emissaries from the Greeks—Odysseus is the other—and it is worth noting that each of them represents something for Philoctetes and for the larger moral order presented in the play. Philoctetes loathes Odysseus, while he loves Neoptolemus' father, Achilles, and soon transfers that love to the son; and so we see how he learns to reconcile conflicting emotions of those who represent his desolation and those who will come to represent his redemption. Moreover, Odysseus is committed to guile in order to accomplish the larger ends of the mission, while Neoptolemus is

---

25. Edmund Wilson, *The Wound and the Bow: Seven Studies in Literature* (Cambridge, MA: Riverside Press, 1941), pp. 294, 283, 295.

committed to an almost deontological sense of uprightness of motive. When Odysseus suggests that they must resort to deceit in order to accomplish their end, Neoptolemus demurs: "I have a natural antipathy / to get my ends by tricks and stratagems" (ll. 87–88). Odysseus, who sees such rigor in ethics as a sign of immature and impolitic youth, counsels him to place in abeyance such conscientiousness: "For one brief shameless portion of a day / give me yourself, and then for all the rest / you may be called most scrupulous of men" (ll. 83–85). Eventually Odysseus succeeds in persuading young Neoptolemus to do what he deems necessary, but the debate between these two ways of thinking runs throughout the play—whether one must be vigilantly truthful or whether it is acceptable, as Odysseus puts it, at "another time" to "prove honest" (l. 83).

For Wilson, Neoptolemus' honesty—"in refusing to break his word"—is what wins the day.[26] I am not so sure that this is quite what the play suggests, though. It strikes me that there are three other points that are equally important.

First, as we saw, Philoctetes must hear, repeatedly, that his rancor is ill-directed and destructive. Part of the cure is for him to recognize that his "insatiable disease" *is* resentment; that is also his wound. Second, Philoctetes must acknowledge the discursive modes that help resolve resentment—especially forgiveness and remorse. Neoptolemus is the bearer of that message, when he chastises Philoctetes for his unremitting anger, and when he asks him, specifically: "Is there no place, then, for repentance?" (l. 1270). Finally, Philoctetes seeks a particular kind of community of fellow-sufferers, and it is only when he feels such community that he is able to take to heart the earlier two points. When Neoptolemus approaches him with the story of his own resentment against Odysseus, Agamemnon, and Menelaus, Philoctetes is particularly eager to welcome him: "Are you, as well as I, a sufferer / and angry?" (ll. 323–24). And so, what Philoctetes requires, then, is to hear a diagnosis, that his illness is resentment, to learn about the practices of repentance and forgiveness that are part of the cure, and to appreciate that he is part of a larger community of people who have suffered ill.

It is worth teasing out the implication of these three points, which, I think, will help us appreciate the subtleties and ambiguities in resentment that the philosophers we have discussed above also found.

---

26. Wilson, *The Wound and the Bow*, p. 295.

The first point reveals what we saw to be the case with Iago earlier, that existential resentment (or envy) seeks to buttress itself with the trappings of the other kind of resentment (umbrage). Philoctetes is not particularly envious, although he is not free of the passion either; mostly, though, he is afflicted with a sense of the absurdity of his condition. We can say that the Chorus is correct to note that Philoctetes is flailing away in trying to identify someone or something culpable for his miserable life—not particularly compassionate, but correct. But we can also say that Philoctetes is right to flail away in search of meaning—that is, within the boundaries with which meaning is constrained in his world. He *feels* resentful, and he knows that rationally his resentment requires a moral, human agent to blame for his condition. He chooses those who seem most plausible—Agamemnon, Menelaus, and Odysseus—because they left him behind. But they acted on the conditions in which they found themselves—with someone whose odor was humanly unbearable, with someone whose groaning was so pitiable and yet disruptive that it interrupted the very acts of worship that led him to the shrine in the first place, and with a war on the horizon for which greater sacrifices had already been made—namely, Iphigenia, Agamemnon's daughter, whose life will eventually cost him his own and the downfall of the house of Atreus. Given this social and historical context, was leaving Philoctetes behind irrational? Was it better to bear him on a ship where his odor might have caused mutiny and his lamentations have a dispiriting effect on warriors on their way to battle? As the Chorus bluntly puts it, "it was the will of the Gods" and it was the decision of a collective on a mission, and not the evil acts of individuals wishing to injure him. Confronted with the inexplicable, Philoctetes is wrong to resent the people he thinks responsible for his fate, but not wrong to feel what is effectively an existential resentment at his fate. He has his wound and he must nurse it, even though the only way he knows to nurse it is by holding a grudge against those easiest to identify as somehow culpable.

The second point is one we will focus on more fully in the chapters that follow, and that is the relationship of resentment to the suite of interactions that are the subjects of this book—remorse, apology, repentance, and forgiveness. These, I argue, are inherently imbricated into one dynamic process: to feel resentment is to feel the need for repentance or apology, and to feel apologetic is to feel the need for forgiveness, and to feel forgiveness is to recognize the need for a peaceful resolution and reconciliation by the negation of resentment. There is a curious and obscure term that helps us better appreciate the dynamic interaction of these emotions and practices: *piacular*. From the classical Latin word *piāculāris*, it is a term that means both something that requires expiation and an act of expiation. In other words, it is both the sin and the repentance. The first usage, something requiring atonement, is now rare. It was less rare in the mid-eighteenth century when Adam Smith used it to describe a particular kind of moral sentiment. On occasions where an individual inadvertently offends, the person, though "not guilty," nonetheless "feels himself to be in the highest degree, what the ancients called, piacular, and is eager to make every sort of atonement in his power." Although Smith was mostly interested in revealing what happens in that peculiar "distress which an innocent person feels," he is also alert to the fact that the term the ancients used to describe it was one that implicated both the loss of innocence and the means by which it may be recuperated to some degree.[27]

Smith offers an example: "in the ancient heathen religion, that holy ground which had been consecrated to some god, was not to be trod upon but upon solemn and necessary occasions, and the man who had even ignorantly violated it, became piacular from that moment, and, until proper atonement should be made, incurred the vengeance of that powerful and invisible being to whom it had been set apart." Smith is referring to the religion of ancient Rome, but the description, as we saw, is also precisely fit for the case of Philoctetes in ancient Greece. He too has performed what Smith calls an "undesigned violation," and he too is struggling to discern what it means to be "piacular."[28] When Neoptolemus asks if there is any place for "repentance," he is referring to his own penitence, his own desire to perform an act showing his remorse at having fooled Philoctetes by lying to him. But the introduction of the idea of repentance is important because it reveals to Philoctetes the other practice of the piacular condition. Philoctetes is unforgiving in his assessments. Once he discovers that Neoptolemus has lied to him, he adds him to the catalogue of offensive people: "Cursed be you all, / first the two sons of Atreus, then Odysseus, / and then yourself!" (ll. 1284–86). What Neoptolemus reveals to him is precisely that such an unforgiving attitude fails to acknowledge the possibility of *change*. In response to Philoctetes' accusations of his treachery, Neoptolemus calmly says: "I am not such now" (l. 1273). He has done wrong, he has felt remorse, atoned for his wrong, and is *now* a different person.

---

27. Adam Smith, *The Theory of Moral Sentiments*, edited by D. D. Raphael and A. L. Macfie (Indianapolis: Liberty Classics, 1976), pp. 338–39, 107.

28. Smith, *The Theory of Moral Sentiments*, p. 107. Smith added both the passages that involve the term *piacular* to the sixth edition of *The Theory of Moral Sentiments* (II.iii.4 and VII.iv.30).

The terms Neoptolemus uses are temporal—he *once was* that, and he is *now* this. He acknowledges the possibility for change and growth *in time*. Philoctetes is mired in time rather than flowing in it, and this inertia is precisely the result and symptom of his resentment. As both Vladimir Jankélévitch and Jean Améry note, the "man of *ressentiment*" fights against the flow of time, either stubbornly hardening "against futurition," as Jankélévitch puts it, or demanding "that time be turned back," as Améry phrases it.[29] For ten years, Philoctetes has been unremittingly fighting this struggle against the future, attempting to understand what caused his suffering, to identify what his wound means, and to resist any act that might imply his being piacular—in either of the two senses. Once Neoptolemus introduces the practice of being piacular—in the second sense of atoning for wrongs, even those inadvertently done—the play changes course and moves toward its resolution. It is not only Neoptolemus' honesty, then, but also his diagnoses of what ails and what will cure Philoctetes that set him free.

The final point is that Philoctetes begins to feel at peace when he recognizes that he is part of a community of suffering, part of a larger order of those who have been wounded. As he exclaims at the end of Neoptolemus' account of how his father's armor had been stolen from him, "your half of sorrow matches that of mine" (1. 403). Philoctetes feels less isolated and more part of a society (of resentment); we are meant to understand this new sense of sharing with another in light of his ten years of isolated and solitary lamentation of his own condition. In recognizing that others have suffered, he feels a new kinship and develops what Smith, and his predecessors in the philosophy of sympathy, will call "fellow-feeling." To show how profoundly he is moved in having this shared sensibility, Philoctetes gives Neoptolemus his famed bow (ll. 762–78). The gift of the bow demonstrates what it meant to him to have someone to share in his resentment, someone who felt his pain as his own, and formed with him a community of rancor against a defined enemy.

Yet, of course, there are two flaws in this logic. First, Philoctetes' emotions were inspired by a ruse and a lie. What Neoptolemus does when he

---

29. Jankélévitch, *Forgiveness*, p. 15; Jean Améry, "Resentments," in *At The Mind's Limits: Contemplations by a Survivor of Auschwitz and Its Realities*, translated by Sidney Rosenfeld and Stella P. Rosenfeld (Bloomington: Indiana University Press, 1980), pp. 62–81, esp. p. 77. Cf. Panu Minkkinen, "*Ressentiment* as Suffering: On Transitional Justice and the Impossibility of Forgiveness," *Law and Literature* 19.3 (Fall, 2007): 513–32, esp. p. 519.

tells Philoctetes his story of suffering at the hands of the same people who have injured him is a fabrication; it is precisely the lie that Odysseus urged him to tell in order to win his allegiance. Second, Neoptolemus was supporting precisely what he and the Chorus and Odysseus understand to be Philoctetes' very problem—his inability to find a suitable person to resent. When Neoptolemus supports him in thinking the best repository of blame and hatred are the three (Agamemnon, Menelaus, and Odysseus), he is enabling his continued persistence in blaming those who are not culpable in the way he thinks them, and not culpable for the fate that is his.

Of course, Neoptolemus returns the bow (ll. 1285–93), and that act reveals how he has upheld his character; Neoptolemus will not operate by the guile of Odysseus, but must be honest in his dealings. Neoptolemus' act demonstrates two things to Philoctetes. First, it shows Philoctetes that he (Philoctetes) is not discriminating; he easily became as enraged and resentful at this lie as he was at the ten years of suffering. Second, it shows him what an act of atonement looks like; Neoptolemus has redressed his wrong. He has shown that he is *now* not what he was *before*.

All of these ideas are important—that Philoctetes has had his wound diagnosed (it is resentment), that he has had revealed to him the way to heal (through repentance and forgiveness), and that he has come better to appreciate what it means to belong to a society (first a society of resentment with Neoptolemus, and then to be part of the Greek army that he joins at the end of the play). Resentment, then, is shown to be not only a wound but also a process, and it is shown to be an instrument. It can create community; the resentment that had been gnawing at him privately became a qualitatively different thing when it became a bond between him and another. What had been his own suppurating wound privately felt and privately mourned became a part of a collective, more public process that eventually leads to healing, for himself and for the society. As we will see in the chapters that follow, that is an important distinction of fruitful tension for the philosophers who write about resentment—between thinking of it as an individual, private sentiment or as a collective, communal sensibility.

IV

At the end of *Notes from Underground*, the Underground Man reflects on what to make of his life of resentment: "I defaulted on my life through moral corruption in a corner, through an insufficiency of milieu, through unaccustom to what is alive, and through vainglorious spite in the underground." It is a curious catalogue of what is presumably meant to describe the *course* of his disease, not its etiology. In the four items in the catalogue, he focuses on places that indicate isolation (a corner, underground) as well as describing states of being that reveal a failure to engage with others in any way other than to envy them or feel rancor toward them. There is, however, one moment of possibility (or perhaps only ambiguity) in the marvelous phrase he uses as the second in his catalogue—"an insufficiency of milieu." It could be that he means to suggest that the milieu he has in mind is, like the "corner" and "underground," another *place* where he has hidden from engagement with life. Or, it could be that he is suggesting a larger sense of "milieu" and indicating that, somehow or other, the resentment he feels is not a result only of his own "moral corruption," but also a product of a social habitus, the environment in which he found himself. Like the odd phrase "unaccustom to what is alive" (which another translator renders less poetically as "losing touch with life"), this one opens up new grounds and suggests that there is more to the Underground Man than a consumptive inability to control his spite for everyone around him.[30]

Those who have been inspired by Dostoevsky have certainly maintained that resentment can be understood not only as an individual ailment but also as a social disease. The one who borrowed his word, Nietzsche, argues precisely that he delineates *ressentiment* as an epochal sensibility. The ones who borrowed his narrative conceit and who traced to this novella the origins of the existential novel of absurdity followed Dostoevsky's example in diagnosing what they identified as a *social* ill. We can perhaps say that the sites for representing resentment fall into two categories—places of isolation and places of judgment. Dostoevsky chose the former, the underground, to suggest how an actual subterranean place can help augment the depiction of subterranean feelings. Likewise, Sophocles chose an island—in this case rendering literally the isolation that he would render metaphorically in Oedipus' blindness in his next and last play, *Oedipus at Colonus*. The other site is the place of judgment, particularly the courtroom. There is a sense of isolation here, too, since the accused is set apart and faces the judgment of society. Since resentment in one form is also about injustice, the court provides

---

30. Dostoevsky, *Notes from Underground*, p. 118. The other translator is Magarshack; see Dostoevsky, *Best Short Stories of Dostoevsky*, p. 258.

a perfect place to show what seething sentiments reside in those who stand falsely accused. Dostoevsky also contributed to this tradition, in *Crime and Punishment* and, especially, *The Brothers Karamazov*.

Avid admirers of Dostoevsky, Kafka and Camus would follow suit—if the pun be allowed—and show us the existential absurdity in *The Trial* and *The Stranger*. What they reveal in these absurdist fables is nothing less than that the society itself—representing its sense of justice in the courts—is cancerously festering with resentment. Josef K is on trial for his life for an alleged crime he is not permitted to know, and Meursault is really on trial for something other than the crime he did commit. It is not ultimately his murder of the Arab for which he is found guilty, but for not following the society's conventions regarding love of motherhood and the rituals of mourning. The jury is most swayed when the prosecutor claims: "I accuse this man of burying his mother with crime in his heart." In his summary statement, he goes further and accuses Meursault of "killing his mother." And in his final peroration, he alludes to the next day's trial of someone accused of parricide, and exclaims that Meursault is "also guilty of the murder to be tried in this court tomorrow. He must be punished accordingly."[31] Meursault will be executed, like Josef K, not for what he did, but for what he did not do.

In the courts, then, in the trials that a society conducts to protect itself from people it estranges, we find an indictment of society itself as the seething resentful entity that requires a particular kind of annihilating revenge against those it identifies randomly or selectively. These become sacrifices to whimsical spite, not criminals who have offended. It is telling, as well, as Camus bitingly revealed, that this society places those on trial for an insufficient show of emotion. Has Meursault "so much as expressed any remorse?" asks the prosecutor of the jury. He is as guilty of being remorseless (for a crime he did commit, presumably, since the prosecutor has confused the charges of murder with matricide) as he was of an absence of indecorous grief in the wake for his mother. He is on trial for his feelings.

What Kafka and Camus and Dostoevsky show us is not simply that there are individuals who are resentful, or even that there is a class resentment among the oppressed that will, in other circumstances, produce revolutionary fervors. What they are showing us, rather, is that the empowered elite

---

31. Albert Camus, *The Stranger*, translated by Matthew Ward (1988; New York: Everyman, 1993), pp. 92, 97–98. I have benefited greatly on how authors represent courts, and the legal profession more generally, in portraits of resentment from Weisberg, *The Failure of the Word*.

attempt to control and disenfranchise and punish because they—sometimes too, sometimes only—are filled with a loathsome *ressentiment* for those they hate. Their resentment is not a product of an injury or an injustice, but a form of that existential envy that Nietzsche so masterfully described. Mastery does not provide immunity from that.

THE BRITISH MORAL TRADITION

CONSCIENCE

Because it was riven with both massive political upheavals (the Civil War, the Restoration, and the Glorious Revolution) and deep economic transformations (the creation of a market society), Britain in the course of the seventeenth century produced a series of philosophers and intellectuals who doggedly asked two related questions—what is the nature of obligation (to country or to contract), and what is the distinctive character of those who participate in either politics or markets? It was during this time that both Hobbes in the 1650s and Locke in the 1680s developed theories of *social contracts*, that is, a defined set of obligations for how a self belongs to the society imagined through a market instrument (a contract). These were coercive contracts, of course, because it turned out that citizens were signatories to them before they were born; this was a contract in which "consent" meant tacit acceptance of what already was, not acknowledged acceptance of what would be. Both Hobbes and Locke offered dystopic visions of what the "state of nature" (that is the state before or beyond the social contract) was like: it was a war of all against all, where no property, including property in life and limb, was safe. Commentators on this historical moment have identified different ways of imagining the kind of autonomous selfhood that developed in these conditions in early modern Britain. C. B. MacPherson suggested that we see the evolution of what he called "possessive individualism" in this period, focusing on how *markets* created the self that one could possess and that was capable of possessing and consuming in turn. This was a self that was produced in and able to participate in the new exchange economy. Focusing more on the *obligations* that political and economic relations entailed, Stephen Darwall suggested that we see the development of what he called "the internal 'ought,'" an interiorized sense of obligation to a particular moral order.[1]

Darwall shows how a passage from Saint Paul's Epistle to the Romans came to be emblematic of that change in sensibility during this era. Paul's words—"For when the Gentiles, which have not the law, do by nature the things contained in the law, these, having not the law, are a law unto themselves" (Romans 2:14)—were traditionally used to justify that a moral community could exist beyond the "boundaries of revelation." In early modern England, though, these words came to be put to a very different purpose, namely, identifying how *obligation* could be understood in terms of the "*autonomy of the moral agent.*" How does one identify a duty, and what set of instruments (laws) or intuitions (nature) motivate one to act on that duty, to fulfill that obligation? In a penetrating study, Darwall traces in a set of thinkers from Hobbes to Hume what he identifies as two traditions in British moral thinking at this time—*empirical naturalist internalism* and *autonomist internalism.* What is important, of course, is that both were "internalisms"; that is, both were committed to the idea that obligation "can be realized only in motives available to a deliberating agent," on what Bishop Joseph Butler, the first thinker on whom we are going to focus in this chapter, called "inward feeling," "inward perception," and "inward conviction."[2] The next chapter in Paul's epistle had emphasized that inward turn, when he defined "a law unto themselves" as showing that the "work of the law" was "written in their hearts" (2:15).

It is not surprising, then, that when *resentment* arose as a topic of moral concern in the eighteenth century, it arose among a set of thinkers who were oriented to imagine what ethics means to autonomous moral agents, with interior spaces and resources to deliberate on when it was appropriate to be obligated and when to be vindictive. And both those values (obligation, vindictiveness) were based on market models. One was obliged to do something because of an implicit contract condition; one was vindictive in response to harm because retribution required a return of like for like. It is worth noting that *resentment*, like *retribution*, was a term that came to mean a particularly negative kind of moral response only. Both terms had earlier been more open.

---

1. C. B. MacPherson, *The Political Theory of Possessive Individualism, Hobbes to Locke* (Oxford: Clarendon Press, 1962); Stephen Darwall, *The British Moralists and the Internal "Ought" 1640–1740* (New York: Cambridge University Press, 1995).

2. Darwall, *The British Moralists and the Internal "Ought"*, pp. 7–8, 11, 259 (for Butler quotations).

Retribution was a term that first meant any kind of exchange (positive or negative) before it came to be understood as returning only evil for evil (and not good for good, as it had originally also implied), and *resentment* came to be understood as taking umbrage at an injury (and not simply to "take well or ill," as Johnson put it in his 1755 *Dictionary*). "To take ill," Johnson wrote, "is now the most usual sense."[3] I wish to examine here a key moment in British thinking when resentment as a negative emotion (its "most usual sense," as Johnson noted) was reclaimed and made part of the apparatus to explain the meaning of obligations, duties, and justice.

The sense of "justice" that is operative here is sentimentalist, as we might expect from a set of thinkers who base it on an *emotion* (resentment). Although he does not go as far as the others whose work we will survey here, David Hume's argument that "the sense of justice is not founded on reason" is precisely representative of them. His is a rejection of the kind of rational models of justice that had been proposed by Samuel Clarke and would flourish later in the eighteenth century with Kant, most notably.[4] And, again, whereas Hume does not talk about resentment as the source of our sense of fairness, he does very much rely on the idea of *benevolence* on which that model of resentment as justice relies. Benevolence in this political discourse is not simply a sense of charitableness for others; it is a process by which we can deeply encounter and fully share in our fellow human beings' feelings. "The sentiments of others can never affect us," writes Hume, "but by becoming, in some measure, our own." That process by which we can understand and make our own what others feel "can proceed from nothing but sympathy," he concludes.[5] Here, then, is the complex of ideas we will trace in the British

---

3. Samuel Johnson, *A Dictionary of the English Language: In Which the Words Are Deduced from Their Originals* (2nd ed., 2 vols.; London: W. Stahan, 1755/56). For a fuller discussion of this shift in meaning, see Lina Minou, "To Take Ill: Resentment in Eighteenth-Century Context," in *On Resentment: Past and Present*, edited by Bernardino Fantini, Dolores Martín Moruno, and Javier Moscoso (Newcastle upon Tyne, UK: Cambridge Scholars Publishing, 2013), pp. 73–90. On the narrowing of meaning of *retribution*, see Marvin Henberg, *Retribution: Evil for Evil in Ethics, Law, and Literature* (Philadelphia: Temple University Press, 1990), pp. 18–21.

4. David Hume, *A Treatise of Human Nature*, edited by David Fate Norton and Mary J. Norton (Oxford: Clarendon Press, 2007), Volume 1, pp. 429–30, cites Samuel Clarke as the one who holds that the "Propositions of Morality" could be "the Objects *merely* of Reason." See also Hume, *A Treatise of Human Nature*, Volume 2, pp. 884–85; J. B. Schneewind, *The Invention of Autonomy: A History of Modern Moral Philosophy* (New York: Cambridge University Press, 1998), pp. 317–19; and Darwall, *The British Moralists and the Internal "Ought"*, p. 328.

5. Hume, *A Treatise of Human Nature*, Volume 1, pp. 318, 378. Although I focus on how Smith drew on Hume's conception of sympathy to formulate his theory of the moral sentiments, there are important differences. For a particularly illuminating discussion of those differences,

moralists we will examine, Joseph Butler and Adam Smith, who both write about the power, danger, and possibilities of resentment as a moral sentiment that was deeply related to forgiveness.

I

In his study of the prehistory of modern forgiveness, David Konstan argues that the concept of interpersonal forgiveness simply did not exist in classical Greece or Rome, did not have its origins in Judaism or Christianity (which focused on the very different concept of divine forgiveness), and appeared sporadically and remained "marginal to philosophical and theological writings" until the nineteenth and twentieth centuries. Even where we might expect to find some systematic consideration of the idea—in the great ethical thinkers of the seventeenth and eighteenth centuries from Hobbes to Rousseau—there appears to be "little attention" paid to it. The one exception, it seems, is Joseph Butler, who entered the Church of England in 1714 and rose to become the bishop of Durham in 1750, two years before he died at the age of sixty. Butler's "contribution to forgiveness," Konstan writes, "would seem to be comparable to what Socrates did for early philosophy: as Cicero put it, he brought it down from the heavens—that is, from the cosmological concerns of the so-called pre-Socratic thinkers, introduced it into cities and homes, and obliged it to inquire about human behavior and the nature of good and evil." Even so, as Konstan concludes, Butler, in the end, concentrated less "on the nature of forgiveness and far more on that of resentment and revenge, both of which he justifies as appropriate when not taken to excess."[6] And that is largely how Butler has assumed his place in our own time, as preeminently the apologist of resentment. Indeed, until he discovered Jean Améry's writings on resentment as the proper response to the experience of Auschwitz, the contemporary philosopher who has made the most supple use of resentment as a prelude to justice, Jeffrie Murphy, thought that Butler's 1726 sermon "Upon Resentment" (supplemented with Peter Strawson's 1962

---

see Darwall, *The Second-Person Standpoint: Morality, Respect and Accountability* (Cambridge, MA: Harvard University Press, 2006), pp. 178–80; and Darwall, "Morality's Distinctiveness," in *Morality, Authority, & Law: Essays in Second-Personal Ethics I* (New York: Oxford University Press, 2013), pp. 3–19, esp. pp. 18–19, on the specific point of how they differ in their conception of resentment as a source for justice.

6. David Konstan, *Before Forgiveness: The Origins of a Moral Idea* (Cambridge: Cambridge University Press, 2010), pp. 152, 154–55, 152–53.

essay "Freedom and Resentment") had "made a case for the nature and value of resentment that could not be improved on."[7]

Bishop Butler would undoubtedly have been surprised had he known that his posthumous fame at the beginning of the twenty-first century would rest on his sermons on forgiveness and resentment, indeed on his sermons at all, as opposed to his magnum opus, *The Analogy of Religion Natural and Revealed*. On the second centenary of *The Analogy*, in 1936, *The Times Literary Supplement* published an appreciation in which the author noted that while Butler published "some sermons which would have sufficed to ensure his philosophical reputation," it was clear that "his fame is most surely grounded on the 'Analogy.'" And that was certainly the case for his admirers and his critics during the eighteenth and nineteenth centuries. It is also worth noting that the topics of resentment and forgiveness barely merit any mention in *The Analogy*. Except for one brief interlude in that tract when he touches on the idea of remorse, resentment, or shame as moral sentiments that arise in humans when they reflect on themselves as having done someone an injury for which they are blameworthy, he steers wide of these topics for which he is now recognized as an early exponent.[8] These facts are important only insofar as we recognize that Butler's sermons on forgiveness and resentment have a place in his larger philosophical system, not that they are tangential, by any means, but that they are part of a greater vision of the place of emotional life in what he presented as a rational world.

We can begin our analysis of Butler by turning first to the topic that, as Konstans and others have noted, clearly has less resonance for him, that is, forgiveness, which he defines primarily as the overcoming of resentment. The "precepts to *forgive*, and to *love our enemies*," he writes, "do not relate to that general indignation against injury and the authors of it, but to this feeling, or resentment when raised by private or personal injury." In other words, to forgive is to forgo resentment. (We will later discuss Butler's distinction between *resentment*, which is felt in response to personal injuries to self, and *indignation*, which is felt at public injuries to others). And the reason to forgive, for Butler, is that holding too firmly to resentment may have deleterious effects. His vision of forgiveness is not the robust version we will find in late twentieth-century

7. Jeffrie G. Murphy, "Foreword," in Thomas Brudholm, *Resentment's Virtue: Jean Améry and the Refusal to Forgive* (Philadelphia: Temple University Press, 2008), p. xii.

8. "'The Analogy of Religion' 1736–1936: Joseph Butler's Achievement," *Times Literary Supplement* 1784 (April 11, 1936): 305–306; Joseph Butler, *The Analogy of Religion Natural and Revealed to the Constitution and Course of Nature*, in *The Works of Joseph Butler, D.C.L. Sometime Lord Bishop of Durham*, edited by W. E. Gladstone (Oxford: Clarendon Press, 1896), Volume 1, pp. 72–73.

psychologists and philosophers, who argue that genuine forgiveness requires a complete eradication of the ill-will felt by the injured party. Butler offers a more tepid forgiveness that certainly has a place in it for lingering resentment. He writes that we may simultaneously "love our enemy, and yet have resentment against him for his injurious behavior towards us." It is only when resentment starts to fester, when it turns "excessive, and becomes malice or revenge," that we need to purge it from our emotional and mental life, and it is forgiveness precisely that prevents resentment from turning bad in this way.[9]

Even in his sermon on forgiveness, then, Butler affirms the value of resentment as a healthy and appropriate response to injury and harm. He had developed these ideas much more fully in his earlier sermon on resentment. He divides resentment into two kinds: "*hasty and sudden*, or *settled and deliberate*." Sudden resentment, or anger, is useful, he writes, primarily in cases of "self-defence," that is, to prevent harm or injury in situations where being "passive is certain destruction" and in which "sudden resistance is the only security." The reason resentment plays a role in such situations is that Butler believes that the "only way in which our reason and understanding can raise anger, is by representing to our mind injustice or injury of some kind or other," which is precisely what animates our sense of resentment.[10]

Butler spends considerably more time discussing the second kind, what he calls "deliberate anger or resentment," which he maintains "seems *in us* plainly connected with a sense of virtue and vice, of moral good and evil." Since "settled resentment" is a *natural* response to injury—not just pain or loss—Butler sees it as a positive boon, something that can be "innocently employed" to "prevent and to remedy such injury, and the miseries arising from it." Here he follows the major argument of *The Analogy*—which, as the title indicates, is meant to find the analogies between natural phenomena and revealed religion—and sees that resentment is effectively "a weapon, put into our hands by nature, against injury, injustice, and cruelty." Like other natural phenomena, or those in revealed religion, it is of course subject to abuse. He details five potential dangers:

> With respect to deliberate resentment, the chief instances of abuse are: when from partiality to ourselves, we imagine an injury done us,

---

9. Butler, *Fifteen Sermons*, in *The Works of Joseph Butler*, Volume 2, pp. 151, 158. All these quotations are taken from the ninth sermon, "Upon Forgiveness of Injuries."

10. Butler, *Fifteen Sermons*, Volume 2, pp. 138, 140, 139. All these quotations are taken from the eighth sermon, "Upon Resentment."

when there is none: when this partiality represents it to us greater than it really is: when we fall into that extravagant and monstrous kind of resentment, towards one who has innocently been the occasion of evil to us; that is, resentment upon account of pain or inconvenience, without injury; which is the same absurdity, as settled anger at a thing that is inanimate: when the indignation against injury and injustice rises too high, and is beyond proportion to the particular ill action it is exercised upon: or, lastly, when pain or harm of any kind is inflicted merely in consequence of, and to gratify, that resentment, though naturally raised.

Resentment, then, becomes pathological, we would say, when someone feels it without reasonable cause or indulges in it beyond reasonable measure. But, in itself, resentment is something that is "implanted in our nature by God" as being "not only innocent, but a generous movement of mind."[11]

It becomes particularly generous when it assumes the form of *indignation*, a more altruistic kind of resentment. Butler insists that the "indignation raised by cruelty and injustice, and the desire of having it punished, which persons unconcerned would feel, is by no means malice. No, it is resentment against vice and wickedness: it is one of the common bonds, by which society is held together; a fellow-feeling, which each individual has in behalf of the whole species, as well as of himself."[12] Indignation, then, that is, resentment against injuries to others, is a socializing sentiment, one that wishes to eradicate injustice at the same time as it inspires a desire for unity ("fellow-feeling"). And here, I think, we can begin to see how the ideas of resentment and forgiveness play a role in Butler's grander vision, which is based on the principles of social life, which in turn is based on the idea of benevolence.

He begins his sermon on resentment by boldly affirming that "general benevolence is the great law of the whole moral creation," and concludes his sermon on forgiveness by noting that it is only "when this resentment entirely destroys our natural benevolence towards" another that we need to forgive in order to avoid falling into one of the abuses of resentment. In another sermon, "Upon Human Nature," he held that benevolence was in fact the natural order of things, which resentment and other forms of envy endangered. There is no such thing as "ill-will in one man towards another, emulation and

---

11. Butler, *Fifteen Sermons*, Volume 2, pp. 140, 141, 143, 145–46, 149.

12. Butler, *Fifteen Sermons*, Volume 2, p. 141.

resentment being away; whereas there is plainly benevolence or good-will."[13] Benevolence, then, the sense of good will towards others, is at the heart of his sense of community, and community—his sense of a social life of people engaged together in more than economic exchanges—is at the heart of his belief of what both natural and revealed religions hold as the good life.

To get a better sense of what role resentment and forgiving play in Butler's vision of social and religious life, we can turn to another sermon on a somewhat different topic. In a sermon preached at the Parish Church of St. Lawrence-Jewry on March 31, 1748, before the founders of the London Infirmary, Butler chose as his text 1 Peter 4:8: "And above all things have fervent charity among yourselves: for charity shall cover the multitude of sins." It was an apt text for a charitable group celebrating its charitable institution, the Infirmary that would later become the Royal London Hospital, and his listeners might well have expected to be applauded for their initiative and their kindness in providing medical aid to manufacturers and merchant seamen. If so, these distinguished listeners, who included Charles Lennox, the Second Duke of Richmond, and the president and governors of the London Infirmary, might well have been disconcerted by the end of the sermon. Butler concludes by distinguishing three strategies available for those aware of their sense of sin—and "charity," in the form that the governors of the Infirmary understood it, as the generous giving of wealth to assist the needy, turns out to be a very distant third.

One way for someone to "cover a multitude of sins," Butler begins his peroration, is through benefaction, donating to public charities. It is through such charitable giving that one may "make amends to society." I suspect his listeners, wealthy men, benefactors, and nobles who employed "their riches in promoting so excellent a design" as the Infirmary, expected it to be higher on the list, or perhaps not on the list at all since they might have felt that their charity was not simply an attempt to "cover a multitude of sins."

The better thing to do, Butler continues, is not to offer general charity to a general population, but specifically to "make amends, in some way or other, to a particular person, against whom we have offended, either by positive injury, or by neglect." Such an act, he says, "is an express condition of our obtaining forgiveness of God, when it is in our power to make it." General charity by the wealthy is what will suffice "when it is not" in "our power to make it," but specific acts of making amends to specific individuals are preferable.

---

13. Butler, *Fifteen Sermons*, Volume 2, pp. 136, 158, 46.

The very best thing, however, is not to make amends but to provide redress, and here Butler offers a capacious definition of what constitutes offense. He includes not only those things that we did to hurt people, but also all those things we did *not* do to help them. Injury can be a positive act, but it is more frequently something caused by our inaction; and it is on this point that Butler dwells. When we "remember, in how many instances we have all left undone those things which we ought to have done," we will have a sense of our deficiency, and we should, ideally, "earnestly desire to supply the good" which we have not supplied, and also to "undo the evil" that we have "neglected to prevent." Our responsibility, then, is both for the commission of our sins and the omission of our benevolence. It is only when we are unable to provide redress, or that it is "impracticable" for us to do so, that amends to individuals becomes a second-best possibility, and only when that in turn is impracticable that general charity becomes a third-best option.[14]

Here, then, we see the hallmark of Butler's theology, evident throughout *The Analogy of Religion Natural and Revealed*, and throughout those sermons focusing on human benevolence.[15] He provides a hierarchy of actions, from acceptable to preferable, and focuses on the ways that human inclinations direct those actions.

It is noteworthy that Butler focuses as much on social and public acts as he does on personal and private faith and devotion. At times, he offers quite traditional Christian homiletics—"the perfection of goodness consists in love to the whole universe," he states in his sermon "Upon the Love of Our Neighbour"—but, even then, he sees love as a social sentiment, and speaks on the same theme of what he calls *benevolence and the pursuit of public good.* His is a humane Protestantism that attends to personal relations among people as indicative of a given person's relationship with God. There is even a hint of a kind of secular pragmatism that we will find fully developed in William James and other American pragmatists at the end

14. Butler, *Six Sermons Preached Upon Public Occasions*, in *The Works of Joseph Butler*, Volume 2, pp. 394, 395.

15. It is important to remember that while he focuses on benevolence, Butler does also reject Hutcheson's argument that virtue can be reduced to benevolence. I am grateful to Stephen Darwall for this point. See Darwall, *The British Moralists and the Internal "Ought"*, esp. pp. 280–83. For a fine reading of the role and limits of benevolence in Butler, see Schneewind, *The Invention of Autonomy*, pp. 342–53. For Smith's somewhat circumscribed sense of benevolence, see Charles L. Griswold, *Adam Smith and the Virtues of Enlightenment* (New York: Cambridge University Press, 1999), pp. 208–209.

of the nineteenth century—that acting "as if" one possessed certain sentiments will work to put one in actual possession of them. "Human nature is
so constituted," Butler sermonizes, "that every good affection implies the
love of itself; i.e. becomes the object of a new affection in the same person.
Thus, to be righteous, implies in it the love or righteousness; to be benevolent, the love of benevolence," and so on. In that sense, then, acting in a
righteous and benevolent way produces what can be described as moral
momentum; one who does something benevolent will find herself or himself impelled onward to do more and, in the end, will develop a sentiment
for the love of "the whole universe" that expresses perfect goodness. The
"sum of morals," Butler sunnily concludes, is that "mankind is a community, that we all stand in a relation to each other, that there is a public end
and interest of society which each particular is obliged to promote."[16]

Here, then, are the grand ideas that animate Butler's Christianity—it is
social, pragmatic, and benevolent. It is within that particular framework, I believe, that we can best understand what he says about the role that resentment
plays in fostering social sensibilities and forgiveness in ensuring their health-
iest manifestation. Resentment is a "generous movement" of mind because it
permits us to comprehend our injuries and to appreciate ourselves as worthy
of better treatment by those who injured us. Indignation is an important
"fellow-feeling" that permits us to imagine the emotional and mental life of
someone other than ourselves, to feel the pain of another as if it were our own.
Forgiveness is an even more potent fellow-feeling that forces us to moderate
the possible excesses to which resentment is subject and to turn away from
revenge, the impulse that destroys social life. In his hierarchical system, forgiving is preferable to resentment; just as in cases of sinning and penitence,
reparation is preferable to apology, which in turn is preferable to benefaction;
just as, in his larger system, revealed religion is preferable to natural. But in
Butler's hierarchy of values, the secondary or tertiary value does not disap-
pear in relation to the primary; charity is not without value in relation to
redress, nor is resentment in relation to forgiveness. They are not devalued
but rather supplementary, not dismissed but seen as analogous to the virtues
they support.

Butler is hailed by many today as the first apostle of the value of resentment, and he might well be; but it is important to recognize that what he
advocates in praising a generous sense of resentment, an altruistic belief in

16. Butler, *Fifteen Sermons*, Volume 2, pp. 201, 210, 228, 155.

indignation at injustice, and a moderating leaven of forgiveness is part of a larger system whose coherence we would do well to appreciate. Let me be clear: appreciating Butler's worldview, and his distinctive form of Christianity that forms it, does not at all weaken the case of those contemporary philosophers who have employed his insights on resentment to make their telling and important case against the frivolity of certain practices of forgiving in personal and public life. It does, however, give us a sense of the broader and specific parameters within which he saw resentment assuming the distinctive forms it does and playing the particular and supplementary roles it plays. And it is only within those parameters—personal, social, communal, public—that we can see how and why Butler, as Konstans perceptively notes, inaugurated a transformation in the meaning and practices of forgiveness.

II

Adam Smith admired Butler—at points he echoed his writings, and he referred to him as "a late ingenious and subtile philosopher"—but he did not share the same depth of belief in or entirely ground his moral system in Christianity, as did Butler. Smith was more influenced by both the Stoics, whose values of holding both life and death in contempt and of uncomplainingly accepting whatever event happened he admired, and by his teacher Francis Hutcheson, whose argument that virtue consisted of benevolence Smith examined sympathetically but critically. In his great tractate of 1759, *The Theory of Moral Sentiments*, Smith developed some of the ideas about the moral sentiments that his teacher and predecessor in the chair of moral philosophy at the University of Glasgow had introduced in his two seminal books of the 1720s, *An Inquiry into the Original of Our Ideas of Beauty and Virtue* (1725) and *An Essay on the Nature and Conduct of the Passions and Affections, with Illustrations of the Moral Sense* (1728). Smith's most important and original contribution—and before he published *The Wealth of Nations* in 1776, his most famous—was the concept of the "impartial spectator." Akin to what George Herbert Mead in the first third of the twentieth century would propose about the development of a socialized self—that is, a sensibility developed in the psyche by virtue of its actual and imagined social interactions with what Mead called "the generalized other"—Smith's "impartial spectator" became a kind of secular conscience. He introduced the phrase "fair and impartial spectator" to describe the perspective each of us should assume when we "endeavour to examine our own conduct" in an unbiased way. He introduced the phrase and concept in Part I of *The Theory of Moral Sentiments* and kept adding explanatory clauses to it, until he concluded in Part VI, in the fullest form in which he expressed it, with the idea of the "impartial spectator, of the great inmate of the breast, the great judge and arbiter of conduct."[17]

For Smith, the impartial spectator, a product of a socialized sensibility, is necessary for the development and maintenance of the moral sentiments as he theorizes them. He is critical of what he identifies as the three major theories or systems of moral philosophy. He feels that they have misidentified the source of virtue and, likewise, that they have mischaracterized the principles that govern our sense of approbation or disapprobation for virtuous or evil actions. The first system defines the source of virtue in *propriety* (Plato, Aristotle, Zeno), the second finds it in *prudence* (Epicurus), and the third argues for its origin in *benevolence* (the Eclectics, Cambridge Platonists, and Hutcheson). One finds the principle of approbation in *self-love* (which we use to judge our own and others' actions), the second finds it in *reason*, and the third in *sentiment*. While in the end, he believes sentiment is the most appropriate source of approbation and disapprobation, he is critical of those who would identify any particular sentiment, instead of seeing the role ascribed to the capaciously constituted "impartial spectator."[18]

That critique of the alternative systems of moral philosophy occupies the seventh and final part of *The Theory of Moral Sentiments*. In the six earlier parts, Smith develops his own theory based especially on *sympathy*, which he defines in the widest sense as any kind of "fellow-feeling with any passion whatever" (as opposed to sympathy narrowly defined as fellow-feeling with the misery of others). He identifies, in particular five kinds of passions: those that originate in the body, those that originate in the imagination, and then three others designated as the "unsocial Passions," the "social Passions," and the "selfish Passions."[19]

---

17. Adam Smith, *The Theory of Moral Sentiments*, edited by D. D. Raphael and A. L. Macfie (Indianapolis: Liberty Classics, 1982), pp. 43, 110, 262. The editors trace the echoes of Butler in Smith on p. 164. Francis Hutcheson, *An Inquiry into the Original of Our Ideas of Beauty and Virtue*, edited by Wolfgang Leidhold (Indianapolis: Liberty Fund, 2008); Hutcheson, *An Essay on the Nature and Conduct of the Passions and Affections, with Illustrations of the Moral Sense*, edited by Aaron Garrett (Indianapolis: Liberty Fund, 2002). For a fuller discussion of the "impartial spectator," including the use of similar terms in Hume and Hutcheson, and the existential status of the "spectator," see Alexander Broadie, "Sympathy and the Impartial Spectator," in *The Cambridge Companion to Adam Smith*, edited by Knud Haakonssen (New York: Cambridge University Press, 2006), pp. 158–88, esp. pp. 180–84.

18. Smith, *The Theory of Moral Sentiments*, pp. 265–305, 314–27.

19. Smith, *The Theory of Moral Sentiments*, pp. 10, 27–43.

He discusses resentment most fully as an unsocial passion. In that form, following the example set before him by Butler, Smith sees resentment as expressing both what is admirable (self-esteem) and what is vicious (a capacity for vengeance). Nobody admires someone who is servile in response to injury since it indicates a failure of self-respect. "Even the mob," he writes, "are enraged to see any man submit patiently to affronts and ill usage. They desire to see this insolence resented, and resented by the person who suffers from it." And, yet, because resentment is in the end an "unsocial" passion, it endangers society because it so easily follows its momentum to vengeance. It affects the person who feels it, but it also expands outward. Part of the reason that resentment constitutes a "disagreeable passion" is that it affects our relations not only with the people who cause it (those who hurt us) but also with our friends who do not hurt us but whose indifference to our resentment we find extremely provoking. It then expands outward to, and endangers, the society as a whole. "Too violent a propensity to those detestable passions," writes Smith, "renders a person the object of universal dread and abhorrence, who, like a wild beast, ought, we think, to be hunted out of all civil society."[20] What begins as an expression of self-respect can end as a wicked failure to respect the rights of the society.

Even more than Butler, considerably more, Smith makes it a point to note the dangers, rather than the benefits, of resentment. "Nature," he insists, "teaches us to be more averse to enter into this passion, and till informed of its cause, to be disposed rather to take part against it." He repeatedly makes the case that resentment requires very particular guards to keep it from expressing itself in vengeance. It is only then, only under very specific conditions, when "resentment is guarded and qualified," that it may "be admitted to be even generous and noble." What guards and qualifies it are a series of preemptive sentiments ranging from being "free from petulance and low scurrility," to being "generous, candid, and full of all proper regards, even for the person who has offended us." It is, in other words, quite a task to be resentful when one has purged oneself of unsocial passions (petulance and scurrility) and immersed oneself in social ones (generosity and candor). He recognizes that most people do not possess these kinds of tempering resources: "experience teaches us how much the greater part of mankind are incapable of this moderation, and how great an effort must be made in

---

20. Smith, *The Theory of Moral Sentiments*, pp. 35, 15, 40.

order to bring down the rude and undisciplined impulse of resentment to this suitable temper."[21]

Because of that difficulty, he concludes that we require in particular the exercise of a heightened sense of propriety to offset resentment. Smith suggests two strategies. In the first, Smith sounds a little like Lord Chesterfield, whose letters to his son regularly advised him of the value of appearances over substance. Smith suggests that we "should resent more from a sense of the propriety of resentment, from a sense that mankind expect and require it of us, than because we feel in ourselves the furies of that disagreeable passion." Resentment, then, should be a strategic presentation rather than an honestly felt sentiment. Of course, to fake resentment, one must first be capable of not succumbing to it. That is the point of the second strategy that Smith urges as the basis of his theory of moral sentiments, and that is the impartial spectator. Because resentment contains the dangers it does, because there is "no passion, of which the human mind is capable, concerning whose justness we ought to be so doubtful," we must control it by carefully consulting "our natural sense of propriety" and by most diligently considering "what will be the sentiments of the cool and impartial spectator."[22]

As we can see, Smith is much more circumspect than Butler in his regard for the potential benefits of resentment, and much more attentive to its dangers. When he does discuss resentment as the source of our sense of justice, he follows Butler in identifying *indignation* as the form of resentment for injuries to others, and as the more "noble and generous" form of resentment. This distinction has been regularly drawn in the modern discussions of resentment. Strawson, for example, writes: "one who experiences the vicarious analogue of resentment is said to be indignant or disapproving, or morally indignant or disapproving. What we have here is, as it were, resentment on behalf of another, where one's own interest and dignity are not involved; and it is this impersonal or vicarious character of this attitude, added to its others,

---

21. Smith, *The Theory of Moral Sentiments*, pp. 11, 38, 77. Writing the year before the publication of *The Theory of Moral Sentiments*, Richard Price likewise saw that the way to keep resentment from degenerating into "*malice* and *cruelty*" was for the individual to resist what Price calls the "instinctive principles" and instead be "guided by reason and virtue." See Richard Price, *A Review of the Principal Questions in Morals*, edited by D. D. Raphael (1948; Oxford: Clarendon Press, 1974), pp. 228–29. Price's book was first published in 1758.

22. Smith, *The Theory of Moral Sentiments*, p. 38. Cf. 172: "Nothing is more graceful than the behaviour of the man who appears to resent the greatest injuries, more from a sense that they deserve, and are the proper objects of resentment, than from feeling himself the furies of that disagreeable passion."

which entitle it to the qualification 'moral.'" John Rawls, too, follows suit, noting that "resentment and indignation have their characteristic resolutions, since the first is aroused by what we regard as wrongs done to ourselves, the second is concerned with wrongs done to others." And Jean Hampton likewise calls the "impersonal form" of resentment "indignation" and reserves "'resentment' for the personally defensive protest."[23]

That distinction is perhaps overdrawn—and, in other writers, has led to some unfortunate dogmatism about precisely what forgiveness can mean and who has standing to forgive. If forgiveness is exclusively the forswearing of resentment, then those who are indignant cannot forgive. That makes intuitive sense, since we largely believe that only those can forgive who are the direct victims of injury, but there are cases where this intuitive sense is limiting and debatable. I will not enter into them here, but suffice it to say that there are debates about whether a survivor can forgive the harm done to a child or parent or relative or friend; and these debates are sometimes foreclosed by the insistence on defining forgiveness as the forswearing only of resentment (and of limiting resentment to the feeling only of those who are injured, and not witnesses to the injury, i.e., the indignant). Smith, who is credited with making that distinction, does not seem to endorse that argument at all. Indeed, at one point, he refers to "the resentment of the sufferer" and the "sympathetic indignation of the spectator." But in cases of murder, he continues, we find the "highest degree of resentment in those who are immediately connected with the slain." In other words, those who are not the primary victims of the crime can feel resentment, and therefore they can forgive a crime committed against their loved ones, if we believe that forgiveness can be the forgoing only of resentment.[24]

---

23. Smith, *The Theory of Moral Sentiments*, p. 24; P. F. Strawson, "Freedom and Resentment," in *Freedom and Resentment and Other Essays* (London: Methuen, 1974), p. 14; John Rawls, *A Theory of Justice* (Cambridge, MA: Belknap Press, 1971), p. 484; Jean Hampton, in Jeffrie G. Murphy and Hampton, *Forgiveness and Mercy* (New York: Oxford University Press, 1988), p. 56.

24. Smith, *The Theory of Moral Sentiments*, pp. 83–84. Strawson is not among those who hold the distinction to be fixed. He holds that "one can feel indignation on one's own account" ("Freedom and Resentment," p. 15).

The question of standing—of who has the "right" to forgive—is a vexed one. Almost all scholars of forgiveness suggest, as Dryden puts it, "Forgiveness to the injured does belong." This passage and the idea it perfectly encapsulates raise questions about forgiveness as a property, of what injury means, and to whether it is singular or extended (primary, secondary, and tertiary injuries). Elsewhere, I challenge the idea and suggest that there are cases where *proxies* can forgive. John Dryden, *The Second Part of the Conquest of Granada*, in *The Works of John Dryden*, edited by John Loftis, David Stuart Rodes, and Vinton A. Dearing (Berkeley: University of

In any case, the philosophers who first gave substance to these terms were not so strict in their usage. Hume regularly wrote of what these philosophers call "indignation" by using the other term, as when he noted that we often feel "a strong resentment of injury done to men" or a "resentment of their misery." Smith is quite inconsistent in his terminology. He sometimes describes those who feel others' harm as feeling resentment, not indignation, and sometimes writes of those who feel indignation for their own harms. He refers, for instance, to "our resentment for what the other has suffered," and the sufferer's "indignation against his enemy." Usually, though, he makes the distinction, and places indignation firmly in the "impartial spectator," as when he refers to the "resentment of the sufferer" and the "sympathetic indignation of the spectator." Even when he conflates the terms, he does wish to place either resentment or indignation in the impartial spectator. As he writes, we "admire that noble and generous resentment which governs its pursuit of the greatest injuries, not by the rage which they are apt to excite in the breast of the sufferer, but by the indignation which they naturally call forth in that of the impartial spectator." The impartial spectator, then, becomes the genuine repository of the only form of the unsocial passion that Smith finds fully acceptable.[25]

The impartial spectator, then, is what controls resentment, directs it into proper channels, and urges its best expression as a "fellow-feeling" of indignation. The focus on the impartial spectator is also finally what distinguishes Smith's treatment of resentment from Butler's, especially in the ways resentment can be controlled and resolved. As we have seen, Butler offers forgiveness as the preeminent strategy for containing the potentially ill effects of resentment, and for bringing resentment to closure for the person suffering it. Smith disagrees. He does comment, briefly and in two isolated places, on how the resentful person demands penitence, which of course is a prelude to forgiveness. Resentment requires that the "offender may be made to repent of

---

California Press, 1978), Volume 11, Act II, Scene 1. For a discussion of that concept as analogous to the role of standing in tort law, see Darwall, "Pufendorf on Morality, Sociability, and Moral Powers," in *Honor, History, and Relationships: Essays in Second-Personal Ethics II* (New York: Oxford University Press, 2013), pp. 189–221, esp. p. 208; and Darwall and Julian Darwall, "Civil Recourse as Mutual Accountability," *Florida State University Law Review* 39.17 (Fall 2011): 17–41, esp. pp. 25–26.

25. David Hume, *Enquiries Concerning Human Understanding and Concerning the Principles of Morals*, edited by L.A. Selby-Bigge, revised by P. H. Nidditch (Oxford: Clarendon Press, 1975), pp. 225, 286; Smith, *The Theory of Moral Sentiments*, pp. 24, 34, 35, 83–84. For his other inconsistent usages, see Smith, *The Theory of Moral Sentiments*, pp. 71, 77, 83–84, 90. Darwall, *The Second-Person Standpoint*, pp. 72–73, is truer to Smith's and Butler's sense in his insistence that forgiveness is "to forbear or withdraw. . . . resentment, indignation, and their kin."

his injustice," he writes at one point, and, in a passage a few chapters earlier, he writes: "Resentment cannot be fully gratified, unless the offender is not only made to grieve in his turn, but to grieve for that particular wrong which we have suffered from him. He must be made to repent and be sorry for this very action, that others, through fear of the like punishment, may be terrified from being guilty of the like offence." Otherwise, though, Smith ignores penitence, forgiveness, and the range of sentiments having to do with atonement. Smith, of course, was deeply influenced by Hume, who derided what he called these "monkish virtues" (including "penance" among a list of other Christian practices).[26]

III

We can end by discerning three major points about the trajectory of thinking about resentment in the British moralists of the eighteenth century.

First, we see in the shift from Butler to Smith a distinct process of secularization. Butler's point is ultimately to justify the ways of God to man, to borrow a phrase, and Smith's is not. We need to qualify this distinction, though. Whereas Butler had seen resentment as a "natural" phenomenon, it was nonetheless part of what he would have argued to be an aspect of "religion, natural or revealed." It is true that Butler is not dogmatic on the point. Even though he wrote what C. D. Broad called "perhaps the ablest and fairest argument for theism that exists," and possessed what Broad characterized as the "sweet reasonableness of an English bishop of the eighteenth century," Butler was in the end more sweetly reasonable than sternly doctrinal in his writings. When he counsels against revenge, for instance, he does not cite scripture ("Vengeance is mine") but instead turns to look at "the nature and reason of the thing itself" in order to show how revenge produces a dynamic that is injurious to self, other, and society. He, like Francis Hutcheson, whom he influenced, can refer to "the providence and wisdom of our Creator" while still believing that we "don't deduce our first notions of duty from the divine Will; but from the constitution of our nature, which is more immediately known." Likewise, Smith draws on the language of religion in key ways, and with a discernible strategy. He refers, for instance, to how "the happiness of every innocent man" is "rendered holy, consecrated, and hedged round against the approach

---

26. Smith, *The Theory of Moral Sentiments*, pp. 79, 69; cf. pp. 338–39; Hume, *Enquiries Concerning Human Understanding*, p. 270.

of every other man," and that any violation of this innocence requires "some expiation, some atonement." Even though Smith refers to the "wisdom of Nature" as the source of these rights, and is drawing on an ancient Roman religion to exemplify them, he is nonetheless clearly using a Christian discourse, both to secularize it but also, I think, because it would have been the one most familiar to his readers. In other words, we should understand that secularization (*in its effects*) might better be seen as a matter of degree, not kind—a modification and change in focus, not a Copernican revolution.[27]

Indeed, we should note the significance of the simple fact that Butler does focus on resentment, a moral sentiment that distinctly sits at odds with other Christian ones. And consider just how he situates his argument about this secular emotion within the religious framework he seems intent on challenging as much as he is supporting it. He begins his sermon on resentment with a text from the Gospel of Matthew, in which Jesus says: "Love your enemies, bless them that curse you, do good to them that hate you, and pray for them which despitefully use you, and persecute you" (Matthew 5:43–44). He then introduces his sermon by asking why God, representing perfect goodness and universal benevolence, should have implanted in humanity a principle "*which appears the direct contrary to benevolence*." The way to proceed in examining and attempting to answer this question, he declares, is "to take human nature as it is, and the circumstances in which it is placed as they are; and then consider the correspondence between that nature and those circumstances, or what course of action and behaviour, respecting those circumstances, any particular affection or passion leads us to." Butler's method is more psychology and social science than theology. Theology is certainly there (he wants to understand resentment as "*placed in our nature by its Author*"), but the major impetus is to examine the phenomenon, its potential uses and applications, its potential abuses and dangers, and then to appreciate "*for what ends it was placed there*." We should not miss the important point—Butler is dwelling

27. C. D. Broad, *Five Types of Ethical Theory* (London: Routledge & Kegan Paul, 1930), pp. 5, 53; Butler, *Fifteen Sermons*, Volume 2, pp. 152–53; Francis Hutcheson, *Philosophiae Moralis Institutio Compendaria, with a Short Introduction to Moral Philosophy*, edited by Luigi Turco (Indianapolis: Liberty Fund, 2007), p. 24; Smith, *The Theory of Moral Sentiments*, p. 107. For an account of what sorts of religious shifts occurred in the eighteenth century, see Schneewind, "The Divine Corporation and the History of Ethics," in *Essays on the History of Moral Philosophy* (New York: Oxford University Press, 2010), pp. 149–69; Schneewind, *The Invention of Autonomy*, pp. 378–79, 388–95, provides an illuminating discussion of Smith's religious beliefs. For an account that sees Smith as being more committed to "Christian virtues," see Ryan Patrick Hanley, *Adam Smith and the Character of Virtue* (New York: Cambridge University Press, 2009), pp. 175–208.

on an emotion that is distinctly contrary to the text on which his sermon is based and challenges the idea of universal benevolence on which his theology is founded.[28] When we turn to the Continental tradition, we will discover a similar debate at the turn from the nineteenth to the twentieth centuries, and discern an uneasy vacillation between a more secular and a more Christian stand on the nature and meaning of resentment.

Second, where perhaps that shift from a religious to a secular focus is most evident in the thinking of British moralists—and matters most—is in the question of forgiveness and its relationship to resentment. For Butler, forgiveness was ultimately a religious principle, and his defense of it as an antidote to resentment came down to a statement of Christian doctrine. He concludes his sermon on forgiveness by noting that a "forgiving spirit is therefore absolutely necessary, as ever we hope for peace of mind in our dying moments, or for the divine mercy at that day when we shall most stand in need of it." His declaration of why forgiveness is necessary, and what ends it serves, unlike his study of the necessity and ends of resentment, is fundamentally based on Christian principles. His ideal of forgiveness, it should be noted, is distinctly in the mode of Jesus, not Paul, and he quotes only the Lord's Prayer and Jesus' gloss on it as his scriptural support for why we ought to forgive injuries.[29] But forgiveness of others is distinctly premised on the Christian belief that it is a prelude and requisite for one's own forgiveness, and the shift is from *earthly* forgiveness of others' injuries to *heavenly* forgiveness of one's own sins.

Smith did not accept these terms, and based his model of how to resolve resentment into something more productive on quite other practices. As we saw, Smith proposed two particular strategies. First, he resorted to what might seem to us as a deceptive practice (but that is largely because we now value other kinds of authenticity than did he or his age). Smith believed that one should appear resentful even when one did not feel particularly resentful because the show of it was socially salutary. And the second was to contain whatever resentment one felt within a strict and constrained limit by considering and following the dictates of the impartial spectator. In these two practices, Smith was following his favored classical philosophical school of the Stoics. The Stoics had maintained, as Smith's friend Hume had argued, that it is sometimes valuable to "counterfeit a Sympathy" in order to give solace to a friend in pain, because it was better to fake such passion than to feel it too

28. Butler, *Fifteen Sermons*, Volume 2, pp. 136–38.

29. Butler, *Fifteen Sermons*, Volume 2, p. 167.

powerfully. Hume was more critical of this idea than was Smith, who saw in it a way to avoid succumbing to the seduction and momentum of felt resentment.[30] The second strategy—the way one can become a Stoic sage—is by constantly consulting the cool impartial spectator whose values are formed not from our own sense of grievances as felt by us, but precisely by the sense of how objective others might perceive them.

Here, it is worth reflecting on what the eighteenth-century sentimentalists as a whole found most objectionable, and that is precisely the theories of Hobbes and Mandeville that self-love is the sole, irreducible motive determining our personal and social activities. Butler, Hume, Smith, Hutcheson, Shaftesbury all took issue with this theory and developed their theories of sympathy and moral sentiments in response. That is why Butler emphasized benevolence (a feeling directed outward and without desiring the kind of interested self-love of Hobbes) and why Smith developed the idea of the impartial spectator who is constituted of the sentiments of others, *not self*. Butler writes that "resentment cannot supersede the obligation to universal benevolence" because resentment is a selfish emotion that leads one to a partiality to oneself (it is, in other words, a manifestation of self-love). It has to be tempered with a sentiment that is wholly outer-directed, and that, for Butler, is forgiveness.[31] For Smith, too, resentment was a manifestation of self-love and therefore had to be guarded against by applying to it an objective view of the injury *as seen from beyond the self*. Hutcheson, too, like Butler, thought that resentment was a danger—when and because it produced what Butler called a "partiality to ourselves." The way to temper what Hutcheson calls the "uneasy affection" of resentment is by seeing it with the eyes of benevolence. From that social and not selfish perspective, what Hutcheson calls one's "deliberate resentment" comes to aim at the "common interest." Although they differ in whether the best moral sentiment to respond to resentment is a Christian forgiveness, a more secular benevolence, or a wholly secular impartial spectator, Butler, Smith, and Hutcheson are motivated to contest the kind of selfishness to which resentment is prone because they, like Hume, believe that "we must

30. Hume, "Of Moral Prejudices," in *Essays Moral, Political, and Literary*, edited by Eugene F. Miller (revised ed.; Indianapolis: Liberty Fund, 1987), pp. 538–44, esp. p. 540; Michael L. Frazer, *The Enlightenment of Sympathy: Justice and Moral Sentiments in the Eighteenth Century and Today* (New York: Oxford University Press, 2010), p. 103, makes the insightful argument that, for Smith, resentment works in two stages: first, by making the offender recognize the impropriety of the injury he inflicted, and, second, by making this "recognition" itself "a kind of reconciliation that brings both offender and offended into a state of sympathetic harmony."

31. Butler, "The Preface," in *The Works of Joseph Butler*, Volume 2, pp. 1–29, esp. p. 20.

renounce the theory, which accounts for every moral sentiment by the principle of self-love."[32]

The third and final point is the shift from understanding resentment as primarily an individual emotion to seeing it as a more social property. Although the British moralists largely see resentment as something that one individual feels—and therefore wish to guard against an indulgence in it that makes one lose focus on the larger social world—it is also clear that they see an intimate relationship between what is individual and what social. Both Butler and Smith follow the example of Shaftesbury in believing that the personal emotion of resentment or anger is indicative of a desire for social emotions, as what Shaftesbury refers to as "*Love of* Justice." It is worth considering what is implied in that set of ideas about the relationship of self to society, and, as is so often the case with the sentimentalists, a good way to understand that is by seeing what it is they oppose—and that in this case is again Hobbes and Mandeville. One of Shaftesbury's most telling points in his critique of them is that the "society" they imagined was pallid and illusory. Shaftesbury argued that "real *Society*" was impossible among "such as had no other *Sense* than that of *private Good*." Self-interest or self-love was inherently an unsocial passion, and one that made genuine "Community" a farce, a collection of suspicious individuals motivated to avoid the prickly behaviors of others' self-love. Instead, writes Shaftesbury, a "publick Spirit can come only from a social Feeling or *Sense of Partnership* with human Kind." For Shaftesbury, what this implies is complex, since he is arguing that there is some kind of intricate interplay between the feeling and the society, which might be described as mutually constitutive. One produces the other that likewise produces it. So, when Shaftesbury sums up by saying that "thus Morality and good Government go together," he is arguing not merely that morally generous individuals will produce a sound society, nor only that a healthy social order will reproduce citizens with a strong sense of fellow-feeling, but something in between, or something that implies both.[33]

That intricate dance between self and society is perhaps less obvious in Butler and Smith, but it is implied most clearly in the fact that they see resentment as an emotion that has the potential either to endanger or to enhance

32. Butler, *Fifteen Sermons*, Volume 2, p. 145; Hutcheson, *A System of Moral Philosophy, in Three Books* (London, 1715), Volume 1, p. 155; Hutcheson, *Philosophiae Moralis Institutio Compendaria*, p. 273; Hume, *Enquiries Concerning Human Understanding*, p. 219.

33. Anthony, Third Earl of Shaftesbury, *Characteristicks of Men, Manners, Opinions, Times* (Indianapolis: Liberty Fund, 2001), Volume 2, p. 224, Volume 1, p. 67.

a larger social world. In both Butler and Smith, resentment is largely an individual emotion; they do not emphasize the possibility that it could be a collective sentiment. And resentment, for Butler, is something implanted in us by God and nature, and for Smith by nature. From that source, resentment felt and transcended becomes a path to a larger social good, especially justice. On the other hand, if resentment becomes delectable and a source of pleasure in itself, then the individual who so broods on her or his ills becomes precisely the kind of self-loving individual Hobbes and Mandeville posit as the norm. Resentment, then, is an individual, moral emotion that can create a healthy "publick Spirit" or can lead one to selfishly seeking only "private Good."

When we turn to the nineteenth-century Continental tradition, God and nature will be largely replaced by society itself. Instead of seeing how individual conscience could form social arrangements, in the way Butler and Smith (and Hutcheson and Shaftesbury) argued, the Continental thinkers posited that it is the social arrangements themselves that produce particular deviations in individual conscience. All that is too tidy, of course, and both the British and Continental thinkers had considerably more complicated arguments about the relationship of individual to social passions, as I hope I have shown in this discussion of the British moralist tradition. Nonetheless, the emphasis is distinctly changed, and we will see more focus on the direction from the collective social order to the individual conscience.[34] We will see how *ressentiment* becomes a shared sentiment, an emotion that marks an age, an epoch, a religious system, rather than being a moral sentiment of a person whose expression of it can reveal the tension between a righteous umbrage and an unacceptable desire for vengeance. Once it is applied to these larger systems—religious and social—*ressentiment* becomes also more attuned to the second form and meaning we outlined in the previous chapter, to envy.

---

34. Another way to read the trajectory of thinking about resentment is to attend to the historical shift from those who focus on resentment as a retaliatory emotion to those who argue that it is a fundamental affirmation of human dignity. I am indebted to Stephen Darwall for pointing out to me the importance of that interpretation.

6 THE CONTINENTAL CULTURAL TRADITION

COLLECTIVE

The British moralists of the eighteenth century wrote in the aftermath of the English Revolution and its economic and political resolutions. The Continental thinkers we are examining here wrote in the wake of the French Revolution. While the English Revolution and the market conditions that produced it and emerged from it promoted a Protestant sensibility about the individual conscience and a sense of obligation to state and soul, so might we say that the French Revolution produced in these later thinkers a somewhat ambivalent sense of romantic nostalgia for the past and a pronounced dread of an emergent mass society. They share with Marc Ferro a sense that in "France, during the revolution, resentment against the privileged gave way to egalitarian madness."[1] Both Søren Kierkegaard and Friedrich Nietzsche referred to exalted figures of the French Revolution to make the point about what a heroic persona in a heroic age might look like, but both also expressed anxiety and fear about the growing power of the crowd that was likewise a manifestation of the French Revolution. Whereas the British moralists depicted an individual conscience wrestling with resentment and trying to tame it into justice, the Continental writers represented resentment as a cultural phenomenon haunting an

1. Marc Ferro, *Resentment in History*, translated by Steven Rendall (Cambridge: Polity, 2010), p. 42. The initial hypothesis of the HIST-EX "Emotional Studies" research group at the Centre for Human and Social Sciences in Madrid was that "the history of resentment" was "intimately linked to the transformations that occurred in late eighteenth-century societies following the impact of the French Revolution on world politics, in which, for the first time, individuals were conceived as having the opportunity to fulfil their expectations under the same social conditions." See Dolores Martín Moruno, "Introduction: On Resentment: Past and Present," in *On Resentment: Past and Present*, edited by Bernardino Fantini, Dolores Martín Moruno, and Javier Moscoso (Newcastle upon Tyne, UK: Cambridge Scholars, 2013), pp. 1–16, esp. p. 4.

epoch in which mobs had assumed a certain kind of destructive power. Their interest was in discerning what a *culture* of resentment looks like, what it produces, and what alternative histories are repressed in its emergence.

The three writers we are examining here differ in their sense of what that alternative history is, but for each of them Christianity plays a key role. For Kierkegaard, Christianity came to represent the glorious alternative history that was destroyed—or disappeared—in the bureaucratic form of "Christendom." For him, that division was most clearly manifest in the distinction between the individual and the "herd." "Christianity is the individual," he writes, "the single individual." But Christendom, in the forms of the state church, in the practices of those who follow but do not understand the morality they are taught, those who believe without knowing what it is to which they claim faith, constitute what he calls the "herd mentality." These are the thoughts of his last writings, but we can find the same topics and concerns about the relationship of individual to collective in the writings of his growing disenchantment a decade earlier, where he explicitly writes about the culture of *ressentiment*. Nietzsche too argued that "*Morality in Europe today is herd animal morality*," and he also felt an anxiety about what he called "the *democratic* movement" of the age. Unlike Kierkegaard, though, who, like the thinkers of the Reformation, wished to return to the pure fount of Christianity to undo the work of Christendom, Nietzsche thought of "the *democratic* movement" as the "heir of Christianity." And when he came to write what is effectively a genealogy of *ressentiment*, he traces that cultural sensibility back to what he calls those slave religions, Christianity and Judaism, which he argued attempted to contain the energies and robust possibilities of more glorious, unbound heroes.[2]

Max Scheler agreed with Kierkegaard and Nietzsche that modern Europe was awash in *ressentiment*, but he differed from them in two significant ways. First, he directly contested Nietzsche that "Christian morality" was the source of that *ressentiment*, tracing it instead to what he called "modern bourgeois

---

2. Søren Kierkegaard, quoted in Bruce H. Kirmmse, "'Out With It!': The Modern Breakthrough, Kierkegaard and Denmark," in *The Cambridge Companion to Kierkegaard*, edited by Alastair Hannay and Gordon D. Marino (New York: Cambridge University Press, 1998), pp. 15–47, esp. p. 44; Kierkegaard, *Kierkegaard's Attack upon "Christendom" 1854–1855*, translated by Walter Lowrie (1944; Princeton, NJ: Princeton University Press, 1968); Kierkegaard, *Concluding Unscientific Postscript to Philosophical Fragments*, edited and translated by Howard V. Hong and Edna H. Hong (Princeton, NJ: Princeton University Press, 1992), Volume 1; Friedrich Nietzsche, *Beyond Good and Evil*, translated by Marion Faber (New York: Oxford University Press, 1998), p. 89.

morality." Second, he saw the French Revolution in more stark terms than his predecessors: whereas they saw a possibility and glimmer of glory in the early Revolution, and in Napoleon, he saw it unromantically as part of a long-term historical process that liberated the evil of "bourgeois morality." What had begun in the thirteenth century with the "rise of the bourgeoisie" culminated "with the emancipation of the Third Estate in the French Revolution." Like Nietzsche, then, he sees the problem of *ressentiment* manifest in what Scheler calls "the political–democratic movement," but he does not think that movement an heir of Christianity but ultimately descended from the French Revolution.[3] So, for Scheler, like Kierkegaard, Christianity continues to represent an ideal that provides liberation from *ressentiment*, while for Nietzsche it is the emblematic source of it. What they shared, though, is the firm belief that they were talking about a social condition, a widespread and hegemonic cultural phenomenon, which stifled the individual's striving to be moral—in a way that was Christian for Kierkegaard and Scheler, in a way that was "beyond good and evil" for Nietzsche.

I

The person widely recognized as introducing the idea of *ressentiment* to modern philosophy did not, in fact, use that term. Kierkegaard used the Danish word *Misundelse* in his lengthy 1846 review "The Two Ages," where he identified and explicated the concept of *ressentiment*. Walter Kaufmann feels the Danish word would be better translated in German as *Neid* and in English as 'envy.' Some translators of Kierkegaard, including the translators of the authoritative Princeton English edition of Kierkegaard, Howard and Edna Hong, have indeed translated the word as 'envy.' The earliest translator of "The Two Ages," however, Alexander Dru, whose 1940 translation we will use here, translated it as '*ressentiment*.'[4] With Kierkegaard, we start to witness

---

3. Max Scheler, *Ressentiment*, translated by Lewis B. Coser and William W. Holdheim (Milwaukee, WI: Marquette University Press, 2007), pp. 110–11.

4. Walter Kaufmann, "Introduction," in Kierkegaard, *The Present Age: On the Death of Rebellion*, translated by Alexander Dru (New York: HarperPerrenial 2010), p. xxv; S. Kierkegaard, "Two Ages: The Age of Revolution and the Present Age: A Literary Review (March 30, 1846)," in *The Essential Kierkegaard*, edited by Howard V. Hong and Edna H. Hong (Princeton, NJ: Princeton University Press, 2000), pp. 252–68. The book Kierkegaard was reviewing was Thomasine Gyllembourg-Ehrensvärd's novel *Two Ages*. I will hereafter be quoting from the Dru translation, cited as *The Present Age*, and citing the passage from the Hongs' translation, cited as "Two Ages."

the shift in meaning from resentment at being injured to resentment at others' success, from umbrage to envy. This shift, as I noted in Chapter 4, is significant but does not constitute a wholesale change in the concept, which in its primary explicators implicitly exhibits both traits, even when only one seems to be emphasized.

Ressentiment for Kierkegaard was a psychological condition. It was manifest in what he called the "constituent principle of want of character"—a moral failing in an individual—who was unable to recognize superior talents. It was a strategy of deriding what was admirable out of that particular sense of envy that manifests itself when one is unable to admire what one cannot be. Instead of marveling at what is distinctive and eminent, *ressentiment* "wants to drag it down, wants to belittle it so that it really ceases to be distinguished." But Kierkegaard, in the end, is considerably less interested in individual than in collective *ressentiment*, less in how a person expresses an odious envy for what he or she cannot be and more in how an entire people might manifest that same sentiment. Kierkegaard's notable contribution is to make *ressentiment* not a response of an individual to an affront but a characteristic mood of a people to a particular epoch. *Ressentiment*, in other words, is not so much a personal reactive attitude to a felt or perceived wrong, a response that was salutary because it was a sign of self-respect but also dangerous because of its possible unruliness and needed to be tempered by equally strong emotional strategies. Instead, *ressentiment* became a collective condition of the collective's failings, like nostalgia (and closely connected to it).[5]

The two "ages" of his title, also the title of the novel he was putatively reviewing, while actually using it only as a pretext for his commentary, are what he called "a revolutionary age" which is "an age of action," and the "present age" which is "the age of advertisement and publicity." The age of revolution was filled with enthusiasm, the current one with "reflection, without passion." The age of revolution was marked by "great and good actions," the present age merely with "anticipation" and indecisiveness. The revolutionary age contained the heroic figures of the French Revolution, like Napoleon, and saw arms "distributed freely" for the struggle for *liberté* and conquest; the present age sees people instead "supplied with rules of careful conduct and ready-reckoners to facilitate judgement." The revolutionary age witnessed the *Encyclopédie*, the intellectual prowess of Diderot and the other thinkers who "wrote gigantic folios with unremitting pain"; the present age, "light-weight

---

5. Kierkegaard, *The Present Age*, p. 23. Cf. Kierkegaard, "Two Ages," p. 258.

encyclopaedists" who produce much that is comprehensive, and nothing that is noteworthy. What Kierkegaard expresses in contrasting these two ages—the revolutionary and the post-revolutionary—is a specific kind of ennui that afflicts an epoch living in the daunting shadow of an earlier glory. In the twentieth century, the Turkish writer Orhan Pamuk writes about a similar ennui that afflicts those in Istanbul who live in the rubbles of what was once Constantinople, a city that housed three world empires. We might call it the malaise of belatedness.[6]

For Kierkegaard, the most remarkable feature of that malaise is its emotional expression. He notes that the passionate "*enthusiasm*" of the revolutionary age has been transformed into the "passionless *envy*" of the present age. In the account Kierkegaard gives of it, that envy becomes both pervasive and deep. It is pervasive precisely because it is not contained at the level of the individual. As a product of "reflection," the envy at the individual level "imprisons man's will and his strength." In other circumstances, or perhaps other times, all the individual has to do to free the self of that envy is "break loose from the bonds of his own reflections." Yet, in the attempt during the post-revolutionary age, he "finds himself in the vast prison formed by the reflection of those around him." The reflection of the individual and the reflection of the society reinforce each other in a negative feedback loop that leave "both the individual and the age . . . imprisoned" by reflective "envy." In addition to being pervasive, that envy is deep because the feedback loop alters it and renders it more potent. Indulged, fed, and reinforced, the "envy of reflection" is transformed into "moral *ressentiment*."[7]

This "moral *ressentiment*" manifests itself socially primarily in the form of "leveling," that is, insisting on the absence or impropriety of eminence. Whereas antiquity and other revolutionary ages had valued the "great individual" who can lead the masses, the present age denies greatness and instead promotes "the negative unity of the negative reciprocity of all individuals." In its *ressentiment* toward the "outstanding and eminent individual," the present age instead posits a "phantom public," an insubstantial collective living in an indecisive age, whose primary interaction seems to be to reinforce the envy that each individual feels and cannot escape. Instead of discovering

6. Kierkegaard, *The Present Age*, pp. 6, 3, 7, 5, 6. Cf. Kierkegaard, "Two Ages," pp. 252, 253. Orhan Pamuk, *Istanbul: Memories and the City*, translated by Maureen Freely (New York: Vintage, 2004). The quotations in *The Present Age* from pp. 3 and 5 are not found in "Two Ages" because the Hongs omit the opening section of the review in their translation.

7. Kierkegaard, *The Present Age*, pp. 19, 20–21. Cf. Kierkegaard, "Two Ages," p. 257.

admiration for genuine eminence, the public is fed advertisement and publicity, manipulative forms of seduction meant to produce desires or the illusion of opinions (instead of felt convictions).[8] In the end, then, Kierkegaard sees the present age's *ressentiment* as profoundly and unalterably destructive, and gaining momentum.

Resentment, as we saw in Butler and Smith, required a brake, a force that could counter its trajectory toward vengeance. For Butler, forgiveness, and for Smith, a form of conscientious remorse in the shape of an impartial spectator, provided that brake. For Kierkegaard, too, *ressentiment* requires a tempering force, and he also proposes penitence and forgiveness as the strategies that would do that work. But because his account is of both a collective and an epochal situation, not of an individual's choices, and because he is temperamentally less hopeful than Butler and Smith, who both saw benevolence as an operative force in the world, Kierkegaard describes moments of failed repentance and failed forgiveness. And the failures are precisely a result of the pervasive and profound *ressentiment* of the age. In an earlier age, two people could mend their differences because they had a distinct and recognized relationship. A father, say, might "curse his son in anger," or a "son defy his father" in rebelliousness, but their conflict could be resolved and would "end in the inwardness of forgiveness." In a present age, such relationships are "ceasing to exist." What used to be a relationship based on love has become "one of indifference"—between fathers and sons, students and schoolmasters, men and women. These are not relationships, but rather "tensions," wrought not of devotion but indifference, an insubstantial and unproductive "tension which exhausts life itself." What used to be a living force has become merely formal, what used to be done vibrantly out of firm belief is now done "on principle"—and "repentance," writes Kierkegaard, "cannot easily strike root in ground where everything is done 'on principle.'"[9]

Ressentiment, then, in its earliest Continental nineteenth-century exponent, has lost much of the moral value that its British advocates had identified, partly because it had shifted from umbrage to envy, but primarily because it was seen as a collective malaise rather than an individual response, a failing rather than an animation of spirit. For moral philosophers like Butler and Smith and Hutcheson, both resentment and forgiveness required an actual

8. Kierkegaard, *The Present Age*, pp. 23, 24, 31, 33. Cf. Kierkegaard, "Two Ages," pp. 258, 259, 260–61.

9. Kierkegaard, *The Present Age*, pp. 16–17, 50. Cf. Kierkegaard, "Two Ages," pp. 255–56. The second passage is omitted in the Hongs' translation.

human relationship, since both were interpersonal emotions. For existential philosophers like Kierkegaard, it was precisely the absence of those relationships that defined the age and the absurd moral condition it suffered. It would likewise be the case in the next, and most influential and important, writer on *ressentiment*, the first who actually used that French word in his writing.

II

With Nietzsche, *ressentiment* assumes its fullest expression in Continental moral philosophy. In a trilogy of works from the mid-1880s—*Thus Spoke Zarathustra* (1883–1885), *Beyond Good and Evil* (1886), and *On The Genealogy of Morals* (1887)—and in the notes he wrote during these years that were collected in what became *The Will to Power*, Nietzsche undertook a complete reevaluation of the historic role that *ressentiment* played in what he argued was the life-negating morality of Judeo–Christian and other religious traditions.

It is quite likely that Nietzsche knew little of Kierkegaard when he undertook the three books in which he most fully examined *ressentiment*. He implied in a letter to the Danish philosopher Georg Brandes in 1888 that he had not yet studied Kierkegaard, although Nietzsche had by then encountered other Danish writers, notably Hans Lassen Martensen and Harald Høffding, who did write about Kierkegaard in books we know Nietzsche owned and read. Nietzsche promised Brandes that he would undertake a more careful study of Kierkegaard, and waxed enthusiastic about the lectures that Brandes was delivering on Nietzsche in Copenhagen, since he felt that the Danish people would be temperamentally primed to accept his concept of warrior and "master morality" from their having been immersed in Icelandic sagas.[10] It is likely, then, that the points of similarity between Kierkegaard and Nietzsche—including their mutual admiration of authoritarian "individuals," disdain for democracy, nostalgia for an earlier and more heroic age, and, especially, their representation of *ressentiment* as a collective, social condition— are less the result of one's reading the other and more the result of their sharing a similar sensibility.

Nietzsche begins *Thus Spoke Zarathustra* by denouncing those phenomena he feels have been employed to constrain an unfettered will to power,

---

10. *Selected Letters of Friedrich Nietzsche*, edited by Oscar Levy, translated by Anthony M. Ludovici (Garden City, NY: Doubleday, Page, and Co, 1921), pp. 325, 327.

that is, the unlimited exercise of forceful actions by the exceptional and the strong who ought, in his system, to impose their forceful will on what he calls the mediocre herd. "God is dead," announces Zarathustra, and "soul," he insists, is "only a word for something about the body." Having purged the world of the immaterial forces (divine and personal) that restrict what he celebrates as "the wholesome, healthy selfishness that wells from a powerful soul," Zarathustra commences to turn what most religions have taught as moral truths on their head. Justice that takes the form of remedying or punishing wrongdoing is merely naked vengeance ("punishment is what revenge calls itself"). Where Christ celebrates a future state for the weak and powerless ("Blessed are the meek"), Zarathustra condemns them as plotters seeking to usurp power ("the tyrannomania of impotence"). Zarathustra dismisses what most religious traditions have held about the value of truth, and applauds the bold lie. "Whoever is unable to lie," he states, "does not know what truth is." Finally, what religious traditions from various epochs and parts of the world have upheld as the Golden Rule—do unto others as you would have them do unto you—Nietzsche transforms into a gangster's piety: "What you do, nobody can do to you in turn." And the principle on which that universal Golden Rule is premised—to love our neighbors as we do ourselves—is likewise codified as *do not spare your neighbor!*" Nietzsche does not use the term *ressentiment* in *Thus Spoke Zarathustra*, although he has certainly started to limn the characteristics he would later condemn in those he diagnosed as suffering from it. Those who resent a harm are seen as weak and abhorrent. A "gruesome sight is a person single-mindedly obsessed by a wrong."[11]

The term likewise does not seem to appear in *Beyond Good and Evil*, the book he published immediately after the first three parts of *Thus Spoke Zarathustra* were published, and the fourth part printed and circulated privately. In drawing out a history of the world divided into three ages (the pre-moral, the moral, and the extra-moral), Nietzsche spends a good deal of energy undermining the sensibility underwriting moral systems, especially Judaism and Christianity. "One must destroy morality if one is to liberate life," he had written in a note in *The Will to Power*, because it constitutes "an opposition movement against the efforts of nature to achieve a higher type." That is, morality was what the herd employed to keep the exceptional from thriving; during the first age, the pre-moral, this was not the case, and,

---

11. Nietzsche, *Thus Spoke Zarathustra*, translated by Walter Kaufmann (New York: Modern Library, 1995), pp. 12, 34, 190, 140, 100, 290, 199, 68.

Nietzsche prophesies, nor will it be the case once the moral age gives way to the extra-moral. Turning his attention to the earliest moral systems of the West, he first dismisses Socrates as an excrescence in an otherwise noble Platonism ("Socratism," he writes, "is not really part of Plato"), and then Judaism. The significance of the Jewish people, he affirms, is that the "*slave revolt in morals* begins with them." A slave morality, as opposed to "master moralities," is a code based on the experiences of an oppressed people who are suspicious of the exercise of unlimited power, and who attempt to constrain it through a code that designates some actions as "good" and some as "evil." A master morality dispenses precisely with this binary (it is "*beyond* good and evil") and celebrates bold, noble actions that are simply expressions of a creative and powerful will. What is distinctive in the Socratic, the Judaic, and the Christian worldviews—in his word, the slave moralities—is that they all share a belief in equality and justice, and they all promote a world in which some forceful wills are hindered from imposing whatever they wish on others. This condition—he terms it in one case in a note in *The Will to Power* as "the psychological problem of Christianity"—is that they are premised on weakness, and, especially, a weakness that, like a slave's, is a response to a history of having been harmed.[12]

The idea that had occupied him for two books and innumerable note entries finally found its proper name in *On the Genealogy of Morals*, and the name was French: *ressentiment*. The eminent translator and scholar of Nietzsche Walter Kaufmann noted that Nietzsche used the French word because "the German language lacks any close equivalent to the French term" and because Nietzsche chose the occasion of his emergence from the shadow of Wagner, of whom he had grown increasingly critical, to distinguish himself as a Francophile (as opposed to the Francophobic, Germanophilic Wagner). And, as we saw, he had read the French translation of Dostoevsky's *Notes from Underground* that used that word.[13]

---

12. Nietzsche, *Beyond Good and Evil*, pp. 32–33; Nietzsche, *The Will to Power*, translated by Walter Kaufmann and R. J. Hollingdale (New York: Vintage, 1968), pp. 189, 216; Nietzsche, *Beyond Good and Evil*, pp. 78, 83, 153–56; Nietzsche, *The Will to Power*, p. 108.

13. Walter Kaufmann, "Editor's Introduction," to Nietzsche, *On the Genealogy of Morals*, in *Basic Writings of Nietzsche* (New York: Modern Library, 1992), p. 441; Yamina Oudai Celso, "Nietzsche: The 'First Psychologist' and the Genealogist of Ressentiment," in *On Resentment: Past and Present*, edited by Bernardino Fantini, Dolores Martín Moruno, and Javier Moscoso (Newcastle upon Tyne, UK: Cambridge Scholars, 2013), pp. 37–54, esp. p. 37. I have profited greatly from Robert C. Solomon, "One Hundred Years of *Ressentiment*: Nietzsche's Genealogy of Morals," in *Nietzsche, Genealogy, Morality: Essays on Nietzsche's Genealogy of Morals*, edited by Richard Schacht (Berkeley: University of California Press, 1994), pp. 95–126.

Nietzsche begins *On the Genealogy of Morals* by identifying the core characteristic of that slave morality he had described in *Beyond Good and Evil*. "While all noble morality grows from triumphant affirmation of itself, slave morality from the outset says no to an 'outside,' to an 'other,' to a 'non-self'; and *this* no is its creative act. The reversal of the evaluating gaze—this *necessary* orientation outwards rather than inwards to the self—belongs characteristically to *ressentiment*." That orientation outward, that "evaluating gaze," one suspects, is the conscience that Adam Smith had designated as the "impartial spectator" and that Nietzsche had already dismissed as "soul." In slave morality, then, because they are in the grip of conscience, those who harm feel remorse and those who are harmed feel *ressentiment*. A noble or master's morality dispenses with both. Nietzsche writes in *The Will to Power*: "Against remorse—I do not like this kind of cowardice toward one's own deeds." The "immoralists" he celebrates "prefer not to believe in 'guilt.'" In such immoralists, what he calls "noble souls" in *On the Genealogy of Morals, ressentiment* rarely appears, and only fleetingly (and "completes and exhausts itself in an immediate reaction"). These "noble souls" feel no remorse for their own acts or resentment for the acts of others against them because they are "incapable of taking one's enemies, accidents, even one's *misdeeds* seriously for long." The reason is that such "strong full natures" have the power that enables them to "forget." Drawing on the French Revolution, Nietzsche offers Mirabeau as an example of someone who "could not forgive simply because he could not—remember." "Such a man with a *single* shrug shakes off much of that which worms and digs its way into others."[14]

Those unable to forget, those who have need either to forgive or to be forgiven, are those who suffer *ressentiment*, and it is their "civilizing" work that Nietzsche condemns. They resort to imagining alternative worlds like heaven where such forgiveness can be found (Nietzsche calls this strategy "the *ressentiment* of metaphysicians"), or denying the will to power in this world by creating systems of repressive culture and justice. Reaction and *ressentiment*, he writes, are precisely the "real *instruments of culture*" that "ruined" the ideals of "the noble races." The mark of that culture, of course, is legislation that affirms and maintains justice. Wherever "justice is practised, wherever justice

---

14. Nietzsche, *On the Genealogy of Morals*, translated by Douglas Smith (New York: Oxford University Press, 1996), p. 22; Nietzsche, *The Will to Power*, p. 136; Nietzsche, *On The Genealogy of Morals*, p. 24. On the effect of *ressentiment* on "noble souls," also see Stephen Darwall, "*Ressentiment* and Second-Personal Resentment," in *Honor, History, & Relationship: Essays in Second-Personal Ethics II* (New York: Oxford University Press, 2013), pp. 72–88, esp. p. 74.

is upheld," wherever laws are legislated to control the will to power of the immoralists and noble races, Nietzsche seethes, "one sees a stronger power seek means to put an end to the senseless raging of *ressentiment* among weaker powers subordinate to it."[15]

Having identified the various spheres where *ressentiment* manifests itself as a constraining force on the will to power (morality, religion, culture, justice), Nietzsche turns finally to what he excoriates as the existential outlook that *ressentiment* represents. And in doing so, he returns to the terminology and complex of ideas proposed by Butler and Smith, involving resentment, indignation, and forgiveness. "The instinct of revenge" that underwrites *ressentiment*, he insists, "has so mastered mankind in the course of millennia that the whole of metaphysics, psychology, conception of history, but above all morality, is impregnated with it." To respond to that history—to move the world from the age of morality to the extra-moral age—requires the immoralists to identify the sources that created it and then diagnose them. First, he identifies what he calls "those apostles of revenge and *ressentiment*, those pessimists from indignation par excellence, who make it their mission to sanctify their filth under the name of 'indignation.' " The "generous and noble" resentment Butler celebrated, the "fellow-feeling" of indignation Smith acknowledged as crucial to the moral sentiments, become in Nietzsche "filth" whose sole purpose is to derail, to stifle, and to reduce the richness of life.[16]

He is emphatic on this point. What *ressentiment* does, in the end, is deny life itself by imposing "upon becoming the character of being," that is denying a process (willing) in order to valorize a state (morality). What such moralities often endorse toward that end is an "ascetic life," a life that urges the transcendence of the material world. An "ascetic life," for Nietzsche, is not only "a contradiction in terms," but it is also where a "particular kind of *ressentiment* rules," that of an "unsatisfied instinct and will to power which seeks not to master some isolated aspect of life but rather life itself, its deepest, strongest, most fundamental conditions." What Nietzsche sees, then, is a struggle between two wills to power—the master immoralists seeking to move the world to the extra-moral age where the exceptional can flourish, and the slave moralists desiring to leave the world mired in the moral age where the herd rules. The immoralist feels the pleasures of imposing will on

---

15. Nietzsche, *The Will to Power*, pp. 310–11; Nietzsche, *On The Genealogy of Morals*, pp. 27, 56.

16. Nietzsche, *The Will to Power*, pp. 401, 402, 330.

the weaker with impunity and a complete absence of conscience, and feeling no pain or immediately forgetting it when such a will is imposed on one. The moralist, on the other hand, feels and seeks pleasure "in failure, atrophy, pain, accident, ugliness, arbitrary atonements, self-denial, self-flagellation, self-sacrifice."[17]

Ressentiment, then, for Nietzsche, is not just the self-pitying state of those individuals who unconscionably nurse the wrongs done them. It is not just a personal and disagreeable response to the world. It is a historic force that governs the moral age, the age Nietzsche feels eclipsed the glorious pre-moral age, and stands as the impediment to the inauguration of the future glorious extra-moral age. *Ressentiment* is the source of all the moralities he would dismantle, all the life-denying ethical systems that dwell on the value and meaning of past actions by remembering and resenting them. It is *ressentiment* that creates both a code of justice (punish those who hurt others in the past) and a code of ethical conduct (forgive those who hurt you in the past). It is this last point that is worth examining in a little more detail. Like Butler and Smith, then, Nietzsche argued for the dynamic between *ressentiment* and forgiveness, but, obviously, he reached a quite different conclusion. Butler felt that forgiveness represented a tempering force on righteous resentment, keeping it from assuming the dangerous aspect of revenge. Smith was even more fearful of the momentum of resentment, and called upon the considerable powers of the "impartial spectator" and the value of repentance to quell what he held to be the most odious of the "unsocial passions." Nietzsche, on the other hand, condemned "self-flagellation" and "arbitrary atonements" out of hand as simply manifestations of weakness. At the same time, though, he equally condemns the *ressentiment* that such atonement and forgiveness are meant to offset. The reason, of course, is that Butler and Smith occupy a wholly different mental world than does Nietzsche. For them, resentment and forgiveness are two distinct forces: resentment is a brutal passion, a product of nature, that cultured reason and religion moderate through rituals of penitence and forgiveness. For Nietzsche, though, they are not distinct or opposed: the one, *ressentiment*, is a historic force that created a morality that promotes the other, forgiveness; and both represent a world he condemns and whose eclipse he prophesies.

---

17. Nietzsche, *On The Genealogy of Morals*, p. 97.

III

A quarter-century after Nietzsche completed his meditations on *ressentiment* as a world-denying, life-defeating force, found in classical and Judaic systems, but most fully manifest in the slave morality of Christianity, the German philosopher Max Scheler responded in a book originally titled *Ressentiment and Moral Value-Judgment* (*Ueber Ressentiment und moralisches Wertureil* [1912]), and then retitled in an expanded, revised edition three years later *The Role of Ressentiment in the Make-Up of Morals* (*Das Ressentiment im Aufbau der Moralen* [1915]).[18]

Scheler's major argument against Nietzsche is not that Nietzsche has mis-characterized the concept of *ressentiment*, but rather that he has misidenti-fied where it occurs and therefore leveled a mistaken and misleading criticism against Christianity. For Scheler, it is bourgeois morality that is rooted in *ressentiment*, not Christian ethics. We can most fully find the *ressentiment* that was the true object of Nietzsche's misdirected critique manifest in what Scheler calls "modern humanitarianism." It was Rousseau, he argues, who first expressed that cultural phenomenon, and he did so while himself being "evi-dently propelled by the fire of a gigantic *ressentiment*."[19]

Although it is doubtful that Nietzsche adopted the idea of *ressentiment* from Kierkegaard, who had first employed it in the modern sense, it is clear that those who followed Nietzsche adopted it precisely because he had him-self made it his own, and had indeed made it his own in French. Scheler openly acknowledges this fact in the opening of his book: "We do not use the word '*ressentiment*' because of a special predilection for the French language, but because we did not succeed in translating it into German." Moreover, he adds, he employs it because "Nietzsche has made it a *terminus technicus*." The French term, for Scheler, introduced something that apparently could not be found in any other European language. The "French word" in its "natural meaning," he writes, implies two things: existential depth and emotional com-plexity. First, because it expresses the "repeated experiencing and reliving of a particular emotional response," the "continual reliving of the emotion sinks it more deeply into the center of the personality, but concomitantly removes it from the person's zone of action and expression." It is therefore felt more pro-foundly and more desperately. In this way, the French term suggests a smol-dering and anxiety-ridden sense that is difficult to express in other languages.

---

18. Manfred S. Frings, "Introduction," in Scheler, *Ressentiment*, p. 3.

19. Scheler, *Ressentiment*, pp. 55–77, 84–85.

Scheler's argument for the second aspect of the French term is considerably less compelling. Second, he writes, "the word implies that the quality of this emotion is negative, i.e., that it contains a movement of hostility." That, however, seems to be the meaning of the term in whatever European language it is expressed. Perhaps, Scheler concludes, "the German word 'Groll' (rancor) comes closest to the essential meaning of the term," although he will continue to use *ressentiment* for the rest of the book in which he placed the term prominently in the title.[20]

As we saw, Scheler's major impetus is to suggest that the *ressentiment* Nietzsche ascribes to Christianity is actually characteristic of the bourgeois morality of modern humanitarianism. *Ressentiment*, then, becomes in Scheler a psychological condition whose most important manifestation is a perversion of the "sense of values," what he calls the "value delusion of *ressentiment*." The process that culminates in this "value delusion" begins in something specific, some event that germinates the "self-poisoning of the mind," and it occurs because the response to that event is repressed. Instead of acting out a response to some harm or expressing what one envies, one represses and this repression produces a series of negative affects. Scheler is somewhat confusing about the sequence of these affects, nor is he altogether clear on how to distinguish some of the emotions that are almost synonymous. At one point, for instance, he argues that the repression leads directly to "value delusions" (which are then expressed in the form of "revenge, hatred, malice, envy, the impulse to detract, and spite"). At another point, however, he argues that the repression produces the emotions first, which in turn produce the value delusion. Consider the following: "When it is repressed, vindictiveness leads to *ressentiment*, a process which is intensified when the *imagination* of vengeance, too, is repressed—and finally the very emotion of revenge itself. Only then does this *state of mind* become associated with the tendency to detract from the other person's value." Vindictiveness, vengeance, and revenge are not easily distinguished; while vindictiveness is generally seen as a disposition, there is not much difference between vengeance and revenge (and, if there is, Scheler has not noted it).[21]

Although his description of *ressentiment* as a psychological condition is not entirely unambiguous, Scheler's insistence on its existential source in a particular spiritual malaise is crystal clear. What is lost in modern humanism

---

20. Scheler, *Ressentiment*, pp. 20, 20–21.

21. Scheler, *Ressentiment*, pp. 48, 34, 25, 27.

is a series of foundational dispositions that Christianity, in particular, had represented—a sense of hereditary good and hereditary guilt, and a sense of genuine love. The modern individual denies the hereditary good and guilt in order to affirm a false sense of moral autonomy, to become self-made, as it were. Moral value, in this modern world, inheres only in those things "which the individual has acquired by his own strength and labor," not things given as gifts. In that moral isolation of the individual divorced from a cosmic history, love, which had represented a "lack" in antiquity, according to Scheler, and a "fullness" in Christianity, is transformed into *ressentiment*. Instead of feeling love, then, a closeness and an obligation, a sense of grateful indebtedness, the man of *ressentiment* feels envy and hatred. Separated from history and a beloved community, he develops values that are subjective, not shared. And it is precisely those subjective values, his value delusion, that recreate his *ressentiment* and spiral into a negative cycle that, in the end, denies the value of life.[22] The *ressentiment* that is life-denying, for Scheler, is not found in Christianity, as Nietzsche maintains, but rather in the world of modern humanism that attempts to deny the moral truths of Christianity.

Like others who make their mark by turning on its head a previous system of thinking, Scheler is important in the philosophy of *ressentiment* not for his originality (he is easily the least original of the writers surveyed here), but rather for his methodical attention to details. First, Scheler most fully delineates the *psychological* condition, making clear just what was implied or taken for granted in Kierkegaard and Nietzsche in what the feeling of *ressentiment* entailed. Second, Scheler teases out the existential character of *ressentiment* that had likewise been presupposed in earlier accounts. He proposed specific forms for that existential *ressentiment*—at one point, he says: "*existential envy*, which is directed against the other person's very *nature*, is the strongest source of *ressentiment*"—but he also noted the despair, absurdity, and anxiety that characterized *ressentiment* in all its forms and manifestations. Finally, Scheler spelled out the possible resolutions to the dynamic of *ressentiment*, which, again, had been largely assumed in earlier writers: retribution or forgiveness. "The desire for revenge," he writes, "disappears when vengeance has been taken, when the person against whom it was directed has been punished or has punished himself, or when one truly forgives him."[23] It is not his

---

22. Scheler, *Ressentiment*, pp. 97–98, 55–77, 102–103, 106–107.

23. Scheler, *Ressentiment*, pp. 30, 29, 26.

originality, then, but the particularities of his argument and the peculiarity of his situation that makes Scheler valuable in this genealogy.

Scheler makes a robust case for forgiveness, as we might expect in someone who is trying to salvage the reputation of Christianity from Nietzsche's condemnation of it as a "slave morality." Nietzsche was mistaken, writes Scheler, in thinking that forgiving an affront is a sign of weakness, a "mere passive acceptance." Instead, forgiving is supremely what "Christian morality" provides as a "new way to guide pain 'correctly.' " As such, it is emphatically a "*positive* act which consists in freely sacrificing the positive value of expiation." One does not forgive by expiating, condoning, excusing, or thinking mercifully. Rather, one forgives through working out the dynamics of vengeful feelings. Forgiving in this sense, he writes, "presupposes the impulse of revenge instead of being based on its absence." In fact, he insists, "one *cannot* 'forgive' if one feels no revenge."[24] What is valuable and significant in Scheler's contribution, then, is what he grants while attempting to rebut the systems he is contesting. Two things in particular stand out. First, he grants that forgiveness, if it is to be genuine, must be based on *ressentiment*; in this, he anticipates much of the current writing on forgiveness for a century after he wrote. Second, he grants that Nietzsche and Kierkegaard are largely correct in their account of the existential condition of the world, while at the same time he urges us to consider a Christian form of resolution (forgiveness) that had not enjoyed much popularity in the genealogy of *ressentiment* since Butler inaugurated this discourse. He grants, then, the importance of *ressentiment*, not as a virtue (as Butler and Smith saw it), but as a condition; and he grants that the world we inhabit is indeed a world filled with *ressentiment* in all its senses, as envy and as umbrage. It is despite these conditions—personal and existential, in us and in the world—that forgiveness can work.

IV

What this genealogy of resentment demonstrates, I hope, is what any philosophical genealogy should demonstrate—that "origins," as Douglas Smith nicely puts it, can be "understood as the complex intersection of a number of different and competing forces."[25] In this particular genealogy, writers with affiliations to Christianity, moral sentiment theory, and existentialism have

---

24. Scheler, *Ressentiment*, pp. 136, note 35; 75.

25. Douglas Smith, "Introduction," in Nietzsche, *Genealogy of Morals*, p. ix.

engaged with the topic, offering alternative descriptions of what resentment involves and what forces operate on it. They have likewise offered alternative accounts of forgiveness as a spiritual, a strategic, or a futile way of containing *ressentiment*, or a complicit agent in the moral systems based on it. What these complex intersections reveal, though, is that, consistently, forgiveness has been part of the discourse of resentment, and, inconsistently, that resentment has been an emotion indicating self-respect that bespeaks a desire for justice, or a social condition that bespeaks an unseemly acquisitiveness or an equally unseemly and morose sensitivity to slights.

There are two reasons Scheler provides a good place for us to end our genealogy of the school of *ressentiment*. First, Scheler represents the end of the discourse precisely because he is attempting to return it to the place where it began, to the forebear who first saw resentment as a human condition that was valuable only insofar as it could be contained by forgiveness. Writers in the eighteenth century suggested that forgiveness provides a means of dissolving resentment, some sincerely advocating it, as does Butler, others, like Smith, seeing it certainly as a demand of resentment but not necessarily an ideal resolution. In the nineteenth century, Kierkegaard saw forgiveness as an illegitimate strategy for encompassing *ressentiment* because the terms of the social contract had so significantly changed, and what were once relationships between human beings were now simply consumer or informational ties between people caught in a nexus of advertising or publicity. Nietzsche went further and saw forgiveness itself as a manifestation of the cult of *ressentiment*, not a strategy for undoing it but rather a part of the ritual practices that continue it. Scheler attempted to resurrect the Christian virtue of forgiveness as the preeminent means of offsetting *ressentiment*, but he offered, in the end, only a compromised defense of its utility in a culture that he himself identified as largely the same as the one Nietzsche diagnosed. Whatever its origin, Christianity or humanism, that culture was marked with the same disjuncture and alienations that rendered humane relationships based on the ability to offer and accept forgiveness difficult, if not impossible.

A second reason for us to end with Scheler is that he gives us an assessment of *ressentiment* before it came to be understood as a historical force in a different sense than he, Nietzsche, or Kierkegaard understood. Scheler is writing at the beginning of the twentieth century, and on the very eve of the first of the mass atrocities (the Great War, the Armenian genocide) that would mark a century in which resentment would come to be understood not only as an individual property requiring discipline to control, and not only as a social malaise that was meant to control and discipline a population, but indeed as a force that determined the life and interactions of societies. Over the course of the twentieth century, beginning with the widespread belief that the "guilt clause" of the Treaty of Versailles inspired a German resentment that produced the conditions for World War II, we see intellectuals and politicians argue that social resentment (felt by nations, by classes, and by peoples) is in fact a motor of history.

This model, we should be clear, is not what the Continental tradition had proposed. Theirs had been a *cultural* model. Kierkegaard saw a debased European society and traced to an invidious sense of pervasive envy and spite the forces that caused that degradation of the culture. Nietzsche and Scheler, too, argued that *ressentiment* was largely a cultural inheritance that kept Europe mired in social relations that thwarted lives that ideally should be more meaningfully creative (Nietzsche) or spiritually enhancing (Scheler). What the new model that emerged in the twentieth century argued was that resentment was a *political* force. If one wished to understand why a given nation or class or people acted as they did, one would have to identify what historical events in the past had inspired in them a sense of being misserved and humiliated in a way that produced the resentment on which they acted. Resentment, in this model, was seen as a historical power that rivaled other forces like political relations or economic allocations or social inequities—in other words, causal forces that permit us to understand the dynamics of intergroup or international relations. To comprehend what happened in Bosnia, Rwanda, Ireland, South Africa, or any number of places where twentieth-century conflicts and mass atrocities occurred, one needed to go back decades or centuries and discern where and how an ancient resentment had been set and then mobilized. Then we would know, as the title of one book (on Rwanda) put it, the prehistory of "when victims become killers."[26]

This third model of resentment is still a work in formation. There are scattered studies of individual nations and peoples that argue how we can understand resentment as a force in particular nations or regions, and there has recently appeared an anthology (*On Resentment: Past and Present*) that contains many insightful essays on different sites in which resentment is seen to play a key political role. That anthology collects papers from the International Workshop "On Resentment" that was inaugurated and planned by the HIST-EX "Emotional Studies" research group housed in Madrid's Centre for

---

26. Mahmood Mamdani, *When Victims Become Killers: Colonialism, Nativism, and the Genocide in Rwanda* (Princeton, NJ: Princeton University Press, 2001).

Human and Social Sciences.[27] The most ambitious attempt to date is Marc Ferro's *Resentment in History*, in which the distinguished *Annales* school historian argues that much of the history of the modern world (the first event for him is the French Revolution) can be understood through an analysis of either the resentful politicians who come to lead revolutions or the resentful nations that either seethe or seek vengeance for what was done to them. Briefly, we can discern three distinct ways Ferro sees resentment operating in history.

First, Ferro sometimes posits class resentment—that is, the amorphous sensibility that emerges and mobilizes a class or group—as the force that moves people to revolutionary action. He does not always see that resentment in the moral sense of people inspired by what they perceive as injustice. Sometimes he does, as when he speaks of the "peasants' resentment" in France at being subject to onerous taxes, unfair rents, and "offenses to their dignity." But at other times, he seems to describe what is more akin to envy and spite by people whose ambitions are the most notable aspect about them, as he does, for instance, when he comments on the French "bourgeois who aped the gentry."

Second, Ferro sometimes suggests that nations are resentful at what they perceive to be their ill-treatment in war or peace. Poland, for instance, he suggests suffers what he calls "a resentment that is still an open wound" at both its being subject to periodic partitions throughout its history and its being underappreciated for the leading political roles it has played in saving Europe from the Turks in the seventeenth century and Communism in the twentieth. For Ferro, this resentment against European powers for events in the distant and recent past can help explain contemporary politics, such as why Poland would send troops in support of George W. Bush's war in Iraq, while the rest of Europe was critical of it. He traces the origins of what he calls "*national* resentment" to the Thirty Years' War (1618–1648).[28]

The third and most striking strategy Ferro employs is to provide more granular studies of particular individuals and show in what ways their resentments inspired them to lead revolutions or counterrevolutions. Piotr Kropotkin's anarchism, for instance, was a product of a "personal resentment" at his father that led him to an "acute awareness of the people's wretchedness." Likewise, Ferro argues that Vladimir Lenin's resentment over the murder of his brother intersected with his "Marxist reasoning regarding the failure of

---

27. Dolores Martín Moruno, "Introduction: On Resentment: Past and Present of an Emotion," in *On Resentment: Past and Present*, pp. 14, 2.

28. Ferro, *Resentment in History*, pp. 24, 25, 74, 77, 84, 96.

past experiences" to lead him to revolution. Likewise, Joseph Goebbels' "personal resentment" at having Jewish editors and publishers frustrate his writing career flourished into an anti-Semitism that led him to the Nazi Party. And Marshall Pétain nursed what Ferro calls "an old personal resentment" against those who stole the honor from his victory in 1918 when he led the Vichy regime in the early 1940s.[29] In other words, we can sometimes understand grand history by examining private spite and envy. (This is not what feminists meant by the slogan, "the personal is the political.")

Ferro, then, sees resentment as a force that operates on individuals, on classes, and in nations—and, in each of these cases, it operates as a *political* force, that is, as a motive for seeking or modifying the power relations in a society or international order. Ferro concludes his book by noting that the developments of the modern global order seem to be producing even more "centers of resentment" that will almost undoubtedly haunt us in the future. Individuals, classes, and nations will seethe and eventually lash out at broken promises, frustrated hopes, and patent injustice. He offers only one hope that can prevent that cyclical process from devolving into greater destruction—what he calls "bursts of magnanimity."[30] I am not entirely sure what he means by this phrase, but it would appear to suggest only one of two processes. On the one hand, it might mean that the magnanimity must come from those who make promises, raise hopes, and commit injustices. They must acknowledge how they have acted and then change their ways, and seek to produce a world order that is fairer for everyone. On the other hand, it could mean that the magnanimity must come from those whose promises and hopes and rights are violated. They must turn away from the seductions of vindictive resentment. In our parlance the one way is atonement or apology, and the other forgiveness.

IV

Here, then, are three robust ways for us to understand how resentment operates in history and in the pursuit of justice. Ferro's three categories—the resentment of classes, of nations, and of individuals—are useful for what they

---

29. Ferro, *Resentment in History*, pp. 33–34, 37, 58, 62. Also see the discussion of Stalin's *ressentiment* in Darwall, *The Second-Person Standpoint: Morality, Respect and Accountability* (Cambridge, MA: Harvard University Press, 2006), pp. 138–40.

30. Ferro, *Resentment in History*, p. 132. In context, and since he mentions South Africa as an example of that kind of "magnanimity," I assume he means that the magnanimity would come from the oppressed rather than the oppressors.

reveal about the multiform aspects that resentment can assume and for what they suggest about the combination of resentments that can accrue to create an identifiable political trajectory. In the case of Goebbels, for instance, we see how an individual seethes at a personal grudge that leads him to anti-Semitism, and how he was able to use that personal resentment to mobilize a national resentment with a very different origin (at the guilt clause in the Treaty of Versailles) into a particular historical tragedy. We notice, of course, that the cases Ferro highlights are drawn from the most notorious historical regimes in the twentieth century—the Nazis, their collaborator Vichy regime, and the Soviet empire at its origins. Likewise, when Pascal Bruckner wants to exemplify what he calls a national "politics of resentment," he gives us Slobodan Milošević and Serbia—another case in which the desire to avenge historical oppression leads to genocidal oppression of others.[31] These, of course, are compelling cases, and they help us understand the destruction that can be wrought when resentment becomes manifest in those individuals, classes, and nations. What strikes me as missing from this otherwise insightful analysis into the operations of resentment in history are those national cases where the regimes are not transparently or obviously evil, and those examples where the class expressing its resentment is not the lower classes that are oppressed or the middle ones that imagine themselves to be.

We can again return to the cases with which we began this study to give some substance to these other possibilities. We saw at the end of the previous section a desire on the part of some intellectuals to see race as a proxy for forgiveness. The Viscount of Falklands, we recall, saw that forgiveness was the *nature* of Africans. While he may think he is praising a people his nation had formerly transported and enslaved—one is reminded of a line in *Seinfeld*, "If I like their race, how can that be racist?"—he is, perhaps, unaware of how much his own sense of his historical place depends on his believing Africans to have a forgiving nature. After all, his acknowledgment of that is also an admission of the fact that there are crimes to forgive; and his preference is to see those injured by those crimes as forgiving rather than resentful. To see them as resentful would be malignant racism, as forgiving benign. It would seem the viscount is caught on the horns of a dilemma. What perhaps might help him escape it is adopting an altogether different perspective—one that neither seeks forgiveness in others nor fears finding resentment in them. He

---

31. Pascal Bruckner, *The Temptation of Innocence: Living in the Age of Entitlement* (New York: Algora Publishing, 2000), p. 221.

might look within—and maybe around him in the House of Lords—and see just what resentment resides there, and try to understand why. It might be precisely what those whose nature he imagines as forgiving are in fact telling him—and the other lords.

We began this section on resentment by looking at Dostoevsky's *Notes from Underground* and those European writers, like Kafka and Camus, who drew on Dostoevsky's vision and his representation of the absurdity of court justice. We can end it by looking at some American writers who drew on the *setting* Dostoevsky made famous and used it to draw attention to a different kind of absurdity. In both "The Man Who Lived Underground" and *Invisible Man*, Richard Wright and Ralph Ellison reveal how the absurdity of American racism is that "insufficiency of milieu" that traps their heroes in underground spaces. The underground is where Fred Daniels learns the key philosophy of the meaning of it all that he is unable to communicate to the police who kill him and return him to the sewer. It is the place ("the hole in the ground") that Ellison's loquacious unnamed narrator equips with 1,369 light bulbs with electricity stolen from the utility company to reveal his own "enlightenment" of what deviations racism causes in American idealism from the founders to the present.[32] These are writers who see that there is something deeper, and more widespread, and *social*, in resentment; if it is an illness, it is a social one—in both senses, that individuals contract it from their social milieu, and that societies are themselves sick with it. Wright and Ellison use the figure of the underground in their writing to expose the same thing that Camus and Kafka use the setting of the court to indict—that the society itself is rife with resentment; and, also like Camus and Kafka, they reveal how innocents must be sacrificed to that resentment. The police kill Daniels as he tries to communicate to them the nature of human guilt, as they kill Brother Tod Clifton in *Invisible Man* as he resists arrest.

In these symbolic scenes—and in the larger philosophical questions they raise and national histories they address in their works—Wright and Ellison are suggesting something even more telling about the resentment of the powerful. The theorists and purveyors of racism, they demonstrate, are driven to their actions—to injure those they identify as others—out of what can only be described as their profound resentment. The intellectuals who accuse others of "identity politics" argue that it is important for those others not to hold

---

32. Richard Wright, *Eight Men: Short Stories* (New York: HarperPerennial, 1996); Ralph Ellison, *Invisible Man* (1952; New York: Random House, 1995).

onto the traumatic past that produces the resentment they deem those others to feel. Don't found modern identities on old oppressions, they urge, but see the possibilities that open up when you release yourselves from that history. What Wright and Ellison, and many other writers, remind us, though, is that it is precisely the oppressors who have founded their identities on that traumatic past. Before they shoot Daniels, the police mock him in the racist terms they have historically inherited and reproduced. Clifton is shot when he fights against the abusive police officer attempting to arrest him for selling paper Sambo dolls without a license. It is a scene rich in symbolic meaning and irony, since the Sambo dolls represent abject acceptance of a slave past, while the person selling them actively resists the police force in a clearly rebellious fashion. He must be killed, as must Daniels, for what he exposes about the fissures and dynamics of American racism. The police in both stories are agents for what Ellison and Wright argue is a nation, and national history, founded on resentment. That, perhaps, is a perspective that would permit an escape from the viscount's dilemma, and it is also a salutary lesson for those who lament that revolutions are destructive upheavals largely inspired and conducted by the resentful. What that perspective exposes for us is the not so hidden and far more destructive resentment of the empowered—those who police others, those who found nations by enslaving others, those who lord it over others, and those who persist in thinking that others are others.

III APOLOGY

There are two ways for us to understand the particular division that we found in the genealogy of *ressentiment*. In spatial terms, we can see the distinction between a British sensibility, in which resentment is an individual property, and a Continental one, in which *ressentiment* is collective and the ethical climate more of an era and culture than the sentiment of a person. In temporal terms, we can see a shift from the eighteenth-century focus on how resentment is a promising but dangerous feature of individual morality to a nineteenth-century attention to *ressentiment* as the debased and corrupting mores of an entire society. Both the geographical and the historical readings strike me as plausible, and are, by no means, incommensurable. In either case, though, we need to notice that the division falls between what we can identify as *private* and *public*. In Smith and Butler, resentment is the moral response of a private person, while in Kierkegaard, Nietzsche, and Scheler, *ressentiment* is the moral ethos of the given public. It is certainly the case that Butler and Smith, and others writing in the eighteenth century, saw that this private response was connected to a social good; resentment and indignation are, of course, the sympathetic moral sentiments that inspire justice. But the location of those sentiments was nonetheless in the private person. As we turn now to the concept of apology, I will argue for this particular distinction—that is, private apologies as one kind of practice, public apologies as another. Each kind of apology takes place in and assumes a particular meaning in a different sphere of moral life. Of course, while there are, as Stuart Hampshire puts it, some "principal differences between public morality and the morality of private life," there are also, as he notes, swathes of obvious "overlap."[1] This will likewise prove the case in the practices of private and public apologies.

There are several different typologies one could formulate to distinguish different kinds of apologies from each other. In recent studies, three have risen to prominence. First, in his groundbreaking 1991 study, *Mea Culpa*, Nicholas Tavuchis determined that there were four kinds of apologies, based on the number of people offering and the number receiving the apology: One to One, One to Many, Many to One, Many to Many. Second, in his 2004 book *On Apology*, Aaron Lazare made the division for which I am indebted— between private and public apologies—and he argues that private ones take place between two people without any "external audience," and public ones "between two individuals in the presence of a broader audience." (Lazare then adds that public apologies include the last three categories Tavuchis named). Finally, in his 2008 book *I Was Wrong*, Nick Smith also defined two kinds of apologies, which he designated as "from individuals" and "collective apologies."[2] All three typologies have much of value in them, and they are not necessarily in much disagreement with each other. Consider the difference between Tavuchis and Smith, which I think is primarily a matter of degree and focus. Whereas Tavuchis focused on the speaker and recipient, Smith focused primarily on the speaker. There are advantages to each approach. By focusing solely on the speaker, Smith is able to identify the specific features of apologies and trace what happens when an act that one person performs becomes one that self-defined groups perform. By highlighting the recipients as well as the speakers, Tavuchis implicitly makes the point that an apology differs in form when it is addressed to an individual or to a large, sometimes amorphous group of people.

Lazare strikes me as providing an important distinction, which focuses on *setting*, on the context within which apologies are offered. This distinction between what happens in private and what happens in public is implicit in Smith's and Tavuchis' typologies, but it is nonetheless worth bringing explicitly to the fore. The distinction I am going to make is precisely that one, be-tween *private* and *public*, but I differ in some important ways from Lazare. For

---

1. Stuart Hampshire, "Public and Private Morality," in *Public and Private Morality*, edited by Stuart Hampshire (Cambridge: Cambridge University Press, 1978), pp. 23–53, esp. p. 48.

2. Nicholas Tavuchis, *Mea Culpa: A Sociology of Apology and Reconciliation* (Stanford, CA: Stanford University Press, 1991); Aaron Lazare, *On Apologies* (New York: Oxford University Press, 2004), pp. 38–39; Nick Smith, *I Was Wrong: The Meanings of Apologies* (Cambridge: Cambridge University Press, 2008).

him, that distinction is one of degree, while for me it is one of kind. He argues that private and public apologies "are more alike than different," and my argument is that they are substantially different, serving quite different purposes, assuming different forms, and having distinctly different meanings.[3] And so while he discusses apologies public and private together throughout his book, I will make that distinction clear by treating one kind of apology in one chapter and the other in the next. A private apology, then, usually involves two people, with one offering an apology to the other, while a public apology is offered from any number of people, although usually one speaking for himself or representing her corporate body (family, state, nation, church and so on), and it takes place in a public setting and *is meant for public consumption*.

There are good reasons for making this private–public distinction in the analysis of apologies. I take Tavuchis' point that an address changes in fundamental ways when it is directed to different types of audiences, singular or collective. I choose to focus on setting because that allows us to attend to the difference not only in the size of the audience, but also the implied conditions in which it is offered for a certain kind of consumption. Private apologies are meant to be heard, public ones overheard. There is one audience for a private apology, but at least two or more for a public one. For that reason, then, we can better appreciate what can be considered two distinct discursive strategies in these two quite different kinds of apologies. The public apology is not just a translation of a discourse from one sphere to another, and not just a transplanting of what usually takes place in private into something that replicates it in public. A public apology is an almost completely different performance. It is, I think, precisely for this problematic reason—we expect in public apologies those features we find in private ones—that so many of us are so frequently disappointed by those public apologies that celebrities and politicians make. Apologies in each of these spheres operate by different, unwritten rules, and they are significantly different in their operation, function, presentation, style, and meanings.

Here, I should add a cautionary note that the distinction I draw is not one in which I have full confidence. There is not a firm division between what is private and what is public, either in the cases of apologizing or in general. These are porous boundaries, and that fact is sometimes a boon and sometimes markedly not. In the case of apologies, there are easily many examples one could devise for showing how porous the boundaries are. Consider: if

---

3. Lazare, *On Apologies*, pp. 38–39.

someone steps on my shoe and offers a quick apology, should I focus on the two strangers who are involved in this interaction and consider it a private affair, or on the physical context in which it takes place, outside of some domestic space, and therefore consider it a public affair? Does the person apologizing intend the apology for me as a private person to redress the offense to my private self, or does he express it to the crowd who might have witnessed it and intend it to show his support of public values of bodily inviolability? I could offer other nuanced examples that show the various problems with the distinction—two reconciling lovers on a park bench, say—but it is more important for us to appreciate that the possibility of overlap, the existence of a large threshold between the two spheres, does not render the distinction itself without some value. In our own cultural moment, awash in social media that permit and encourage people to share almost all aspects of their lives, we may use the words of one philosopher and call the division between private and public a "rough and vanishing distinction."[4] Its roughness is not especially problematic, and it is certainly worth making that distinction for those of us who might lament that it does in fact appear to be vanishing. The major tenet of the distinction is, in the end, whether or not the apology is meant for public consumption, whether, in other words, it is an act of *privacy* or an act of *publicity*.

I

An implicit point that Kierkegaard, Nietzsche, and Scheler presuppose is that public morals produce private morality, that a society that is fundamentally based on *ressentiment* will create citizens who are plagued in their private relationships by it. Another understated implication in the Continental, nineteenth-century conception of *ressentiment* is that cultures *become* infested with the sentiment. For Kierkegaard, a pre–French Revolutionary order, for Nietzsche, a pre-Christian, for Scheler, a pre-European humanist one, were all free of *ressentiment*; the emergence and spread of a certain set of conditions and ideas caused the social orders to fall into it. And the assumption—unstated in all but Nietzsche, who states it with considerable relish—is that those social orders can also emerge from *ressentiment*. These two points—cultures are productive of private values, and cultures undergo

---

4. J. L. Austin, *How to Do Things with Words*, edited by J. O. Urmson and Marina Sbisà (2nd ed.; Oxford: Oxford University Press, 1975), p. 35.

transitions—converge to form a good place for us to start our exploration of apology. The two cases I will examine here are not national cultures, indeed not nations at all in any meaningful sense, but rather defined by their geographical relationship to another social order. The first is the American West, the second East Germany.

In American lore, the West of gunslingers and vigilantes is explicitly defined against the eastern American establishment, and its rules of order, decorum, and sense of justice are posed against that establishment. Texts that deal with the interaction of the East and West in the American nineteenth century reveal precisely the ways that the order of the West has its own logic and mores, which the interloper from the East either accepts and adopts or rejects and leaves. Owen Wister's 1902 novel *The Virginian*, for instance, shows us how one person, the Virginian, has already adopted the values of the vigilante justice when he lives in Wyoming, and then reveals the ways that Molly Wood, called "the New England girl," comes to accept them as she accepts the Virginian for her husband.[5] The West, then, is part of a nation, but a society apart. Likewise, East Germany is cast as distinct from West Germany, divided by the Allies and then formed into distinct societies, and part of an international order in the Communist bloc. While literally a nation by virtue of its state apparatus, its status as a "nation" is compromised by its enduring history with the old nation against which it defines itself and its political affiliation with the new empire to which it putatively belongs.

In these cases, I think it makes more sense to speak of a social order rather than a culture, but it is, nonetheless, a social order that operates very much like a culture in many ways, and especially in the ways it defines what is private and what public in the society, and what relationship between private and public acts can obtain in it. The two works that can help lead us into the discussion of apology to which this final section of this study is devoted are Clint Eastwood's *Unforgiven* (1992) and Florian Henckel von Donnersmarck's *The Lives of Others* (2006). Each of these films—one an American western, the other a German eastern—critically reveals just what social texts underwrite a particular order, and, given our interest, what those social texts reveal about the interactions possible for apologizing and forgiving, for private and public actions.

---

5. Owen Wister, *The Virginian: A Horseman of the Plains* (1902; New York: Oxford University Press, 1998), pp. 283–84.

II

The plot of *Unforgiven* follows the intersection of two major crimes: the first creates the conditions for the second, and the second produces the vengeance that ends the film. The first crime is a crime against Delilah, the prostitute in Big Whiskey, Wyoming, whose face is slashed by Quick Mike when she laughs at his small penis. We are shown two options for justice for this crime. The sheriff, Little Bill, sees it as a crime against property, while the prostitutes see it as a crime against human dignity. For the sheriff, justice is fulfilled through economic compensation. He orders Quick Mike (and his accomplice Davey) to give a string of horses to Skinny, the owner of the saloon where the prostitutes work, to compensate *him* for the loss of Delilah's earning power. (The meaning of crimes against women in the Old West is one of the several large and important questions the movie raises that I cannot treat here, given our focus.) The prostitutes see this as a crime, not against property, but against their dignity. They organize as a union, pool their money to finance a substantial reward, and demand nothing less than the life of the wrongdoers. The incentive of the reward draws vigilantes to Big Whiskey. In an effort to maintain control of his town and to send a message to the other hired guns, the sheriff beats up one of them, English Bob.

The second crime follows when the main group of three hired guns arrives in Big Whiskey. William Munny, a gunfighter who is failing at life as a widowed father and farmer, arrives with his friend Ned Logan, and the young gunslinger who lured them into the game, the Schofield Kid. After they ingloriously and unheroically kill Quick Mike and Davey—one is killed in an outhouse—the sheriff tortures and kills Ned, and then displays his desecrated corpse in front of the saloon. (Another question the movie poses in having the African American Ned tortured and then his corpse brazenly displayed concerns the relationship of institutional to vigilante policing, especially in terms of the history of lynching, where the two were frequently complicit.) This second crime drives Munny to Homeric vengeance as he ends the film by killing six men, including the sheriff, to avenge the murder of his friend. The final exchange in the film returns us to the question that began the movie about what kind of punishment ought to be meted out for particular kinds of crimes, in other words, the question of desert. When the injured sheriff reaches for his gun, he complains to Munny: "I don't deserve to die like this . . . I was building a house." Munny's response, as he shoots and kills the sheriff—"Deserve's got nothing to do with it"—seems either an indictment of a particular kind of justice or an existential plea about the complete absence of it in human life.

As numerous commentators have pointed out, the film raises crucial questions about the nature of desert, punishment, and justice. I would like to focus here on two interpretations in particular and see how each one reads this film as a commentary on justice and forgiveness.

Peter French claims that the theme of *Unforgiven* is the "matter of proportionality in punishment." Looking at the two options for justice the movie proposes for the crime of mutilating Delilah, compensation and retribution, French notes that the prostitutes reject the crime as "an issue of tort" and see it as a "criminal matter." What Delilah deserves is justice, and what Quick Mike deserves is punishment more fit for his crime, which is not a crime against property. In terms of the second crime, too, French sees it not as a matter of what the sheriff might deserve—"Desert is not an issue," he writes—but rather about proportionality. The "whole movie might be described as about fit," he concludes. It is worth noting the distinction French makes between these two concepts. Desert is the condition of the person in question; if he is a wrongdoer, he deserves punishment, if innocent not. To "deserve something," for French, is to merit it, to warrant it, to be entitled to it, be worthy of it, rate it, have earned it, and have it coming. And this is the case for both reward and punishment. Fitness is a condition of the punishment, the proportionate act of retribution appropriate for the particular wrong. Both are contested, perhaps even defeasible, concepts, and French sees them as defined and contested through the "moral dialogue of the community."[6]

For French, *Unforgiven*, a film about fitness, shows us how the punishment must fit the crime. The sheriff's punishing Quick Mike with a fine did not fit the first crime, while Munny's killing six people in the final shootout in the saloon did fit the second. French perspicaciously notes how Munny is cast as effectively two different characters. In the first, as "Munny the assassin," he is a clumsy and inept failure whose actions in that role "cannot be virtuous," while in the second, as "Munny the avenger of Ned," he is filled with "grace" and becomes a model of what French calls "virtuous vengeance." Realizing that some could think the killing of six people for the murder of one might seem "exorbitant," French notes that we need to consider that some of the six killed by Munny "probably participated in some measure in the torture of

---

6. Peter A. French, *The Virtues of Vengeance* (Lawrence: University Press of Kansas, 2001), pp. 39, 116, 205–206, 229.

Ned," and that the others followed the sheriff's order to kill Munny and did fire on him. In other words, Munny killed some in vengeance for what they did, some for their complicity, and some in self-defense. That, writes French, "may be what makes the six corpses in the saloon a morally satisfying act of vengeance despite the apparent excess."[7]

French concludes by taking up the question of desert as it is raised in the final exchange between the sheriff and Munny. French reads Munny's final words as a statement that affirms desert—not one that dismisses it, and perhaps dismisses justice too, in an expression of existential angst. In other words, Munny's final words mean that there is "no question" that the sheriff *deserves* what he is going to get. On this point, French is firm. "Any other reading of 'Deserve's got nothing to do with it' introduces a doubt about the satisfaction of both the communication and the desert conditions, conditions Munny clearly believes are satisfied as he takes revenge. Desert is crucial to perhaps the only morally legitimate act of vengeance Munny did, or ever will, commit." The sheriff deserves the fit punishment Munny metes out to him in a righteous, "morally legitimate," and indeed "virtuous vengeance." Justice is served in this movie, then, when the authorized agent of policing is punished for his failures by the lone vigilante, who is emblematic of what French calls "the virtues of vengeance." What, then, about forgiveness in *Unforgiven*? For French, this is a film entirely about retribution, and the title of this film serves primarily to remind "us that the characters will not and cannot be forgiven."[8] In other words, "unforgiven" is not a state of gracelessness, but a condition of desert.

Like French, Austin Sarat also sees *Unforgiven* as a "classic of the revenge genre," but for him it is one that "complicates the story" of what the revenge is supposed to accomplish. Revenge is very much about the past: something in the past motivates it and is somehow put to rest when the proper punishment is inflicted. It is, then, about memory, or, as Sarat puts it, "commemoration." Vengeance, writes Sarat, "re-enacts the past" and represents the place where "the present speaks to the future through acts of commemoration." In Eastwood's movie, though, "commemoration is not celebration." For one

---

7. French, *The Virtues of Vengeance*, pp. 39, 40, 116, 39, 116, 40. French also discusses the film throughout his earlier book, *Cowboy Metaphysics: Ethics and Death in Westerns* (Lanham, MD: Rowman & Littlefield Publishers, 1997).

8. French, *The Virtues of Vengeance*, pp. 117, 39: "Unless Munny's final words to the sheriff are read as claiming that there can be no question as to desert, they would seem to negate somewhat his communicating the appropriate message of vengeance" (117).

thing, the movie troubles just what memory means when there are various versions of the past. Sarat focuses in particular on two, opposing forms of remembering that Nietzsche called "monumental" and "critical." Two of the characters in the film live in and reproduce what Sarat describes as a "mythic world." The Schofield Kid draws on his uncle's memories of relentlessly heroic acts of violence in his own aspirations to be part of the world his uncle had delivered him. W. W. Beauchamp, a dime novelist and hired writer, likewise operates to create myths of the Old West by writing fabricated texts of heroism that "work to sustain a culture of vengeful violence by eliding the grim realities that vengeful violence produces." Even more than the Schofield Kid, Beauchamp operates in the mode of "monumental history," since he makes public those memories that the Kid uses in his private fantasies.[9]

Munny is the representative of "critical history," the kind of history Nietzsche describes as bringing the past "to the bar of judgment, interrogat[ing] it remorselessly, and finally condemn[ing] it." Haunted by the memories of the people he killed, Munny anxiously replays the acts of violence he inflicted, and is subject to grim fantasies of the afterlife of their corpses. His memory, as Sarat notes, "is anything but monumental, anything but heroic." At the end of the film, Munny responds to the sheriff's taunt by accepting that he, Munny, is indeed a killer of the innocent. Sarat sees this final moment as an indictment of the kind of vengeance that French sees as virtuous. "Even as he embraces a vengeful violence Munny insists on debunking as heroic pretensions, linking revenge to killing 'women,' 'children,' and 'everything that walks or crawls.'"[10] What was celebrated by the Kid's uncle in private, and by Beauchamp in public, is revealed to be not only a fabrication, but indeed a fabrication that hides the murderousness that is seemingly more important for the vigilante than the wild justice that vengeance purports to accomplish.

What animates the revenge genre, and what gives vengeance an acceptable patina, is the notion of desert. Whether or not one believes that those who punish should be authorized state agents or vigilantes, formal or informal justice depends on the notion that those who are punished deserve it. We saw that what Sarat calls "the signature line of the film" can be read in two distinct

9. Austin Sarat, "When Memory Speaks: Remembrance and Revenge in *Unforgiven*," in *Breaking the Cycles of Hatred: Memory, Law, and Repair*, edited by Martha Minow (Princeton, NJ: Princeton University Press, 2002), pp. 236–59, esp. pp. 241, 245, 247.

10. Friedrich Nietzsche, *The Use and Abuse of History*, translated by Adrian Collins (Indianapolis: Bobbs-Merrill, 1949), p. 20; Sarat, "When Memory Speaks," pp. 252, 253.

ways. French argues that Munny's statement—"Deserve's got nothing to do with it"—is an affirmative commentary on the fact that the sheriff does deserve what he is going to get. Sarat disagrees, as does William Ian Miller, who argues that Munny's "self-doubts about his life of violence, the fact that no one ever brought him to justice for his past deeds, makes him think the delivery of justice [is] purely random, a matter of good or bad luck." Desert, in other words, has nothing to do with life. Sarat points to another scene in which the Schofield Kid responds with horror to his first (and now final) act of killing. To justify what he did, the Kid mutters: "Yeah, well, I guess they had it coming." Munny's response challenges the very notion of desert: "We all have it coming, Kid." By shifting from the notion of crime (he deserved to be punished) to the concept of death (we all have that coming), Munny mutes the question of justice in the face of what to him is the more critical question of finality.[11] Desert becomes a matter of moral luck in a perhaps absurd world.

What, then, does "forgiveness" mean in this bleak vision of a social order determined more by death than desert? We saw that, for French, to be unforgiven was a condition of desert; those who deserved to be punished *ought* not to be forgiven, and the act of vengeance against them is justified. What happens to forgiveness when the question of desert is absent? For Sarat, it would seem that everything is unforgiven: "In this film, a past of purposeless violence is unforgiven. Injuries unredressed are unforgiven. But doing vengeance violently is also unforgiven." Sarat had focused on two points especially: first, vengeance is a commemorative redressing of past wrongs and, second, stories of the past can be constructed monumentally or critically. In a world in which desert is random, it is impossible to say that an act of vengeance is righteous and commemorates a past wrong virtuously. Vengeance, for Sarat, is shown to be both necessary but awful, since acts motivated by it both "sanctify but also dishonor those in whose names vengeance is taken as well as those who take revenge." What a critical history does to a monumental one is render our motivations suspect. What it also does is render questionable what options

---

11. Sarat, "When Memory Speaks," p. 250; William Miller, "Clint Eastwood and Equity: The Virtues of Revenge and the Shortcomings of Law in Popular Culture," in *Law and the Domains of Culture*, edited by Austin Sarat and Thomas Kearns (Ann Arbor: University of Michigan Press, 1998), pp. 161–202, esp. p. 195; Sarat, "When Memory Speaks," p. 249. There is another scene in the film when Munny talks explicitly about desert, as he tells Ned about another past murder: "Ned, you remember that drover I shot through the mouth and his teeth came out the back of his head? I think about him now and again. He didn't do anything to deserve to get shot." This comment suggests that there are some circumstances where it is possible to discern desert, perhaps leavening somewhat Munny's otherwise dismal description of a world without justice or meaning.

we have for both recollecting the past and redressing it. "While we are called on to remember unforgivable injury," Sarat argues, "certain kinds of remembering and certain kinds of action, too, may be unforgivable."[12]

Sarat does not say what the film suggests about the kinds of actions that would not be unforgivable, and that is largely, I think, because the film does not offer an example of those options. The sheriff is corrupt, misunderstands justice, and deals in his own form of disproportionate punishment, and so the formal mechanisms of justice are shown to be part of the problem, and not the solution, to social problems in this society. For French, that representation of the failures of formal policing and justice opens the door to vengeful vigilantes as virtuous punishers. Sarat disagrees, and suggests that the film indicts them too. In French's reading, justice is possible because desert is obvious, while in Sarat's it would appear that justice is on some distant horizon and not realized, primarily because we do not have a means of telling the stories we need to tell in order to give substance that is meaningful (but not mythical) to explain our actions and motivations.

There is one final point I would like to address about these readings of this film. It has to do with what both Sarat and French do with its title. When he was working on the original screenplay, the writer David Webb Peoples had employed the working titles *The Cut-Whore Killings* and *The William Munny Killings*; and it was optioned to Eastwood—fifteen years before the film was finally produced—under one of those titles (accounts differ as to which). At some point, as one biographer of Eastwood put it, the script would "quietly undergo a title change to *Unforgiven*," before it was announced as Eastwood's next film in 1991 trade publications.[13] How that change was made, or by whom, is, for me, not that important; what is important is that the title constitutes part of the film's overall message. The film's final title is significant because it poignantly establishes the setting for the very questions the film raises about the nature of justice and equity and desert. What is striking, though, is that the commentators seem intent on altering the term. French stays truer to the title, and he simply notes that the point Eastwood is making is that these are crimes that "will not and cannot be forgiven." For Sarat, it is not a matter

12. Sarat, "When Memory Speaks," pp. 242, 254, 242.

13. See Patrick McGilligan, *Clint: The Life and the Legend* (London: Harper-Collins, 1999), p. 467; and Tim Grierson, "FilmCraft Screenwriting: Interview with David Webb Peoples," at http://masteringfilm.com/filmcraft-screenwriting-interview-with-david-webb-peoples/; McGilligan, *Clint*, p. 462. For the fascinating backstory about how the screenplay came into Eastwood's hands through his then-love interest Megan Rose, a story analyst at Warner, who also played a key role in the evolution of the script, see McGilligan, *Clint*, pp. 462 ff.

of will, but rather that both the original crimes and the vengeful responses to them are in some unstated prima facie way "unforgivable." "Unforgiven," it seems to me, does not suggest so much a determination (it will not be forgiven, it cannot be forgiven) as it describes a condition.

Like purgatory, to be unforgiven is to be in a situation of limbo and waiting. And, in a film that complicates the representation of resolution itself, whether the issue is justice, vengeance, or the absurdity of life, that condition of waiting for resolution strikes the right note. To be unforgiven is to be guilty of something, but expectant too. At one point in the movie, there is a wonderful riposte that the sheriff, Little Bill, offers to someone who objects that he has beaten an "innocent" man: "Innocent? Innocent of what?" As Miller astutely notes, this humorous comment reminds us that in the genre of revenge films innocence is "a true moral and social condition, not a legal conclusion." No one is presumed innocent. And, in a world where no one is presumed innocent, all are unforgiven.[14]

III

The plot of *The Lives of Others* dwells on what the film considers most criminal in a state, and that is the evisceration of the concept of the private. The movie is about a Stasi officer's work in spying on a suspected playwright's private life, and reveals how the Stasi officer goes from being a dispassionate state functionary who performs the work he does in idealistic pursuit of a superior Socialist order to becoming a compassionate rebel against a state that requires an apparatus that makes it impossible for people to have privacy. The Stasi officer, Gerd Wiesler (code name HGW XX/7), bugs the apartment of the playwright, Georg Dreyman, and his actress lover, Christa-Maria Sieland, and spends the rest of the film as an intrusive presence in their private lives. Wiesler is not the one who selects his victims; the Minister of Culture, Bruno Hempf, orders it on the pretense of questioning Dreyman's loyalty to the party, but in reality because he, Hempf, is sexually attracted to Sieland. Over the course of his surveillance, Wiesler begins to change. He discovers Hempf's ploy, begins to suspect that the social order he serves is not as sound as he believed, nor

---

14. Miller, "Clint Eastwood and Equity," p. 179. Miller also makes a profoundly insightful point about the near impossibility of forgiveness in the saga world (and revenge cultures more generally): "such a model does not allow for easy forgiveness of wrongs or harms; in fact, it makes it conceptually incoherent. I can forgive what you owe me, but not what I owe you, and I owe you for what you have done to and for me. To forgive is thus to act like a coward, or a welsher" (166).

motivated by the same exalted principles in which he believes. He also tearfully listens to a piece of music that Dreyman plays, "Sonata for a Good Man." After he plays the sonata, Dreyman asks Sieland, "Can anyone who has heard this music, I mean truly heard it, really be a bad person?"

Following the suicide of his blacklisted friend, the theater director Albert Jerska, who gave him the sheet music for "Sonata for a Good Man," Dreyman begins his active resistance to the state. Using a typewriter that cannot be traced back to him, Dreyman begins composing an article that exposes the way the party hides the high suicide rates of East Germany. The article is published in West Germany, and immediately places Dreyman under suspicion. Wiesler now operates fully to save Dreyman rather than indict him. In the climactic moment in the film, he rushes to the apartment to remove the typewriter from its hiding place under the floorboards, and does so. Sieland, who has given the incriminating information to the Stasi about the hiding place of the typewriter, does not know it has been removed, and rushes out of the apartment to throw herself into the path of a truck. As she lies dying, Wiesler furtively speaks to her first, and then Dreyman, who had initially suspected her of being the informant against him, and now believes her to have removed the typewriter, apologizes to her. Suspected of being the agent who foiled the plot, Wiesler is then exiled to a basement office with the job of steaming open letters. In the denouement of the film, five years later, Wiesler hears that the Berlin Wall has fallen, and walks out of the dreary basement to which he had been confined. Dreyman, meanwhile, reads the Stasi file on himself, and discovers that Wiesler, and not Sieland, had saved him. The film ends, two years after the fall of the Wall, with a scene in which Wiesler buys a book by Dreyman, entitled *Sonata for a Good Man*, and gratefully dedicated to HGW XX/7.

Von Donnersmarck's film is, as the title indicates, about the lives of others, about how to define self and otherness, in a sphere in which privacy is so compromised. The film reveals how each site of private life is affected by a totalitarian state. Dreyman's apartment, like so many others in East Germany, is bugged. There is a scene in which the Stasi agent threatens Dreyman's neighbor not to reveal what she sees when they are setting up surveillance equipment; fearful of losing her freedom and meager state-granted rights, she is silent and thereby fails to act as a true neighbor. This is a state in which there is no sanctity in places—private residences, neighborhoods—and therefore no sanctity in personal relationships, from the romantic to the neighborly.

What, then, does the movie say about the relationship between private and public? It is worth noting that the surveillance of Dreyman is called

"Operation Lazlo," in a nod, I think, to *Casablanca*, where Ingrid Bergman's character has to choose between her original love, Rick Blaine, and her duty to her husband, Victor Laszlo, which is cast in the movie as a choice between private desire (her love) and public duty (Laszlo's political work to defeat the Nazis). *Casablanca* has it both ways, of course, since she chooses Rick, who then sends her off to Laszlo. The important point is that choices are permitted; one can give up private wishes to fulfill more important public goals. In *The Lives of Others*, though, choice, like privacy, is largely an illusion.

In such a social order, the film asks, where physical spaces are so compromised, what emotional space is there for genuine expression, whether of love or of political defiance? Without such space, the film suggests, in a stifling social order in which nothing is private, there can be only alienation and anomie. And suicide, it would appear, becomes the only possible expression of such anomie. Shunned by his friends because he is blacklisted, Jerska kills himself; ashamed of herself for betraying her lover, Sieland does the same.

So, what, then, does *The Lives of Others* have to say about forgiveness? We saw that *Unforgiven* represented a social order in which all are unforgiven because everyone has some kind of existential guilt ("Innocent of what?") and the society itself seems arbitrary in its justice ("Deserve's got nothing to do with it"). *The Lives of Others* raises the same questions about forgiveness, and particularly the possibility of it in what has come to be called "transitional justice," that is, the forms of resolution possible in societies transitioning from one political order to another. Some forms that nations have adopted in pursuing transitional justice are political trials, truth and reconciliation commissions, and blanket amnesties.

In what was formerly East Germany, the problem was how to reach some kind of resolution in a nation that had what Tina Rosenberg describes as the most extensive spy organization in world history, and a population that constituted "the most spied-upon people who ever lived." After reunification, what was now one Germany pursued what we can identify as three major strategies. The first was *punishment*, as the president of East Germany (Honecker) and the head of the Stasi (Mielke) were both put on trial, as were border guards who had shot fleeing fugitives at the Berlin Wall. And like the Czech Republic, Albania, and Bulgaria, Germany passed *lustrace* laws that prohibited former Communists from holding significant political posts. The second strategy was *exposure*, as the Bundestag formed an inquiry commission to hold public hearings. In this, Germany followed the course of other nations that also formed "truth commissions," to collect evidence of what crimes the whole state had committed. The third was *remediation*. Numerous nonstate agencies created spaces for informal mediation sessions between those who spied and those spied upon to meet and talk. The Insider's Committee for Illumination was formed to facilitate meetings in which former Stasi officers could "admit their abuses and talk about the harm they had done" to their victims. These sessions soon migrated and transformed into media spectacles, like the television show *My Friend the Stasi Informer*, in which a former Stasi agent publicly apologized to his victim. German television soon produced other episodes that were broadcast from the highly symbolic place at the former Berlin Wall known as Checkpoint Charlie in which *Opfer* and *Täter*—victims and victimizers—went through a ritual of something like penitence and reconciliation.[15] Here, then, was a society that simultaneously pursued retribution, revelation, and remorse.

The film shows us a world in which the injustices of the past are not redressed through punishment, at least not obviously. The former minister of culture is thriving in the post-fall world, while Wiesler, as a mailman, is clearly not. Appropriately, I suppose, he is now delivering the mail that he used to steam open, but the dreariness of the scene and his trudging gait reveal that it is a chore. It could, of course, be the director's wish to contrast his downcast look at his current job with the sunniness that the dedication of the book will bring to his face. But, it is clear nonetheless that those who manipulated the system have not suffered by it. It would appear, then, that the film endorses the other two forms of reconciliation. While it is not stated what Dreyman's book is about, it would seem to be a book that reveals who is and, by implication, who is not a "good man." The fact that he wrote it after he read the files the Stasi compiled on him also suggests that it will be an exposé. Moreover, the dedication would seem to imply an act of forgiveness. Unlike the tortured, televised broadcasts on German television of forced rituals of apology and forgiveness, this novel's dedication seems a genuine act of acceptance and reconciliation. *The Lives of Others*, then, favors revelation and forgiveness as the modes for recreating a society in which privacy matters, and personal relationships can presumably thrive. The fact that the book is just being published, and the exposure not yet complete, and the fact that Dreyman and Wiesler do not meet, nor do we see any evidence of newly refreshed romances or neighborly camaraderie, also suggest that such flourishing is still in the future.

---

15. Tina Rosenberg, *The Haunted Land: Facing Europe's Ghosts After Communism* (New York: Random House, 1995), pp. 289, 374, 385–93.

IV

Both these films deal more with forgiveness than with apology, which is very much in keeping with film history, in which apology is generally treated with evident discomfort. It is worth noting that one of the more famous scenes of apology in contemporary cinema is Tom Hanks' apology to a volleyball in the 2000 film *Castaway* (it is a moving scene, but we must wonder what it tells us about how we think about apologizing, given the recipient of the apology and the near absence of reason for it). In more conventional filmic representations, apology is presented as a symptom either of failed strength (John Wayne's signature line in the 1949 film *She Wore a Yellow Ribbon* is "Never apologize. . . . It's a sign of weakness") or of insufficient love (the signature line of the 1970 film *Love Story* is "Love means never having to say you're sorry"). (Perhaps, one is tempted to say, but being loved certainly does!) *Unforgiven* follows this pattern of rendering the act of apologizing as something foreign to its social order.

In *Unforgiven*, the word *sorry* occurs three times (and *apologize* appears once, in the Beauchamp book that the sheriff reads aloud). But the film departs from the original script in one usage of *sorry* in a telling way. In the original script, Little Sue tells Munny that the sheriff "didn't mean to kill" Ned, and "he said he was sorry an' all." That scene does not appear in the film. The other use of *sorry* to appear in the film, that was not in the original script, was one in which Munny apologizes after calling his horse a "no good pig-fucking whore." "Sorry old horse," he ends. Miller acutely notes that this scene enhances the film's play with the pun on *whores* and *horses* (one of the prostitutes in Big Whiskey comments: "we ain't nothing but whores, but, by God, we ain't horses").[16] It also perhaps echoes another famous Eastwood scene in *The Good, the Bad, and the Ugly*, when Eastwood's character demands that the villains "apologize to my mule" before shooting four of them dead when they refuse. Horses and mules get what humans do not. In a western called *Unforgiven*, a movie about precisely the state in which the absence of remorse seems endemic, apology seems an inconceivable gesture.

We cannot say the same of *The Lives of Others*, where there is, as we have seen, one important scene of apologizing in which Dreyman apologizes to

---

16. David Webb Peoples, "The William Munny Killings" (production draft, April 23, 1984), at http://www.dailyscript.com/scripts/unforgiven.html; "Unforgiven: A Transcript," at http://www.clinteastwood.net/filmography/unforgiven/script/unforgivenscript.txt. Hereafter all passages from the original script will be taken from this text. Miller, "Clint Eastwood and Equity," p. 185, n. 26.

Sieland as she lays dying in the street. It would appear that he is apologizing for thinking that she had betrayed him, which she had. In other words, what is most significant about this apology is that it is given to someone undeserving of it (it is an inapt apology). In a more conventional scenario, we would expect that when we have an inapt apology extended to the wrong person, the narrative will eventually reveal to the person who apologized the identity of the right person, in the same way that someone who rewards or expresses gratitude to the wrong person will eventually discover her or his mistake and correct it. *The Lives of Others* plays with our expectation. There is a moment of revelation, of course, when Dreyman discovers that Wiesler did the good deed he thought Sieland had performed. What reveals to Dreyman that Wiesler had saved him is the red fingerprint on the Stasi files in ink that he recognizes as coming from his typewriter. The irony, of course, is that the typewriter that was sought in order to prove Dreyman an enemy of the state turns out to prove that Wiesler is a "good man." That discovery leads Dreyman to see that his apology to Sieland was misplaced, but *not* to think that Wiesler should have been the one to receive it.

Instead, what that revelation does is inspire Dreyman to write a book and dedicate it to Wiesler. I think we can see those two gestures—when Dreyman apologizes to Sieland and when Dreyman dedicates his book to Wiesler—as reflecting on each other. One is a misplaced apology, and the other what I have suggested we can think of as an indirect act of forgiveness. The two characters (Sieland and Wiesler) are deeply connected. Each of them, for instance, responds to the recognition of the harm they have done through a suicide of sorts—Sieland literally by throwing herself into traffic to escape her coercion, Wiesler politically by defying his. And so we are meant to understand that Dreyman can forgive Wiesler only when he discovers that he was mistaken in apologizing to Sieland. She did not deserve his apology, but Wiesler does deserve his forgiveness. We are also meant to understand a larger social transition, from communist to democratic, and that too is tied to a transition from resentment to forgiveness. Like other societies undergoing regime changes, and employing the mechanisms of transitional justice, forgiveness proved to be a strategy and sentiment deemed essential to marking the new social order.

What, then, might *The Lives of Others* be saying by drawing our attention to this connection between Sieland and Wiesler, between the recipient of an undeserved apology and a deserved forgiveness? It seems to me that the film is making a bold statement about personal responsibility. Even in the state with the most thorough spying apparatus in the history of the world, with the most coercive policing structures and informal modes of controlling its citizens, there is room for moral choice; and the supreme value of moral choice this film endorses is right in its title—how we think about other people's lives. In other words, we can think of this movie as Kantian, with its focus on how we can think of others' lives as *means* or *ends*, as things we can betray for our own profit or safety or things we treat as inviolate. Sieland is obviously not the most culpable character in the film, but we are nonetheless meant to indict her choices because she has chosen to harm another person, however much she might be coerced into doing so. Wiesler, who also had much to lose, made choices that we are meant to admire because he chose to reject the state and its values in order to protect the integrity of "the lives of others."

This is a film that we can say endorses a certain kind of apology and forgiveness, and one that, I think, distinguishes that apology–forgiveness dynamic from the specious ones that German television was broadcasting. The question for us is: how does the film do that? The answer, I think, is threefold, and at three levels: first, it shows that apologizing requires assuming the place of the offended (we can call this the empathic level); what Wiesler demonstrates by weeping at the playing of the sonata is that he can feel, and what he reveals through his saving Dreyman is that he can feel what another feels. He is empathic. Second, it shows us that apologizing can be most sincere and personal when it is sometimes hidden (the personal level); if we think of Wiesler's actions, recorded in the Stasi file, and in his actions in saving Dreyman, as apologies (or, more properly, apologetic acts of redemption), then we see how he performs these in private and hidden places. Apologies, this movie seems to suggest, can be more effective when they are discovered belatedly than when they are televised farcically. Finally, it shows us that the apology can make sense only when it is part of the specific cultural milieu in which it takes place (the social level). I will return to this point in the next section.

The Lives of Others, then, complicates the idea of forgiveness and apology. The dedication to *Sonata for a Good Man* seems to constitute an act of forgiveness, but one that is complicated for several reasons. First, it is a dedication, and one given in gratitude, not forgiveness; second, it is not given directly or privately to the person; and third, the dedication is addressed to the spy's code name, not the actual name of the individual, which Dreyman has indeed discovered. So, it might appear highly unorthodox, since it is a gesture of gratitude, a public and not a private one, and given to an office and not a person (and, moreover, an office that no longer exists). And yet in the terms the film establishes, this is indeed an act of forgiveness. And it is one, apparently, that is given without a typical apology inspiring it. The film complicates apology by showing us an inapt apology (given to a person undeserving of it) and, perhaps, suggesting that a Stasi file might constitute an act of apology if it is read as revealing what a "good man" had done to guard privacy in a totalitarian state. The two texts—Stasi file and novel—are clearly in a dialectical relationship with each other. One inspires the other—the Stasi file moves Dreyman to publish his novel—in the same way apology inspires forgiveness. What is also worth noting is the play between private and public in the connections the film makes among all these gestures and acts. Dreyman's apology to Sieland is intimately private, Wiesler's Stasi file is a semiprivate bureaucratic document that becomes public when the regime falls, and Wiesler's dedication-forgiveness of Wiesler occurs in a public sphere, literally a *publishing* event.

The two films, then, offer different representations of the place apology and forgiveness can occupy in those societies. In the American western, there is no apology, and its occupants seem to occupy a liminal place that is described as "unforgiven." In the German eastern, communications are thwarted and need to take covert forms, and this sometimes leads to mistakes (apologies given to the undeserving) or require deciphering (a file might be an apology, a dedication might be forgiveness), but there nonetheless appears to be a place and a need for these moral acts that express and reveal a change of heart in those who formerly oppressed and those who were formerly oppressed. A society that had been mercilessly secretive, the film suggests, requires new mores and gestures to make a meaningful transition to a society that is open. The two films offer us very different visions of quite distinct social orders. What the two movies share, though, is a commitment to revealing what scripts underwrite each kind of society—what are the texts that operate to produce a social order in which these moral acts may or may not be resonant. It is, finally, to what we can call the social scripts that each film represents that we can now turn.

V

The root word for *apologia*, from which we derive our contemporary term *apology*, is *apologus*, which means a story or narrative or fable. In our modern usage, apologies tend to produce concise narrative accounts that reveal the incidents for which the apology is being offered. Most commentators focus in particular on what that narrative can become if it in any way exceeds its minimal purpose. Too much detail explaining the context can strike some as an excuse rather than apology, too little as an insufficient understanding of just what event has offended or the depth of the offense. The point I would like to address is somewhat different. Apologies are indeed accounts, stories, but they, like all other stories, can be understood only within a social context that permits them to bear the meanings they have. I want to suggest that in particular kinds of societies, represented here by the world Munny occupies in *Unforgiven*, there is no place for apology because the world itself is organized around concepts and terms antagonistic to it. This is a world of strict retribution, punishment, vengeance, and violence. Apology is premised on the idea that we have some determination in our actions; we are remorseful at having done what we wished we hadn't or not having done what we wished we had. If we had no choice or will or capacity, we could not be apologetic. But the world of *Unforgiven*, as we saw, is in some way determined by an absurdist sense of moral luck rather than a sense of free will or choice. One of the last lines in the movie is Munny's statement to Beauchamp, "I've always been lucky when it comes to killing folks." Beauchamp is hoping to hear about rational strategy—with what kind of aim and in what order should one shoot multiple victims—but what he gets instead is a statement of randomness.

In other societies, there are places for apology, even under almost equivalent conditions of retribution, punishment, vindictiveness, and violence. The world of *The Lives of Others* represents that kind of society, in which pockets of morally autonomous individuals can indeed effect a change in the agents of that society, and then a transformation in the entire political order of that society. Here, we see a vision of a world in which, even under the most oppressive conditions and limitations on freedoms of thought and expression, one may still possess free will and choice. Dreyman makes a choice to resist the state by expressing how its stifling culture is producing suicidal anomie, and Wiesler chooses to resist the state in order to protect Dreyman's right to that freedom of thought and expression. It is telling that Dreyman apologizes to Sieland for having ill thoughts about her betraying him. In other words, he apologizes because he thinks he underestimated how she acted on her free will and was instead coerced to betray him. In a state that has the power to stall professional and college careers, the choice to resist is the choice to seek truth and virtue rather than advancement. It is the choice Dreyman and Wiesler make, and the one Sieland does not. The social order of *The Lives of Others*, then, provides hard but nonetheless real opportunities for the expression of moral responses to injury; the coded but understood acts of apology and forgiveness are the movements of this society's sonata.

Each film also reveals to us the social scripts that promote that social order, that produce the ethos that leads to the impossibility or possibility of a discursive place for acts of apology or forgiveness.

In *Unforgiven*, Beauchamp, the English writer who is the mythologist of the "western," is the author of the primary social script. Sarat is right to note that Beauchamp and the Schofield Kid both represent Nietzsche's "monumental history." It is, however, important to note the distinct roles they play in producing and reproducing that history. The Kid draws on familial tales, that is, personal narratives that his uncle has told him that aggrandize violence. He reproduces that history by being sufficiently inspired by the familial narratives to act on them and seek out opportunities for establishing himself as the hero of future ones. He takes what is private and acts on it in public. Beauchamp, on the other hand, produces for public consumption precisely those kinds of large narratives that indeed form sensibilities like the uncle's. In other words, the Kid, as his name implies, is a product of a larger order, and Beauchamp, as his name suggests, is the one who champions that social order. His published narratives are not the same, and do not exert the same limited force, as the Kid's. They are indeed monumental because they are foundational. It is texts like his that give birth to boys who want to grow up and be like the Kid.

Beauchamp, then, is the one who produces the social scripts that promote the world of *Unforgiven*, and therefore the person whose mythic stories are the ones that the "critical" history contests. For that reason, critics are right to see the deep significance of Munny's rejection of Beauchamp at the end of the movie. As Beauchamp advances with the intent to tell a heroic version of Munny's story, Munny threatens and then dismisses him. In some ways, this is the sign of the victory of the critical over the monumental history of the West. What Beauchamp wants to make mythic, Munny casts as simple luck—not justice, not desert, not heroic. Sarat makes a fine point in noting that Munny's final threat to Beauchamp is "an ill-disguised threat to kill the author, the myth-maker, before he can ply his death-doing, violence-inducing trade again." But, likewise, I think Miller makes an equally fine point in noting that Beauchamp represents "a stand-in for Clint Eastwood the director. He is the one who holds the power to tell the story any way he wants to."[17] There is a tension, in other words, between celebration and denunciation, and that, I think, is also represented in the fact that Munny kills five people in the end (or six, as some suggest). The number five had been important

---

17. Sarat, "When Memory Speaks," p. 253; Miller, "Clint Eastwood and Equity," p. 198. Miller also sees Beauchamp as more a consumer than producer of myths, although he sees that Beauchamp's presence in the world of *Unforgiven* "is no less corrupting to realists than to sentimental romantics" (196–97).

throughout the movie (the Schofield Kid lied that he had killed five, and Ned and Munny ponder whether it is true). Of course, the five had been killed in a messy fashion, but, still, they were killed by one lone vigilante. We can compare this scene, for instance, with the one in *The Good, the Bad, and the Ugly*, where Eastwood's character shoots four villains who won't apologize to his mule with five clean shots. That scene in the earlier movie is purely myth-making, while the scene in *Unforgiven* seems to be a resistant debunking of the possible myth. It is more temperate, or more ambivalent, and, largely, I think, because Eastwood is revealing the ways misperception (Beauchamp has many) is at the heart of the project.

That ambivalence about the culture of violence, perhaps, might reveal what other culture is possible, hinted at but not realized, in the film.[18] Munny, of course, is lured back into his vigilante role after years of attempting and failing to live as a pig farmer; and in the end of the movie, we are informed that he has gone to San Francisco to attempt a new life at running a dry-goods store. In other words, what we see in the world of *Unforgiven* is akin to a *lapse* from what he had been striving to become and would, after the killings, re-turn to striving to become. One of the stage directions in the script as Kate tells him about the murder of Ned is: "As she talked MUNNY has begun to drink slowly from the bottle of whiskey. It is as if his past is coming back to him and with it all his old habits." Munny hasn't had a drink for ten years, and this act of imbibing signals, as the stage directions suggest, a return to his old ways. Repeatedly, he tells his friends that his wife "cured [him] of drink and wickedness." His wife represents the reformation of character, of chang-ing him from a sodden, vicious killer to something closer to a good man. He also emphasizes that she had "showed him the error" of his ways about being cruel to animals. Indeed, when he has trouble mounting his horse, he suggests that the "horse is getting even with me for the sins of my youth" and "for the cruelty I inflicted," that is, the time before his wife had reformed him.

Perhaps, then, the apology he makes to the horse—the one apology in the film that Eastwood added to the script—suggests something about the role that Munny's wife plays in *Unforgiven*, since the film had made the connec-tion between his previous and present relations to the horse in terms of his wife's intervention in his life. In other words, his apology suggests his having

---

18. Everett L. Worthington, Jr., *Forgiving and Reconciling: Bridges to Wholeness and Hope* (Downers Grove, IL: InterVarsity Press, 2003), pp. 150–52, suggests that the film also plays with the idea that unforgiveness is not a "terminal character trait" by showing us "the spark of good in the characters at times."

imbibed the lesson his wife taught him about the place of empathy and re-morse in a well-lived life. Munny's wife represents, then, the possibility of another culture, one not of intemperate violence (an unforgiving world in which all are unforgiven), but rather one that permits recovery and reconcili-ation through remorse (a forgiving world). The movie begins and ends with a crawling script that refers to the puzzle of Claudia Feathers Munny's marrying a man of "notoriously vicious and intemperate disposition." *Unforgiven*, then, is framed by references to the woman who never appears in the film, but the one who represents forgiveness (she forgave Munny his disposition), reform (she cured him of it), and remorse (she taught him the empathy that precedes apologizing). We might think of this infusion of the possibility of another culture of apology and forgiveness into *Unforgiven* as one more element in the movie's dismantling both the revenge motif and the monumental histor-ical sensibility that creates and celebrates it. But, of course, the only propo-nent of that culture is dead, buried, and absent; and the one person who did learn from her demonstrates a very limited sense of what values he did learn, or how deeply. *Unforgiven*, in the end, hints at the evolution of a society in which apology to humans and animals might have a place, but that society is not this one.

The social scripts of *The Lives of Others*, on the other hand, are clearly placed in a way that shows that this society is undergoing a transition. There are two important texts in the film, one that Wiesler authors and one that Dreyman publishes, or, to put it in terms of consumption, one that Dreyman reads and one that he writes. The first is the Stasi file, and the second the novel *Sonata for a Good Man*. We have already suggested that Wiesler's Stasi file represents something like an act of apology, and Dreyman reads it as such when he finds the red fingerprint on one of the pages. It is worth consid-ering what that file contains, though, and not only what it symbolizes. What it contains is a fabrication of a play that Dreyman was supposed to be writ-ing, the play that celebrates the fortieth anniversary of the founding of the Communist state. In order to protect Dreyman, who is authoring an exposé of East German politics by showing the anomie that living in a totalitarian state produces, Wiesler writes into the Stasi file a fake script (literally a script). And the film makes it clear that we are to think of these two texts as being involved in a dialogue, since Dreyman writes his novel after reading the Stasi file; and clearly it is hinted that the fake play tells one story, while the novel tells quite another.

We don't know what either text does in fact say, but we may plausibly be-lieve that Dreyman's novel, *Sonata for a Good Man*, celebrates the individual and not the collective. He is *one* good man in a corrupt, collectivist state. The play, on the other hand, would have promoted the values of collectivity and the creation of a totalitarian state. Here, then, are the scripts for the old order and the new—one attempting to create a monument to the founding of the police state, and the other inaugurating the moral choices and values of individualism in a new democratic society. The fabricated play in the Stasi file is entirely subsumed and replaced by the novel, *Sonata for a Good Man*. And the place each text occupies is very much a statement about the transition from one kind of society to another. The play about the monumental founding of the collectivist state sits in a musty file, not published, not performed, not regarded, while the novel about individual, moral merit is a major publishing event. One is a defunct script for a dead society, and the other is a robust script for a new social order.

Unlike *Unforgiven*, in which the representative of a culture of apology and forgiving is buried and absent, *The Lives of Others* shows us how the text that promotes the values of remorse and reconciliation, of apology and forgiveness, is a living document. The social script for *Unforgiven* exists in a private past and possible future, that of *The Lives of Others* in a public present that makes the future possible. What each of these films reveals, then, is that apology is possible only in certain social conditions—those in which it is imaginable not to be unforgiven, and one in which we can respect, enter into, and, when necessary, express remorse for how we think about and treat the lives of others.

8 PRIVATE APOLOGIES

On April 23, 1641, Charles I of England wrote a letter to the Earl of Strafford, promising him "upon the word of a king," that he would not permit him to suffer loss of life, honor, or fortune. At the time, Strafford was being tried for treason, which, he argued, was illogical since he was only carrying out the king's wishes. How could obedience to the king be treason against the person he was obeying? Strafford had made many enemies who wanted to see him executed, but he had made one very loyal friend in the king whose assurance he possessed. After Strafford was found guilty and sentenced to death, Charles faltered. He did not want to sign the death warrant for his former privy counselor to whom he had made such a sincere promise. Yet, he knew that there was a great danger in defying the newly formed Long Parliament. He consulted his bishops, one of whom told him that he could not in good conscience break his promise and one of whom told him that a king could do so when reasons of state demanded it. After Strafford wrote him a letter releasing him from his promises, Charles reluctantly signed the order. Eight years later, as Charles faced his own execution, he reflected that his own impending death was God's punishment for his failure to protect the friend whom he had promised to save. For Charles, the issue was that *promise*: it was what he had consulted his bishops about, what he felt he had violated, and what tormented his conscience until his own death. There are differing accounts of what Strafford said when he learned that Charles had signed his death warrant; one of them—"Put not your trust in princes"— shows us that he too was thinking about the meaning of promises, as well as the fickleness of monarchs.[1]

---

1. *The Letters, Speeches, and Proclamations of King Charles I*, edited by Charles Petrie (1935; Oxford: Oxford University Press, 1968), p. 115. For the account of

A promise is a particular kind of ethical statement, an implied moral contract that assumes its meaning because of how it sets the terms for and establishes a particular kind of relationship. One of the most astute commentators on the meaning of promises, Hannah Arendt, wrote that promises are the "remedy for unpredictability." In a world in which we cannot control what is to come, in "the ocean of uncertainty, which the future is by definition," writes Arendt, promises are "islands of security without which not even continuity, let alone durability of any kind, would be possible in the relationships between men."[2] In other words, promises, explicit ones that take the form of contracts and implicit ones that depend on the bonds between or among people, create conditions possible for trust, for human sociability, for relationships.

In a letter five years earlier, September 3, 1636, Charles had written to Strafford (then Lord Thomas Wentworth) with a pithy comment about another kind of ethical statement: "I will end with a rule that may serve for a statesman, a courtier, or a lover—never make a defence or apology before you be accused." Both the recipient and the writer of this letter were eventually accused, both offered some kind of "defence" (for Charles it was "the divine right of kings," for Strafford obedience to those who had the divine right), and neither apologized.[3] It is intriguing to consider that their fates might have been different if either of them had; it is doubtful, but, of course, the counterfactual past is just as unpredictable as the future. Here, then, are two "words of a king"—one a promise that he did not keep, and another an apology he did not make. We can begin by noting the key differences between them. A promise addresses the future, an apology the past; one is predictive, the other retrospective; one is marked by hope, the other by remorse.

But the two forms—promising and apologizing—also share a great deal. They are both speech-acts, and they both establish or re-establish a

---

Strafford, I have relied largely on C. V. Wedgewood, *Thomas Wentworth: First Earl of Strafford, 1593–1641: A Revaluation* (London: Jonathan Cape, 1961).

2. Hannah Arendt, *The Human Condition* (Chicago: University of Chicago Press, 1958), p. 237.

3. *The Letters, Speeches, and Proclamations of King Charles I*, p. 98. *Apology* in its seventeenth-century usage could have either its older meaning of being an account or its modern one of being an expression of remorse; it is not clear which Charles had in mind. Strafford did apologize in general on the scaffold—"I desire heartily to be forgiven of every man if any rash or unadvised words or deeds have passed from me"—but did not apologize for the crime with which he was charged and maintained his innocence with his final statement before his beheading. See Wedgewood, *Thomas Wentworth*, pp. 387–88.

relationship. They operate, that is, as linguistic performances and as social ones. In this chapter, I want to explore *apology*, and see how it can be understood for what it is and does in both roles (as performative speech and as restorative gesture within a relationship). Although apologizing is, of course, an ancient practice—in the forms of penance and atonement in religious practices and other kinds of appeasement and repentance in social life—it has recently become a more pronounced topic of interest for those who write philosophy, or write about business, therapy, politics, and many other spheres of intellectual and social life. As I noted in the previous chapter, the major distinction I am making is between *private* and *public* apologies. Here, I focus on the former.

I

We can begin our analysis by returning to what are arguably the two most important analytical models for understanding apologies, both of which were products of the 1950s and 1960s. It was clear that apologies had at least two easily identifiable and easily distinguished features—their medium and their intentions, or their form and their functions. It is not surprising, then, that ordinary language philosophers turned to apologies with their focus on the first feature (medium, form) and explored what they meant as speech-acts or performative utterances. Likewise, it made sense for sociologists to focus on the second feature (intention, function) and inquire into the work that apologies do in repairing the frequent failures of human sociability. The former group attended to what apologies do as utterances, as *words that do things*, in the formulation of one of the philosophers; the latter with how they matter as received, how they operate as a practice of *remedial interactions*, in the formulation of one of the sociologists. The two most influential practitioners of these two modes of studying the practice—both of whom made passing rather than extended studies of apologies—were the ordinary language philosopher J. L. Austin and the sociologist Erving Goffman.

My interest here is in neither critique nor application. I do not wish to show the drawbacks and problems in either model; I also don't wish to adopt and apply either model to a series of apologies and tease out its deeper applications. Others have done that work, and done it well. I am more interested in returning to the formulation of these theorists, and seeing what questions they raise about the practice and what those questions, the moments of tension and slippage they reveal, might tell us about what apologies are as spoken words and parts of social interactions. After that, I turn to some contemporary theories of what apologies are and mean, and address what it is that we can learn from these earlier theorists that could correct what seems to be missing or understated in these contemporary formulations.

It is highly significant that Austin and Goffman were writing at precisely the time when the form they were studying—the apology—was undergoing a dramatic evolution from being a private to becoming a public act. While some forms of apologizing have a long history as social performances—religious confessions made in some of the Abrahamic faiths, for instance, and somewhat secular apologies of the sort Charles considered and did not make— there emerged in the postwar period a discernibly novel form of public apologizing for personal, political, collective, and historical crimes. Why this happened in the wake of World War II is not the subject of this chapter; I have written about it elsewhere.[4] But it is important to recognize what might have stimulated it. My argument is that the turn to public apology was a response to a new notion of public guilt.

The postwar period witnessed a widespread and concentrated attention on the question of *metaphysical guilt*. That term is Karl Jaspers', and it is the fourth kind of guilt that he identifies in his analysis of how a citizen of Germany could be responsible for the crimes of the Third Reich. In light of those crimes, he writes, we need a concept of responsibility that reconsidered the ideas of autonomy that we inherited from the Enlightenment. Metaphysical guilt, for Jaspers, meant that each individual is "co-responsible for every wrong and every injustice in the world." Even those who suffered directly at the hands of the Third Reich felt that kind of encompassing guilt. Primo Levi, for example, who was a prisoner in Auschwitz, wrote that he felt "guilty at being a man, because men had built Auschwitz." This is an existential guilt that "the just man experiences at another man's crime," because one feels responsible for things one has not done. In *The Origins of Totalitarianism*, Arendt called it "our consequent responsibility for all deeds and misdeeds committed by people different from ourselves." What existentialism means by saying that a "man is responsible for what he is," writes Jean-Paul Sartre in a postwar essay, is that "he is responsible for all men."[5] Here, then, in the

---

4. Ashraf H. A. Rushdy, *A Guilted Age: Apologies for the Past* (Philadelphia: Temple University Press, 2015).

5. Karl Jaspers, *The Question of German Guilt*, translated by E. B. Ashton (Westport, CT: Greenwood Press, 1978), p. 32. Jasper's book was first published in 1948. Primo Levi, *The Periodic Table*, translated by Raymond Rosenthal (New York: Everyman's Library, 1995), p. 157; Levi, *The Reawakening*, translated by Stuart Wolf (New York: Simon & Schuster, 1995), p. 16; cf. Levi, *The Drowned and the Saved*, translated by Raymond Rosenthal

immediate postwar period, we find repeated descriptions of this concerted sense of being responsible for the lives of others, and an attendant guilt for the acts of others. That widespread condition of existential guilt demanded a social form of atonement that arguably the new public apology provided. What Austin and Goffman give us, then, are theories of the apology at that very critical moment when that practice was just beginning to assume a new setting and meaning.

II

The speech-act that most challenged Austin was the apology. The reason is not hard to discern. In a 1956 BBC Third Programme talk he delivered, he gave four examples of what he called "performative utterances," that is, those forms of speech that do not *report* something but *indulge* in it, statements that don't merely *say* something but *do* something. The four cases he offered are: marrying, christening, betting, and apologizing. In the appropriate circumstances, we make particular, appropriate utterances—I do, I christen, I bet, I apologize. These are not descriptions or reports. Rather, as Austin insists, "in saying what I do, I actually perform that action." For these performative utterances to be actions, they need the right situations: an unwed person standing with another unwed person in front of an officiant, an authorized official standing over a child or in front of a ship, one gambler next to another, or someone who has offended another. Austin wants very much to insist that it is the public use of speech or what we can term a *statement* that does the work, not any sentiment behind it. The "one thing we must not suppose," he declares, "is that what is needed in addition to the saying of the words in such cases is the performance of some internal spiritual act, of which the words then are to be the report."[6] Applied to his four examples, we can see that the only one that conventionally represents, or, for some, requires an "internal spiritual act" is

(New York: Summit Books, 1988), pp. 70–87; Arendt, *The Origins of Totalitarianism* (1948; New York: Schocken Books, 2004), p. 631. On this point, also see Arendt, "What Is Existential Philosophy," in *Essays in Understanding, 1930–1954: Formation, Exile, and Totalitarianism*, edited by Jerome Kohn (New York: Schocken Books, 1994), pp. 163–87, esp. p. 181; Jean-Paul Sartre, "Existentialism," translated by Bernard Frechtman, in *Existentialism and the Human Emotions* (New York: Philosophical Library, 1957), pp. 9–51, esp. p. 16.

6. J. L. Austin, "Performative Utterances," in *Philosophical Papers* (Oxford: Clarendon Press, 1961), pp. 220–39, esp. pp. 222, 223. There is a point in "Performative Utterances" where Austin notes: "It's very easy to slip into this view at least in difficult, portentous cases, though perhaps not so easy in simple cases like apologizing."

apologizing. One can christen, bet, or marry without emotion; the ship or child is no less named, the gamble no less undertaken, or the marriage no less legally binding (if impoverished in other ways) by virtue of the insincerity of the person speaking. It is not at all clear, and much disputed, whether this is the case for apologizing.

Later in his talk, Austin returns to this point and seems to rebut what he had earlier said. One way that a performative utterance can fail to be felicitous is that the person making it does not "have certain feelings or intentions." When someone makes an utterance without holding the requisite feeling, we have cases of what Austin calls "insincerity." The problem of insincerity, which we also discerned as a crucial one in our discussion of forgiveness, might also be described in the term that Austin's colleague Gilbert Ryle used, as the "problem of other minds." In an essay of that title, "Other Minds," published a decade before his BBC talk, Austin had addressed this key question of what it can mean for utterances to perform something when people can be insincere, when, as he puts it, we live in a world in which we confront "the birthright of all speakers, that of speaking unclearly and untruly." In "Other Minds," Austin identifies three kinds of doubt that arise and "occasion genuine worry" when we consider what we think to be another mind's emotions.[7] We can be deceived by someone who suppresses or feigns emotions; we can misunderstand because we might believe that the other mind feels or expresses emotions in the same way we do; or we can be fooled by thinking an action intentional or deliberate when it might be inadvertent or involuntary. In the case of apology, for instance, someone can fake remorse, or feel or express something that we do not identify as remorse, or fool us by having a facial tic that we interpret as looking remorseful.

This problem, this "genuine worry," of sincerity and other minds is, in some ways for Austin, an epistemological problem. How can we know? And the answer he gave in the BBC talk, dissatisfying as it might be, is that we cannot. One "can't just make statements about other people's feelings," he concludes, although one "can make guesses" if one wishes. Austin was not particularly troubled by this insoluble condition—it is a human condition, after all—and he recognized that the best we can do in that condition, the human one, is be humble in our assessments. In commenting on another feeling, in another essay, he noted that it was a grave mistake to believe that "pleasure is always a

---

7. Austin, "Performative Utterances," p. 223; Austin, "Other Minds," in *Philosophical Papers*, pp. 44–84, esp. pp. 79–80.

single similar feeling."[8] The same could be said of remorse. So, if the feelings of other minds always elude us, what can we make of performative utterances where we expect that feelings are being expressed? Is an apology an apology, if remorse is faked or expressed in an incomprehensible way?

The BBC talk was broadcast the year after Austin delivered the 1955 William James lectures at Harvard, in the course of which he provided the most complete statement of his speech-act theory; and the BBC talk is truncated in points in the argument where the Harvard lectures offer greater elaboration. Nonetheless, that same tension that we find in the radio talk can be found in the Harvard lectures. On the one hand, Austin made the question of sincerity a key point in his discussion. He identifies six "necessary conditions" for a performative utterance to be happy or felicitous. The first four concern external contexts—the propriety of the speaker, the circumstances, the procedure, and its execution (correctly and completely performed). The last two concern cases where "certain thoughts or feelings" are involved, in which case persons who perform that utterance must have those thoughts and feelings, intend to conduct themselves by them, and do in fact "conduct themselves subsequently." On the other hand, he also remained troubled by this concession. He laments that the focus on some "inward and spiritual act" somehow debases morality. This insistence on "the invisible depths of ethical space"— some inward set of feelings and thoughts—strikes him as a breakdown of a social order in which "*our word is our bond*."[9] We should not have to inquire into whether the person who says "I promise" does indeed feel, somewhere deep down, that she intends to promise, and thinks that her promise is going to govern her future behavior.

It is not clear to me just what world Austin was lamenting we had lost, what social order in which a word was a bond and the question of the sincerity behind it was not questioned. It is certainly a desirable one, and would have been so especially in the midst and wake of World War II when Austin was writing, but it is illusory. In some respects, though, speech-act theory insists on that particular abstraction, even if it does not always base it on Austin's longing for an honorable social order. When John Searle writes that to "study speech acts of promising or apologizing we need only study *sentences* whose literal and correct utterance would constitute making a promise or issuing

---

8. Austin, "Performative Utterances," p. 236; Austin, "The Meaning of a Word," in *Philosophical Papers*, pp. 23–43, esp. p. 41.

9. Austin, *How to Do Things with Words*, edited by J. O. Urmson and Marina Shisà (1962; New York: Oxford University Press, 1975), pp. 14–15, 10.

an apology," it is not hard to see the felt need to exclude what seems to him extraneous rather than essential to the speech-act.[10] What is extraneous is the sentiment behind the expression, and what is essential the abstraction of the words from the feelings. Searle is not nostalgic like Austin, but rather entirely focused on the object of his analysis, but both, it seems to me, give away too much in defining an object of study freed from what they feel is the constraint of accounting for internal states.

In the end, of course, Austin, who is our focus here, did account for them. We can note that he did so reluctantly. For instance, he distinguished the rules about sincerity from the other four rules by giving them Greek rather than Latin letters in delineating their place in the rules, and he called their placement the "first big distinction" in his system. More significantly, he also noted that the failure of those last two rules concerning "thoughts and feelings," and, later, intentions, is a violation of a different order from failure of the first four rules. A violation of any of the first four rules constitutes a *misfire*, while a violation of the last two is designated an *abuse*. Those violations of "insincerity" (not having the right feelings during the utterance) and what he came to call "infractions" and "breaches" (not conducting oneself appropriately subsequent to the utterance) render a performative utterance not felicitous, but also "*not* void."[11] In other words, there was some curious middle space in which a performative utterance could be unhappy but nonetheless effective. If someone is not an authorized officiant, the words "I christen" do not name the baby or the ship; but if someone is not sincere, the words "I apologize" have some kind of meaning. They are not void.

As we saw in our discussion of his BBC address, Austin makes these distinctions because that particular kind of performative utterance—what he eventually defined as a behabitive illocutionary act—depended on unanswerable questions in ways that other kinds of performative utterances did not. Behabitives as a whole—that is, performative utterances that "have to do with attitudes and *social behaviour*"—offer what Austin called a "special scope for insincerity" precisely because they dealt with *social* behavior, with interactions between those who express something and those who assess whether the expression is sincere. Austin did not dwell on apologies in either the BBC talk or the Harvard lectures, one suspects, because they were troublesome

10. John Searle, *Speech Acts: An Essay in the Philosophy of Language* (Cambridge: Cambridge University Press, 1969), p. 21.

11. Austin, *How to Do Things with Words*, pp. 15–18, 39.

and somewhat awkward features in an otherwise quite elegant theory. In the Harvard lectures, he does not discuss apologies so much as employ them as examples of a larger point—the distinction between constative and performative utterances, for instance, or the difference between seeking truth or felicity in a particular kind of utterance.[12] On the whole, then, he found apologies problematic. They were the Greek-designated rules in his Latinate system, the speech acts that could not be void but continue to have meaning even when they are performed abusively, and the sticky utterances that require us to seek something deeper, beyond the words themselves.

What I think we can best take away from Austin's analysis of apologies are precisely the difficulties he identified with them, the features that made them especially problematic for him. The questions we ask of apologies involve deeper issues, and appropriate behaviors. In a word, insincerity matters. If a person who says "I do" is insincere and does not perform the appropriate subsequent behaviors associated with that sincerity—let's say, acts in a way unbecoming to a married person and consistently has sex with several different partners—that insincerity does not void the wed state. It will require another act to do that. But if someone who says "I apologize" is insincere—and who behaves in ways that demonstrate that insincerity by doing the same thing for which the apology was offered—then that apology occupies a more difficult status; as Austin says, it is not felicitous and it is an abuse, but it might also not be void. The person who apologized might continue to think it an apology, even if the person receiving it does not. And the person who does not accept it might, in some circumstances, wonder if perhaps there has been a misunderstanding because remorse is not a singular feeling, and that there might be ways for someone to express remorse in ways that are not immediately clear to us. In the case of apologies, we are inevitably faced with the problem of other minds. Austin did have a cheery enough, and satisfying enough, answer to that problem. We humbly give up our claim to certainty, and we act in accord with our previous experiences as our best guides. Sometimes, as he Platonically says in "Other Minds," to know is "to *recognize*," and recognizing, as he continues, is to discern "a feature or features which we are sure are similar to something noted (and usually named) before, or some earlier occasion in our experience."[13] We can recognize sincerity in other minds by dint of our hoping that we have witnessed it in our earlier lives. All this is uncertain, and

---

12. Austin, *How to Do Things with Words*, pp. 152, 161, 45–47, 53.

13. Austin, "Other Minds," p. 84.

that, as Austin implies, is fine because that uncertainty is our condition (just as our discomfort with it is likewise our condition).

III

Goffman, on the other hand, was concerned less with questions of epistemology and more with questions of politics. His attention, in other words, was not directed to the question of how we can know other minds, but rather to the question of how we can operate in the midst of other bodies. Apologies, for Goffman, are examples of what he calls "remedial exchanges," that is, those rituals that deal with offenses that require remediation, both for those involved directly in them and for the larger public order. Remedial exchanges involve interpretation, the work of taking what seems to mean one thing and altering it, through the remedial exchange, so that it may mean something else that is palatable. The function of remedial work, as Goffman puts it, is "to change the meaning that otherwise might be given to an act, transforming what could be seen as offensive into what can be seen as acceptable." The three kinds of remedial exchanges he highlights in his most extended study of the phenomenon are accounts, apologies, and requests. All deal with the key question of responsibility, which in turn deals with the crucial issue of how we can understand an act. If there is a dispute about responsibility, then those disputants cannot agree on the act in question. Without "knowing how those involved in an act attribute responsibility for it," Goffman writes, "we cannot in the last analysis know what it is that has occurred."[14] Let's say, one feels that the other holds responsibility for immediate causation (he pushed me), while the other feels that he pushed her only because he was in turn pushed by a third party. What was seen as an intentional push, once responsibility is more fully ascribed, is now seen as part of an unintentional chain reaction.

In this case, an *account* provides a larger context in which the act must be discerned more accurately, and appropriate responsibility ascribed. Goffman gives numerous examples of accounts—drawing in places on Austin's famous essay "A Plea for Excuses"—because they are easily the most studied of the three forms of remedial work he highlights. Accounts, in general, attempt to reduce responsibility by offering stories, or providing contexts, in which there are mitigating circumstances that change the interpretation of the offense

---

14. Erving Goffman, *Relations in Public: Microstudies of the Public Order* (New York: Basic Books, 1971), pp. 109, 99.

from what it seemed to be (an act of intentional malice, say) into something else (an unintentional and unavoidable accident). Accounts are offered after the event, while *requests* are made before the act. A request, as Goffman puts it, "consists of asking license of a potentially offended person to engage in what could be considered a violation of his rights." The example Goffman gives is of police officers asking the suspect to empty her purse or his pockets instead of doing it themselves; this request gives the suspect "a slight sense of the autonomy and self-determination the law presumably guarantees him."[15] The request, in other words, participates in remedial work prior to the offense, while accounts operate after, but both recognize that there has been, or will be, an offense.

For Goffman, these offenses are largely tied to the integrity of the body. His essay on remedial work in his 1971 book *Relations in Public* is an extension of a 1955 essay he had written entitled "On Face-Work," where *face* was of course used in a symbolic sense (as in "losing face"), but where Goffman was also attentive to, and implied the importance of, the physical property itself—the face that would be lost symbolically but crestfallen or express embarrassment physiologically. In *Relations in Public*, he defines "interactional offenses" as those that "pertain mainly to claims regarding territories of the self." Again, as with *face, self* here means an entity that is not properly or entirely physical but is also nonetheless physical. As he notes, these claims really do "amount to expectations regarding forms of respect."[16] But Goffman is also careful to note that these are not easily divided properties—a self has what he specifically identifies as a territory, an inviolable space that surrounds the physical, corporal being encasing or representing the self (depending on what mind–body interpretation one favors). It is disrespectful for someone to get up into my face because it is a violation of my personal space, the space I believe physically belongs to my self because it is immediately surrounding my body. An offense, then, can be someone stepping on my foot (a violation of my physical body), intruding on my personal space (a violation of my presumed "territory of the self"), or insulting me (an offense against my sense of my self in the world at large).

---

15. Goffman, *Relations in Public*, pp. 114, 115.

16. Goffman, "On Face-Work: An Analysis of Ritual Elements in Social Interaction," *Psychiatry: Journal for the Study of Interpersonal Processes* 18.3 (August, 1955): 213–31; reprinted in Goffman, *Interaction Ritual: Essays in Face-to-Face Behavior* (New York: Pantheon Books, 1967), pp. 5–45. Goffman, *Relations in Public*, p. 107.

The final form of remedial work is the *apology*, and Goffman gives an ingenious interpretation of just what is at stake in apologizing. An apology differs from the other forms of remedial work in a specific way. While accounts reduce the agent's responsibility, and requests reduce the victim's rights, apologies do not reduce anything for either party, but instead affirm the responsibility and the right. The person apologizing is responsible, and the person offended has the right that was violated. Goffman defines apology, in a much-cited quotation, as follows: "An apology is a gesture through which an individual splits himself into two parts, the part that is guilty of an offense and the part that dissociates itself from the delict and affirms a belief in the offended rule."[17] Goffman's insistence on seeing apology as involving a "split" has elicited some important commentary, and we should attend to it first.

Nick Smith, for instance, finds it deeply problematic because he believes that the split "risks stripping" the person apologizing "of the intentionality required to accept blame." The fracturing of "moral agency in this way drifts toward offering an excuse for the act or understanding it as a sort of intrapersonal accident." Smith argues that apologies require "unified moral agents possessing a suite of values and accepting blame for their violations of these values." Smith offers some examples of deeply troubled, and troubling, apologies that seem to do just what he fears, apologies that employ the formula of "that wasn't me" or "I don't know what got into me." Such apologies, he suggests, differ little from a self-description that is not an apology. The example he gives is of a sailor who beat a gay shipmate to death and then claims: "It was horrible, but I am not a horrible person."[18]

I am not certain what to make of Smith's examples. The case of the homophobic sailor raises an additional but also entirely different problem than the split self, since it is largely about the dissociation of act and agent. Inspired by Augustine's expression of "hate the sin, but love the sinner," many writers on forgiveness have expressed what are the metaphysical questions involved in our affirming or denying that an agent is irreversibly associated with a particular act; for them, it comes down to the key question of whether or not there exists something or someone we can claim is "unforgivable."[19] But, let's assume that the sailor also does now have a split self—one part that committed the

---

17. Goffman, *Relations in Public*, p. 113.

18. Nick Smith, *I Was Wrong: The Meaning of Apologies* (New York: Cambridge University Press, 2008), pp. 63–64; Aaron Lazare, *On Apology* (New York: Oxford University Press, 2004), p. 126, cites the same sailor example and suggests that it "would have been better had the sailor not tried to separate himself from the crime he had committed."

19. For discussions and debates about the concept of the "unforgivable," see Trudy Govier, "Forgiveness and the Unforgivable," *American Philosophical Quarterly* 36.1 (January

horrible crime and another that now recognizes it as horrible. Like the expressions Smith offers as examples, this one assumes a "me" that occupies two places—one *me* having committed an act that the second *me* now recognizes as wrong. That does not strike me as a repudiation of responsibility—when it is expressed properly—but rather as an expression of it. The moral agent is no less "unified" at the moment of apologizing for past actions; it is as a unified moral agent (the second *me*) that she renounces a previous self (the first *me*) that acted against the moral order she now wholeheartedly upholds. Of course, there are ways of testing whether one assumes responsibility or not when employing the split self model of apologizing. If someone says, for instance, that the present self shouldn't be punished for the previous self because it is now redeemed by the knowledge of the moral values, then we can sense the presence of insincerity and feel that the split is being exploited for ulterior purposes. But if someone feels otherwise, and the apology here can be seen as the expression of self-imposed punishment, then we have no reason to believe that the split self does not accept blame and responsibility.

Indeed, it is hard to imagine any model of apology or accepting responsibility that does not posit something very like Goffman's model of the split self. The religious practices from which our secular notions of apology and forgiveness emerge demand it, and use terms like *conversion* and *mortification* and *renovation* to describe the process by which one turns from sin, dies as a sinner, and is reborn as someone who rejects her earlier sinning. In each case, the new self judges the old self's actions as inappropriate. In the rabbinical tradition, we see the same thing. Maimonides, for instance, urges the penitent person to exile himself or to change her name as a way of creating, and marking, distance between the person who sinned and the person who repents. Even Kant, no mystic at all, held, as we saw, that repentance transformed the "old human being" into the "new human being."[20]

1999): 59–75; and Govier, *Forgiveness and Revenge* (New York: Routledge, 2002); and Charles L. Griswold, *Forgiveness: A Philosophical Exploration* (Cambridge: Cambridge University Press, 2007), pp. 90–98. For a discussion of the concept in political relations, see P. E. Digeser, "Forgiveness, the Unforgivable and International Relations," *International Relations* 18.4 (2004): 48–97. For a discussion of it in therapeutic terms, see Beverly Flanagan, "Forgivers and the Unforgivable," in *Exploring Forgiveness*, edited by Robert D. Enright and Joanna North (Madison: University of Wisconsin Press, 1998), pp. 95–105; and Flanagan, *Forgiving the Unforgivable: Overcoming the Bitter Legacy of Intimate Wounds* (New York: Macmillan, 1992).

20. Maimonides, *Maimonides—Essential Teachings on Jewish Faith & Ethics*, translated by Rabbi Marc D. Angel (Woodstock, VT: Jewish Lights Publishing, 2012), pp. 113, 143; cf. Maimonides, *The Book of Knowledge: From the Mishnah Torah of Maimonides*, translated by H. M. Russell and Rabbi J. Weinberg (Edinburgh: Royal College of Physicians of Edinburgh,

Or consider Smith's own model. An apology requires what he calls "categorical regret," that is, the "offender's recognition that her actions, which caused the harm at issue, constitute a moral failure, and the wish "that the transgression could be undone." An expression of categorical regret is as follows: "She explains that she regrets what she has done because it was wrong, she wishes she had done otherwise, and in accordance with this realization she commits to not making the same mistake again." I have written elsewhere about this curious notion in the discourse of apology and forgiveness about something's being "undone."[21] The expression can mean many things, ranging from those, like Smith, who see it as an expression of a desire (I wish I could undo this), to those who don't have as much faith in the physical laws of our universe as they do in other systems, and believe that it is actually possible for events to be undone, not psychologically but physically. In its nonmystical form, it is an expression of a wish, as Smith says, that someone can "undo" the past or had "done otherwise" in the past. It posits a present self who looks back at a past self's actions and laments them by wishing for what is physically impossible (until time travel becomes a reality). Is there any difference between someone's wishing for a different past (in which I would have done otherwise) and someone's splitting a self in order to express the same point (the person I am now would not do what the earlier self did)? In both cases, there is a unified moral agent in the present, and both are ways of expressing retrospection (through either an impossible split or an impossible wish).[22]

1983), p. 113. The passage is taken from Maimonides' Mishnah Torah, but the actual Mishnah passage is found in "The Fifth Tractate Yoma (The Day)," in *The Talmud: A Selection*, translated by Norman Solomon (New York: Penguin, 2009), pp. 193–207, esp. p. 202 (85b). Also see *The Book of Legends: Sefer Ha-Aggadah: Legends from the Talmud and Midrash*, edited by Hayim Nahman Bialik and Yehoshua Hana Ravnitzky, translated by William G. Braude (New York: Schocken Books, 1992), p. 651; Immanuel Kant, *Religion Within the Boundaries of Mere Reason*, translated by George di Giovanni, in *Religion and Rational Theology*, edited by Allan W. Wood and Giovanni (Cambridge: Cambridge University Press, 1996), pp. 55–215, esp. p. 114.

21. Smith, *I Was Wrong*, p. 68. See Rushdy, *The Guilted Age*, chapter 6.

22. Nicholas Tavuchis, *Mea Culpa: A Sociology of Apology and Reconciliation* (Stanford, CA: Stanford University Press, 1991), p. 138 n. 41, likewise criticizes Goffman for "'splitting' the self" in his model of apologizing, whereas he (Tavuchis) holds for the "necessity of 'attachment' to the offense in response to a call." I think Tavuchis misses Goffman's point in the same way as does Smith, and, likewise, I think Tavuchis' model of apology depends on precisely the same structure of division as does Smith's (and Goffman's). Tavuchis, too, uses the concept of *undoing* as his primary explanation of the work apology performs: "an apology, no matter how sincere or effective, does not and cannot *undo* what has been done. And yet, in a mysterious way and according to its own logic, this is precisely what it manages to do" (5). As I state above,

Let's return now to Goffman, and see just what this "split" does in his model of apology as remedial work, and why it is important for that model. Partly, of course, he follows the same imperatives that had driven the religious practices we saw above, the need to provide a model for expressing the process of dramatic change in the same person. But, for Goffman, there are additional imperatives that have to do with a series of *splits* in his model of the social world. We can begin by noting just what Goffman means by *public* in *Relations in Public*. (It is not what I will mean in the next chapter, which involves *publicity* in public apologies.) Rather, what Goffman means is simply a social interaction involving more than one person. He describes the "public realm" as the site where we can find "people co-mingling." The opposite of *public* in his model is not *private* (as it is in mine) but *isolation*. When he talks about "public life" in the case of remedial work, he is talking explicitly about cases "in which the offended and offender are present together and the offense is something that occurs while they are thusly placed." In what he calls *public relations*, then, and what we might call *interpersonal ones*, remedial work is required to re-establish what he calls "ritual equilibrium."[23]

In this model, we can see that healing gestures are meant primarily to reduce the two kinds of *splits* that an offense creates. There is, first, the split between two people in public, one of whom becomes the "obligated person" by dint of committing the offense, and the other the "expectant person" who has suffered it. The split creates two new roles in the public exchange, and the ritual of remedial work produces the equilibrium that returns the obligated and expectant person to the public in which they are not melded into only those roles. In other words, it is not only the person apologizing who is split, but likewise the person who was the victim of the offense. There is, secondly, a split within the social order itself since the offense violated the rules of the order. Remedial work helps restore that order by revealing that offenses are "one-shot deviations from ordinary rules," not revolutionary or anarchic breaks from the rules.[24] An apology, then, affirms respect for both the victim and the social order that were violated.

But those are not the only kind of splits or divisions in his model. There are others not meant to be reduced and healed, but indeed constitute the

---

I see no difference between a self that is able to divide itself in order to see its previous action as wrong and a self that divides itself in order to wish to undo what it had done.

23. Goffman, *Relations in Public*, pp. 106, 122,149.

24. Goffman, *Relations in Public*, pp. 105, 165.

possibility of a public, social order. Let me note two here. First, there are splits that are necessary for the social order, the kind that render people divided enough to require and desire communion. For Goffman, that split is what makes dialogue possible, and dialogue is likewise what makes equilibrium and communion desirable. Goffman's model is premised on dialogue, even when words are not employed. Interactions involve what he calls "statement-like moves directed to particular others who respond in a replying-like fashion." Where Austin focused on *utterances* that perform a particular kind of work, Goffman focuses on statements or gestures that elicit particular kinds of responses that, together, do a particular kind of work. That work, for Goffman, is always cooperative and always follows a particular script: the initial *deed*, the offense that initiates what he calls the "remedial dialogue," and then the *remedy*, the *relief*, the *appreciation*, and the *minimization*. (This is the language of his mature model revising his earlier model of "corrective interchanges" involving what he had then called *challenge, offering, acceptance*, and *thanks*). Even when the remedial activity is rushed, and parts of it appear to be missing, he argues that they are signaled in some way so that the "dialogic character" of the remedial interchange remains. In some cases where the whole exchange involves effectively a "single act"—an accidental bump by someone rushing forward, a hurried "Sorry!," and a quick departure without waiting for formal acknowledgment—the "single act" nonetheless "stands for the completed interchange."[25]

Dialogue permits more than social life between two people, though; it also permits social life for the individual alone. Goffman gives several examples of how a person performs bodily actions as if she were in dialogue with a presumed other who is somehow watching her. These are the kinds of exaggerated gestures that we make after a mistake—Goffman calls them "body glosses"—in order to signal to some generalized Other that we recognize our mistake. We trip over our feet while walking alone on the sidewalk, and we turn and pointedly stare at the sidewalk in a way meant to indicate that there is something there that caused this incidence of clumsiness. Goffman's point, then, is that we are always in dialogue, whether with actual others, presumed others—or ourselves. Here, then, is where the split in an apology becomes imperative for Goffman's model. The "capacity and the right [of the person apologizing] to turn upon himself and to cut himself off from what he once

---

25. Goffman, *Relations in Public*, pp. 138, 140; Goffman, *Interaction Rituals*, pp. 20–22; Goffman, *Relations in Public*, p. 151.

was" is part of the ritual processes that permit social life because they reveal that the offender is also in dialogue with himself.[26] He chastises his earlier offensive self from the perspective and standing of his newer offended self.

And yet, crucially for Goffman, that split in the offender does not permit the kind of solipsism involved in what some call self-forgiveness. What Goffman describes is an *apology*, a direct address to the other who is offended, an indirect appeal to the social order that has been violated, and only implicitly a statement to the sense of self that has suffered disruption. And it is only through dialogue with the other that the new self can take form. When the individual "makes an apology," writes Goffman, that individual "becomes needful of the addressee's providing a comment of some kind in return; for only in this way can he be sure that his corrective message has been received and that it has been deemed sufficient to reestablish him as a proper person." He can be returned to the social order through a dialogic exchange because the dialogue he is now having with the offended (expectant) person affirms his new identity of the kind of person who condemns the act performed by his earlier (obligated) self. Goffman returns to this point later in the chapter to insist on its importance: "When, then, the individual splits himself in two, he becomes very needful of evidence from others that the dissociation is perceived and accepted as he defines it."[27] That interpretation requires validation.

For Goffman, this split, this dissociation from an earlier self, and the dialogue that permits it, is part of a process of not only possessing an identifiable self—what he calls in another essay the "ritual game of having a self"—but might also be described as the very process by which he believes we become human. As a theorist committed to the self as a social construction—at one point, he writes that "the self, for many purposes, consists merely of the application of legitimate organizational principles to one's self"—Goffman believes that we *become* rather than simply *are* humans. At the end of his "On Face-Work" essay where he first assayed the meaning of apologies, he writes: "The general capacity to be bound by moral rules may well belong to the individual, but the particular set of rules which transforms him into a human being derives from requirements established in the ritual organization of social encounters." We are humans because the rituals of public, social

26. Goffman, *Relations in Public*, pp. 130, 122.

27. Goffman, *Relations in Public*, pp. 119, 161. On the topic of self-forgiveness, see Nancy E. Snow, "Self-Forgiveness," *Journal of Value Inquiry* 27 (1993): 75–80, esp. p. 75; Jon K. Mills, "On Self-Forgiveness and Moral Self-Representation," *Journal of Value Inquiry* 29 (1995): 405–406, esp. p. 406.

dialogues we have with ourselves and others—the "little worlds sustained in face-to-face encounters"—make us such.[28] Apologizing, then, that small gesture within remedial rituals in general, like other rituals that we employ (presentational, avoidance), is a micro-political act within a considerably larger organization that provides us with a sense of who we are becoming through the rituals that make us human. For Goffman, then, apologizing, and the split self on which it is presumed, is part of his psychology, his metaphysics, his politics, and his sense of how we create worlds within worlds, selves within selves.

IV

We can describe the main differences between Austin's representation of what an apology is and what it does and Goffman's by noting that one sees it as an *act* and the other as a *process*, and that one focuses on *words* and the other on *gestures*. For Austin, an apology was a performative utterance that was not void when insincere because what mattered was that it was an act, an abused one, but nonetheless one whose existence was not nullified by that fact. Its being an act defined it as a particular thing in the world (and the world is defined, in this case, as a population of speech-acts). For Goffman, on the other hand, an apology is a gesture, and therefore does not come to exist as an apology until it is registered as such by the other participant in the exchange. An apology that might or might not be sincere can *assume* sincerity in the course of an interchange. What Goffman calls a "remedial interchange" is one kind of "naturally bounded ritual dialogue." It has a script—actions that follow upon other actions—that constitutes what he describes as a "total set of moves made in connection" with a particular offense.[29] The dialogue is not closed until those moves are completed; if the apology seems insufficient to the other person in the dialogue, then the dialogue continues in that state of disequilibrium. The world is defined, in this case, as a population of interactions, some of which are in words and some in gestures.

Perhaps the clearest way for us to appreciate that difference is in how each thinker defines *performative*. For Austin, utterances are performative; they are words that do things. For Goffman, though, "performative" means something else. Even when "verbal utterances are often employed" in interchanges, he

---

28. Goffman, *Interaction Rituals*, pp. 91, 111, 45, 118.

29. Goffman, *Relations in Public*, p. 120.

writes, "it is not communication in the narrow sense of that term that is at the heart of what is occurring." Rather, he sees the people involved in the interchange taking stands, making moves, providing displays, and establishing alignments. It is a full set of gestures at play, sometimes vocalized and sometimes expressed through other bodily moves. Utterances, when used are "performative," but they are part of a larger performance—what he describes as "something closer to a minuet than to a conversation."[30]

What they share, albeit somewhat tenuously, is a desire to situate apology within a particular framework—linguistic or social—in which it plays a particular role. Both Austin and Goffman see apologizing as part of a larger system within which it operates in particular ways, through specific strategies, and with certain intentions. For Austin, an apology was a kind of illocutionary act that did something, an utterance that performed what it said and thus exemplified one kind of practice of language as a social system. For Goffman, apologies were one sort of remedial exchange, and remedial exchanges are one structuring ritual in the panoply of others that constitute social life in public. Goffman, because he was a sociologist and because he presented a theory of remedial rituals that was much more grounded on a wider set of social actions, exemplified this particular desire to situate apologies in a broader framework. And what he presents in his thinking about apologies strikes me as salutary. They are best thought of not simply as expressions that follow particular schemes of emotion and expression, or that have a paradigmatic structure, but rather as a wide range of possible scripts and exchanges that serve a greater purpose—remedial, restorative, rehabilitative.

V

As we turn now from the first modern commentators on apology, Austin and Goffman, to the contemporary ones writing in their wake, we notice two discernible differences. First, those who write about apology since the 1990s employ specific examples taken from newspapers and other media, while Austin and Goffman do not (they offer generalized statements or imagined dialogues). Second, these writers focus more on situating apology within a narrower gambit, and isolating it as a phenomenon from its contexts. Much of the contemporary writing has given a great deal more attention to defining *apology*—what specific features make a speech-act an apology—and assessing

---

30. Goffman, *Relations in Public*, p. 120.

apologies—what makes for a successful, what for a failed one—rather than situating apologizing into a richer, broader framework—linguistic or social. These two phenomena are related, I think. It is precisely because apologizing has gained more of a public profile in our postmodern world—and because these public examples are frequently so patently self-serving and shockingly shabby—that these commentators feel compelled to see in just what ways these public examples are shameful ones (they fail) and therefore attempt to define what particular acts make for successful ones. While I understand that imperative, it is, I think, one that needs some modifications. I will suggest two. First, as I have already noted, it is important for us to distinguish personal and public apologies as almost wholly different phenomena; and so the examples that make it to newspapers and other media do not strike me as particularly salient in understanding private apologies. Publicity alters everything about an apology, as we will see in the following chapter. Second, in looking at private apologies, I think we would do well to return to an appreciation of context rather than thinking more particularly about the text of a particular apology. Context alters much about an apology, as I hope to demonstrate below.

First, it is important to make the point, as Edwin Battistella does so well, that Goffman, who is frequently the object of criticism of these modern writers, is much more nuanced than he is often represented as being, and much more aware of the moral principles underwriting apology than he is often recognized for being.[31] Let me turn to two critics of Goffman. One asserts that we should return to a model that favors moral sentiment as a baseline for defining apologies, and the other proposes a set of restrictive aspects of apology that renders it an almost impossible ideal.

Nicholas Tavuchis emphasizes the emotional content and expressiveness of apologizing. An apology for Tavuchis is premised on sincerity and founded on a specific suite of emotions. His primary critique of Goffman, what he calls the "pivotal" difference between their approaches, is that Goffman makes no reference to what Tavuchis takes to be *central to apology: sorrow and regret*." Indeed, Tavuchis calls "sorrow" the "motor and organizing principle of apology." There are a couple of points worth raising here. First, it is not entirely clear that Goffman was silent about the emotions involved in apologies. In defining the elements of apology in its "fullest form," Goffman notes that

---

31. Edwin L. Battistella, *Sorry About That: The Language of Public Apology* (New York: Oxford University Press, 2014), p. 8.

an apology expresses "embarrassment and chagrin," involves "vilification" of the self that performed the offense, and represents the "performance of penance."[32] Can these elements not be considered an adequate representation of sorrow and regret? Second, there is a question about whether it is the feeling or the expression that matters more. Can we say an apology occurs if someone feels sorrow and regret but does not express them? Is the "motor" more important than the vehicle? I think Tavuchis makes an important point, but it also focuses our attention on the person apologizing, what he or she feels, rather than on the apology as a communicative act that assumes the meaning it does when it is received.

Nick Smith has offered the most extended—indeed, multivolume—study of apologies to date, and he has defined what he identifies as the thirteen elements or concerns of what he calls "categorical apologies." There are, I think, at least two ways we can understand Smith's use of the term *categorical*. The first is what we might call the dictionary usage, that is, that whatever is categorical is indisputably that thing, unquestionably, unconditionally *it*. An apology that expresses all the features he describes is an apology that cannot be faulted, that is, it cannot be found to be anything but an apology, just as what he calls "categorical regret" cannot be anything but regret. In that sense, then, *categorical* simply indicates something close to perfection, something that is not ambiguous or indefinite or in any way compromised. The second is what we might call the Kantian usage, and it is hard to imagine a contemporary philosopher using the term *categorical* who would not have expected his readership to consider at least a nod to Kant. It is worthwhile teasing out that possible Kantian usage for a moment.

Given his repeated use of *categorical*, it would seem that Smith wants us to consider the apology as "categorical" in the same way Kant argued that the "imperative"—that is the "formula of the command" for an ethical will to pursue an objective principle—should be *categorical*. All imperatives, as Kant writes, "are expressed by an *ought*," what the British moralists writing a century before Kant called "the internal ought." For Kant, the imperative had to be categorical, which meant that it "represented an action as objectively necessary of itself, without reference to another end." The opposite of the categorical imperative is the "hypothetical" imperative, which represents "the practical necessity of a possible action as a means to achieving something else that one wills." In his summary statement, Kant writes: "if the action would

32. Tavuchis, *Mea Culpa*, pp. 138, n. 41; 120; Goffman, *Relations in Public*, p. 113.

be good merely as a means *to something else* the imperative is *hypothetical*; if the action is represented as *in itself* good, hence as necessary in a will in itself conforming to reason, as its principle, *then it is categorical.*"[33]

Let's assume that this is the distinction Smith has in mind—and, again, I am not sure it is. Is that how we want to think of apologizing, as an act that is in itself good? I am not sure. There is something solipsistic about that conception of apology. In his more famous pronouncements, Kant made the same distinction he made here—something as an end in itself, something as a means to another end—in order to affirm the inherent and inviolable dignity of each human being. Ethically, we ought to treat each other *person* as an end in herself, and not as a means to some end of our own. But should an apology, or, for that matter, any kind of performative utterance, be conceived in that way? Apologies would seem designed to serve other purposes, other ends, such as reconciliation, sociability, mutual recognition, respect, all sorts of things that apologies and other acts of remediation facilitate. It is inherently a *means* and not an *end*, at least in the ethical models with which I am familiar. In virtue ethics, apologizing promotes a particular kind of character aware of one's own faults and recognizing the other's need for reassurance. In utilitarian models, apologizing is an action that promotes a superior happiness since it ends two miseries—remorse and resentment—by giving speech to the former and permitting the abeyance of the latter. And in deontological models, it would seem to promote the kingdom of ends rather than represent it.

In the Kantian usage, then, a "categorical apology" seems to miss the point because it, unlike a person, is inherently not an end, but a means. As an end in itself, an apology is meaningless (at least as a social act). But, likewise, in the dictionary usage, there is something amiss in describing something as a "categorical apology." It requires us to think of apologies as capable of being categorized, or for us to believe that what makes an apology indisputably an apology is that it follows this particular strategy, expresses these specific emotions, and operates in this specific way. As with Tavuchis' insistence on remorse, Smith's model focuses primarily on the one expressing the apology, and gives scant attention to the one hearing it.

---

33. Smith, *I Was Wrong: The Meanings of Apologies*, pp. 28–107. Smith changes the twelve elements to thirteen in his sequel volume, dividing one element into two; see Smith, *Justice Through Apologies: Remorse, Reform, and Punishment* (New York: Cambridge University Press, 2014), pp. 17–37; Kant, *Groundwork of the Metaphysics of Morals*, in *Practical Philosophy*, translated and edited by Mary J. Gregor (New York: Cambridge University Press, 1996), pp. 43–108, esp. pp. 66–67. For the British moralists, see Stephen Darwall, *The British Moralists and the Internal "Ought": 1640–1740* (New York: Cambridge University Press, 1995).

Smith is aware of these problems, and attempts to address them. He notes, for instance, that he wants to focus on "social meanings rather than definitions," but he seems unwilling to accept the wider latitude that would permit us to appreciate what social meanings apologies hold when they are not so restrictively defined. "Ultimately," he declares, "something is a categorical apology because it satisfies necessary conditions or it is not." That insistence, it seems to me, prohibits us from appreciating the social meanings of apologies. Finally, Smith is also quite clear that what he is presenting is an almost impossible ideal. By his own account, a "categorical apology amounts to a rare and burdensome act." He has his reasons for insisting on a strict and limiting definition, and they are plausible, indeed good, ones. He notes that we are unable to "judge apologies" primarily for three reasons: first, we are uncertain about "what a full apology is"; second, we are liable to consider lesser acts with a "family resemblance to an apology" to be "equal to a full apology"; and third, "we may accept whatever satisfies our lowest standards for apologies so that we can consider ourselves 'apologized to.'" In other words, we lack a rigorous definition of a full apology, and our own confusions and desires can lead us to be fooled by some gestures that are not full apologies. His account of categorical apologies answers the first problem by giving a definition that acts as "a kind of *prescriptive stipulation*" or a "regulative ideal," and would presumably equip us to avoid the second and third problems by expecting more of those who apologize to us.[34]

I think Smith is onto something, and missing something else. He is right in noting that we often do receive and accept apologies that are insincere and wanting in many ways. What he misses, though, is that we often do so for good reasons, and those good reasons have to do with the social meanings that apologies can hold and the social work they do perform—not because they are prescribed and regulated or even because they are "judged"—but rather because they assume a certain value and importance by virtue of being part of a dialogic exchange. Let me offer an example, and let me do so by also taking up the topic I raised in the section on forgiveness about the problems associated with regulative and prescriptive models of forgiveness.

Suppose a husband has tracked mud onto the living room carpet five minutes before his wife was hosting a party that was crucially important for her budding business career. She is upset, and feels that it is not only inconsiderate of her attempts to keep the house clean, but that it is also an unconscious

---

34. Smith, *I Was Wrong*, pp. 25, 17, 10, 17.

expression of resentment at her attempt to establish herself in business. The next day, the husband rents a carpet cleaner, and spends hours shampooing the carpet until it is spotless. He says nothing, and she also says nothing. Four days later, he hands her a box that has come in the mail, and says, "I'm sorry." She opens up what turns out to be one thousand business cards with her name and the name of her new business venture on it. She hugs him, and thanks him. Has he apologized? Has she forgiven him?

Note that I am giving an example that violates as many of the usual rules as I can. Here is what he does not do. He does not give a full account or "corroborated factual record" of what is offensive in his behavior; he does not directly imply each harm, or identify the moral principles underlying each harm; he does not explicitly promise to reform. And here is what is implied rather than stated in his act: his acceptance of blame, recognition of his wife as a moral interlocutor, categorical regret, and expression of emotions. Here is what the wife does not do: she does not say, "I forgive you." (This is a phrase that I think we rarely hear; it again is usually expressed through other phrases, "don't worry about it," "it's okay," "thanks," or through actions that reincorporate the offender, like hugging.)

Can we say of this exchange that it is not a categorical apology and a paradigmatic forgiveness? If we employ the models provided by Griswold and Smith, yes, we would have to say that. These are compromised acts—not categorical, not paradigmatic. Now, I don't imagine anyone would be churlish enough to consider them failures per se. They are simply not pristine examples of the practice at its most fully expressive. But that tepid endorsement seems to me quite problematic. An apology is not like a cardinal or a blue jay, which we can place in some Linnean order by noting what features define each of them from other phyla, classes, orders, families, genera, and species. An apology, as Goffman sagely noted, is something that becomes, not something that is. If the wife feels forgiving, and expresses it in a way that indicates that feeling to the husband, then she has forgiven him; and if the husband's actions have been taken as an adequate expression of remorse that addresses the wife's concerns, in a manner that makes sense to her and within their communicative norms, then he has apologized.

The way for us to think about apologizing, then, is not by defining it through its features or its elements, but rather through the local practices that make sense within a given tradition. That is the language of Alasdair MacIntyre, of course, and it seems to me to make sense here, to a large extent, precisely because it values variation within traditions. There is a longer trajectory to the tradition—expressing contrition and remorse through an evolving set of strategies and modes that make local sense to participants in that tradition in different moments.[35] Instead of regulating what are wide-ranging and indefinite practices, we need to attend more to what precisely these practices do involve. That strategy, let me hasten to add, is not a recipe for anarchy. Not everything one does or says can be taken as an apology, and Smith is absolutely right to note that we are all too able to fool ourselves about what it is we intend, and all too willing to be fooled by others whose intentions we cannot know and might suspect. In the case, I mentioned above, if the husband had knelt down, put his face in the dirt he had tracked, and uttered "mea culpa" in a loud voice instead of cleaning the carpet and giving his wife the business cards, we might have good reason to think his act not an apology. There are degrees and gradations of the practice within what are blurry and indefinable borders—but the more important point is that those actions might well be an apology if the wife and husband have a certain history, a particular communicative pattern, and set of expectations of each other in which that is what it is taken to be. Apologies, like forgiveness, become those things in relationships; and they are both features of and constitutive of those relationships. Rather than thinking of these features as categorical or paradigmatic, then, I think we might be better advised to think of them as local practices within a larger tradition.

VI

What we have seen, then, is that there are several ways to study apologies: one can focus on their verbal performance (what do they do as words, and how do they do it) or their social function (what do they do in relationships, and how) or their expression of particular sentiments (how they communicate remorse) or their fulfillment of certain ideal elements. There is value in all these methods we associate with Austin and Goffman, and there is likewise value in the contemporary studies that focus on the emotional or categorical particularities of apologizing. My tendency here has been to focus more on the purpose rather than the form of apologies, largely because I fear that too great an attention to form makes us disregard the largely informal practices that mark our daily lives and think of them as less than, or failures as, categorical apologies. Many of them are failures, of course; but many of them, and

---

35. Alasdair MacIntyre, *After Virtue: A Study in Moral Theory* (1981; South Bend, IN: University of Notre Dame Press, 2007); and MacIntyre, *Three Rival Versions of Moral Inquiry* (South Bend, IN: University of Notre Dame Press, 1991).

many of those that violate the formal tenets of apologizing, are not. They are successful in achieving the greater purpose and end that they intended—to re-establish relationships by performing acts meant to be and accepted as remedial, restorative ones. Perhaps the best way to make the point about what is most important about private apologies, and to direct us to the questions we will address in the next chapter about public apologies, is to look at a book that troubles that very distinction.

Dave Bry's 2013 book *Public Apology: In Which a Man Grapples with a Lifetime of Regret, One Incident at a Time* is presumably a memoir, or a parody of one, but, as we will see, it is also an uncomfortable memoir or parody. First, though, we need to appreciate its humor. There are many things that are funny about Bry's apologies. Sometimes, they are clearly unnecessary, since the events for which he is apologizing are the kinds of regular pranks and tricks children and adolescents play on their elders, whether the elders are camp counselors, teachers and principals, or parents. In other words, he seems to be apologizing not for an offense, but for a whole period of life. Here, what makes it humorous is the self-aware self-indulgence in those apologies. At other times, what makes it funny is that he is not apologizing at all. One of his most sincere statements, for instance—"It's hard for me to describe how sorry I felt at that moment"—is written to a girl he was too cowardly to try to kiss. When he finds out that his advances "to fool around" would have been welcome—but he finds out too late since she is on a plane back to California—he feels, as he puts it, indescribably sorry. It is, of course, for himself that he feels sorry, and self-pity, not remorse, he is expressing. At other times, he comes to the awareness that he feels something other than remorse, such as gratitude, in the letter he addresses to a friend who had supported him shortly after his father's death and on whom he had drunkenly vomited: "So this is more of a thank-you than an apology, I guess. For being a good friend, for making me feel better. But, you know, I am sorry about your shirt."[36]

There are also places in the book in which he parodies the form assumed in his title, namely, those celebrity public apologies that so frequently fail. In one case, he shows us what awkward tensions are often found in those apologies between a need to accept responsibility and an inability to do so. Apologizing to a college roommate for eating his slice of carrot cake in a fit of marijuana-induced munchies, Bry couches his overdone apology—"So I officially

---

36. David Bry, *Public Apology: In Which a Man Grapples with a Lifetime of Regrets, One Incident at a Time* (New York: Grand Central Publishing, 2013), pp. 87, 128.

apologize. I hereby accept full responsibility for my actions. And I owe you a piece of carrot cake"—with a preliminary statement condemning the whole American collegiate experience: "I'll slough responsibility again now and blame the environment: our life at college was just that divorced from reality." In another case, he parodies the whole situation of celebrities apologizing to fans by reversing the roles. Usually, celebrities offend the public with some (sometimes drunk) comment—when I am writing this, think Mel Gibson, Alec Baldwin, Reese Witherspoon—and then offer a sober and remorseful statement. Here, Bry presents himself as a fan who apologizes to the celebrities for his drunken behavior, as he does when he apologizes to Bon Jovi for throwing empty beer cans on his lawn.[37]

Finally, Bry also reveals what kind of skewed values are often expressed in those formulaic public apologies because those who offer them don't understand the meaning of remorse. For instance, he offers an apology for an entire lifetime of failure as a brother: "This is perhaps a good time to make a blanket apology for my behavior as an older sibling." Such a "blanket apology" is of course self-serving, saving him from having to identify particular failures, reflect on them and feel the pang of remorse for each one, and instead simply write off an entire relationship with a blank check. In another apology, the one to Bon Jovi for littering his lawn, Bry takes the opportunity to criticize Bon Jovi's music, in a way that he recognizes as wholly inappropriate. This note, he writes, "must be the least apologetic-sounding apology you've ever gotten." He adds: a "couple years from now, I'll probably be writing you another apology just for the tone of this one." Apologies are so cheap that one can predict the need for future ones. What is funny, of course, is the compulsion of the person who can't help himself as he follows a train of associations in his mind that are irrelevant to the task at hand and betray his self-indulgence. In these cases, he shows us someone who does not understand what an apology should be. In another, he shows us someone who misunderstands forgiveness. As he is himself apologizing to his principal for cheating, lying, and insulting her intelligence through an attempted fraud, he takes the opportunity to indict the musician Sting for a particular television commercial in which he endorses a luxury car that he dreams about while singing a concert. "I try to be as forgiving a person as I can be," he writes (and, remember, this is in an apology), and yet "this I will never be able to forgive."[38] This television

---

37. Bry, *Public Apology*, pp. 191, 107–108.

38. Bry, *Public Apology*, pp. 106, 108, 93.

commercial might strike most of us as lower in importance than all the things in the history of the world that might be described as "unforgivable."

Those, then, are some of the things that make *Public Apology* funny; what makes it uncomfortable, and wise, is something else. The whole premise of *Public Apology* seems based on the ninth step in Alcoholics Anonymous, which states: "Make direct amends to such people [those we had harmed] wherever possible, except when to do so would injure them or others."[39] Bry, it must be noted, does not declare that he is an alcoholic anywhere in the book, although there are plenty of scenes in which he shows how much it was the abuse of alcohol, marijuana, and cocaine that were at the root of his behaviors. If this principle was indeed in Bry's mind, it is one that he partly follows, partly mocks. After all, it is precisely that many of his apologies do in fact "injure" the person to whom he is apologizing that makes them even more humorous. In a letter addressed to "Dear Sean Something," in which he apologizes for having sex with his girlfriend, Bry writes: "Forgive me for not being able to remember your last name. We haven't seen each other for twenty-two years. Perhaps it's better that way, too, in light of my writing publicly about this. I figure it's not such a big deal. But I realize that it is a sensitive subject."[40] Here we see many of the things that make this book a rich parody—the indifference, the lack of remorse, and the acute awareness in the letters of their being either unnecessary or insufficient, as well as their being clearly violations of the protocols of apologizing for what is private in public.

The last thing I wish to say about Bry's book is that while it is primarily, and entertainingly, funny as a parody of public apologies, it is also a book that reveals what is necessary about apologizing. There are three moments in the book where we can sense a more somber side, where the parody gives way to sincerity. One is the apology to his fiancée on the eve of their wedding, one to his son, and one to his dead father. The apology to his fiancée is not actually addressed to her. In the letter addressed to her, he apologizes for wearing sweat pants on their first date and for being stoned when he first met her parents. It is in a letter to the actor Robert Sean Leonard, apologizing for confusing him with Matthew Broderick as the star of *The Producers*, that Bry reveals that he did in fact apologize to her—in person—for not calling and coming home at six in the morning after a cocaine-fueled night just days

---

39. Alcoholics Anonymous, *Twelve Steps and Twelve Traditions* (1953; New York: Alcoholics Anonymous World Services, Inc., 2004), p. 83.

40. Bry, *Public Apology*, pp. 95, 98.

before their wedding. It dawns on him that he was now responsible for more than himself—"My behavior carried ramifications for her"—and that apologizing to her was part of the process necessary for actually changing himself into the person she deserved. The apology to his son, for allowing him to get lost in Prospect Park, reveals even more poignantly his sense of responsibility for someone other than himself. When he says that his guilt takes the form of "a feeling of essential worthlessness," we are meant to reflect on all those earlier apologies where he had felt no such remorse. The apology to his father is the most moving in the book: "Sorry I didn't come right away when you called me. This happened on December 25, 1990, the day you died."[41] Each of these moments in *Public Apology* shows us what is crucial about *private* apologies: we apologize because our lives are connected, because we are responsible for others, and because we can become disconnected and lose others. The reason we apologize, in other words, is that we live *in* relationships, and that is the only way we can and know how to live.

---

41. Bry, *Public Apology*, pp. 212, 226–28, 150.

PUBLIC APOLOGIES

Jay Rayner's 2004 novel *Eating Crow* is a smart and funny parody of the mania for public apologies that marked the end of the last millennium, and continues to mark the first decades of this one. It also reveals just what can happen when the distinction between public and private apologies is ignored. The story follows the career of a viciously acid-tongued newspaper restaurant critic, Marc Basset, whose savage review of one restaurant led the demoralized chef to tape the review to the door of the bread oven in which he then baked himself to death. At the urging of his newspaper's publicity department, Basset attempts to control the fallout from this episode by appearing on radio and television in order to express what the director of the department calls a "certain amount of regret." She adds, "don't overdo it and certainly don't accept any responsibility." After his broadcast appearances, Basset decides on his own that he wants to apologize to the chef's widow, does so, and feels a "lightness and joy" he had never before felt. Inspired by what he describes as the "buzz" he gets from saying sorry, he then begins a series of apologies to people he had offended throughout his life—the restaurant critic whose job he had stolen, a woman whose overweight adolescence he had tormented, another of whom he had publicly boasted as a sexual conquest, his brother whose youth he had made miserable—and gets varying highs from each one. (He describes one that was less robust and shorter than the others as "an espresso of apology.") He is eventually "discovered" when a former love interest videotapes his apology, which becomes an Internet sensation, and he is then recruited to become the chief apologist of the newly inaugurated United Nations Office of Apology and Reconciliation. Drawing on an academic's theory of "penitential engagement" as a form of diplomacy and international relations, the UN has sponsored a series of ritualized conferences in which the chief apologist effectively apologizes to groups and nations for past atrocities like enslavement, colonization, and historical oppression. It turns out that Basset is perfect for the job, not only because he is gifted at emotional apologies, but also because his family tree is populated with ancestors who have participated in each of these historical crimes. He has, in the words of the theory of "penitential engagement," what is called "plausible apologibility," that is, some familial connection to the event.[1]

Rayner is parodying several different things in his novel. First, and ob-viously, he mocks academics (an easy target, sigh) who create theories like "penitential engagement." Professor Thomas Schenke is the primary target, as is his tome *Grievance Settlement Within a Global Context*, and the ghost-written popular versions of his academic book, *A Very Sorry Business: Further Apologies for Home and Hearth* and *Sorry Situations: Perfect Apologies for Weddings, Funerals, and Bar Mitzvahs*. He is also parodying the shameless ec-onomic motive on which that theory is based, that is, the idea that an apology by a corporation can prevent lawsuits and reduce the amount of settlements (the percentage of reduction in reparation settlements comes to be called the "Schenke scale differential"). Schenke may be fictional (let us hope), but the theory and the practice he represents are not. Corporations do recognize that timely apologies by significant representatives do indeed reduce tort claims, and, as Nick Smith has shown in his recent book, some, like the Toro Company, have made it explicitly a part of their business model (at appreci-able savings in legal fees).[2] Finally, Rayner is also parodying the ritual we have come to expect of nations' apologizing for the crimes of their past, but that aspect of the novel, it seems to me, is less harsh than the other parodies, and understandably so. Oppressed groups and nations are less funny than unstable academics, and less crass than greedy corporations.

What Rayner is most parodying, though, it seems to me, is what happens when we ignore the division between private and public apologies. Because Basset had always associated his private apologies with food, for instance, he decides to apologize for American slavery by cooking a meal (with fried chicken, cornbread, and milk gravy!) for the African American representa-tive to whom he is to offer the world's apology. (The representative rejects the meal, and requests filet mignon, seared foie gras, and outrageously expen-sive wines with each course). What had worked in private affairs—an apology

---

1. Jay Rayner, *Eating Crow* (New York: Simon & Schuster, 2004), pp. 15, 28, 34–35, 55, 58, 95.

2. Rayner, *Eating Crow*, pp. 237n, 101; Nick Smith, *Justice Through Apologies: Remorse, Reform, and Punishment* (New York: Cambridge University Press, 2014), pp. 243–58, and esp. pp. 255–56 on the Toro Company.

over lunch—becomes the formal structure for international diplomacy. Rayner pitilessly skewers the failure to regard the distinction between what is private and what is public, what is appropriate in one sphere and not in another. Throughout the novel, UN strategists use a discourse of private mental health to discuss public global politics. One refers to "the enormous weight of emotional baggage that world history has given us." Another leaves the UN apology unit to start working at the "new psychotherapy unit for dysfunctional nation-states" that uses the talking cure to look into "various events in the childhoods of the referred countries." But it is not only the idea that practices (apology, psychotherapy) meant for individual use become awkwardly co-opted for collective cases that Rayner finds laughable; it is the idea that these collective (public) practices then come to define the private use of them. After Basset makes apologizing chic, individuals and families around the world begin creating "apology ceremonies" and adapting the "Schenke Laws" to "more domestic circumstances."[3]

Like many of us, I think, Rayner traces the inability to gauge the difference between public and private to the media phenomenon of reality television, especially those that have debased the concept of remorse by making entertainment of it. Basset's appearance on one such show raises the bar and critics now must search for new terms for the genre: "ultra-reality," "meta-reality," "reality max." And it is precisely the failure to respect privacy that Rayner most powerfully condemns. Basset appears on one such program, Helen Treasure's *Powertalk*—a television show so filled with "Kleenex moments" that to watch it is to suspect that the nation was governed by "a tight coterie of emotionally incontinent men"—and apologizes to a friend whose romantic relationship he had intentionally ruined. When he finally meets that former friend, his friend condemns the invasion of privacy, in having "broadcast every sodding detail of my sodding humiliation on global television." Private lives should not be fodder for public entertainment, just as private practices are not entirely appropriate for public acts. Basset finally comes to that recognition when he realizes the division he had elided—things private and things public each "have their time and their place."[4] In the end, what Rayner finds risible is the idea that these public apologies are exactly like, and mean the same things as, private ones.

---

3. Rayner, *Eating Crow*, pp. 95, 247, 203.

4. Rayner, *Eating Crow*, pp. 185, 274, 1.

Rayner's is a very funny romp through a modern sensibility that he rightly mocks for failing to see how ridiculous it is to apply concepts meant for private psyches to public entities. People have emotional baggage and require psychotherapy; nations cannot. His larger point is that we live in a culture awash with the effects of the failure of modern agencies—political, media, business—not to see and mark the distinction between what is appropriate for private and what for public life. Television shows that bare the soul of individuals for entertainment value debase the souls of all of us when they take for granted that anything can be fodder for public consumption. Corporations that see the dollar value of apologies are shown to be *calculating* in the more morally dubious way that term can be understood. It is those kinds of public apologies that Rayner most skews.

Because Rayner's novel is a satire—and therefore relatively merciless in its mockery of public apologies—it does not ask, nor could be expected to ask, questions about what might motivate public apologies, other than the rank greed of the kinds of corporations he indicts. How, then, can we understand the practice of public apologies, how can we discern what motivates those who make and those who desire them, and how can we appreciate what role they have come to assume in the absence of other mechanisms for performing the restorative work these public apologies are assumed to undertake? There are no easy answers to these questions, and that is largely because there are so many different kinds of public apologies that serve quite different purposes. The best way for us to proceed in this case, then, is to offer a typology of public apologies and see how each kind expresses a particular dynamic. By showing more sympathy for particular groups, that is, by being more understanding of how a long history of oppression might create in certain ethnic and national populations the desire for accountability and redress, Rayner also highlights what is true of all types of public apologies—there are few public resources, discursive forms, and mediation forms and venues for raising and resolving those concerns.

I

There are a number of ways for creating a finer taxonomy of types of apologies within the large categories of private and public apologies. I have resisted doing so in the case of private apologies because I wished to focus on apologies as reconciliatory acts within particular situations, or of what Goffman called interactions or relations. In the previous chapter, I argued that we learn something valuable about private apologies when we turn our focus from what they are as *texts* and turn it instead to what they do and how they operate in specific *contexts*. In this chapter, though, I will follow a different strategy and argue that it is important for us to draw some important distinctions among the types of public apologies. I have two reasons for doing so. First, in the past few decades we have witnessed a dramatic increase in public apologies that occupy different spheres of activity, and it is worthwhile to see what this expansion of apologetic discourse can mean. Second, while there are different spheres of private life, and, no doubt, different kinds of private apologies within each sphere (and not just different communicative norms within relationships and traditions), it is nonetheless likely that the form and meaning of apologies do not significantly change in those different spheres. That is emphatically not the case with public apologies. In the same way that a political stump speech differs in form and meaning from a closing argument in a trial, so too does a public apology offered by a politician for saying something atrocious, say, differ from a public apology by a convicted criminal during the sentencing phase of the trial. They both seek to control the damage, obviously, but they differ in the stakes at issue and the meanings attached to the apologies by virtue of the different settings within which they take place, the different audiences they address, and the different precedent acts in the traditions in which they participate. Given the range of public spheres in our contemporary societies, then, and given to what extent apologies are coming to play increasingly important roles within them, it is important to make finer distinctions about the different kinds of public apologies.

I will explore six kinds of apologies here: (1) celebrity apologies, (2) corporation apologies, (3) diplomacy apologies, (4) regime apologies, (5) court apologies, and (6) apologies for the past. These apologies differ in important ways. Some apologies, for instance, are concerned with controlling public perception (celebrity and corporation), while others are more concerned with limiting liability (court and corporation). Some are focused on alleviating immediate political crises (diplomacy and regime), while others are intently attempts to foster more intricate trade, treaty, and political relations with the nations to which they're offered (diplomacy, apologies for the past). Some are defined by the venues where they take place (courts), others by a political calendar on which they mark anniversaries of historical atrocities (apologies for the past). What distinguishes all of them, of course, is that they are expressly public, and meant for public consumption, in other words, they are acts of publicity. A defining feature of public apologies is that they are delivered in venues where they can intentionally be overheard.

II

All public apologies are negotiated and staged, to some degree, but perhaps we may make finer distinctions and note how they are negotiated differently and staged differently.

Let us first consider celebrity apologies, that is, those apologies offered by those who live in public perception, and whose personae are primarily defined by what they represent as public figures. Under celebrity apologies, we would include those made by politicians who are apologizing for personal and not political errors of judgment, gaffes, and actions. So, for instance, in the example we will use here, President Bill Clinton's apology for the Monica Lewinsky affair counts as a celebrity apology since he is addressing a failing in his personal life, while his apology for the Rwandan genocide or the Tuskegee syphilis experiment would not count since he is there representing a larger entity (the United States) in his role as political representative. The reason these apologies assume a place in public is that the figure is a celebrity (that is, living in public) and that the damage is often public too and therefore needs to be redressed in public. Quite often, the damage is local and merely a matter of the celebrity's reputation; and therefore these apologies constitute a form of public relations damage control. In other cases, though, the damage is not local and what might look like simply repairing a reputation actually carries greater weight. So, in the case before us—Clinton's apology for the Lewinsky affair—we can see that Clinton had to repair his image, but he had to do so in order to govern effectively.

In celebrity apologies, the negotiations are almost wholly informal and amorphous; responses to an initial apology are almost entirely to be found in the news and social media, unlike a diplomacy apology, for instance, where the negotiations are through designated and recognized channels of communication between nations.

We can see this dynamic at work in the Clinton apology. Clinton's first public apology came on August 17, 1998, in the form of a televised 546-word statement. He expressed remorse—"I deeply regret that"—but a good part of his statement was actually spent trying to distinguish what was private— "Even presidents have private lives"—and what was more properly the domain of the public. The response to his first apology was considerably critical. Editorials by major newspapers expressed dissatisfaction with the apology, and polls taken in the immediate aftermath and long-term polling assessing his approval rating showed that a majority of Americans polled agreed. Clinton used the White House prayer breakfast a month later as his next occasion for addressing the topic. He began by saying that he had indeed received the message sent him by editorials and polls and letters directly addressed to him: "I agree with those who have said that in my first statement after I testified I was not contrite enough." Because the occasion was perfect—it was a prayer breakfast before religious leaders—he was able to express what he had failed to express a month earlier in a discourse that both his immediate audience at the prayer breakfast and his larger American audience understood. He now expressed his *contrition*, articulated his "genuine repentance," and sought forgiveness from God—"I must have God's help to be the person I want to be"—as he openly declared: "I have sinned." He ended by reading a long passage from the Yom Kippur liturgy—on turning from sin and seeking atonement.[5] The response to this second apology was almost universally positive.

Those who have written about the Clinton apologies have identified the key features that made the second apology so much more successful than the first. I wish to focus on something else, and that is that the second apology, as Clinton himself noted in the course of delivering it, was largely a result of a public discussion about the merits of the first. It was, in other words, a product of that informal negotiation in the public sphere. I suppose that some private apologies might also involve those kinds of negotiations, but I suspect that those discussions are more directed toward defining the offense rather than negotiating the proper words to address it. In response to an initial apology, the victim might tell the offender that he has it wrong, and that what really hurt was something else altogether, or the kind of disrespect that the more superficial offense expressed; and then the second apology would address the deeper issues involved. Negotiations over public apologies, in this case, and many others, are not about defining the offense but rather about identifying what sort of tenor and affect the apology should strike. What Clinton was told through the informal channels in which he received the communications—including the gift of the Yom Kippur liturgy from which he read at the prayer breakfast—is that a nation with the religious sensibilities

5. "Testing of a President: In His Own Words: Last Night's Address," *New York Times* (August 18, 1998); "Clinton's Prayer Breakfast Speech," *Washington Post* (September 11, 1998). For coverage, commentary, and representative editorial responses to each of these speeches, see Peter Baker and John F. Harris, "Clinton Admits to Lewinsky Relationship, Challenges Starr to End Personal 'Prying,'" *Washington Post* (August 18, 1998); and Brian Knowlton, "'I Sinned,' He Says in Apology that Includes Lewinsky: Clinton Vows He Will Stay and Fight," *New York Times* (September 12, 1998). There is a great deal of commentary on these apologies. For a recent, informative discussion see Edwin L. Battistella, *Sorry About That: The Language of Public Apologies* (New York: Oxford University Press, 2014), pp. 79–85.

of the United States wanted to hear the discourse of penitence and remorse more than that of defiance. The public wanted an apology.

Second, it also became clear that it wanted a *public* apology. That is not surprising, given that the negotiations took place in the public sphere, but it should not be downplayed that those comments in the public sphere rejected what Clinton had first proposed in his attempt to divide what was private and what was public. He had urged in his August 17 statement that he would deal with this matter in private, with his wife, daughter, and their God. He made a crucial distinction between what he called "private lives"—where he felt this matter belonged—and what he called "national life," where this matter, he argued, had no bearing. It was partly that division that the public disputed.

There is a more vexed and larger problem than I am addressing here, but it should be acknowledged as a backdrop to debates about the meanings and value of public celebrity apologies. What is it the public has claim to from its celebrities, especially its political ones? Before the Internet and social media made a grotesque art form of acts of self-revelation and other-shaming, there was a question of whether particular kinds of curiosity were relevant or prurient (a term that used to have resonance). Is the demand for the scandalous details part of what makes a celebrity apology complete—an account of what was the wrong done, and for which an act of atonement is being offered—or something that simply satisfies a very different sensibility or need in the public? Celebrity apologies are, I argue, inherently problematic for reasons I will discuss below, but they are made even more troubling when we consider that the audience for them likely brings expectations that have little to do with the discourse of apology, and much more to do with the desire for certain kinds of spectacle.

III

Whereas celebrity apologies are implicitly negotiated—in an informal but choreographed minuet between an undefined public and a set of handlers, advisors, and publicity specialists for the celebrity—corporation apologies are explicitly negotiated. We can take as our case study an apology the Ford Motor Company offered to Donna Bailey, a woman who was paralyzed from the neck down after her SUV rolled over because of design flaws in the vehicle and the Bridgestone/Firestone tires that came with it. So, how was the apology negotiated? It began when Bailey sued the company for over $100 million. Ford responded, and, after negotiations between her lawyers and the company's, she decided to settle for three things: an undisclosed sum, a public disclosure of thousands of pages of company memos and reports on the safety of the vehicles and tires, and a public apology. The public apology came in two forms. First, three lawyers for the Ford corporation flew to the Texas Institute for Rehabilitation and Recovery, where Bailey had been hospitalized for months, and apologized to her. By her request, the apology was videotaped; and by Ford's request, the sound was turned off. Her lawyer, Tab Turner, says that Ford negotiated "to keep the audio off of the videotape because they didn't want anyone hearing what they said." Meanwhile, the chair of Firestone, a unit of the Bridgestone Corporation, sent Bailey a handwritten note that began: "There is nothing any of us at Firestone can say or do to return what you and your family have lost."[6]

It is worth noting the steps in this negotiation of a public apology. It began in court, when Bailey filed a lawsuit against the corporation. It then went to lawyers' offices where the terms of the settlement were hammered out. It then ended at the hospital bed where the public apology was delivered. Bailey initiated the negotiations that led to the public apology through one venue (courts), had it agreed to in another (lawyers' offices), and finally made public in a muted videotape that was shown on network television when her lawyers released the tape (media). These were all strictly formal agreements that were set in decidedly corporate venues (tort courts, law offices, network television). Moreover, it is important for us to recognize the bizarre combination of publicity and privacy in this corporation apology. There are two things that are especially hidden from the public and rendered private—the amount of money Ford gave Bailey and the actual wording of the three lawyers' apology. (It is not clear whether part of the settlement was that Bailey could not disclose how much she was paid, but such a nondisclosure clause is a common feature of such settlements.) At the same time, Ford made public the thousands of pages of reports that would reveal how much the two corporations were at fault for covering up what they knew was dangerous. The question that seems necessary to ask is why the sound was turned off on the video? Why was that not public in this public apology?

In an insightful discussion of this case, Nick Smith argues this as an example of a corporation winning on both sides. It gets public credit for

6. Michael Winirip, "Ford and Firestone Settle Suit Over Explorer Crash," *New York Times* (January 9, 2001); "Tire Victim: Apology Seemed Sincere," CBS News (December 20, 2000). I have benefited from Nick Smith's commentary on this case. See Smith, *I Was Wrong: The Meaning of Apologies* (New York: Cambridge University Press, 2008), pp. 254–55; and Smith, *Justice Through Apologies*, pp. 243–45.

apologizing (it is a moral corporation) but it also avoids having to admit wrongdoing or "otherwise undertaking legal risk." He speculates that the muting of the sound likely permitted Ford to avoid accepting blame.[7] It is not clear just what that would serve, though. If the sound is turned off, and there is a disclosure clause written into the settlement contract, might Ford not then be able to produce an enhanced rather than a redacted apology, one in which they accepted responsibility, admitted wrongdoing, and expressed their heartfelt sorrow for what Bailey was suffering? This is unlikely, of course, since nondisclosure clauses are only as binding as the person who receives them is willing to be bound by them. Ford would not want to offer sufficiently tempting information that Bailey would be willing to violate the terms of her settlement to make them public. (It is also hard to imagine that Ford would then have the gall to go to court and sue a quadriplegic woman for not abiding by that clause; that would cause them much more of a public relations disaster than it was worth.) This example, I think, serves to show what are the most pressing constraints on public corporation apologies. Corporations cannot tell the truth or accept blame precisely because they are pressured by the two venues in which this negotiation began and ended. Tort courts on one side and public media outlets on the other are the Scylla and the Charybdis of the corporate world.

I offer this fact not as an explanation for or a defense of why corporations do not produce more robust apologies for their failures, apologies that more resemble what Smith describes as "categorical." I offer it instead so that we can understand just why our expectations might be skewed when we imagine public apologies to share the same properties as private apologies. In spite of American laws that declare it so, corporations are not people—or, at least, not people enough to feel remorse. To the extent that people find it satisfying to hear a corporation apologize for its malfeasances—and many do, and they have good reasons to do so—then corporate apologies will likely remain a feature of our public life. To the extent that we believe or expect that they abide by the same set of norms as private apologies, though, we delude ourselves. The Ford apology is not an anomaly, at all; it strikes me as emblematic of precisely all corporate apologies. They are always muted—just not always literally so—because they are offered by unfeeling entities, because they are part of negotiated settlements, and because they operate within venues (tort courts,

_____

7. Smith, *Justice Through Apologies*, p. 244.

law offices, and media) where they become a fungible item: public apology or public exposure (and both reducible to a bottom line).

IV

The diplomacy apology, like all diplomatic negotiations, is largely about defining what is formally permitted in a particular relationship between nations. We can use as our case study one that the United States gave to China in 2001. There remains some dispute over precisely what happened on April 1, 2001, but when a Chinese interceptor fighter jet approached a US Navy intelligence aircraft over the South China Sea, there was an accident that forced the American plane to land on Hainan Island, where China had a military installation. The pilot of the Chinese interceptor jet, Wang Wei, was killed in the accident. Several things are in dispute, including the legality of the American flights, which had been taking place since the early 1950s, and the cause of the accident, which America claimed was due to the Chinese pilot's bumping the wing of the American plane on a precariously close approach, while China claimed it was caused by the American pilot's veering at and ramming the Chinese plane. The American plane was now on Chinese terrain, and China demanded an apology from America before it would release the plane and its crew of twenty-four. After much diplomatic negotiation, and many public statements by both sides, US Ambassador Joseph Prueher sent a letter to the Chinese Minister of Foreign Affairs, Tan Jiaxuan, on April 11. That text used the word "sorry" (or cognate expressions) in three places. It began by stating that both "President Bush and Secretary of State Powell have expressed their sincere regret over your missing pilot and aircraft." In the second instance, Prueher wrote: "Please convey to the Chinese people and to the family of pilot Wang Wei that we are very sorry for their loss." The final instance addressed the American plane's landing on Hainan Island: "We are very sorry the entering of China's airspace and the landing did not have verbal clearance." As numerous commentators have noted, America's apology was intentionally meant to express sorrow, not remorse.[8] It is the same thing as saying, "I am sorry for your loss."

Because this was an issue of diplomacy, the apology was negotiated (as we have seen to be the case in celebrity and corporation apologies). The

---

8. For the text of Ambassador Prueher's letter, see "We Are Very Sorry," *The Guardian* (April 11, 2001); Aaron Lazare, *On Apology* (New York: Oxford University Press, 2004), pp. 214–17; Battistela, *Sorry About That*, pp. 15–51. Also see Smith, *I Was Wrong*, pp. 123–24.

negotiations were particularly over who would deliver the apology, and what precisely it would say. It was decided that the ambassador, and not the president or secretary of state, would deliver it, whereas China would have preferred a higher-level official to do so; but the letter would also make reference to the president's and secretary's saying sorry. As well, in the first draft, the second and third appearances of "sorry" had not been qualified; in the final draft, both were changed to "very sorry." This negotiated diplomacy apology intentionally left enough room for each country to claim what it wished. China called the letter an American *daoquian*, and translated the two instances of "very sorry" as *shenbiao qianyi*. Both translations denote an apology in its remorseful sense (we express regret and accept responsibility). America, meanwhile, made it clear that it was expressing something entirely different. As Secretary of State Powell stated in his appearance on *Face the Nation*, the apology, such as it was, was strictly for the violation of Chinese airspace during the emergency landing: "We do acknowledge that we violated their air space . . . [a]nd we regret that, and we've expressed sorrow for it, and we're sorry that that happened. But that can't be seen as an apology, accepting responsibility."[9]

It turns out, then, that what quickly became known as the "letter of the two 'very sorries'" produced two very different ways of reading those sorries. America claimed it did not apologize, while China claimed that it did. In this case, the possibility for reading it either way had much to do with the ambiguity in the English word (*sorry* as sorrow or remorse), but we must also be clear that it is not simply a matter of mistranslation or cultural misunderstanding. It is a matter of coordinated and negotiated misunderstanding. The document permitted each nation to present to *its* public its own interpretation of what happened. There are two curiosities here. The first is that there are distinct publics. In 2001, that was possible, and as of this writing (2015) it remains possible; it might not be for long, though, as the Internet transforms what used to be distinct national media into one conglomerate body of media, and as China is eventually forced to end its imposed restrictions on Internet content and its monitoring of individuals' Internet usage. In that future world, it will be difficult for such diverse interpretations to have much chance of success. Second, it is curious that the obfuscation seems driven by the perceived importance in the apology. It was as important for China to

---

9. Colin Powell on *Face the Nation*, http://www.cbsnews.com/news/ftn-transcript-april-8-2001/. Powell's appearance was in the midst of the negotiations, but clearly reflects what the United States intended the apology to do and sets the stage for how it would be interpreted.

receive one as it was for America not to offer it. Perhaps that was only a case of whether or not the entity apologizing claims responsibility with the apology, but one suspects that there is something deeper at stake than responsibility. It had much more to do with "saving face."

Even though it seems an anomaly, I would suggest that this apology is a paradigmatic example of a diplomacy apology. Consider those features that make it seem peculiarly anomalous as an apology—it was negotiated, it was in some ways coerced by the fact that there were "detainees" whose freedom depended on it, and it contained a purposeful ambiguity that permitted each side to interpret it as each saw fit. These are arguably the features we can find in other kinds of international agreements, such as treaties or conventions. They are all negotiated, they all involve what happens to government agents when they are outside their acknowledged territories, and they are documents capable of bearing many meanings. The diplomacy apology too is a document that not only changes meaning over time, but, crucially, is capable of bearing different meanings by differing entities at the same time. Consider the document that was at issue over whether or not American flight was permitted over the South China Sea, the United Nations Convention on the Law of the Sea. The United States interprets the particular, relevant provision of that convention as permitting free navigation, while China interprets it as not permitting it. Like the convention, the diplomacy apology is not just capable of being interpreted in different ways, but must, to some extent, be so capable in order to do the work it is supposed to do, that is, achieve a peaceful resolution to a political crisis. If that strikes us a form of deception—and we disapprove of it in an apology—then we are applying values to diplomacy apologies that do not properly belong to them.

Diplomacy is not about truth, and nor are diplomacy apologies. As Sir Henry Wooton famously claimed, "An ambassador is an honest gentleman sent to lie abroad for the good of his country." Wooton, who was a diplomat for England during the reign of James I, made this claim while he was on his way to a mission in Italy in 1604. It was later to cause him serious problems when one of the king's antagonists used it to criticize James I, who, the antagonist claimed, sent a confessed liar to represent him abroad. Wooton's crime was not in being a liar, but to make public what everyone knew—that diplomacy depended on deceptions of various sorts. It is perhaps as ironic as it was tragic that his honesty about what was involved in an ambassador's job cost him his job as an ambassador. There is no extant copy of Wooton's written apology to his king—James declared somewhat ambiguously that it "commuted sufficiently for a greater offence"—but it was an apology that did not permit him to keep his job.[10] We can see here, then, the difference between a *diplomat's* apology, where sincerity is key, and the interpretation belongs solely to the person receiving it, and the *diplomacy* apology, where sincerity is unimportant and where interpretation is not so restricted.

V

The regime apology is a part of a larger process that has come to be called "transitional justice." In the second half of the twentieth century, several nations underwent "regime changes," shifting from one kind of order, such as a military junta, single-party communist or fascist rule, or an apartheid government, to a democratic order in which the population repressed by the former regime would elect a new regime that represented them. At those moments in those several countries, a debate took place about what sort of justice to apply to the former government, which was now frequently defined as a criminal regime. Different options were proposed in what became a global debate. Some held for strict retributive justice and the punishment of those responsible, based on the example of the Nuremberg trials. Others feared that such trials would distract and endanger a fragile democratic movement and they proposed instead either amnesty (specific or blanket) or acts of exclusion of those associated with the previous regime (lustration, decommunization, denazification), or a tribunal that would perform an act of collecting information and producing a report that demonstrated just what that regime's crimes were. All these strategies came to be understood under the umbrella term *transitional justice* because they described processes by which a nation would best be able to complete a shift from an oppressive to an open order.

The most regnant symbol of transitional justice in the last quarter of the twentieth century became the truth and reconciliation commission reports that about a score of countries produced. Much has been written about these truth commissions and the work they performed.[11] I would like to

---

10. See "Wooton, Henry," *Dictionary of National Biography*, edited by Sidney Lee (London: Smith, Elder & Co., 1904), Volume 63, p. 53. The antagonist was Gasper Scioppius, and his target was James I's theological stances. Also see "Sir Henry Wooton's Aphorism," *European Magazine and London Review* 59 (1811): 109–10.

11. See, especially, *Transitional Justice: How Emerging Democracies Reckon with Former Regimes*, edited by Neil J. Kritz (Washington, DC: United States Institutes of Peace Press, 1995), 3 volumes; Ruti Teitel, *Transitional Justice* (New York: Oxford University Press, 2000); Priscilla B. Hayner, *Unspeakable Truths: Confronting State Terror and Atrocity* (New York and London: Routledge, 2001). For debates in South Africa, in particular, see Antjie

focus here on one aspect of them, and that is the regime apologies that often took place in the midst of these commissions' proposal, operation, and conclusion. While the primary terms of the debate were whether a new regime should prosecute the previous regime (retributive justice) or grant it amnesty in order to permit the gathering of truth and the fostering of reconciliation (transitional justice), other terms also came into play, and especially the terms *forgiveness* and *apology*. In South Africa, in particular, as we have seen, the Truth and Reconciliation Commission headed by Archbishop Desmond Tutu produced a series of wrenching scenes in which perpetrators of crimes would apologize to and sometimes be forgiven by the survivors of the victims. And so, the dynamic of apology and forgiveness came to inhabit—some say, "haunt"—the process of transitional justice. Those scenes, jarring and moving as many of them are, are not acts of regime apology per se, since those offering the apologies are often police agents and not the more responsible political representatives of the state. Those are apologies for crimes of policing, not for crimes of creating and maintaining the political state that required those policing strategies.

Regime apologies come from the head of the state whose apology accepts responsibility for the regime. That is what happened when President De Klerk apologized for the crimes of apartheid in a 1993 press conference, for instance. In that case, it was the leader of the outgoing regime that apologized. In other cases, intriguingly, it is the leader of the incoming regime that apologizes for a predecessor that the whole process of regime change has implicitly indicted. In Chile, for example, it was the democratically elected President Patricio Aylwin who offered an apology and assumed the state's accountability for the crimes of his predecessor—and, with great symbolism, staged the affair in the very sports stadium that the previous regime had used for the torture for which he was apologizing.[12] It is these regime apologies, I think, that most fit what both Nicholas Tavuchis and Aaron Lazare believe to be a distinguishing feature of public apologies, namely, a "public record" of them.

Krog, *Country of My Skull: Guilt, Sorrow, and the Limits of Forgiveness in the New South Africa* (New York: Three Rivers Press, 2000), pp. 21–22; Kader Asmal, Louise Asmal, and Ronald Suresh Roberts, *Reconciliation Through Truth: A Reckoning of Apartheid's Criminal Governance* (2nd ed.; New York: St. Martin's, 1997); and *Truth v. Justice: The Morality of Truth Commissions*, edited by Robert I. Rotberg and Dennis Thompson (Princeton, NJ: Princeton University Press, 2000).

12. Liz Sly, "De Klerk Apologizes for Apartheid's Abuses," *Chicago Tribune* (April 30, 1993). For President Aylwin's apology and its terms and settings, see Teitel, *Transitional Justice*, p. 84. Teitel calls "transitional apologies" what I am calling "regime apologies."

This public record is part of the political process, as Ruti Teitel insightfully notes, since it performs that delicate dance of transition, which requires both "the continuity of state responsibility" as well as the "discontinuity" of "letting go of the past."[13] In that way, regime apologies are like the apologies for the past we will discuss presently, in that they become political statements marking a particular shift in policy and history, but they are also like the diplomacy apologies we've just discussed in that they are meant to be overheard by the international community, even as they are addressed to the citizens of that particular nation. They are statements of change and invitations to new diplomatic relations, as much as they are statements of regret for the crimes of the previous regime.

VI

Court apologies, unlike the types we've looked at so far, are named not for those who offer them (celebrities, corporations, diplomats, or regimes) but for the particular public venue in which they occur—court. And these apologies are quickly assuming a critical place in discussions of jurisprudence. In light of a judicial system in which the state largely displaces the victim in the prosecution of crimes, restorative justice theorists are asking critical questions about just what retributive justice is supposed to accomplish, and whether it is not more humane for the victim, the criminal, and the society for us to think about processes that are more *restorative*. Ought not the courts and the penal system work to restore dignity and hearing for the victim, create the possibility for reintegration for the criminal, and thereby deliver a more meaningful sense of justice for the society? Given the sharp rise in rates of incarceration, especially in the United States, is there not some way to produce a court system that is less punitive, and less enduringly punitive? Many other cultures have mechanisms for mediating disputes that do not assume that the victim should have no place, or that the only fit response to a wrong is punishment that takes away freedom or life.[14] Cannot Western cultures learn

---

13. Nicholas Tavuchis, *Mea Culpa: A Sociology of Apology and Reconciliation* (Stanford, CA: Stanford University Press, 1991), p. 109: "the major structural requirement and ultimate task of collective apologetic speech is to put things on record"; Aaron Lazare, *On Apologies* (New York: Oxford University Press, 2004), p. 40: "The precise written statement of the apology for the public record is essential to public apologies"; Teitel, *Transitional Justice*, p. 84.

14. See, for instance, *Traditional Justice and Reconciliation After Violent Conflict: Learning from African Experiences* (Stockholm: International Institute for Democracy and Electoral

from these cultural practices? In some cases, it seems that they are trying to do just that.

And the practice of court apologies is a centerpiece of that attempt. There are two ways to think of that practice. One is that apologies are, and should be, shaming rituals. John Braithwaite, the most prominent restorative justice theorist who advocates the practice of apologizing in courts, argues that "apology is the most powerful and symbolically meaningful form of shaming," and can thus promote the greatest satisfaction in victims who receive such an apology. He notes that apologizing as an aspect of a public shaming ritual is very much part of Japan's judicial system, which he shows to have significantly lower rates of incarceration and recidivism. Some American localities are practicing this form of symbolic reparation. In Oregon, for instance, in the mid-1980s the district attorney for Lincoln County established a program in which "people found guilty of crimes against property can take out advertisements apologizing for their crimes instead of serving prison terms." The apology is not meant only for the victim, but for the entire readership of the newspaper where the advertisement is taken out; and so it is, prima facie, an act of public shaming. The second way of thinking about the court apology is to see it as *practice*, literally—not *a* practice, but an act that permits those involved to learn and get better at doing a particular thing. In mediation sessions, criminals face their victims and apologize to them. Margaret Walker sees these sessions as transformative because they permit the inauguration and performance of new relationships. When people who were wronged and the people who wronged them engage with each other, one to apologize and the other to forgive, they "begin to *act out* the more morally adequate relationships at which they aim."[15] They begin to develop the discursive strategies that will assist them in maintaining instead of violating relationships.

At a second level, though, court apologies are beginning to appear in other manifestations that strike many as more problematic. Consider two of them. The first is the court-ordered apology, which some see as meaningless since

Assistance, 2008); and *Justice as Healing: Indigenous Ways*, edited by Wanda D. McCaslin (St. Paul, MN: Living Justice Press, 2005).

15. Eliza Ahmed, Nathan Harris, John Braithwaite, and Valerie Braithwaite, *Shame Management Through Reintegration* (New York: Cambridge University Press, 2001), p. 52; John Braithwaite, *Restorative Justice and Responsive Regulation* (New York: Oxford University Press, 2002), p. 52; see Braithwaite, *Crime, Shame, and Reintegration* (New York: Cambridge University Press, 1989) on Japan; Tavuchis, *Mea Culpa*, p. 140, for Lincoln County; Margaret Walker, *Moral Repair: Reconstructing Moral Relations After Wrongdoing* (Cambridge: Cambridge University Press, 2006), p. 212.

it is mandated from without, and some see as coercive. I am sympathetic to the first objection, since it is hard to imagine what sincerity an apology can contain that a judge imposes on a criminal to perform. The second objection that it is coercive seems to me to miss the point. Nick Smith gives an example of someone who believes in the legalization of marijuana being ordered by the court to apologize for possession of drugs. "Requiring such a person to contradict his beliefs under the threat of punishment evokes the most authoritarian examples of forced conversions."[16] Since the person has the choice—offer an apology or serve time—it seems to me that it is not so coercive, no more coercive, in any case, than any other example of someone who has violated the laws of the state. If one disagrees with those laws, then one performs acts of civil disobedience, and, like the originator of that term and practice, goes to jail for those acts as part of the process. The "threat of punishment," in other words, is for the crime, and the option of apologizing is to remove that threat; the choice, like that of Lincoln County criminals, is up to the individual.

The second is the "apology reduction"—in which an apology by the criminal in court would potentially reduce the sentence imposed. The major text for those who write about this matter is the section entitled "Acceptance of Responsibility" in the US Sentencing Commission *Guidelines Manual*. In cases where a defendant "clearly demonstrates acceptance of responsibility for his offense," the judge may decrease the offense level by two levels, and, if the defendant furthermore in a timely way tells the court that he plans to plead guilty, thereby "permitting the government and court to allocate their resources efficiently," the judge may reduce the offense level by one additional level. As Smith notes, a three-level reduction typically reduces a sentence by 35%. The guidelines are clear in the commentary on what *timely* in particular means: "This adjustment is not intended to apply to a defendant who puts the government to its burden of proof at trial by denying the essential factual elements of guilt, is convicted, and only then admits guilt and expresses remorse." As several commentators have noted, these guidelines largely reward compliance rather than apology, since they expressly state that saving the state money is what counts.[17]

---

16. Smith, *Justice Through Apologies*, p. 64.

17. US Sentencing Commission, *Guidelines Manual*, §3E1.1 (Nov. 2014), p. 371, Part E— "Acceptance of Responsibility"; Smith, *Justice Through Apologies*, p. 193; US Sentencing Commission, *Guidelines Manual*, p. 372; see Jeffrey G. Murphy, "Well, Excuse Me!: Remorse, Apology, and Criminal Sentencing," 38 *Ariz. St. L.J.* (Summer 2006): 371–86; and Murphy,

There are many who advocate that apology reductions, whether or not they can be teased out of the sentencing guidelines, *ought* to be part of our judicial system.[18] The key problem raised by this possibility, the same one we identified in our discussions of Austin and earlier of forgiveness, is *sincerity*. Some, like Jeffrie Murphy, argue that having that option clearly invites abuse; those who are not remorseful will act as if they are since there is excellent incentive to do so. Others, like Smith, see more promise in it, largely because he believes that his model of "categorical apology" permits us better to discern whether or not apologies are insincere, and courts have to make judgments of

---

"Remorse, Apology, and Mercy," in *Punishment and the Moral Emotions: Essays in Love, Morality, and Religion* (New York: Oxford University Press, 2012), pp. 129–80, esp. p. 156 n. 34; and Smith, *Justice Through Apologies*, pp. 94–240.

18. Another set of discussions about sentencing guidelines and the law in general has also occurred in those who write on *forgiveness*. Cesare Beccaria had pointed out that in practice a small crime "is sometimes pardoned, if the person offended chuses to forgive the offender." As Susan Jacoby notes, there was a long tradition in Greek law, repudiated in both Hebrew and Roman law, which held that acts of private forgiveness could override public punishment. If the injured person was willing to forgive the crime, then the state could do the same. The modern Milanese Beccaria agreed with the ancient Romans. While it appears to be "an act of good-nature and humanity," such forgiveness, he writes, when applied to reduce or remove the punishment is "contrary to the good of the public." Beccaria works with the premise that a crime committed against an individual is also a crime committed against the public order; and the individual injured has no more than his or her minor share in determining that order. Modern advocates of restorative justice in criminal trials challenge that premise, believing that modern systems of criminal justice often alienate the victim (and do not attempt to "restore" what the crime took away, including the peace of mind that comes from participating in the administration of justice). Some restorative justice advocates suggest that that peace of mind might be found by permitting victims of crimes to have a more prominent role, including the right to proclaim their forgiveness, in court proceedings, just what Beccaria identified as contrary to public good.

Contemporary retributivists wholeheartedly agree with Beccaria. Criminal justice is for apportioning punishment based on fitness, whereas forgiveness is an act of mercy based precisely on *disproportion* (a gift of grace for an injury). "Retributivism does not forbid forgiveness," Kathleen Dean Moore concludes, simply because the two occupy quite different realms. Retributive justice is about acts that constitute proportionality, in other words, it is about the requirement of "punishment under specified circumstances." Forgiveness, on the other hand, is an emotion (how people "feel toward someone who wrongs them"), and retributivists, like everyone else, can maintain "an attitude of goodwill toward a transgressor." Forgiveness, then, is a virtue that has no place in the courtroom, and yet it has certainly been present. Cesare Beccaria, *An Essay on Crimes and Punishments: by the Marquis Beccaria of Milan. With a Commentary by M. de Voltaire* (Philadelphia: William Young, 1793), p. 159; Susan Jacoby, *Wild Justice: The Evolution of Revenge* (New York: Harper & Row, 1983), p. 128; Kathleen Dean Moore, *Pardons: Justice, Mercy, and the Public Interest* (New York: Oxford University Press, 1989), p. 196; Paul Tullis, "Can Forgiveness Play a Role in Criminal Justice?" *New York Times Magazine* (January 4, 2013). The most recent study on forgiveness that raises the question of its place in courts is Margret R. Holmgren, *Forgiveness and Retribution: Responding to Wrongdoing* (New York: Cambridge University Press, 2012).

the value of many other features of evidence as well. And, finally, some, like Christopher Bennett, steer another course altogether, and argue that sincerity is not important, but that the apology ritual is, since it serves the needs of the victims who would like to hear that the criminal sides with them in acknowledging his previous actions as wrong. Murphy's answer is caution, and he implies that a sincerely remorseful defendant might actually wish to suffer the imposed punishment. Smith's is hopefulness, and he argues that we can establish guidelines and logistics and training that would enable judges and juries to gauge sincerity. Bennett's is a somewhat formalist approach in which he dispenses with the question of sincerity altogether, and argues that restorative and retributive justice can be reconciled through an approach that sees sentences of hard treatment completed by "proportionate apologetic action regardless of the spirit in which one does this."[19]

I think the appearance of the word *remorse* in the commentary of the sentencing guidelines might tell us something else, as well. It might reveal to what extent *apology* is being *implicitly* considered in this dynamic. There is a fear, in other words, that defendants are being judged on particular postures (apologetic or not) that are not clearly part of the charge or the understood procedure. It is worth reminding ourselves that for a long time judicial forms had the discourse of apology built into their workings, since "remorseless" was a category of a kind of criminal who deserved no, and received no, special consideration in reduced sentencing. It is only recently, however, that the category of "remorseful" seems to be coming into formal play in sentencing, but it is also not entirely spelt out in a formal way just what role it is playing. When the legal standards are unclear, the people most misserved are those who cannot afford lawyers who know how to present their clients to most advantage in that system, that is, poorer defendants and those who have historically been perceived as being criminals because of their race rather than their actions. The history of American race relations has shown us that people of African descent have long suffered greater rates of arrest, indictment, and death penalty imposition; and part of that reason, a clear one for those of us who have written about these issues, is that their postures—including postures of defiance or remorse, resistance or apology—are read and misread

---

19. Murphy, "Well, Excuse Me," p. 379; Smith, *Justice Through Apologies*, pp. 202–15, 215–20, 220–24, respectively, for the guidelines, the logistics, and the training of personnel; Christopher Bennett, *The Apology Ritual: A Philosophical Theory of Punishment* (New York: Cambridge University Press, 2008), p. 173; also see Bennett, "Taking the Sincerity Out of Saying Sorry: Restorative Justice as Ritual," *Journal of Applied Philosophy* 23.2 (2006): 127–43.

through the lens of primarily white juries, judges, and society.[20] The danger, then, is that sentence reductions will apply more to those who have been punished less because of how the "remorse" of which the sentencing guidelines speak is going to be understood.

VII

The final kind of apology we will consider here is the apology for the past. I will make here a distinction I have made elsewhere between two different kinds of apologies within this category—one I call *political apologies*, which address the near past, say the period from World War II to the present, and the other *historical apologies*, which address events from the distant past. An apology by the United States for the internment of Japanese citizens is a political apology, while an apology by the United States for slavery would be a historical apology. Both, to be clear, are *political* in the sense of being part of a public discourse about the relationship of the state to its citizens, its past, and its place in the international order; in other words, historical apologies are not apolitical simply because they address events that are five hundred years old instead of fifty. The division is somewhat arbitrary, but it is primarily based on whether there is anyone living from the event for which the apology is offered. If an event still has survivors, then it is political because they are frequently the ones directly addressed; if there are no survivors, then the apology is historical. So, apologies that are political will all eventually become apologies that are historical. The distinction is worth making, I argue, because there is a difference between an apology directly addressed to a living constituency and one that is offered directly to a more nebulous and clearly not living one, even as it is also indirectly addressed to an audience descended from those historical victims. When the pope apologizes for the Crusades, for instance, he is addressing a long history of the Vatican's aggressive disrespect for other religions, and because he does not apologize to anyone directly victimized by the Crusades, he is able to frame the apology in a particular way that addresses those larger concerns. When the pope apologizes for Vatican inaction during the Holocaust, on the other hand, he is addressing a specific group of survivors, and he therefore has to frame his apology in a way that does not seem indifferent to the fact that there are people who have standing (by their

---

20. See Ashraf H. A. Rushdy, *American Lynching* (New Haven, CT: Yale University Press, 2012).

experience) of accepting or rejecting the apology.[21] I will turn first to political apologies to show what work they do, and then to historical apologies.

At the time I was writing this chapter (April 2015), Prime Minister Shinzo Abe of Japan was scheduled for an official state visit to the United States. It would be historic, in one sense, because he would become the first Japanese leader to address a joint meeting of Congress, but it was a different sense of "historic" that was even more to the fore in the debates in advance of his visit. As the editorial board of the *New York Times* phrased it: "the success of the visit also depends on whether and how honestly Mr. Abe confronts Japan's wartime history, including its decision to wage war, its brutal occupation of China and Korea, its atrocities and its enslavement of thousands of women forced to work as sex slaves or 'comfort women' in wartime brothels." Those historical facts are in dispute in certain sectors of Japanese society—especially by the conservative, militaristic sectors of it—who express their dissatisfaction through organizations committed to revising school textbooks, keeping alive Shinto religion, and making visits and donations to Yasukuni Shrine, a symbol for them of Japan's military glory and a symbol for its enemies of its militaristic, ultranationalist crimes. In addition to its symbolic value, Yasukuni Shrine houses the crypts of several class A war criminals. Because of that association, the last two emperors have boycotted visits to the shrine, but many of Japan's conservative premiers have made their visits in defiance of international concern. No one has done that as much as Premier Abe, who sent a gift to the shrine the day after the *New York Times* editorial board statement.[22] Previous visits to the shrine, and gifts, are attempts by Abe to express support for his conservative political base.

These, then, are the vectors of Japanese politics on the issue of its wartime conduct: the Yasukuni Shrine as a symbol of a militaristic past and school textbooks as encasing different versions of that past. The other, and perhaps most important, vector in this suite of symbols for Japanese politics is the *apology*. Previous prime ministers, especially Tomiichi Murayama, have apologized on the ritual date of August 15, for Japan's wartime aggression, colonization, and exploitation of the comfort women. (August 15 is the anniversary of the end of the Pacific War.) Murayama's 1995 apology has been the most robust and

---

21. See Ashraf H. A. Rushdy, *A Guilted Age: Apologies for the Past* (Philadelphia: Temple University Press, 2015).

22. Editorial Board, "Shinzo Abe and Japan's History," *New York Times* (April 20, 2015); Martin Fackler, "Shinzo Abe, Japanese Premier, Sends Gift to Contentious Yasukuni Shrine," *New York Times* (April 21, 2015).

important of the anniversary apologies, and it represents the zenith of Japan's expressed remorse for its wartime conduct. Abe has taken special delight in toying publicly with the idea that he would repudiate Murayama's apology. Regularly, he would throw out an offensive comment—something along the lines of, "Korean comfort women were not coerced but willing participants in their prostitution"—and then suggest that he might revoke the apology previous premiers had made for that wartime crime of Japan's. A media furor would follow, and then Abe would walk it back.[23] Like his periodic visits and donations to the Yasukuni Shrine, these attempts to rile the waters are meant to address his conservative base. His repeated re-elections suggest that it works.

So, the apology, then, delivered on the fiftieth anniversary of the end of World War II has become a pristine symbol of Japanese politics. Although each anniversary has been important, the decennial anniversaries of the end of World War II have been more important—for obvious reasons—and so what Abe would do or say on the seventieth anniversary on August 15, 2015, assumed especial significance. The *New York Times* addressed this specific point: what the joint session of Congress should watch for is "how clearly he acknowledges Japan's wartime aggression, and for whether he tries to water down past apologies."[24] Some of us, I suppose, might be in relationships where the individual who apologizes threatens to take it back, but I suspect most of us don't think of those acts as apologies, nor seek to continue that kind of relationship for long. But that is precisely the dynamic of the political apology, and, especially, in the case of Japan. The political apology is part of a public record that is subject to revision. It is part of a political script. Political apologies, then, are just like other discursive acts within the sphere of governance, that is, for instance, legislative bills, policies, legal codes, and sentencing guidelines. They are acts that determine, set, and act on a policy stance at a particular moment by a political agency that may more closely represent one part of the larger constituency, and is always subject to revocation by a later political agency. Political apologies, then, do a particular kind of political

---

23. Julian Littler, "Japan's Nationalist Prime Minister Wants to Revise War Apology," *Telegraph* (January 1, 2013); "Japan 'May Revisit Second World War Statement,'" *Telegraph* (February 1, 2013); "Former PM Murayama Cautions Japan on Reviewing 1995 War Apology," *Japan Daily Press* (July 2, 2013); Martin Fackler, "Japan Says It Will Abide by Apologies over Actions in World War II," *New York Times* (May 7, 2013). For a fuller treatment of Japan's political apologies, see Rushdy, *A Guilted Age*, Chapters 2 and 3.

24. Fackler, "Shinzo Abe, Japanese Premier"; Editorial Board, "Shinzo Abe and Japan's History."

work—they represent a discursive act that can be evoked or revoked, can be supported or challenged—and in that evocation or revocation they represent a contemporary political stance. It is not their sincerity that matters—as is the case in all public apologies, as we have seen—but their maintenance.

Historical apologies are also part of a political script, but in a different way, I think, than the political ones because they raise a different set of questions. We can say that political apologies raise questions about *power*—who has the power to make an apology, who to repudiate it—while historical apologies raise questions about the nature of *belonging*. Many historical apologies are offered by citizens, and they are using these apologies to express a sense of being what Michael Sandel has called "thickly constituted, encumbered" citizens, that is, individuals who accept that the nature of belonging to a place carries with it a set of affiliations and responsibilities that come with the history of that place.[25] These are apologies that do not say, "it is not my responsibility; I did not do it," but rather say, "what was done here constitutes who I am." They value a less autonomous sense of self, and a more fluid sense of responsibility. These are apologies that do not say, "my family was not here when that happened," but rather say, "What was done here was done in my name and done so that people like me could occupy these lands when we arrived." They value citizenship over genetics, and accept responsibility for acts of colonization, enslavement, exploitation, and genocide to show that they accept, fully, the responsibilities and the rights of citizenship.

Even when offered by political personages—presidents, popes, and political bodies—these historical apologies are also about belonging. When members of the US Congress, for instance, apologize for slavery, as the House of Representatives did in 2008 and the Senate in 2009, they are making statements as the *representatives* of the people who elected them, and this particular act of representation makes it clear that these bodies acknowledge the sins of the past and articulate anew a different sense of what makes an American *representable*. Rejecting the odious, exclusionary ideas of race that the Constitution had accepted, about who belonged and who was owned, this apology is a form of symbolic redress that states the wrongness of a historical stance—we now recognize that all should have belonged—and presumably opens up the possibility for that renewed sense of belonging. It is likewise the case when a church leadership does this, as did the Southern

---

25. Michael J. Sandel, *Democracy's Discontent: America in Search of a Public Philosophy* (Cambridge, MA: Belknap Press, 1996), p. 15.

Baptist Convention in its apology for slavery in 1995, and the pope on several occasions. They are addressing the terms of belonging to the congregation through an act of contrition that recognizes how one kind of reintegration through atonement (becoming one with God) is applicable to other kinds of reintegration socially (opening up the doors of the church to all). These are ideals, of course, but they are, I think, the ideals for which these historical apologies strive.[26]

VIII

There is something both hopeful and fresh and yet melancholic and desperate in public apologies. The attempt to judge these public apologies as either successes or failures—the most dominant way of approaching them—strikes me as insufficient, and not only because we have limited paradigms or models or traditions for assessing what makes for success in a public apology. It is better, at this point anyhow, for us to appreciate how they strive to do a particular kind of work—often unstated—that might be deemed important or not. I will outline two opposing ways of thinking about them, two poles—one *cynical* and one *romantic*—that represent possible ways of imagining what these discursive acts do, how they serve to make certain statements or urge us to think of the events they address in particular ways.

The cynical way is for us to see these public apologies as being largely about economics. In some cases more than others, it is easier for us to see the shameless idea of apologies as commodities. Not only corporations, obviously, but celebrities too depend on a public that consumes what they produce, even political ones. Reputation, in other words, becomes an asset that is necessary to remain competitive in the marketplace. In the background of both diplomacy apologies and regime apologies are questions of what sort of relations will exist between the two countries negotiating a diplomacy apology (using the same forms they do for a treaty or trade agreement) or what sort of general commercial possibilities will exist if a government apologizes or not for the previous regime's violation of human rights. (South Africa is an interesting

---

26. H.Res.194—Apologizing for the enslavement and racial segregation of African-Americans (110th Congress, 2007–2008); S.Con.Res.26—Apologizing for the enslavement and racial segregation of African-Americans (111th Congress, 1st Session); Jeannine Lee, "Southern Baptists Offer an Apology," *USA Today* (June 21,1995): 5A; E. J. Dionne, Jr., "Pope Apologizes to Africans for Slavery," *New York Times* (August 14, 1985): A-3; also see Luigi Accattoli, *When a Pope Asks Forgiveness: The Mea Culpa's of John Paul II*, translated by Jordan Aumann, OP (New York: Alba House, 1998).

example, because the Truth and Reconciliation Commission highlighted the apologies that were supposed to attract new international investment, while at the same time downplaying, and then all but rejecting, calls for reparations to the oppressed victims of apartheid because that kind of redress would repel foreign investors.) The same is true for apologies for the past, in which the debate is often couched in terms of what this apology would mean as either an invitation to or a replacement for reparations of some sort. Court apologies too are liable to abuse by those who see in them an easy way to escape or reduce punishment.

That, then, is the cynical interpretation, and it is not, I think, entirely misplaced. Some of the public apologies—especially those by celebrities and corporations—are clearly designed to curtail the loss of cultural or material capital. They are seen as symbolic investments to prevent public divestments. It is hard to read them in other ways (not impossible, just hard). Diplomacy apologies and regime apologies seem to me less obviously crass acts meant to control the loss of material wealth. These are acts that are more clearly meant to control international perception and to demonstrate shifts in political values and alignments. The fact that they can be understood by different nations as saying different things demonstrates how they operate as open-ended but nonetheless meaningful statements that can be emptied and filled with particular kinds of meanings. They are, therefore, like treaties, which are always subject to interpretation and reinterpretation.[27] Court apologies are more difficult cases, because they are obviously statements by deeply interested individuals, within a venue and within a system of sentencing guidelines that reward the appearance of contrition. There are cases where those who wish to apologize can make it clear that their primary interest is in the apology, and not the rewards for making it, by directly addressing and rejecting the possible reward. At her parole hearing, for instance, Katherine Ann Power ensured that her sincerity would not be questioned by withdrawing her parole appeal immediately after she apologized to the family of the guard killed during the robbery in which she was the getaway driver.[28]

27. See, for instance, Steven Mailloux, "Interpretation," in *Critical Terms for Literary Study*, edited by Frank Lentricchia and Thomas McLaughlin (2nd ed.; Chicago: University of Chicago Press, 1995), pp. 121–34, for an engaging case study of the reinterpretation of the 1972 Anti-Ballistic Missile Treaty.

28. Janet Landman, "Earning Forgiveness: The Story of a Perpetrator, Katherine Ann Power," in *Before Forgiving: Cautionary Views of Forgiveness in Psychotherapy*, edited by Sharon Lamb and Jeffrie G. Murphy (New York: Oxford University Press, 2002), pp. 232–64, esp. pp. 257–58. Murphy notes more generally the paradox involved in assessing the sincerity of someone

That leaves us, then, with the apologies for the past. These apologies, I think, have been subject to just as much cynical interpretation as have the other kinds of public apologies, but they have also been seen more charitably as desiring a certain kind of civic, national, global sense of belonging premised on accepting responsibility for the past, the kind of responsibility that Karl Jaspers described as "metaphysical."[29] They strike me as the best, and perhaps only, candidates for the romantic interpretation of public apologies. What I mean to suggest by *romantic* is that these apologies can be seen as expressing imperatives that reject the materialism that the cynical interpretation implies. Consider the case of the so-called comfort women who rejected offers of reparations that were not accompanied by an apology from the Diet itself, or those who see any reparation for a past atrocity as "hush" money or "blood" money. It seems to me that these are groups and individuals fighting an up-hill battle against what might be seen as the very tenets of the modern world order—the belief that all offenses, tragedies, losses, accidents, harms, and values can be reduced to a monetary figure. Nick Smith began his research on apologies while he was working on a project on the "increasing commodification in law." As he investigated the way that lawyers and courts brazenly used "economic cost–benefit analyses" to measure the value of any given harm, and therefore put a price on it, he saw that this expansion of economic thinking was offensive (what price a limb, a child?) and dangerous to what he called "certain forms of meaning incommensurable with money." His research on apologies, especially his work on apologies in judicial and corporate settings, showed him that the expansion of commercial thinking was even greater than he suspected. He in the end cannot find fault with those victims who seek redress in the form of pecuniary reparations because, as he notes, "there is a certain social gravity to money that can make its meaning more real than any others." And that social gravity is hegemonic. Michael Sandel's superb book *What Money Can't Buy* shows us just how invasively money determines moral choices, and to what extent fewer and fewer things are not for sale. That includes not only vital organs and life insurance options on open markets, but apology itself. The Tianjin Apology Company in China, whose motto is "We

---

appealing for amnesty in Murphy, "Repentance, Punishment, and Mercy," in *Repentance: A Comparative Perspective*, edited by Amitai Etzioni and David E. Carney (Lanham, MD: Rowman & Littlefield, 1997), pp. 143–70, esp. p. 158.

29. Karl Jaspers, *The Question of German Guilt*, translated by E. B. Ashton (Westport, CT: Greenwood Press, 1978).

say sorry for you," permits the affluently remorseful to hire someone to do the actual work of delivery for them.[30]

We can see this demand for an apology in some ways as a statement against this hegemonic view that everything is reducible to money, or that one must accept this common currency. Apology, like other acts of moral discourse, is a challenge to that belief. Something matters more than money for correcting offenses, for restoring balance, and for repairing relationships. The individuals who wish to apologize for things they have done, or things done in their name, or things done in the distant past that assured the dominance of people like them over people defined as not like them, are seeking not simply what some call the "cheap grace" of atonement. They are challenging the premise of that charge and its language (why *cheap*, another of the terms that belong to markets, like the apology some feel they are "owed"?). The atonement they seek is neither "cheap" nor "expensive," but rather vital in a way that has nothing to do with material exchanges. When Australians apologize for the "stolen generations" and the exploitation of Aborigines, when Canadians apologize for their destruction of the cultures of First Nations, when the British apologize for colonization, and Americans and French for enslavement and the slave trade, they are apologizing for precisely those historical events that created a market in bodies, and permitted the creation of a world order in which there would be precious little that money can't buy. They are apologizing for the history of the commodification of things and people and souls and lands that ought never to have suffered such disgrace.

What their apologies—at their best—bespeak, or, more accurately, imply and implore, is a hope that there can be other relations between us based on more fundamentally important kinds of exchanges (moral rather than monetary) and presuming more soulful relationships. Some are driven to that imperative because of the religious beliefs they hold in atonement and forgiveness, some because of the cultural values they want to draw on from many cultures they feel to be more immune to market forces. Many restorative justice advocates, as we saw, draw on forgiveness rituals from African cultures, from Native American ones, and those of other ancient peoples because they feel that these more integrally communal cultures provide a remedy for the kind of thinking that treats wrongdoers as alien and alienable instead of wayward souls who should be reintegrated. What they are seeking is not only an

---

30. Smith, *I Was Wrong*, pp. 2, 238; Sandel, *What Money Can't Buy: The Moral Limits of Markets* (New York: Farrar, Straus and Giroux, 2012), pp. 96–97.

escape from a world produced by these crimes of the past, but also what they believe that world lost, which is, admittedly, a kind of fantasy of communal, close-knit and deeply meaningful relations among peoples. It does not matter whether that world existed or was lost. Theirs is not a historical analysis. What matters is that they believe that these acts of atonement are a necessary first step in regaining or attaining something that the lost world represents— and that something is *a moral value based on moral values*. An apology is not something that can be purchased, or something that can reduce reparations, or some *thing* at all. It *is* a relationship, as well as a gesture presuming one and attempting to repair one.

So, what then do these public apologies *mean*? I can frankly say I am not sure, because they surely mean many different things for many different people who offer them, expect them, accept them, and reject them. I have offered two opposing ways of seeing them—cynical and romantic—and those are assuredly too narrow a set of terms to define the variety of responses these apologies elicit. The basest examples of public apologies reveal the deep cynicism of those who offer them as crass and jejune attempts to maintain economic relations—the only kind they can imagine. The most heartfelt examples express a deep need to escape those kinds of relations as if they defined human striving—instead seeking value that is not reducible to monetary terms, seeking communion where there might not yet be community, and seeking a sort of morality where there isn't yet a shared ethic validating it. So, can public apologies do that work of establishing a new moral order, one that challenges monetary exchange as the basis of human relationships? The answer has to be, obviously not—not by themselves, not in isolated instances, and not without foundational structural changes. One way of seeing them, then, is as failures; another, as attempts.

IX

Apology is, in fundamental ways, a more curious practice than resentment and forgiveness for at least three discernible reasons. First, apology is a second-order practice that is more complicated than resentment and forgiveness because it involves more transitions from passion to expression. Apology, of course, is not an emotion, but an expression of one (remorse) that itself follows on the heels of another (guilt). And, yet, it is also the pivot on which the two emotions of resentment and forgiveness can turn. Apology can dissipate resentment, and it can elicit forgiveness. Although resentment can be dissipated and forgiveness proffered without an apology, of course, apology conventionally remains the fulcrum between those two emotions.

Second, apology is the only one of these three practices that has a discernible, voluntary collective expression. Resentment, as we saw, is an immanent social condition, according to those nineteenth-century existentialists who argued the case; there is nothing voluntary about it, and, as Nietzsche suggested, it requires something voluntary (a will-to-power) to counter it. Forgiveness, as we will see in the Conclusion, has a quite limited collective expression. Apology, though, does, and indeed seems in the near past to have become a significant feature of public discourse.

Finally, apology is also the most coercive of the three practices because it focuses on and forces a choice by the person or people who may not yet have chosen to make that choice. The person who chooses to apologize has made a choice to forgo impenitence, and that is, usually, a choice made by someone who has worked through her or his feelings from guilt to remorse. But the person who receives an apology is now forced to what amounts to a forced choice between rejecting the apology (and abiding in resentment) or accepting it (and thereby moving into forgiveness). There is a fundamental difference between having a choice and being confronted with one. And, let us not forget, the person who has a choice is the one who originally injured the person now confronted with one.

We can return one last time to the cases we have been using to give substance to our theoretical discussions of the three moral practices—drawn from debates and hearings about racial incidents in South Africa, Britain, and the United States—to appreciate what burdens an apology can place on a person or people. We saw those cases in South Africa where individuals found themselves being coerced to accept an apology they did not expect, or others who had to choose to reject an apology they were not yet ready to accept. There is something profoundly troubling in these cases, not only for the coercive setting in which these injured individuals found themselves, but also for the racial dynamics of that setting. Here were white police officers— the same ones who had controlled the mobility and lives of black people in apartheid—effectively controlling the discursive options of black victims after apartheid. Each apology places a moral burden on the one to whom it is offered because it forces a resolution; in these cases, there is an additional moral burden in that the person receiving it is expected to fulfill a particular social and racial mandate. In a situation where the commissioner of the Truth and Reconciliation Commission holds that forgiving is what he calls "a central feature of the African *Weltanschauung*," what exactly is the choice confronted by a black woman receiving a premature apology from the white man who killed her family? Is it the choice to declare that she does or does not inhabit that African *Weltsanschauung*? Or, to use the Viscount of Falkland's terms, does not to be forgiving mean that one has a different "nature" than the Africans he knows? Is it, effectively, to be less African?

We recall that the viscount made his comment in response to Lord Gifford's proposal for reparations for Britain's involvement in the slave trade. The viscount's assertion that reparations "would go against the grain" of Africans' nature alerts us to the two choices he felt Africans had—to desire reparations (and thereby exemplify resentment) or to be forgiving (which amounted to rejecting reparations). The lord and the viscount clearly have two different ways of thinking about reparations. Lord Gifford sees them as restitution, that is, a form of apology for historical oppression, while the viscount sees them as a complicated accounting problem—how much, to whom, and how to calculate mitigating factors like African involvement in the trade? And so, in the final accounting, while Lord Gifford believes in monetary reparations, the viscount believes that what "we owe to Africans is a renewed and more energetic attitude, and a greater amount of material, constructive and well-thought out aid for sub-Saharan Africa." Both insist that money should go to Africa, but in one case, it is restitution for the past, in the other, foreign aid for the future. One need not deny the value of either strategy to acknowledge that there is a difference between accepting and not accepting the responsibility for redressing past oppressions. For Lord Gifford, reparations are an acknowledgment of unjust enrichment; it is a statement that British wealth and stature are connected to the historical oppression of Africa. For the viscount, the attitude and aid that Britain offers occlude just where the nation's wealth was acquired. It is like the acts of those "great reformers," the British abolitionists whom the viscount celebrated in his speech, an act of magnanimity and not of acknowledgment.[31]

The topic of reparations as apology returns us to the topic of apologies and their relationship to monetary exchange. The viscount here represents what we have seen to be a desirable alternative—one that severs the relationship between moral practices and monetary exchanges—while the call for reparations is one that very much insists on that relationship. Apologies are

---

31. "The Official Record from Hansard of the Debate Initiated by Lord Gifford, QC in the House of Lords of the British Parliament on 14th March 1996 Concerning the African Reparations," In *Reparations for Slavery: A Reader*, edited by Ronald P. Salzberger and Mary C. Turck (Lanham, MD: Rowman and Littlefield Publishers, 2004), pp. 96–115, esp. p. 106.

not only acts of moral restitution, but they are meaningful, for some, only to the extent that they are accompanied by expressions of material restitution. In that case, apologies become failures because money or its material equivalent is assumed to be the sign of the sincerity of the one apologizing. Here, then, is another dilemma, another burden, facing those to whom apologies are offered. Accepting reparations seems to support the cynical, and reject the romantic, views I have outlined above. But, as we saw in our concluding discussion of resentment, the way to solve a dilemma is sometimes to adopt a different perspective; and in this case, the perspective must be historical and moral. The reason that money is an issue in debates over reparations is that it has historically been made an issue; land, resources, and bodies were ascribed a value by those who appropriated them, and so the language of reparations is what it is because that is, to quote Caliban in a doubly meaningful sense, the victims' "profit on't." But it is also not the only issue, nor the only language, and the desire for genuine atonement, as Roy Brooks so eloquently puts it, is very much part of the black redress movements he expertly delineates.[32] Reparations, understood from this perspective, are about repair in every sense, and absolution in none.

---

32. Roy L. Brooks, *Atonement and Forgiveness: A New Model for Black Reparations* (Berkeley: University of California Press, 2004). For other studies of the discourse around reparation, especially in an American context, see Eric K. Yamamoto, *Interracial Justice: Conflict and Reconciliation in Post Civil-Rights America* (New York: New York University Press, 1999); Randall Robinson, *The Debt: What America Owes to Blacks* (New York: Dutton, 2000); Ellis Cose, *Bone to Pick: Of Forgiveness, Reconciliation, Reparation, and Revenge* (New York: Atria, 2004); Charles P. Henry, *Long Overdue: The Politics of Racial Reparations* (New York: New York University Press, 2007); and Boris I. Bittker, *The Case for Black Reparations* (1973; Boston: Beacon Press, 2003). Two anthologies that are also useful are *Should America Pay?: Slavery and the Raging Debate on Reparations*, edited by Raymond A. Winbush (New York: Amistad, 2003); and Salzberger and Turck, Eds., *Reparations for Slavery: A Reader*.

CONCLUSION

By focusing on a key critical moment in the history of each these three moral practices, we have been able to appreciate the cultural background within which each of them shifted from one sphere to another. Forgiveness, at the dawn of the Christian era, went from being a form of divine absolution to a strategy for interpersonal reconciliation, resentment at the turn from the eighteenth to the nineteenth centuries from being an individual property inspiring justice to a collective malaise of cultural spite, and apology at the end of World War II from being an essentially private to a manifestly public act. These moments constitute an *expansion* of the practice in question, not a replacement of the prior practice with a new one that supplants it. What used to be a form of forgiveness that could only come from God could now come from both God and our fellow sinners. And people continue to resent and apologize in private, even as we are shown how groups can and do so in public. At each of those critical moments, we see a certain slippage as the old and new meanings jostle and shift. We see Paul subtly challenge the meaning Jesus has given to forgiveness as a new practice for human amity, denying it conditions that Jesus affirmed and ascribing to it powers that Jesus did not suggest. We see Kierkegaard and Nietzsche argue that resentment is an existential condition of a sham culture without depth and sustained meaning, picking up and transforming an idea that Adam Smith had toyed with—that resentment was so dangerous a stance, and yet so respectable a one, that it was sometimes better to fake it. We see how public apology, when it emerged from its tradition as a private practice, continued uneasily to bear certain properties that gave private apologies their meaning, and sometimes too easily shed others that gave private apologies their raison d'être.

In focusing on the contemporary debates over these practices, we sometimes see the residues of that slippage. We find, for instance, a set of philosophers who argue that secular forgiveness is impossible precisely because they have exclusively adopted a Pauline perspective on what forgiveness can do. In the case of resentment, we see that most modern writers, with a few notable exceptions, have followed Nietzsche in seeing only one aspect of what is a multiform and deeply ambivalent emotion. And in the case of apology, there has been a discernible shift toward identifying the paradigmatic discursive elements of it as an isolated act and a turn away from appreciating it as one of a repertoire of strategies for social reconciliation. In the modern discussions of these practices, then, one finds a forgiveness that is represented as impossible, a resentment that should be castigated, and an apology that must be formulaic. What is lost, it seems to me, is an appreciation and understanding of what it is these practices do, what they mean, and what purpose they serve in our daily lives in which we regularly resent, apologize, and forgive in ways that are rich and textured (and neither formulaic nor impossible).

I will conclude this study by focusing on two related points. The first is for us to appreciate better the shift or expansion from private to public practices. In our discussion of resentment and apology, especially, we have most clearly seen that shift. Resentment evolved from what British moralists cast as a private sentiment to becoming what Continental existentialists argued to be a public ethos. Apology, a personal act between two people in private, has increasingly assumed a public profile as a practice that collective bodies of all sorts employ. We have, then, largely been talking about the distinction between what happens in an interpersonal relationship and what happens in a social one, and that perhaps puzzling distinction is based on *setting*—whether this relationship is premised on *privacy* (this statement is meant for and intended to be heard by you) or *publicity* (this statement is meant and intended to be overheard by others). Here I wish to examine more closely that tension between what is involved in the practices of resentment, apology, and forgiveness when they are performed in private or in public, and tease out what it means that these practices take on the forms and meanings they do in each of these spheres. The second point involves the question of how that public aspect of these practices has implicated the discourse of race into its workings.

I

In its private form, resentment has two distinct aspects. In one, there is a genuine desire for privacy. Consider the curious phenomenon of what the eighteenth century called "cards of resentment." In his book of familiar letters and providing models for the writing of them, Charles Hallifax gives us three unfolding dramas as examples of how a card of resentment can be composed and answered. Two of the examples are of women who feel neglected by other women, one because her cards requesting information have not been answered and the other because a friend kept her waiting and made her miss the beginning of the play they were to attend together. Both of these cases end with conciliatory gestures. The lady who has not answered the cards sends a card saying she will attend in person on the morrow. The one who has kept the lady waiting for the play apologizes and gives the reasons for the delay and begs the lady not to break off their next engagement. It seems important that the emotion these cards are expressing be named by the recipient, and not the sender. When the neglectful correspondent responds, she notes that "she is most seriously concerned to have received a Card from her with so much Resentment." Having named what the card is supposed to express, she can then work toward removing it. Both of those cases involved an exchange of one card for another. In the most extended case, covering a sequence of six cards, Hallifax offers us the story of two men.

A gentleman (Lennox) hears from a mutual acquaintance (Miss Watson) that he has been insulted and sends a card requesting that the person who insulted him (Fowke) should refrain from public conversation about him: "Silence from certain Persons being the only Civility," he sententiously ends his note. Fowke sends back a note that becomes even more rude in its insult, after which Lennox sends a note titled: "From a Gentleman whose Rudeness had been resented." In that note, he again requests that Fowke keep these sentiments "within his own Breast," and hints that "if he should hear that Breath had been given to them in any Company, the Consequences might be very disagreeable." The card of resentment, now, has assumed a more traditional form in the discourse of honor—and that is the prelude to an invitation to a duel. Eventually Lennox learns that the original cause of their dispute has been misrepresented to him, and admits to having "been in the wrong in two Cards which he has sent to Mr. *Fowke*." He then makes the final request of Fowke regarding those cards: "He begs they may be burnt, and the Contents of them forgotten." He offers an explicit apology ("very sorry") and ends by repeating "the Entreaty that every Thing may be forgotten." Fowke's answer is not conciliatory at all, and effectively ends the relationship. Playing on Lennox's desire that "every Thing may be forgotten," Fowke says that "he shall not after this remember there ever was such a Man in the World. This will not be difficult since there is no such *Man* as the supposed Mr. *Lennox*."[1]

---

1. Charles Hallifax, *Familiar Letters on Various Subjects of Business and Amusement* (2nd ed.; London, 1754), pp. 272–76. Hallifax insists in the preface that he is the author of only a minority of the letters and the rest are authentic (pp. i–xviii).

Lina Minou has ingeniously argued that these cards of resentment, appearing at a "time when writings against duelling and its consequences are a main part of the call for social, and male, reformation," do a particular kind of work. Instead of "multiplying the injury, as happens in a duel, a card of resentment bears the potential to 'undo' it: the burning of the papers being the tangible erasure of the offence." In other words, the card of resentment operates to indicate the need for apology, and the burning of the papers suggests the closure of forgiveness—often cast, in moral philosophy, as an act of "undoing." While I agree with this reading that the cards of resentment and the act of their disposal replay the dynamic of apology and forgiveness, I also see another dynamic at work in this exchange—the dynamic between public and private. Lennox's request that the cards all be burnt is another part of his consistent request that the matter be *private*. His final entreaty that everything be burnt and forgotten is of a piece with his earlier request that Fowke keep his "Sentiments" within "his own Breast," and his opening salvo that "he should be most satisfied if that Gentleman would never mention it at all: Silence from certain Persons being the only Civility."[2] In other words, the burning is another form of returning to privacy what had been public—which, remember, is the entire cause of this disagreement: that Lennox thought Fowke had talked about him in *public*. What this episode reveals is that resentment is a fine private sentiment—what an impartial spectator might recommend, say—and that it is part of a suite of values of privacy that was important to eighteenth-century British mores.

In its other aspect, though, private resentment desires publicity. Consider the case of Dostoevsky's Underground Man. In the second section of the novella, he tells three interrelated stories that show his spitefulness in three formats. The first involves his seeking out debaucheries in hidden, out of the way places so that he would not be noticed. "I was terribly afraid of somehow being seen, met, recognized." As a result of this fear of publicity, he seeks out "various rather murky places." It is in one of these ("a wretched little tavern") that he has his first encounter. As he is standing beside a billiard table, unwittingly impeding the flow of traffic, an officer wishing to pass by the narrow

---

2. Lina Minou, "To Take Ill: Resentment in Eighteenth-Century Context," in *On Resentment: Past and Present*, edited by Bernardino Fantini, Dolores Martín Moruno, and Javier Moscoso (Newcastle upon Tyne, UK: Cambridge Scholars Publishing, 2013), pp. 73–90, esp. p. 87. For an analysis of the logic and illogic of "undoing" in the practice of apologizing and forgiving, see Ashraf H. A. Rushdy, *A Guilted Age: Apologies for the Past* (Philadelphia: Temple University Press, 2015), Chapter 6; Hallifax, *Familiar Letters on Various Subjects of Business and Amusement*, p. 272.

space took the Underground Man by the shoulders, lifted, and moved him, "and then passed by as if without noticing." He is tormented by this episode and what it seems to mean. He goes the next day to confront the officer but ends up avoiding any confrontation. He continues to muse on how he can get either acknowledgment of the fault or revenge, each time failing to muster the courage to confront the officer. For the next two years, he continues to be obsessed with this incident. Describing himself as "choking with spite," he writes a letter—a card of resentment—that invites the officer to a duel, but does not send it. He then discovers that the officer regularly walks on Nevsky Prospect, and plans to have the confrontation there. He spends more time equipping himself for the encounter—buying new "black gloves and a respectable hat at Churkin's," and then a "good shirt with white bone cuf-flinks," and finally a new beaver collar for his overcoat. Properly accoutered, he goes to Nevsky but keeps walking past the officer on repeated occasions, each time moving out of the way instead of bumping into him, shoulder to shoulder, as he had planned. Finally, he musters his courage and bumps into the officer, who does not notice—or, as the Underground Man insists, "he only pretended, I'm sure of that."[3]

What particularly irks the Underground Man about the encounter with the officer is not that the officer violated him; he states that he could "have forgiven a beating." What he finds unacceptable is another kind of insult: "I simply could not forgive his moving me and in the end just not noticing me." That not "noticing" is telling. In one way, it tells us that he wanted recogni-tion; he wanted the officer to notice him in the sense of seeing him as a person with rights and integrity. But the Underground Man does not just seek the kind of recognition of one person who regards another, an I that notices the Thou. He seeks a more public "noticing." For that reason, he dresses him-self fastidiously for the encounter, and chooses to have it in a public venue in the open rather than a private tavern. When the officer first moved him, he wanted to be acknowledged publicly but instead, as he puts it, "I changed my mind and preferred . . . to efface myself spitefully." Many obsessed years later, in public Nevsky Prospect, the Underground Man, even though he is not noticed by the officer who bumps him, feels nonetheless that he had, as he concludes, "placed myself publicly on an equal footing with him."[4] What he

3. Fydor Dostoevsky, *Notes from Underground*, translated by Richard Pevear and Larissa Volokhonsky (New York: Everyman, 2004), pp. 46, 47, 49, 51, 52.

4. Dostoevsky, *Notes from Underground*, pp. 47, 53.

desires is *publicity*, which, of course, is why he writes about the whole course of his resentment in what he intends to be a public document (*Notes*) that addresses a public "you" throughout.

Resentment, as we have seen, took at least three forms. In one, it was what British moralists considered a conscientious sentinel guarding the honor and self-esteem of its possessor and, as indignation, operating to reveal injustices in the larger world. In the second, it was what Continental existentialists saw as a social malaise that afflicted entire eras, institutions, and societies, causing those reared within them to feel enviously resentful at the world instead of seeking to change it in the act of living meaningful, heroic lives. In the third form, it manifests itself as a class sentiment (of all sorts, including economic, social, ethnic, racial, and gendered classes) that inspires a desire for and moves toward social justice. It might originate in private acts of resentment at ill-treatment, but its trajectory is toward reform or revolution, that is, changing the society that had permitted that oppression.

II

Whereas the concept of resentment slowly evolved from its private to its public aspect, from being a moral guide to becoming a social condition, the concept of apology has undergone a rather dramatic and recent change from its private to its public performance. What we see when heads of states or churches apologize for past atrocities is clearly not the same thing we find in earlier epochs, in which we see acts of penitence or confession. When the Holy Roman Emperor Henry IV stood for three days in the snow outside the castle of Canossa in January 1077, he was performing an act of penance so that the pope would lift his excommunication. It was a religious performance (and a political one). Likewise, when King Henry II of England performed a public act of penance at Canterbury in July 1174, it was a religious performance (and, again, a political one). What each of these monarchs did was appease the papacy through the understood forms of expressing public penitence through physical acts—wearing a hair shirt in one case, accepting blows from a rod in the other—that represent a desire for spiritual absolution. Likewise, it was a religious performance when Judge Samuel Sewell in 1697 repented of his role in the Salem witch trials. In the church on a fast day, he asked Samuel Willard, the pastor of the South Church, to read a statement while he stood penitent. The statement accepted the "Guilt contracted," and stated Sewell's desire to "take the Blame and Shame of it, Asking pardon of Men, And especially desiring prayers that God, who has an Unlimited Authority, would pardon that Sin and all other his Sins; personal and Relative."[5] While Sewall sought the pardon of his fellow citizens, it was in context of a religious act in a religious space that sought primarily the remission of sins from God.

The modern forms of public apology, as we saw, differ significantly in that they are performed in secular places. In the case of celebrity, corporation, and diplomacy apologies, these are often media-staged events in media-saturated sites. In the case of court apologies, these are in courtrooms where the consequences at stake (guilt or freedom) and the social ideals (justice) determine the meaning of the practice. In the case of apologies for the past, these performances often take place at sites where the past event itself occurred. Here we can most clearly discern the difference between those past practices of penance and the modern one of apologizing. An act of penance in a church highlights the sacred space where absolution is sought; an apology at the site of an atrocity instead makes us aware of the atrocity and its enduring significance. An apology for the Crusades, for instance, in which those apologizing retrace the steps of the Crusaders and then arrive ultimately in Jerusalem is making a very different statement about *place* and, implicitly, about what kind of practice they are performing. It is not an act seeking penance in a sacred space; it is an act that seeks to atone for the acts that took place here before, and to exorcise the evil of those atrocities and the abiding effect on this space through a peaceful and apologetic revision of the original acts.

That kind of public apology is relatively new and has assumed a relatively important place in modern culture. Many date that practice to Willy Brandt's famous *kniefall* in Poland in 1970, when he, as the chancellor of West Germany, knelt with bowed head before the Warsaw Ghetto Memorial. Most commentators take his symbolic act to be an apology, and he himself eventually came to represent it as such. What he was doing by humbling himself before a memorial erected to the victims of a nation of which he was the leader was accepting responsibility, expressing remorse, and offering a symbolic restitution. Since then, many heads of state have offered similar apologies, often for the same set of crimes that we trace to World War II. Leaders in Austria and Japan have regularly made these apologies, and, in the case of Japan, they have become so routine a practice on the August 15 anniversary of the end of the Pacific War that media analysts like to speculate on what sort

---

5. Samuel Sewall, *The Diary of Samuel Sewall, 1674–1729*, edited by M. Halsey Thomas (New York: Farrar, Straus and Giroux, 1973), Volume 1, p. 367.

of political message the prime minister of the moment will send out with this year's apology.

Eventually, around the mid-1980s, it would appear, heads of state and heads of churches began to offer apologies for events that were not within living memory at all. Chancellor Brandt stood at a site whose devastation happened while he was alive; Prime Minister Murayama apologized for Japanese war crimes that happened during his lifetime. Neither was the leader at the time of the atrocities, and indeed both were politically resistant to the regimes that committed them; but both belonged to and represented the nation that was perceived to be guilty of them. The apologies that leaders began to make for events well before anyone was living, and events or systems that were international, like the transatlantic slave trade or the Crusades, were qualitatively different than apologies made by leaders for things that happened while they were alive. What can we make of this widespread effort by contemporary national and religious leaders, as well as some heads of families, and, in some cases, a swathe of the citizenry of a country, to take responsibility and express remorse for these historic crimes? For some, it bespeaks an urge to find a substantial identity, an "encumbered" one as communitarians put it, that accepts that affinity means acceptance, that belonging to a place means being involved and responsible for its formation and historical trajectory. It is about an enlarged sense of selfhood. For others, it is indicative of a presumption that they find repulsive, either because it misconstrues the crime by thinking it can be apologized for or because it devalues national heroes and founding fathers by casting their historic acts as historic crimes or because they find themselves baffled by that enlarged sense of selfhood where one claims responsibility for things that fall outside one's control, one's will, and one's lifetime.

I suggested at the end of the last chapter that apologies for the past could also be seen as the ones that most express many people's uneasiness with the bases of our modern world. These are not only expressions of remorse directed *to* those who passed away a hundred or a thousand years ago, and not only *for* events that took place that long ago, but also statements of remorse *expressive of* the malaise of our epoch. If we were given to thinking of large groups of people, or nations, or eras, as having a similarly structured sensibility or consciousness as individual persons have, then we might say that these historical apologies reveal an epoch's existential shame. As I write this book (2015), we are marking the seventieth anniversary of the end of World War II, and the centenary of the Great War, the events that produced our modern age. Those who reflect back on a century cratered with a series of horrors for which we had to find new names—*genocide, World War, nuclear holocaust, ethnic cleansing*—can imagine what might drive many politicians and citizens of several nations to seek solace in a gesture they know well from their private lives. These were crimes so great and so intimate that they required more than policies or principles or legislation. Brandt fell to his knees the day after he signed the Treaty of Warsaw accepting the Allied-imposed Oder-Neisse Line and thereby renouncing land that many Germans thought as theirs. A treaty was one kind of political act; an apology was another.

One was a traditional form that established protocols for future behavior and set terms of agreement for how the two nations would regulate their relations and their trade practices. The other was an unconventional and new form that, in many ways, repudiates the very premises of the treaty as a political instrument. What we have seen in our discussion of these moral practices of apologizing and forgiving is that they can be seen as an exchange—one offers an apology and receives forgiveness. Indeed, in many languages the terms are drawn from the discourse of commerce. *Forgiveness* is derived from *give* in English, just as *pardon* from *donner* ('to give') in French. What is striking, though, is that the primary terms for that exchange—apology and forgiveness—are inherently about an *unequal* exchange. To apologize is implicitly to recognize the *insufficiency* of the action. No one apologizes and thinks she has done more than enough in saying the words. That is why so many writers about apology think that it does, or ought to, express a desire to "undo" the event. That impossibility of altering the past would be an appropriate and equal exchange. What was done is undone. But the fact that it is impossible, and the fact that we often say that we wish for that impossibility in the midst of our apologies, show us that we see our apologies as inherently insufficient. Likewise, to forgive, as commentators from the earliest religious traditions have recognized, is about *excess*. Forgiving is an act of grace because it is willing not to demand what is *due*. When we are *owed* an apology, we know that it cannot fully cover the debt. And forgiveness is excessive precisely because it covers the distance between what an injury means and what an apology can do. It is the gift of the difference.

I think it is important for us to consider what it means that an apology and forgiveness are unequal, because I believe it addresses that point that I raised at the conclusion of the last chapter about understanding the apologies for the past as expressions that recognize that they need a discursive form that challenges the very idea of exchange. That, of course, is the only way that nations regulate their relations—by treaties that establish norms for trade, whether that trade is explicitly economic or implicitly so because it is based on defining borders. What such apologies might be saying is that we need a world order premised on other kinds of agreements—moral ones—than those that define the terms of exchange. Public apologies, especially the apologies for the past, are sometimes acts that suggest just that, haltingly and perhaps without much faith in the hope, but they are, in what I called the romantic view in the previous chapter, at least attempts for those descended from the wronged and those descended from the victors at establishing a relationship in which they might also be able, over time, to discern a common descent.

That, in any case, is what public apologies might be able to suggest, and it is premised on one of the only ways, I argue, in which we profitably see how they are similar to private apologies (in that both acknowledge *insufficiency* as part of what they are expressing). Otherwise, public apologies should be seen as a quite distinct kind of practice, governed by different norms and expectations than those that we use to understand private apologies.

III

It will be clear by now, I suspect, that in this book I have treated only two of the three practices—resentment and apology—in the terms we have been using to explore moral acts that are either personal or collective, private or public. That is largely because there is, as of yet, no such thing as a clearly discernible act of collective public forgiveness in the same way as there is such a thing as an act of collective public apology. When we speak about a public as being forgiving—which we do usually when celebrities or politicians do something unconscionable and then repent for it and are then returned to grace—we are actually talking about the ways that a celebrity can be made palatable again for public consumption. In other words, a forgiving public is something a good publicist produces by calling it that. It is important to note that "forgiving" in this scenario is not an *act* but a *disposition*, not something a society does but something it seems to exemplify (or, often, something it is best to represent it as exemplifying). That is what is meant when a disgraced celebrity's publicist states that we are a forgiving society and that he therefore predicts that the public will soon forget the racial slur, sexual impropriety, domestic abuse, or marital infidelity his client has committed and quickly be returned to radio, television, the sport's league, or Congress.

When we think of it as an act, we find cases where those who make public apologies in the expectation of public forgiveness are frequently embarrassed. In 1995, for instance, the Southern Baptist Convention apologized for its historic support of slavery. It produced a document, entitled "Declaration of Repentance and Rededication," in which it stated: "We apologize to all

African-Americans for condoning and/or perpetuating individual and systematic racism. . . . We ask for forgiveness from our African-American brothers and sisters. . . . We hereby commit ourselves to eradicate racism in all its forms from Southern Baptist life and ministry." The convention debated the apology, voted on it (with the support of twenty thousand and the dissent of three who spoke against the motion), and then staged a performance in which the president of the convention, who was white, presented the apology to the second vice president, who was black. The vice president then forgave the convention: "On behalf of my black brothers and sisters, we accept your apology and we extend to you our forgiveness in the name of Jesus Christ. We pray that the genuineness of your repentance will be demonstrated in your attitude and your action." Later, when he was grilled by the media for his presumptuous act of forgiveness, he hastily retreated, saying that was "not receiving (that apology) for all blacks." He kept retreating until he eventually made it clear that the forgiveness, and the question of reparation that the apology opened up, was strictly a "family affair" (that is, within the family of the Southern Baptist Convention). That is what happens when organizations attempt to stage *acts* of public forgiveness (and don't hire talented publicists first).[6]

There are cases where it seems that we find what can be considered acts of public collective forgiveness, but a closer examination reveals what I believe to be a different dynamic. Let us examine two.

When the prime minister of Canada, Steven Harper, apologized to the First Nations in 2008 for the abusive mistreatment of students in Indian residential schools, he did not receive any indication that the Canadian government had been or would be forgiven. Indeed, some, including the executive director of the organization of the abused students, Residential School Survivors of Canada, sternly noted that the apology was the beginning of a long process of restitution and reformation that might, or might not, conclude with forgiveness and reconciliation. There would be no staged act of public forgiveness simply to give validity to the official government apology; more, much more, political action was required to give the apology the substance it needed to matter. Only after two more years did some of Canada's aboriginal

---

6. "SBC Renounces Racist Past," *Christian Century* 112.21 (July 5, 1995): 671; Jeannine Lee, "Southern Baptists Offer an Apology," *USA Today* (June 21,1995): 5A; Judith Lynn Howard, "Baptists Apologize for Racism; Resolution Says Funding of SBC Rooted in Slavery," *Dallas Morning News* (June 21, 1995): 1A; Howard, "Black Scholars Question Baptists; Some Say Convention's Apology Must Include Remedy for Racism," *Dallas Morning News* (June 22, 1995): 23A.

leaders offer forgiveness, and they gave it in a way congruent with the values they held, and the kinds of values that the abusive schools had violated. A co-alition of Inuit, Métis, and other First Nation peoples, under the umbrella organization Gathering Nations International, undertook a five-month Journey of Freedom across Canada, meeting with groups of non-native Canadians to explain the historical crime in question. They concluded their journey at the National Forgiven Summit in the nation's capital, where they gave the prime minister an unsigned copy of the "Charter of Forgiveness and Freedom." At the summit that followed, five thousand survivors and children of survivors signed the charter.[7] The act of forgiveness, in other words, was not an *act*: it was a journey, an unsigned charter, and a process that required non-native Canadians to be informed and the Canadian government to exemplify what its apology meant. Most importantly, it was also presented as formally a gathering of individual acts of forgiveness—each signature attesting to the forgiveness of that person—rather than a collective one.

That is also the case in the second example. In South Africa, we are often led to believe, the entire post-apartheid society participated in the collective act of reconciliation and forgiveness. Individuals who appeared before the Truth and Reconciliation Commission were sometimes encouraged to forgive the state agents who harmed them and their families, and, sometimes, people who appeared before the commission expressed a wish to forgive those who did those things if only they knew who they were. But these were acts of individuals forgiving state agents who confessed to their political crimes, not a collective, public forgiveness on behalf of the population subjugated by the state terrorism used to support and buttress apartheid. There was slippage in the language and thinking, especially in those who truly held that South Africa could exemplify a kind of widespread social forgiveness that would be transformative. Archbishop Desmond Tutu held, for instance that "to forgive is indeed the best form of self-interest since anger, resentment, and revenge are corrosive." But what had been "self-interest" quickly became something else, as he continued to argue that such acts of forgiveness would produce "communal harmony that enhances the humanity and personhood of all in the community." It would seem that "self" and "community" are conflated in this conception, and this slippage certainly influenced those who

7. "Prime Minister Stephen Harper's Statement of Apology," CBC News (June 11, 2008); Ted Quewezance, "RSCC Welcome Apology but Expect More," *Windspeaker* 26.4 (2008); "Native Residential School Forgiveness Granted," CBC News (June 12, 2010); Gathering Nations International, "The Charter of Forgiveness and Freedom," http://gni.arlenbresh.ca/charter/.

appeared before the commission. Cynthia Ngewu, for instance, whose son, Christopher Piet, was murdered by state agents, stated to the commission that if forgiveness and reconciliation mean that "this perpetrator, this man who has killed Christopher Piet, if it means he becomes human again, this man, so that I, so that all of us, get our humanity back . . . then I agree, then I support it all."[8] Tutu might have idealistically seen that individual and communal acts were deeply connected, and he is certainly right that they are related; but what Ngewu did, and what many other South Africans did, is forgive individually, even as they did it in the hope that "all of us" would benefit.

It is true that public apologies are also frequently contested—those who disapprove of them speaking out against them or performing acts that symbolically repudiate them—but those acts do not render the public apologies meaningless. When a group of Japanese politicians visit the Yasukuni Shrine—a building that symbolizes the Allied-proscribed Shinto belief in the divinity of the emperor, represents Japan's military glory, and houses the remains of several World War II war criminals—their act of defiance does not invalidate the prime minister's public apology for the crimes Japan committed during the Pacific War. It demonstrates dissent, but the prime minister's speech continues to matter as the statement of the appropriate representative of the nation. It is for that reason that Japan continues to debate that apology—because it registered as the *official* statement. Such acts of official forgiveness may exist, but they are likely those made by a small group and may also have required the suppression of dissent. The examples we offer above are more representative of the unbearable pressures to which acts of collective public forgiveness are subject. When they are offered by someone who presents himself as a representative, his representative status will be examined until it is shown to be immaterial—and that what had been an encompassing act of historical forgiveness turns out to be massively overblown rhetoric that might, or might not, even represent the miniscule population of people of African descent in the Southern Baptist Convention. In the more plausible cases, we see that we have not collective but individual acts of public forgiveness.

Where individuals do forgive in public—and for wrongs that were done in public and, in the case of Canada and South Africa, for what were deemed

---

8. Desmond Mpilo Tutu, *No Future Without Forgiveness* (New York: Doubleday, 1999), p. 35; Cynthia Ngewu, quoted in Antijie Krog, *Country of My Skull: Guilt, Sorrow, and the Limits of Forgiveness in the New South Africa* (1998; New York: Three Rivers Press, 1999), p. 142.

to be the values and security of the public—then we occupy a curious middle ground between what is private and what public. When, for instance, Eugene de Kock asked to apologize to the widows of some of the many men he had killed during apartheid, he was granted a private room where he met directly with the widows (and their lawyers). He apologized and they forgave. As one of the widows, Pearl Faku, expressed it: "I could hear him, but I was over-whelmed by emotion, and I was just nodding, as a way of saying yes, I forgive you."[9] What I think we can understand in this scene, at least one thing anyhow, is that de Kock and the widows needed some kind of privacy in the midst of what was an overwhelming amount of publicity. It is not clear whether they got it, since the room might have been private, but it was, after all, arranged by the Truth and Reconciliation Commission, and reported to at least one of the commissioners, and then reported widely in the South African media. To that extent, it cannot be considered private, but I think we can sense that the participants desired that it could be. And that, I believe, tells us something important about how some sites still strike participants as unusual and un-comfortable places for the performance of these practices.

These are examples of what happens when an interaction that might be best conducted privately becomes enmeshed in publicity, what happens, in other words, when the players in the drama are forced to perform in a way that is at odds with their desires to have a different kind of relationship or communication. That perhaps reveals what we might think of as the grow-ing pains of an evolving process. As public apology becomes a more regular and understood feature that is performed in different public sites—including courtrooms, mediation offices, and parole board gatherings—we could see emerge a different set of expectations that will, maybe, leave the participants with less cognitive dissonance about the practices in which they are engaged.

That discomfort of what is private being conducted in public, of course, is not the only possible scenario involving these practices, as we have seen. There are situations where public performances of these practices have a spe-cial value and express something important about the societies where they take place. There are occasions where public resentment or indignation expresses a desire for social justice, where public apologies permit a society to express its sense of grief and remorse at the immoral acts of the past that gave

---

9. Pearl Faku, quoted in Pumla Gobodo-Madikizela, *A Human Being Died that Night: A South African Story of Forgiveness* (Boston: Houghton Mifflin, 2003), pp. 14–15.

that society its current shape, and where individuals' public acts of forgiveness might together, as an ensemble set of performances, add up to something that resembles a larger-scale reconciliation. As I have attempted to show, the norms governing these practices when they occur in private and when they are performed in public differ, and we cannot ignore the crucial difference if we want to understand—rather than judge or dismiss—them.

IV

We have seen that many of the exchanges about political and historical injuries are between groups of people who inhabit what are considered different social identities, and that many of them follow a particular script in which those who are widely considered racially "white" are apologizing to those who are widely considered not "white." These are the dynamics we find in countries seeking transitions from one regime to another, as is the case in post-apartheid South Africa; white settler nations that wish to address the lengthy colonization of indigenous people, as is the case in Canada and Australia; and the executives of corporations, governments, and religious bodies around the world where these leaders wish belatedly to record and apologize for the involvement of their institutions, states, and churches in the slave trade. What at the end of the nineteenth century had been dubbed "the white man's burden" had become by the end of the twentieth "white man's guilt." Many, of course, challenged both the idea of the guilt and the practice of apologizing that seemed to have evolved from it. Pascal Bruckner, to take one notable example, thought it paternalism in another guise. In his 1983 book *The Tears of a White Man*, he referred to this kind of "compassion" as nothing more than a transformed "contempt" for those populations for whom the tears were shed. Finding the sobbing unabated almost a quarter-century later, he wrote another book, *The Tyranny of Guilt*, in which he diagnosed this whole misadventure as a form of what he called "Western masochism."[10]

What Bruckner and many others critical of these practices thought a farcical misconstruing of the past appeared to others sympathetic to them as a historical accounting, a moment of taking stock of how the modern world had been created, and a recognition of who had borne the costs of that

---

10. Pascal Bruckner, *The Tears of a White Man: Compassion as Contempt*, translated by William R. Beer (New York: Free Press, 1983); Bruckner, *The Tyranny of Guilt: An Essay on Western Masochism*, translated by Steven Rendall (Princeton, NJ: Princeton University Press, 2010).

creation. Their belief was that the guilt was a manifestation not of masochism but of conscience; and the strategy they developed was the public apology for the past which they held to be not an inappropriate response to the past but rather an effort to alter the terms inherited from the past. For both individuals and collectives, injuries mark a transformative moment fraught with potential choices. Those who injure are presumed to have a choice between remaining impenitent and redeeming themselves by apology, while those injured are often forced into an invidious choice of rejecting the apology (and abiding in resentment) or accepting it (and thereby exemplifying forgiveness). What might seem like choices of a moment—an isolated act—turn out also to be revelations of a disposition. We apologize or not, but, depending on what we do, we are perceived as conscientious or remorseless; we may resent or forgive a wrong, but we also demonstrate a resentful or forgiving character in our choice of what we do. These practices constitute not just transitional acts or moments, but defining ones, both in interpersonal relationships and in social orders. Those choices define us morally—and in some cases, according to some writers, identify us socially and racially.

Race, we have been told for the past century, is a social construction, that is, it is a category of existence that does not have much biological or genetic depth or meaning. More and more, we are shown that race was historically produced through particular political and economic dynamics and fissures in the past half-millennium, and that in our modern world it is largely reproduced through systems of social power and discourse. Given that, then, it might be worth more critically examining how the discourses we have seen emerge in these three moral practices are recreating race. We have seen, in some cases, an altogether predictable smuggling in of older conceptions of race. Those who were presumed to be racially pliable and therefore exploitable are now cast as racially forgiving. Their "nature" has not changed so much; it is simply manifest in a different way. It is this way of thinking that Soyinka mocks when he satirically comments that "To forgive [is] African." It is, he points out, yet another method for those who hold tightly to race as meaningful to distinguish Africans (those who forgive) from the larger category of human (those who err).

The aim of those who apologize is presumably to return the relationship to what it was before the injury; the point of recalling the injury is to identify it and thereby see it as an event. In public apologies for the cases we have been examining here—enslavement and apartheid, in particular—we must see that the crimes are both those institutional structures that exploit people of African descent *and* the creation of an intellectual system that buttresses, supports, and rationalizes that exploitation. The crime, in other words, was also *race itself* as a way of thinking. We will not have returned to an earlier world prior to those crimes if we continue to reproduce the intellectual crime that made possible the material ones. We do, of course, occupy a vastly superior world than the one in which those crimes took place, but I suspect that we will not advance to a more desirable world in which the effects of those crimes are less destructive as long as we continue to recreate race in our discursive assumptions and acts.

Is that possible, though—or is it as impossible as the kind of forgiveness that absolves us of the past, as impossible as the "undoing" that many proponents of apology believe it to be able to perform? Perhaps, perhaps not. As I suggested earlier in this study, what look like failures in the short term can appear as attempts in retrospect. It will clearly be difficult, and assuredly require more than the moral practices we have been discussing here, although they will also be involved because they constitute the evolved practices we have for responding to injury, to guilt, and to remorse.

What will make it difficult, initially, is that it appears that these interactions reinforce those divisions since those apologizing look white and those to whom the apology is offered do not. Appearances are deceptive, though, and what the best analyses of race are showing us is the fragility of those social identities that had earlier seemed solid enough to bear the burden of an empire. The social history that emerged in the middle of the twentieth century has made possible those analyses, since much of it is precisely focused on showing us how what seemed eternal and natural is in fact historical and social. C. Vann Woodward's *The Strange Career of Jim Crow*, for instance, a book written the year after *Brown v. Board of Education*, helped dispel the belief that segregation in America had a long and enduring life. What had been made, Woodward implied, could be unmade; a social order that came into being to serve particular interests at a specific time could be disordered and reordered to serve new interests in new times. Artists before him had insisted that the same thing is true of social identities. "Black is . . . an' black ain't," sermonizes the preacher in Ralph Ellison's *Invisible Man*: "Black will make you . . . or black will un-make you."[11] Ellison, I think it safe to say, believed that

---

11. C. Vann Woodward, *The Strange Career of Jim* (1955: New York: Oxford University Press, 1963); Ralph Ellison, *Invisible Man* (1952; New York: Vintage, 1980), pp. 9–10.

to be true of all identities; and he focused on blackness only because it was, in an American context, hypervisible just as whiteness was the truly invisible category. Perhaps then, we can say, part of what seems to be happening in these public rituals that involve these three moral practices is a simultaneous affirmation and disavowal of the meanings of whiteness, blackness, and indigeneity, a working through and possible shedding or reformation of identities that can make or unmake us.

AFTERWORD

THE ARTS OF EMPATHY

At the beginning of the twenty-first century, we are living in what primatologist Frans de Waal and economist Jeremy Rifkin each calls "the age of empathy." These two thinkers differ significantly in their approaches. De Waal argues that by studying our fellow primates and other nonhuman animals, and by looking more attentively at how the human species has evolved, we can learn that nature and evolution have not made us an entirely selfish species (composed, say, of "selfish genes"), but also one that values trust and altruism and all the practices that make us communal and social beings. Rifkin looks at critical transformations in what he calls "energy regimes"—the rise of hydraulic agricultural systems, for instance, or those based on wind, steam, coal, or fossil fuels—in order to show us how the evolution of these energy regimes produced particular kinds of civilizations that evolved specific sorts of relations among those living in them, and how those relations became increasingly empathic. While de Waal focuses on biological evolution to show how our empathy is producing a "kinder society," Rifkin examines social evolutions in the harnessing of energy and the production of communication patterns tied to those energy regimes to show how moments in our past may help us see that our trajectory is inexorably leading us to a "global consciousness." Empathy is in our nature and in our history, and a product of our nature and our history—and, in either case, an aspect of who we are as individuals and what we are as a society or world.[1]

---

1. Frans de Waal, *The Age of Empathy: Nature's Lessons for a Kinder Society* (New York: Harmony Books, 2009); Jeremy Rifkin, *The Empathic Civilization: The Race to Global Consciousness in a World in Crisis* (New York: Jeremy P. Tarcher/Penguin, 2009), p. 421. Some have recently argued that we can find a neurological substrate for that kind of empathy in the so-called mirror neurons that were discovered in the 1990s.

At its core, empathy is about connectedness, about being able to imagine what another feels or experiences and to share deeply in those feelings. The "age of empathy" that de Waals and Rifkin describe is premised on an expansion of that gift or ability so that it becomes a marked feature of all our relations—of person to person, of group to group, of species to species, of ourselves to the world. It is an ethic of connectedness with everything. When Peter Singer wrote the first edition of *The Expanding Circle* in 1981, he limited our concern to sentient beings. The "only justifiable stopping place for the expansion of altruism," he wrote, "is the point at which all whose welfare can be affected by our actions are included within the circle of altruism." That included most animals, but not plants or minerals, not trees or land or streams or mountains. It is not that we should not care about those things or protect them and recognize that they provide a habitat for species that do fall within the circle of altruism, he was quick to add, but since there is "nothing we can do that matters to them" we need not consider them in defining the boundaries of "the expansion of our moral horizons." There is probably nothing new to make us change our mind about that, but the emergence of climate change and the ecological destructiveness that has produced it, and threatens us and our planet, perhaps makes us rethink how far we want to expand our empathy. Perhaps our moral horizons need more fully to include our physical horizons—these inanimate things—into the circle of our concern precisely because we are connected to them, and they to us, in ways that make our existence, and therefore our sentience, possible. In the age of empathy, as Rifkin argues, "the new science takes us from a colonial vision of nature as an enemy to pillage and enslave, to a new vision of nature as a community to nurture."[2] Within what he calls "biosphere consciousness" we empathize with the whole world.

The three practices I have been discussing in this book are all, in their own way, expressions of empathy, and have developed particular forms of expression and performance in our contemporary "age of empathy." Since apology and forgiveness are practices of responding to injury and remorse, it is not surprising that we witness the rise of more public forms of apologizing for past injuries at a time when people are educated to understand their connectedness to those they had earlier been taught to think of as "others," nor is it surprising that this emergent consciousness should come as a result of their

2. Peter Singer, *The Expanding Circle: Ethics, Evolution, and Moral Progress* (1981; Princeton: Princeton University Press, 2011), pp. 120–21, 124; Rifkin, *The Empathic Civilization*, p. 600.

seeing their own existence as connected to the historical generations that came before them. White Australians who apologize to aboriginal peoples, white Canadians who apologize to First Nations peoples, and white Americans and Europeans who apologize for the enslavement of people of African descent are expressing their connectedness to those who have been oppressed and recognizing their connectedness to those who oppressed them. These are acts of recognition, recovery, and reconciliation, but they are also acts of empathy that falteringly attempt to express a sense of shared sorrow, grief, and hope. Empathy, then, might be the source of the moral practices that we have been most engaged in exploring here—resentment, apology, and forgiveness—and empathy might also be what they are striving to express. (Many commentators have also called ours "the age of apology.")[3] I would like to end, then, by seeing in what ways each of these moral practices may be said to belong to the arts of empathy.

Empathy is a relatively new term, just a little over a century old in English and only slightly older in its German origins. Edward Bradford Titchner coined the term in 1909 in his *Lectures on the Experimental Psychology of the Thought-Processes* to capture the German word *Einfühlung*, which had been introduced into the discourse of aesthetics by Robert Vischer in 1873 and then developed by Theodor Lipps in 1903. Lipps used the term in his book *Aesthetik*, which he was writing at the very time that he was also translating David Hume's *Treatise on Human Nature* into German (1904–1906), which of course had employed *sympathy* to describe something very close to what we mean by *empathy* today.[4]

Hume used *sympathy* to refer to more than one kind of practice (by some accounts, he uses it in four different senses), and much has been written in general to demonstrate the key distinctions between sympathy and empathy. I am not going to enter that debate, and the meaning of *sympathy* in Hume that particularly interests me here is the one that is closest to our sense of *empathy*. If empathy means, as one influential definition has it, "the involvement of psychological processes that make a person have feelings that are more congruent with another's situation than with his own situation," then Hume's account of what happens when "we sympathize with the passions and sentiments of

3. Mark Gibney, Rhoda E. Howard-Hassmann, Jean-Marc Coicaud, and Niklaus Steiner, Eds., *The Age of Apology: Facing Up To the Past* (Philadelphia: University of Pennsylvania Press, 2008).

4. Edward B. Titchner, *Lectures on the Experimental Psychology of the Thought-Processes* (New York: Macmillan, 1909); T. Lipps, *Aesthetik* (Hamburg, Germany: Leopold Voss, 1903).

others" and thereby "receive by communication their inclinations and sentiments" is a description of empathy. When we sympathize with another, Hume notes, we feel what the other feels; the other's passion "acquires such a degree of force and vivacity, as to become the very passion itself, and produce an equal emotion, as any original affection."[5] That is empathy—where our capacity to feel imaginatively what another is feeling is so powerful that we can sometimes be confused about the source of it.

Hume—like Joseph Butler, Francis Hutcheson, and Adam Smith—used the term *fellow-feeling* as a synonym for *sympathy*, or what Hume on other occasions also called *social sympathy*. The term *fellow-feeling* appears to be a coinage of the seventeenth century; the earliest entry in the *Oxford English Dictionary* is 1604, and Hobbes refers to it in 1651 as "the phrase of this present time." It was a phrase and sentiment Hobbes represented as being precisely the opposite of sympathy. For Hobbes, pity and compassion (which antedated the new term *fellow-feeling*) were responses not of sympathy for another's plight in the present, but rather of what we feel when we imagine ourselves subject to the same plight in the future (it is "imagination or fiction of future calamity to ourselves," as he put it in *Human Nature*). In other words, fellow-feeling in Hobbes follows his conception of humanity as selfish and appetitive. Shaftesbury challenged Hobbes on this point, as on virtually every other, by affirming that if "*Appetite* or *Sense* be natural, the *Sense of Fellowship* is the same." In the state of "nature," then, Shaftesbury argued, we can find the glimmer of another sensibility that finds expression in family, offspring, companions, clan, tribe, and eventually what he called "*a Publick*." Here, then, was another way for us to imagine the formation of a social order, premised not on the ever-present fear of devolution or regression to barbarism that Hobbes feared, but rather on a sense of fellowship that inspired and created an ever-expanding circle of concern and care.[6]

---

5. Martin L. Hoffman, *Empathy and Moral Development: Implications for Caring and Justice* (New York: Cambridge University Press, 2000), p. 30; David Hume, *A Treatise of Human Nature: A Critical Edition*, edited by David Fate Norton and Mary J. Norton (Oxford: Clarendon Press, 2007), Volume 1, pp. 208, 206; also see Lou Agosta, "Empathy and Sympathy in Ethics," in *Internet Encyclopedia of Philosophy*, http://www.iep.utm.edu/emp-symp/#SH3b.

6. Hume, *An Enquiry Concerning the Principles of Morals: A Critical Edition*, edited by Tom L. Beauchamp (Oxford: Clarendon Press, 1998), p. 66; Thomas Hobbes, *Leviathan*, edited by Richard Tuck (revised student edition; New York: Cambridge University Press, 1996), p. 43; Hobbes, *Human Nature* and *De Corpore Politico*, edited by J. C. A. Gaskin (New York: Oxford University Press, 1994), p. 53; Anthony, Third Earl of Shaftesbury, *Characteristicks of Men, Manners, Opinions, Times* (Indianapolis, IN: Liberty Fund Books, 2001), Volume 1, pp.

Others who challenged Hobbes (and Mandeville) argued for the importance of sympathy and fellow-feeling as the basis of a morality and of a social order. Hutcheson referred to the "sympathetick" sense "by which, when we apprehend the state of others, our hearts naturally have a fellow-feeling with them." Butler directly challenged Hobbes' *Human Nature* statement, and argued, in a long footnote in his sermon "Compassion," that what Hobbes describes as "imagination or fiction" in such circumstances is precisely the opposite of what Hobbes thought it exemplified (self-regard), but was instead a perfect example of "mutual sympathy between each particular of the species, a fellow-feeling common to mankind." Hume likewise dismissed Hobbes' suggestion in his chapter "Of Compassion" in the *Treatise of Human Nature*. Finally, Adam Smith, too, in his opening chapter "Of Sympathy," argued that the "source of our fellow-feeling" is our capacity for "changing places in fancy with the sufferer" so "that we come either to conceive or to be affected by what he feels."[7] While the term did not yet exist, what these eighteenth-century philosophers were talking about was what we today call *empathy*. And it is not surprising, then, that the first expression of *resentment* as a moral response to injury should arise at this time, among these thinkers.

Resentment is the most clearly empathic of the three practices, odd as that sounds since it is also the most clearly self-regarding of them.[8] It is the response

---

69–70. Once asked by a religious magazine what he would change about the human species, "if he were God," de Waal claimed: "if I could change one thing, it would be to expand the range of fellow feeling." See de Waal, *Age of Empathy*, p. 203.

7. Francis Hutcheson, *A System of Moral Philosophy* (London, 1755), Volume 1, p. 19; Joseph Butler, *Fifteen Sermons*, in *The Works of Joseph Butler*, edited by W. E. Gladstone (Oxford: Clarendon Press, 1896), Volume 2, p. 97; Hume, *A Treatise of Human Nature*, Volume 1, p. 239; Adam Smith, *The Theory of Moral Sentiments*, edited by D. D. Raphael and A. L. Mackie (Indianapolis, IN: Liberty Fund Books, 1982), p. 10; Stephen Darwall, *The Second-Person Standpoint: Morality, Respect, and Accountability* (Cambridge, MA: Harvard University Press, 2006), pp. 43–48, insightfully discusses Smith on empathy, and compellingly argues for the centrality of empathy for second-person ethics.

8. In an essay published the year before his more famous "Freedom and Resentment," P. F. Strawson discussed what he would come to call "the participant reactive attitudes"—such as resentment for injury and gratitude for benefits—by noting their "natural sources," and the natural source he seemed most to have in mind is something like empathy. The "appeal to the concept of sympathy," he continues, "will scarcely now seem adequate. But, however we explain it, there is no need to sophisticate ourselves into denying altogether the existence or fundamental importance of this recognition of others' claims." In his more famous essay the next year, he likewise lamented that we might not have the language to describe that need for what he called "a certain sort of demand for inter-personal regard." "It is a pity," he concluded, "that talk of the moral sentiments has fallen out of fashion." These terms—*recognition* and *regard*—strike me as descriptions of how we hope to see manifest in ourselves and others what the theorists who did write about the "concept of sympathy" and the "moral sentiments" called "fellow-feeling,"

we have to injuries to ourselves, and an expression of insulted self-esteem. As we saw, however, its earliest and most insightful theorists in the eighteenth century regarded it as not just a self-centered sentiment, but rather a deeply sociable one. We are resentful at being misused ourselves, and likewise resentful at seeing others misused because we feel their pain and share their sensibilities. Sometimes, but not always or consistently, the earliest theorists used the term *indignation* for the social response, *resentment* for the personal one. But their larger point is that the response is functionally and emotionally the same. What we feel in either case is a sense of the injustice of the action. What sympathy does, as Hume, Butler, and Smith so emphatically insist, is produce a sense that what happens to others is not so distant and distinct from what happens to us that we can't be fooled sometimes into thinking ourselves feeling "the very passion itself." It is perhaps because of its contagion-like quality that it evolved from its British eighteenth-century form as an act of sympathy to its nineteenth-century Continental form as a social condition.

If resentment is an act of empathy, apology, we might say, is an indirect expression of it. What apology does express—remorse—requires us to see and understand how another feels, and has been made to feel by our actions. It requires a kind of reflective empathy since it requires us to occupy the place of the offended and recognize the offense from the place it is felt. Consider, again, the case of Katherine Ann Power's parole board hearing in front of the Schroeder family. Overcoming what she acknowledged as her "defensiveness" required Power to see her actions not as she had intended them or from an "objective" perspective as a legal issue, but as they created the conditions for, led inexorably toward, and culminated in the Schroeder family's loss. What Power recognized, and expressed in retrospect, is that she most wanted the Schroeder family to "*know* that I *know* that I hurt them." She wanted them to see that she felt, or at least understood, what they felt, that she was at a point where she could now imagine what it must feel like to lose what they lost, and at a point where she recognized that she extended rather than alleviated that pain by the denial of it. "Without empathy," writes Nick Smith, "the apology becomes so concerned with the violated principle, the offender's failures, or the process of the offender's redemption that the victim's felt

---

and what we today call "empathy." See Strawson, "Social Morality and Individual Ideal," in *Freedom and Resentment and Other Essays* (1974; New York: Routledge, 2008), pp. 29–49, esp. p. 43; and Strawson, "Freedom and Resentment," in *Freedom and Resentment and Other Essays*, pp. 1–28, esp. pp. 17, 25–26.

suffering becomes incidental."[9] With empathy, that is, when it is a result of the offender's empathic reconsideration of the offense, an apology becomes a sharing of perspective and feeling about the injury. Apology, we might say, is an exercised empathy—not so much an act of empathy in the way resentful indignation is, but the product of an empathic act.

Forgiveness, as the forswearing of resentment, is an empathic act because it is motivated by the sense that the offender has been *heard*—that the apology registered as sincere and meaningful—and that therefore one wishes to relieve the oppressive sense of remaining unforgiven. It is a response to an empathic act, and is itself an act of empathy in relieving what is acknowledged as distress in another who is feeling guilty or ashamed. We feel their pain, and relieve it. For some scholars of forgiveness as a secular practice, such an act would not constitute forgiveness because it is less about the forswearing of resentment (and all the related emotions) than it is about relieving distress (our own or others'); for them, forgiveness should be less an act of empathy and more a contract. If I hear remorse, I will forgive, and I forgive because that remorse binds you to a particular future. But most people, I wager, do forgive out of empathy. That, I think, is what people mean when they say that we ought to forgive because we are ourselves in need of forgiveness. It is one of what I would argue are the two most resonant reasons people claim for the virtue of forgiving.

The second resonant reason is also based on empathy: we should forgive because we otherwise fix the humanity of the offender into one static condition, believing that one act defines him or her. In its popular, Augustinian form, that wisdom—we should hate the sin and forgive the sinner—means that we forgive the person because that is not the only performance we know of or expect of that person. As Trudy Govier put it, to "regard people as absolutely unforgivable on the grounds that what they have done is atrocious to extend attitudes, unwarrantedly, from acts to persons, to argue from acts to character in such a way as to mark an irrecoverable stain on the agents." This "line of reasoning," she concludes, "is mistaken: logically, metaphysically, and psychologically, the act is not the agent." To argue that the act is the agent— that a "moral agent is reducible to those deeds and is thus absolutely unforgivable"—is "to ignore the human capacity for remorse, choice, and moral transformation." Forgiveness acknowledges that capacity, and enables it. As

---

9. Nick Smith, *I Was Wrong: The Meanings of Apologies* (New York: Cambridge University Press, 2008), p. 100; also see Charles L. Griswold, *Forgiveness: A Philosophical Exploration* (New York: Cambridge University Press, 2007), pp. 83–90.

Paul Ricoeur notes, each mysterious "utterance" of forgiveness says: "you are better than your actions."[10]

The first reason is based on a respect for reciprocity and the second on a respect for human freedom. Both reasons, I think, are based on empathy, our ability to imagine what it would feel like not to be forgiven or to imagine what it might mean to be condemned by one act that then and thereafter defines us and our future relationships. Nobody more fully or insightfully examined that condition than Hannah Arendt. Her more famous point is that without forgiveness "we would be the victims of an automatic necessity," that is, un-free. Her less famous, but perhaps more remarkable point, is that with for-giveness we open up a sphere of personal and public life in which empathic imagination—the capacity to see another—becomes an even more wondrous capacity to see ourselves through others' imaginations. We "are dependent upon others," she writes, "to whom we appear in a distinctness which we our-selves are unable to perceive." An empathic act of forgiveness accepts that wisdom, and creates a new, shared space for a novel kind of self-knowledge. Forgiveness, then, might best be considered a "fellow-feeling."[11] That, in the end, strikes me as truer to the conception that we found in Jesus' statements than in the Pauline model of forgiveness. We do not forgive as God, as Paul implied, but as humans who do so precisely because we recognize ourselves as *not* God (we are in need of forgiveness), and recognize ourselves as sharing that very condition with our fellow fellows (we are all better than our acts).

---

10. Trudy Govier, *Forgiveness and Revenge* (New York: Routledge, 2002), p. 112. Cf. Govier, "Forgiveness and the Unforgivable," *American Philosophical Quarterly* 36.1 (January 1999): 59–75; Paul Ricoeur, *Memory, History, Forgetting*, translated by Kathleen Blamey and David Pellauer (Chicago: University of Chicago Press, 2004), p. 493.

11. Hannah Arendt, *The Human Condition* (Chicago: University of Chicago Press, 1958), pp. 246, 243.

INDEX